Psycholinguistics and Cognition in Language Processing

Duygu Buğa
Independent Researcher, Turkey

Muhlise Coşgun Ögeyik
Trakya University, Turkey

A volume in the Advances in Linguistics and Communication Studies (ALCS) Book Series

IGI Global
DISSEMINATOR OF KNOWLEDGE

Published in the United States of America by
IGI Global
Information Science Reference (an imprint of IGI Global)
701 E. Chocolate Avenue
Hershey PA, USA 17033
Tel: 717-533-8845
Fax: 717-533-8661
E-mail: cust@igi-global.com
Web site: http://www.igi-global.com

Library of Congress Cataloging-in-Publication Data

Names: Buga, Duygu, 1991- editor. | Ogeyik, Muhlise Cosgun, 1974- editor.
Title: Psycholinguistics and cognition in language processing / Duygu Buga and Muhlise Cosgun Ogeyik, editors.
Description: Hershey PA : Information Science Reference, [2018] | Includes bibliographical references and index.
Identifiers: LCCN 2017026111| ISBN 9781522540090 (hardcover) | ISBN 9781522540106 (ebook)
Subjects: LCSH: Psycholinguistics. | Cognitive grammar. | Bilingualism. | Second language acquisition.
Classification: LCC P37 .P7593 2018 | DDC 401/.9--dc23 LC record available at https://lccn.loc.gov/2017026111

This book is published in the IGI Global book series Advances in Linguistics and Communication Studies (ALCS) (ISSN: 2372-109X; eISSN: 2372-1111)

British Cataloguing in Publication Data
A Cataloguing in Publication record for this book is available from the British Library.

Advances in Linguistics and Communication Studies (ALCS) Book Series

ISSN:2372-109X
EISSN:2372-1111

Editor-in-Chief: Abigail G. Scheg, Western Governors University, USA

MISSION

The scope of language and communication is constantly changing as society evolves, new modes of communication are developed through technological advancement, and novel words enter our lexicon as the result of cultural change. Understanding how we communicate and use language is crucial in all industries and updated research is necessary in order to promote further knowledge in this field.

The **Advances in Linguistics and Communication Studies (ALCS)** book series presents the latest research in diverse topics relating to language and communication. Interdisciplinary in its coverage, ALCS presents comprehensive research on the use of language and communication in various industries including business, education, government, and healthcare.

COVERAGE

- Discourse Analysis
- Dialectology
- Computational linguistics
- Non-Verbal Communication
- Semantics
- Language and Identity
- Cross-Cultural Communication
- Language Acquisition
- Youth Language
- Sociolinguistics

IGI Global is currently accepting manuscripts for publication within this series. To submit a proposal for a volume in this series, please contact our Acquisition Editors at Acquisitions@igi-global.com or visit: http://www.igi-global.com/publish/.

The Advances in Linguistics and Communication Studies (ALCS) Book Series (ISSN 2372-109X) is published by IGI Global, 701 E. Chocolate Avenue, Hershey, PA 17033-1240, USA, www.igi-global.com. This series is composed of titles available for purchase individually; each title is edited to be contextually exclusive from any other title within the series. For pricing and ordering information please visit http://www.igi-global.com/book-series/advances-linguistics-communication-studies/78950. Postmaster: Send all address changes to above address.

Titles in this Series

For a list of additional titles in this series, please visit:
https://www.igi-global.com/book-series/advances-linguistics-communication-studies/78950

Establishing and Evaluating Digital Ethos and Online Credibility
Moe Folk (Kutztown University of Pennsylvania, USA) and Shawn Apostel (Bellarmine University, USA)
Information Science Reference • ©2017 • 400pp • H/C (ISBN: 9781522510727) • US $200.00

Computational and Cognitive Approaches to Narratology
Takashi Ogata (Iwate Prefectural University, Japan) and Taisuke Akimoto (The University of Electoro-Communications, Japan)
Information Science Reference • ©2016 • 467pp • H/C (ISBN: 9781522504320) • US $215.00

Analyzing Language and Humor in Online Communication
Rotimi Taiwo (Obafemi Awolowo University, Nigeria) Akinola Odebunmi (University of Ibadan, Nigeria) and Akin Adetunji (Emmanuel Alayande College of Education, Nigeria)
Information Science Reference • ©2016 • 324pp • H/C (ISBN: 9781522503385) • US $185.00

Discourse Analysis as a Tool for Understanding Gender Identity, Representation, and...
Nazmunnessa Mahtab (University of Dhaka, Bangladesh) Sara Parker (John Moores University, UK) Farah Kabir (Action Aid, Bangladesh) Tania Haque (University of Dhaka, Bangladesh) Aditi Sabur (University of Dhaka, Bangladesh) and Abu Saleh Mohammad Sowad (University of Dhaka, Bangladesh)
Information Science Reference • ©2016 • 323pp • H/C (ISBN: 9781522502258) • US $185.00

Revealing Gender Inequalities and Perceptions in South Asian Countries...
Nazmunnessa Mahtab (University of Dhaka, Bangladesh) Sara Parker (John Moores University, UK) Farah Kabir (Action Aid, Bangladesh) Tania Haque (University of Dhaka, Bangladesh) Aditi Sabur (University of Dhaka, Bangladesh) and Abu Saleh Mohammad Sowad (University of Dhaka, Bangladesh)
Information Science Reference • ©2016 • 286pp • H/C (ISBN: 9781522502791) • US $185.00

For an entire list of titles in this series, please visit:
https://www.igi-global.com/book-series/advances-linguistics-communication-studies/78950

Editorial Advisory Board

Table of Contents

Detailed Table of Contents

The purpose of this chapter is to define and present central language integration by neurolinguistic and psycholinguistic aspects in bilingual and multilingual persons in emotion-based circumstances. Central language hypothesis (CLH) imparts that one language in the subconscious mind of bilingual and multilingual individuals is more suppressive and it is structured as central language. It has an emotional background such that if limbic cortex of the brain gets any stimulus (e.g., fear, anxiety, sorrow, etc.), the brain directly produces the CL. This phenomenon distinguishes CL from the notion of mother tongue because mother tongue is the first language that is acquired at home, but CL may be the second language as well.

Processes involved in converting print to sound are reported to be flexible and under the strategic control of skilled readers even in transparent orthographies. In this respect, word frequency effect, regularity, and lexicality have been the topic of much research and debate in understanding how context is involved in the emergence of strategies. However, whether age of acquisition (AoA) effects are influenced by context and under the strategic control of readers have yet to be established. A series of single-word naming experiments addresses this issue and examines the role of filler type critically manipulated on lexicality, frequency, and imageability on the size of AoA effect in word naming in an entirely transparent orthography. Overall, results, which are discussed within the current theoretical frameworks, suggest that context plays a significant role on AoA.

Marked and unmarked language forms can be distinguished with the level of simplicity or complexity denotations of the forms. Unmarked target language forms may create little or no difficulty, even if they do not exist in the native language of the learner, while marked forms can be relatively difficult for language learners. In addition to the notions of markedness/unmarkedness, there has also been an emphasis on similarity and dissimilarity between the items of first (L1) and second languages (L2). Along with similarity or dissimilarity of L1 and L2 forms, the level of difficulty may vary enormously in different language-specific procedures. In this chapter, therefore, it is intended to build an understanding of the recognized pronunciation and orthographic problems of similar loanwords in both Turkish (L1 of the participants) and English (L2).

Language is one of the most essential features of humans. Another basic feature that is common for all mankind is emotions, and expression of emotions is through the use of language whether it is verbally uttered or represented by body language. This interrelated and human-specific nature of language and emotions gains a place in foreign or second language learning process studies as well. However, the emotional aspect in learning a second or foreign language has mostly been neglected, or in other words, it has commonly taken the backseat. From this point forth, this chapter descriptively represents how the emotional development of an individual—specifically the child's—fosters the foreign language learning process. In doing this, learning/ acquisition theories and a child's emotional development process—as a foreign language learner—are reviewed and assumptions/suggestions are displayed through a detailed literature review.

Identifying and exploring factors that influence bilingual language processing has been the topic of much psycholinguistic research. Semantic priming is typically used to examine semantic processing and refers to the phenomenon in which semantically related items (doctor-nurse) are processed faster and more accurately than semantically unrelated items (doctor-butter). The aim of the chapter is to address two key questions: 1) how the two languages of a bilingual are organised or stored and 2) how the two languages are processed. A review of the literature shows that there are currently no theoretical frameworks that explain Russian monolingual or Russian (L1)-English (L2) bilingual storage or processing. Monolingual Russian speakers and bilingual Russian (L1)-English (L2) speaking university students were asked to name target words under related or unrelated conditions. The results show that the magnitude of the semantic priming effect was determined by L2 proficiency. The implications for these findings is discussed within the current bilingual theoretical models.

Linguistics as the study of the nature of languages has a visible impact on various fields such as education, language teaching, philosophy, computer science, and anthropology. However, the nature of language is a broad idea, which makes it hard to give a clear, simple definition. One of the most fundamental assumptions is the rule-governed feature of the human language interrelated with pronunciation, word formation, and grammatical construction. The aim of this chapter is to discuss how the rules of the language have an impact on foreign language learning process and how it affects foreign language learners' storing and processing the language in the brain. In doing so, some predetermined samples of lexical items and formal structures of language are analyzed in terms of the foreign language learners' cognition as prospective teachers of English in the teacher training process.

Children in bilingual communities are frequently exposed to speech from nonnative speakers, but little research has described how that input might differ from the input of native speakers. There is evidence that input from nonnative speakers might be less useful to language learning children, but little research has asked why. This chapter analyzes the frequency of complex structures in the child-directed speech of 30 native English speakers and 36 nonnative speakers who were late learners of

This chapter examines the relationship between teachers' picture story book reading activities and 48- to 60-month-old children's language development and to identify the effect of different variables on this relationship. The study sample was composed of 208 children in classrooms for 48- to 60-month-old children and 10 teachers in five independent pre-schools in the province of Kırşehir. The data obtained in the study were analyzed by using appropriate statistical methods. Based on the study results, a significant relationship was identified between pre-school teachers' picture story book reading activities during their daily programs and language development of children. The result of the study presents the importance of picture story book reading activities for language development. Longitudinal studies that will investigate teachers' and parents' involvement in picture story book reading activities in detail and development of programs that will support children's language development are suggested in the chapter.

The chapter starts with a definition and models of mental dictionary. It then builds on the bilingual lexical activation models and goes on to discuss formulaic language (collocations in particular). After explaining the basics of formulaic language processing, the author attempts to address the issue of lexical and collocational priming theory by Hoey, which has its roots in cognitive linguistics and usage-based language models. Last but not least, some suggestions for future research are provided in an attempt to address the needs of the lexical research literature in the Turkish setting.

Fossilization is a common linguistic phenomenon among learners. It presents an obstacle that hinders the process of learning and prevents learners from acquiring the target language. The present chapter explores this phenomenon. It gives an overview of the theory of interlanguage and the concept of fossilization. The chapter presents the history of pronunciation teaching. It also reviews a previous study on pronunciation problems and fossilized errors that face learners of English as a second or a foreign language. The present chapter also raises an important question. It attempts to show the matter behind this linguistic phenomenon. There seems to be different views. Some researchers claim that phonetic fossilization is a matter of intelligibility. Other researchers state that achieving perfection in pronunciation is preferable. Another trend of researchers assumes that fossilization cannot be applied to the multilingual context.

Preface

Language and psychology are two fields which have been studied for centuries to uncover the building stones of them and find out how human mind processes. It is an apodeictic fact that language and psychology are interrelated, and these fields influence one another. Psycholinguistics is the title of the field where you may study how language and psychology affect each other. Although there are varied proposed studies and theories in psycholinguistics, the mystery of the language and the infinite obscurity of psychology impel researchers to do new research studies.

The book, *Psycholinguistics and Cognition in Language Processing,* aims to bring novelty to the field of psycholinguistics and include innovative studies which may light the way of further studies. In this book, the reader will be able to find both ground-breaking, innovative studies and informative chapters for practitioners.

Chapter 1 defines and presents Central Language occurring in bilingual and multilingual brain in some emotion based circumstances. Central Language Hypothesis (CLH) imparts that one language in the subconscious mind of bilingual and multilingual individuals is more suppressive and it is structured as Central Language. It has an emotional background and such that if limbic cortex of the brain gets any stimulus (e.g. fear, anxiety, and sorrow etc.), brain directly produces the CL. This phenomenon distinguishes CL from the notion of mother tongue, because mother tongue is the first language which is acquired at home but CL may be the second language as well. The chapter begins with an Introduction followed by the section discusses the process of centralizing of language and Neurolinguistic aspect to the Central Language. The next section explains the method of the study and the results of the survey used in this study. The Discussion section provide additional information about the questionnaire and synthesize the data, followed by Future Research Directions and finally Conclusion.

Chapter 2 focuses on the processes involved in converting print to sound; it is stated that they are reported to be flexible and under the strategic control of skilled readers even in transparent orthographies. In this respect, word frequency effect, regularity and lexicality have been the topic of much research and debate in understanding how context is involved in the emergence of strategies. However, whether Age of Acquisition (AoA) effects are influenced by context and under the strategic control of readers have yet to be established. A series of single-word naming experiments address this issue and examine the role of filler type critically manipulated on lexicality, frequency and imageability on the size of AoA effect in word naming in an entirely transparent orthography. Overall, the results suggest that context plays a significant role on AoA which are discussed within the current theoretical frameworks.

Chapter 3 explains that marked and unmarked language forms can be distinguished with the level of simplicity or complexity denotations of the forms. Unmarked target language forms may create little or no difficulty, even if they do not exist in the native language of the learner; while marked forms can be relatively difficult for language learners. In addition to the notions of markedness/unmarkedness, there has also been an emphasis on the similarity and dissimilarity between the items of first (L1) and second languages (L2). Along with the similarity or dissimilarity of L1 and L2 forms, the level of difficulty may vary enormously in different language-specific procedures. In this chapter, therefore, it is intended to build an understanding of the recognized pronunciation and orthographic problems of similar loanwords in both Turkish (L1 of the participants) and English (L2).

Chapter 4 explains the role of emotional development in child's foreign language learning. Language is one of the most essential features of humans which conduce to make distinction with other living organisms. Another basic feature that is common for all mankind is emotions, and expression of emotions is through the use of language whether it is verbally uttered or represented by body language. This interrelated and human-specific nature of language and emotions gain a place in foreign or second language learning process studies as well. However, emotional aspect in learning a second or foreign language has mostly been neglected or in other words, it has commonly taken the backseat. From this point forth, this chapter descriptively represents how emotional development of an individual -specifically the child's- fosters foreign language learning process. In doing this, learning/ acquisition theories and a child's emotional development process –as a foreign language learner- are reviewed and assumptions/ suggestions are displayed through a detailed literature review.

Chapter 5 analyses semantic priming in monolingual Russian and bilingual Russian (L1)-English (L2). It aims to address two key questions: 1) how the two languages of a bilingual are organised or stored and 2) how the two languages are processed. A review of the literature showed that there are currently no theoretical frameworks that explain Russian monolingual or Russian (L1)-English (L2) bilingual storage or processing. Monolingual Russian speakers and bilingual Russian (L1)-English (L2) speaking university students were asked to name target words under related or unrelated conditions. The results showed that the magnitude of the semantic priming effect was determined by L2 proficiency. The implications for these findings will be discussed within the current bilingual theoretical models.

Chapter 6 discusses how the rules of the language have an impact on foreign language learning process and how it affects foreign language learners' storing and processing the language in the brain. In doing so, some predetermined samples of lexical items and formal structures of language are analysed in terms of the foreign language learners' cognition as prospective teachers of English in teacher training process.

Chapter 7 analyses the frequency of complex structures in the child-directed speech of 30 native English speakers and 36 non-native speakers who were late learners of English, all speaking English to their two and a half year-old children. All instances of nine categories of complex structures were coded in transcripts of mother-child interaction. The frequency of all but one category was greater in the speech of native speakers. These findings suggest that input provided by native speakers provides more frequent models of complex structures than non-native input.

Chapter 8 examines context word in picture naming and it aims to understand the nuances involved in experimental manipulations that may influence the pattern of results and be responsible for differences in outcomes. The series of experiments reported in this chapter was aimed at refining our understanding of mechanisms in the way bilinguals process language production by examining two different paradigms—primed picture naming and picture-word interference. This was investigated by manipulating both the type of visual context words presented with the picture and the time interval between the presentation of context word and picture. The results are interpreted within the context of current models of lexical access

Chapter 9 focuses on the signification processes that are constituted during enunciation by subjects who, due to brain dysfunction, appropriate reality and produce conscience of themselves in a particular fashion. Linguistic monitoring articulated with neurolinguistics is suggested in order to promote rhythmic, lexical and syntactic modifications in such subjects' discourse so as to place the significant chain in order as regards its oral or written production. The Chapter begins with an Introduction followed by a section explains The Discourse Theory to Observe the Subject. The next sections are Linguistic education for social inclusion, Linguistic Evaluation for Social Inclusion, The Literacy Theory to Achieve Social Inclusion, and Authorship: Finding A Way for The Viability of Being followed by Future Research Directions and finally Conclusion.

Chapter 10 examines the relationship between teachers' picture story book reading activities and 48-60-month-old children's language development and to identify the effect of different variables on this relationship. Based on the study results, a significant relationship is identified between pre-school teachers' picture story book reading activities during their daily programs and language development of children. The result of the study presents the importance of picture story book reading activities for language development. Longitudinal studies that will investigate teachers' and parents' involvement in picture story book reading activities in detail and development of programs that will support children's language development are suggested in the study.

Chapter 11 is focused on bilingual mental lexicon. The chapter starts with a definition and models of mental dictionary. It then builds on the bilingual lexical activation models and goes on to discuss formulaic language (collocations in particular). After explaining the basics of formulaic language processing, the writer attempts to address the issue of lexical and collocational priming theory by Hoey (2005), which has its roots in cognitive linguistics and usage-based language models (Barlow and Kemmer, 2000). Some suggestions for future research are provided in an attempt to address the needs of the lexical research literature in the Turkish setting.

Chapter 12 presents the history of pronunciation teaching. It also tries to review previous study on pronunciation problems and fossilized errors that face learners of English as a second or a foreign language. The present chapter also raises an important question. It attempts to show the matter behind this linguistic phenomenon.

While conducting this book project, our purpose was to contribute to the field of Psycholinguistics and Cognitive Science and provide a useful resource for academics, practitioners and researchers. We hope this book will spark interest among scientists, researchers, and others who are interested in this field and additionally would be a promotive factor for further studies and surveys.

Duygu Buğa
Independent Researcher, Turkey

Muhlise Coşgun Ögeyik
Trakya University, Turkey

Acknowledgment

We would like to thank all chapter authors for their excellent contributions regarding this publication effort, as well as all the Editorial Board members and chapter authors who took the time to review the following work during their busy schedules. Without your cooperation and assistance this publication would not have been possible.

Duygu Buğa
Independent Researcher, Turkey

Muhlise Coşgun Ögeyik
Trakya University, Turkey

Chapter 1
Central Language Hypothesis

Duygu Buğa
Independent Researcher, Turkey

ABSTRACT

The purpose of this chapter is to define and present central language integration by neurolinguistic and psycholinguistic aspects in bilingual and multilingual persons in emotion-based circumstances. Central language hypothesis (CLH) imparts that one language in the subconscious mind of bilingual and multilingual individuals is more suppressive and it is structured as central language. It has an emotional background such that if limbic cortex of the brain gets any stimulus (e.g., fear, anxiety, sorrow, etc.), the brain directly produces the CL. This phenomenon distinguishes CL from the notion of mother tongue because mother tongue is the first language that is acquired at home, but CL may be the second language as well.

INTRODUCTION

The current paper, by neurolinguistic and psycholinguistic aspects, defines and presents Central Language which ingenerates in bilingual and multilingual brain in some emotion based circumstances. It is a fact that the number of multilingual and bilingual individuals is increasing day by day. Distinctive studies about bilingualism and multilingualism are presented to understand the bilingual and multilingual brain and mind by researchers (see Wei & Moyer, 2008). There are various statements about the description of bilingualism. For instance, according to Bhatia (2006), to be bilingual, end result of the second language acquisition is required. That is to say, the end result of second language acquisition is bilingualism. In addition, Bilingual speaker is fluent in two languages (Harley, 2008). Moreover, childhood is critical on bilingual acquisition that acquiring two languages in childhood means bilingual

DOI: 10.4018/978-1-5225-4009-0.ch001

acquisition (Deuchar & Quay, 2000). On the other hand, Edwards (2006) states that everybody who knows at least a few words in another language is bilingual speaker. Grosjean (2013): "Bilinguals use their languages for different purposes, in different domains of life, to accomplish different things. Their level of fluency in a language depends on their need for that language. Hence many bilinguals are more fluent in a given language, and some cannot read or write one of their languages" (p. 7). Discrepant phenomena point that there isn't any consensus among researchers on what the bilingualism is. Also Li Wei (2000) presents different types of bilingualism and it can be seen from the Table 1.

No matter what bilingualism means, when bilingual/multilingual individuals switch in languages what happens on their mind is not definite and should be studied. Bilingual individuals are flexible to control their language output and they can use only one language or intentionally switch another as well, however how they choose the intended language and what mechanisms are used when they switch between languages remain as questions (Christoffels, Firk, & Schiller, 2007).

In daily lives, Bilingual/Multilingual people use code-switching while communicating. Individual differences about why and when they switch to another language is not clear. It is substantial to examine psychology of bilingual/multilingual individuals in order to comprehend aforesaid individual differences. Central Language Hypothesis clarifies the dilemma and puts emphasis on psychological perspective of language switching in bilingual/multilingual brain. In the brains of bilingual and multilingual individuals, one language is more suppressive as it dominates reflexes, emotions and senses. It is at the centre of the limbic cortex of the brain. This language is defined as *Central Language (CL)* in this paper. CL is the language which lies within the subconscious mind of a person. According to the Piaget's theory of development, sensory development is the first in the brain so it is the core or centre of the brain, in this case, the language based on the sensory system (senses, reflexes and emotions) in bilinguals and multilinguals is the Central one. That's why it is called as Central Language in this hypothesis. It is basically related to the sensory system of the brain. By the help of sufficient exposure, mind structures a language as CL. Central Language captures the subconscious so when there is a stimulus on limbic cortex (e.g. fear, anxiety, sadness or etc.) brain produces the Central Language. A bilingual/multilingual person who is in those situations reacts in CL unconsciously/reflexively. A bilingual/multilingual person might not be fluent or very competent in his/her CL. In that case it substantially means that being fluent or very competent in a language isn't a clue or key of CL. And it's possible to say that in some cases mother tongue of an individual might not be the CL of him/her. These phenomena distinguish CL from the notion of mother tongue (L1), because as the Harley (2008) defines that "mother tongue is the first language which is acquired at home" but CL may be the second language

Table 1. Varieties of bilingualism

Achieved Bilingual: Same as late bilingual.

Additive Bilingual: Someone whose two languages combine in a complementary and enriching fashion.

Ambilingual: Same as balanced bilingual.

Ascendant Bilingual: Someone whose ability to function in a second language is developing due to increased use.

Ascribed Bilingual: Same as early bilingual.

Asymmetrical Bilingual: See receptive bilingual.

Balanced Bilingual: Someone whose mastery of two languages is roughly equivalent.

Compound Bilingual: Someone whose two languages are learnt at the same time, often in the same context.

Consecutive Bilingual: Same as successive bilingual.

Co-ordinate Bilingual: Someone whose two languages are learnt in distinctively separate contexts.

Covert Bilingual: Someone who conceals his or her knowledge of a given language due to an attitudinal disposition.

Diagonal Bilingual: Someone who is bilingual in a non-standard language or a dialect and an unrelated standard language.

Dominant Bilingual: Someone with greater proficiency in one of his or her languages and uses it significantly more than the other language(s).

Dormant Bilingual: Someone who has emigrated to a foreign country for a considerable period of time and has little opportunity to keep the first language actively in use.

Early Bilingual: Someone who has acquired two languages early in childhood.

Equilingual: Same as balanced bilingual.

Functional Bilingual: Someone who can operate in two languages with or without full fluency for the task in hand.

Horizontal Bilingual: Someone who is bilingual in two distinct languages which have a similar or equal status.

Incipient Bilingual: Someone at the early stages of bilingualism where one language is not fully developed.

Late Bilingual: Someone who has become a bilingual later than childhood.

Maximal Bilingual: Someone with near native control of two or more languages.

Minimal Bilingual: Someone with only a few words and phrases in a second language.

Natural Bilingual: Someone who has not undergone any specific training and

Passive Bilingual: Same as receptive bilingual.

Primary Bilingual: Same as natural bilingual.

Productive Bilingual: Someone who not only understands but also speaks and possibly writes in two or more languages.

Receptive Bilingual: Someone who understands a second language, in either its spoken or written form, or both, but does not necessarily speak or write it.

Recessive Bilingual: Someone who begins to feel some difficulty in either understanding or expressing him or herself with ease, due to lack of use.

Secondary Bilingual: Someone whose second language has been added to a first language via instruction.

Semibilingual: Same as receptive bilingual.

Semilingual: Someone with insufficient knowledge of either language.

Simultaneous Bilingual: Someone whose two languages are present from the onset of speech.

Subordinate Bilingual: Someone who exhibits interference in his or her language usage by reducing the patterns of the second language to those of the first.

Subtractive Bilingual: Someone whose second language is acquired at the expense of the aptitudes already acquired in the first language.

Successive Bilingual: Someone whose second language is added at some stage after the first has begun to develop.

Symmetrical Bilingual: Same as balanced bilingual.

Vertical Bilingual: Someone who is bilingual in a standard language and a distinct but related language or dialect.

(L2) as well. L1 is commonly regarded as language of the self to express ourselves in daily life but L2 is for other purposes such as business, education etc. Contrary to this "us versus them" dichotomy where "us" means L1 and "them" represents L2 flops because, in some cases the second language may become another language of the self (Pavlenko, 2005). Surely centralizing of a language depends on being highly exposed to it, because of this, it doesn't matter to be simultaneous bilingual or sequential bilingual. Reflexive and emotional utterances are basic clues to get which language is the central in the brain of an individual. On the other hand it's essential to say that there is not any age limit to centralize a language in the brain for the human psychology till the end of puberty because, it is entirely based on exposure, senses, emotions and reflexes.

While experiencing different situations throughout years before the end of puberty, emotional experiences lead the mind to structure one of the languages as Central and after puberty CL of a bilingual/multilingual individual cannot change. Puberty has a critical role on this matter. Furthermore emotional density of the situation is substantial that the language which the bilingual/multilingual individual is exposed in this emotionally dense situation is structured as CL in the mind. In other words, immersion has undeniable influence of generation of CL, nevertheless, in the mind; sensational effect of the situation where one language appeared is the linchpin. That is to say, mind encodes an emotional lexicon and it dominates to the reflexes. Christoffels, Firk, and Schiller (2007, p. 193) stated, "Lexical selection refers to the process of selecting a lexical item from the mental lexicon." It contributes to the statement "Mental/emotional conditions have effects on language".

Process of Centralizing of Language

Exposure and immersion have critical roles in language acquisition. It is a critical point that in bi- or multilingual mind, centralization of a language occurs after acquisition process. An individual exposes to a language during acquisition process. Second language acquisition process pursues 5 steps: *apperceived input*, *comprehended input*, *intake*, *integration* and *outcome* (Gass & Selinker, 2008). In centralization process after acquisition, there should be an immersion to hear the language repeatedly in human interaction. Without human interaction, emotional transmission in the discourse cannot be comprehended exactly so internalization cannot come. Birkner (2016) states:

Jacqueline Sachs (1981) studied Jim´s case and when he was given an oral assessment at the age of 3 years and 9 months, it was detected that he was way below other children his age in all aspects of language. When he tried to express ideas appropriate to his age, his utterances contained ungrammatical and unusual order. When he was

4 years and 2 months, after some time he spent engaged in conversational sessions with an adult, he was already able to produce language typical of his age and the strange and ungrammatical patterns had disappeared. This shows that input, though comprehensible (TV= sounds, images, movement, colours, different topics, available anytime) is not enough, especially if it is something impersonal. The same might happen if the input comes from an Audio-based course and no human interaction is provided. The same could be said about an online language course that is practiced on a computer. (p.21)

Another main element of centralization process is where and under what conditions the individual exposes to the language. Condition which triggers the individual's emotions is the *Sensory Encoding* step of the language. Sensory Encoding step corresponds to a mind activity in which brain exposes to an emotional situation (e.g. requiem, cheer, scream etc.) and a language there so brain matches the language with that emotion. The next step is *Cognitive Encoding* that there is another mind activity; brain comprehends and makes sense of the expressions and the discourse in the exposed emotional situation. The process of structuring a language as CL is completed with *Decoding CL*. Individual decodes that exposed language as CL so produces it in other similar situations. In other words, under corresponding circumstances bilingual/multilingual individual is in need of imitating what she/he is exposed to.

Neurolinguistic Aspect to the Central Language

In this paper it is claimed that Central Language is composed unconsciously. Remembering something without awareness in an automatic way is the implicit memory (Cherry, 2003). Thereby, the implicit memory takes part in this centralising process fundamentally. Additionally, as an output Central Language occurs under emotionally intense circumstances. In connection with that, primarily Limbic cortex and then other parts of the brain should be analysed to define CL in neurolinguistics base.

Parts of the Brain which have roles on centralising process:

- **Basal Ganglia and Caudate:** Language selection, language planning and lexical selection.
- **Prefrontal Cortex:** Decision making, response selection, response inhibition, working memory, executive functions.
- **Anterior Cingulate Cortex**: Emotion formation and processing, attention, error detection.

Figure 1. Stages of the structure of CL in the mind

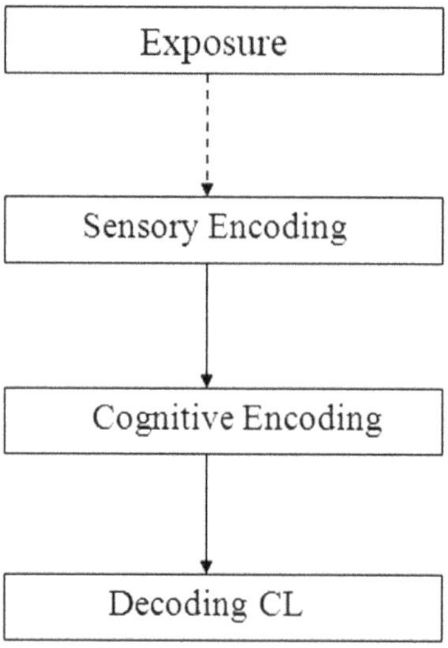

- **Anterior Speech Cortex (Broca's Area):** Speech production.
- **Posterior Speech Cortex (Wernicke's Area):** Speech comprehension.

In the brain, limbic lobe lies along the Parietal, Frontal and Temporal lobes. In limbic lobe, senses and emotional phenomena are formed and it is the core of the CL; the limbic cortex ought to be considered predominantly in the CL process so that the structure of CL is utterly based on emotions and senses (see means in Figure 4).

Figure 2. Basal Ganglia and Caudate Nucleus

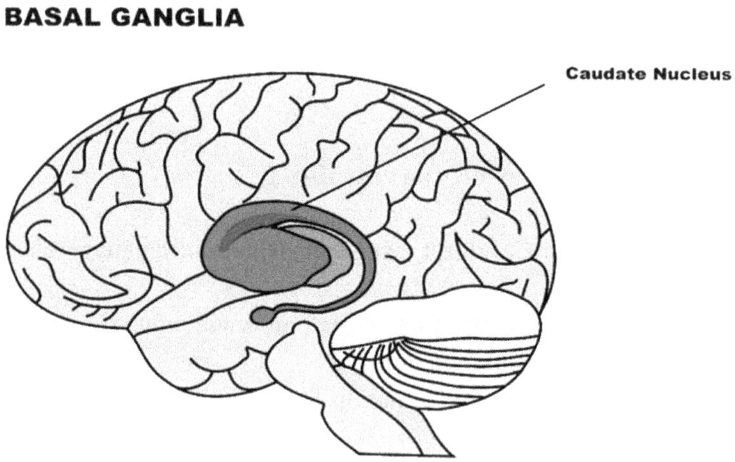

Figure 3. Broca's area and Wenicke's area

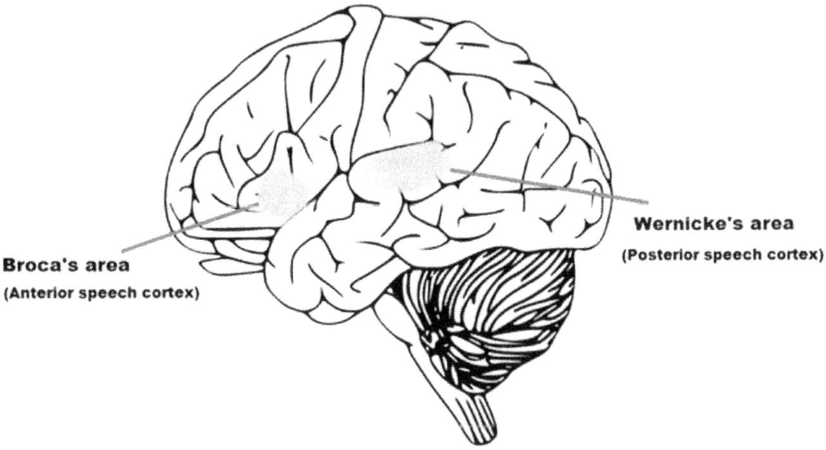

METHOD

In this study a survey is used to identify the language in potential and possible utterances of bilingual/multilingual individuals in specific emotion based situations. The language identification survey consists of 8 written questions (see means in Table 1) and these questions are intended to grasp the subconscious mind of individuals. The first and third question are related to reflexive utterances so they trigger limbic cortex, hence these two questions would be linchpin to identify the CL so as expression in the reflexive situations is in CL of individual.

Figure 4. Medial view of major subdivisions of cortex

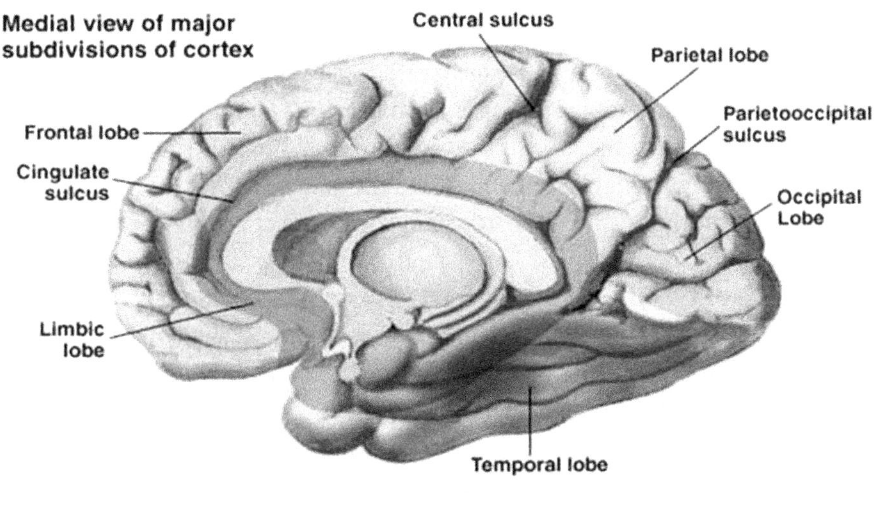

Table 2. Sample of the language ıdentification survey

<u>Age</u> :
<u>Languages spoken as native languages</u>:
<u>Origin</u>:

QUESTIONS

1. When you witness a shocking situation (e.g., A terrible crash or a bloody body on the floor) which language do you use abruptly and directly to show your reaction
2. Imagine that you are in court and blamed for killing a friend of you, but you are innocent and you will defend yourself, they will understand you whichever language you use. Think about your native languages and which one would you prefer to defend yourself?
3. Imagine that you are in a wooden house alone and that is a jungle your house is in. Sky is hazy and you go out to wander, and while walking you notice a tiger running towards you. What would be your first word in this situation? Imagine the atmosphere and then jot down the word directly, <u>do not translate it into English</u>.
4. In which language do you pray?
5. Which language do you use <u>mostly</u> in your dreams while sleeping?
6. Which language do you use in your daily life? How often do you use it and why do you prefer to use that language? Discuss it please by giving reasons. (e.g., I am Turkish but I use Italian at school because I live in Italy and mostly my friends are Italian at school however when I come home I turn back to Turkish, I speak Turkish with my family even though they can speak Italian fluently.)
7. What language do you use to talk inwardly?
8. Which language did you first acquire? (Your mother language)

This survey was implemented to more than 30 bilingual and multilingual people and 30 clear outcomes are obtained and analysed. Jean-Marc Dewaele and Aneta Pavlenko (2001-2003) conducted a webquestionnaire to elicit bi and multilinguals' own views and perceptions of the connections between their languages and emotions. The survey questions of CL and the webquestionnaire have some mutual parts. Both of them aimed to understand the emotion lying behind the language and the language lying behind the emotion.

In the first question it is intended to grasp the language which is especially in the case of fear and shock. In the second question with the part: "*they will understand you whichever language you use*" it is aimed to understand the individual's emotion towards the language because she/he is free to use any language she/he knows. The third question is to catch what language (word or phrase in this language) comes to an individual's mind initially in the case of anxiety and fear. It is asked in the third question not to translate the word or the phrase into English because test takers cannot be proficient in English or cannot find the exact English equivalent of their utterances. The fourth question is in order to bring out what language has the highest spiritual power on individual. The language in the subconscious/unconscious mind is the objective of the fifth question. What we experienced composes the content of dreams (Freud, 1900) and Freud also defines dreams as "*royal road to the unconscious*". Therefore the language using while dreaming indicates the language in unconscious mind that the central language. On the other hand the sixth question tells us the daily-life language of individual. Inward talking is associated with the reflexes because; when an individual starts to talk in her/his mind, the language is produced directly and suddenly that it is out of the control. That is why it may be called as reflexive talking.

RESULT

It is explicitly seen that each of the investigated individuals has an emotionally dominant language. Highlighted columns demonstrate elicitation of CL and they are compatible in most. Other answers of questions are also remarkable to figure out the language in subconscious mind of people. However there might be some discrepancies in answers; presumably the reason is not to be able to settle down to imagine the written situation. It is acknowledged that written questions don't have strong effect to understand individual's spoken utterance. By reading the written form of some specific situation, an individual cannot anticipate herself/himself in the situation perceptibly because reading merely cannot dominate the limbic cortex exactly as it happens in experienced situation (Buğa, 2016).

Buğa (2016) states that imagining a situation just by reading the written form of it has 2D effect in the brain however to experience a situation is a part of real-life so it can directly influence the limbic cortex of the brain, thus the 3D effect. Hernandez (2016) states: remembering something actually changes the content of memory; eyewitness testimony can actually lead to changes when compared to original written accounts of what someone said. What is needed to elicit CL is primarily to stimulate the limbic cortex. That's why, the survey needs to be strengthened by providing an environment including 3D effect. For further studies it will convey more valid outcomes.

DISCUSSION

At the present time, it is clear that bilingual and multilingual individuals have different cognitive system than monolinguals. Central language hypothesis comprises a part of this cognitive difference. Subconscious mind has a crucial role in the centralization process. That's why, what bilinguals/multilinguals experienced is quite important in terms of psychology and linguistics. The language they exposed in an emotion based situation starts to structure the centralization in subconscious mind and it can be seen as output in some other similar situation after a long time. Puberty has another critical role in this process that according to observations, bi-multilingual individuals have so many changes on their central language before puberty. To get a stabile result, testing on central language should be performed after puberty.

Central Language is considerably different than *mother tongue* and the *first language* because CL is sometimes the first language but sometimes the second or third language would be the central one. Thereby, the term "Central Language" covers the mother tongue, first and second language too. In a study of him, Foster includes (1996):

I was born in urban New York to parents who migrated to the U.S. from Cuba and the Dominican Republic in the 1930s. Spanish and English were expressive, vivid, and equally used modes of communicating in our daily lives....In the world of relationships within my family, each language included instructions about what part of me I could express, articulate, and develop through its use within a particular relationship. I used Spanish for loving my father, English for anger with my mother, Spanish for political discourse with everyone, and English for witty sarcasm with my aunts. These were rules about domains of language use and experience in my home that were finer than the gross distinctions of Spanish for home and English for school, or Spanish for early trauma and English for defense. (p.142, 143)

The language that dominates the emotions constructs the building blocks of central language. In the example above, individual has some emotions (e.g. love, anger etc.) in Spanish so it can be noted that presumably Spanish is the Central Language of this person.

In some cases and even more often, the first language would be the Central one however there are various, totally opposite situations. A retired teacher narrated her story (2015):

I was born in Georgia, my mother is Georgian but my father is Turkish. My mother and father had divorced and I had lived with my mother until 5ages in Georgia. My first language is Georgian and it was the only language I know. Afterwards my father and mother came together; however I did not speak Turkish so I could not speak Turkish with my father, in addition I did not understand what my father said me. We moved to Turkey after a period of time and I began school in Turkey and learned Turkish and I live in Turkey till now from those years and at the moment it is interesting that I don't know even one Georgian word; I cannot speak Georgian right now, I completely forgot that language. Whereas I was speaking only Georgian fluently till my 5 ages.

There is a language loss so this experience puts forward a contradiction about the notion of mother tongue or first language. Language forgetting which covers language loss or language attrition can be seen in bilinguals (Grosjean, 2013). It may open us a door to examine the notion of mother tongue (L1) again.

One of the studies of emotion-memory effects on bilinguals includes that in comparison with L2, L1 has many more emotional connotations on bilingual individuals (Ayçiçeği-Dinn & Caldwell-Harris, 2009). In native language, emotion and emotion-laden words are recalled much more than the second language (Pavlenko, 2005). Nevertheless the experience of Georgian bilingual person above has a discrepancy with those results of emotion-memory effects studies. Moreover, results of the other emotion-memory effect tasks include that L2 is also equally intense in emotion-memory of bilinguals (Ayçiçeği-Dinn & Caldwell-Harris, 2009).

There are different aspects of using different language that Grosjean stated (1997):

Bilinguals usually acquire and use their languages for different purposes, in different domains of life, with different people. Different aspects of life often require different languages.

In these different domains, purposes and aspects; emotion based ones cause bilinguals to produce the Central language.

Central language might be the second language of an individual. The concept of "mother tongue" does not mean the language which dominates the emotions of individuals. Based on the exposure and experiences of individual, the second or the third language may be emotionally dominant (see *Table 3*) because it is possible to be competent in a language after years of the first language acquisition. Hernandez stated (2016):

Even when this window presumably closes, it isn't completely closed. It can be reopened. And it offers us some answers to how it is that someone who's older, maybe three or five years of age, could actually learn a language and sound like a native, and perceive it very similarly to a native. Specifically, it appears that their window reopened.

There, Hernandez's statements overlap the concept of the Central Language so that it may be the second language as well. In spite of the fact that it takes years, notably socialized L2 user can be competent and confident in expressing her/his emotions (Dewaele J.-M., 2013).

Largely L1 has more emotional intensity in childhood memories than L2 (Schrauf & Rubin, 1998). Dewaele (2013) points out that L2 has less emotional effect than L1. On the other hand L2 is not always the language of detachment; for some bi-multilingual speakers L1 may be away from emotions (Pavlenko, 2005). In the language identification survey (see Table 3) *G2* states that the first acquired language of him is Spanish but in reflexive and emotional situations he uses English. He says "I mostly use English because it is the language which exists at my home, my

Table 3. Compiled results of the survey (The identity of the interviewees are reserved)

NAMES / Age/ First Language	Native Languages	In Shocking Sit.1	To Defend Own Self Better	In Shocking Sit. 2	Language to Pray	Language in Dreams	Language in Daily Life	Inward Language
A1 / 22 / Turkish	Turkish & Dutch	Dutch	Dutch	Dutch	Turkish	Dutch	Dutch-Turkish	Dutch
B1/ 21/ Turkish	Turkish & English	English	English	English	English-Turkish	English-Turkish	Turkish	Turkish
C1/ 23/ Greek	Greek & Dutch	Greek	Greek	Greek	Greek	Greek	Greek-Dutch	Greek
D1/23/Turkish	German & Turkish	German	Turkish	German	Turkish	Turkish	Turkish	Turkish
E1/26/Kurdish	Turkish & Kurdish	Kurdish	Turkish	-	Turkish	Kurdish	Kurdish	Kurdish
F1/26/Japan	Turkish & Japan	Japan	-	Japan	Japan	Japan	Turkish	Turkish
G1/26/Kurdish	Turkish & Kurdish	Kurdish	Turkish	Turkish	Kurdish	Turkish-Kurdish	Turkish	Turkish
H1/55/Zazaki	Zazaki & Turkish	Turkish	Turkish	Turkish	Turkish	Turkish	Turkish	Turkish
I1/ 21/ Kurdish	Turkish & Kurdish	Turkish	Turkish	Turkish	Turkish	Turkish	Turkish	Turkish
J1/ 21/ Turkish	Albanian & Turkish	Turkish	Turkish	Turkish	Turkish	Turkish	Turkish-Albanian	Turkish-Albanian
K1/24/ Galician	Galician & Spanish	Galician	Galician	Spanish	Galician	Spanish	Spanish	Galician
L1/22/ Turkish	German & Turkish	Turkish	German	Turkish	Turkish	Turkish	Turkish-German	Turkish
M1/22/ Turkish	German & Turkish	Turkish	Turkish	Turkish	Turkish	Turkish	German	Turkish
N1/23/ Turkish	German & Turkish	German	Turkish	German	Turkish	Turkish	Turkish	Turkish
O1/21/Urdu	Urdu & German	German	German	German	German	German	German-Urdu	German
P1/36/Turkish	Turkish & German	German	German	German	Turkish	German	German-Turkish	German
Q1/49/Zazaki	Zazaki & Turkish	Zazaki	Turkish	Zazaki	Zazaki	Turkish	Turkish	Turkish
R1/36/Turkish	German & Turkish	German	German	German	Turkish	-	German	-
S1/24/ Cantonese	Cantonese & Mandarin &English	Mandarin	Mandarin	English	Cantonese	Cantonese	Cantonese	Mandarin
T1/23/ Cantonese	Cantonese & Mandarin & English	Cantonese	Cantonese	English	Cantonese	Cantonese	Cantonese	Cantonese
U1/24/ Mandarin	Mandarin & English	Mandarin	Mandarin	Mandarin	Mandarin	English	English	Mandarin-English
V1/21/Urdu	German & Urdu	German	German	German	German	German	German	German
Y1/27/Arabic	Turkmen & Arabic & English & Turkish	English	Turkish	Turkish	Arabic	Turkish	English	Turkish
W1 /20/ Azerbaijani	Azerbaijani & Russian	Russian	Azerbaijani	Russian	Azerbaijani	Azerbaijani	-	-
X1/23/Greek	Greek & Dutch	Greek	Greek	Greek	Greek	Greek	Dutch	Greek
Y1/21/Dutch	Dutch & English & Arabic	English	English	English	-	English	English	English
Z1/35/Arabic	Arabic & Turkish	Turkish	Turkish	Turkish	Arabic	Turkish	Turkish	Turkish

continued on following page

Table 3. Continued

NAMES / Age/ First Language	Native Languages	In Shocking Sit.1	To Defend Own Self Better	In Shocking Sit. 2	Language to Pray	Language in Dreams	Language in Daily Life	Inward Language
A2/65/ Georgian	Georgian & Turkish	Turkish	Turkish	Turkish	Turkish	Turkish	Turkish	Turkish
B2/30/ Ukranian & Russian	Russian & Ukranian & English	Russian	Russian	English	Russian	Russian	English	Russian
C2/38/Uzbek & Turkish	Uzbek & Turkish & Russian	Uzbek	-	Turkish	Uzbek-Turkish	Turkish	Uzbek-Turkish	Uzbek - Turkish
D2/29 /Arabic	Arabic & French & English	English	Arabic – English	English	Arabic	English	English	English
E2 /31/ Greek	English & Greek	English	English	English	-	English	English	English
F2/28/Arabic	English & Arabic & French	English	English	English	Arabic	Arabic	English	English
G2/27/Spanish	English & Kurdish & Russian & Spanish & Turkish	English	English	English	-	English	English	English
H2/23/Arabic	English/Arabic/ French	Arabic	English	French	Arabic	English	English	English

office and the most common language of the majority of my friends". Based upon his statements, Central Language of him is English not his first language "Spanish". Dewaele (2008) defines the language which has a strong effect on emotions as the language of heart and states that it can shift. In his multilingual study Dewaele (2008) presents that emotional weight of "I love you" depends on the people. In this survey, large amount of people reported that *I love you* in L1 has much more emotional influence but according to some of the participants, influence of the phrase is equal both in L1 and LX (any language which is not the L1). Furthermore some other participants reported that the phrase "I love you" is the strongest in an LX. Regarding these matters, Central language of a bi-multilingual person may change till the end of puberty and differ from another one that has the same conditions. It depends on personal experiences and emotional encoding of the language. To be structured a language as CL, exposure is the main element and more substantial part for interlocutors is emotional weight of the situation in which a language appeared. Any language learnt in classroom environment cannot be used to express emotions as effectively as the language acquired in authentic interactions outside the classroom (Dewaele, 2013). It is a crystal-clear fact that in majority, bi-multilingual people's central languages are their first languages because of the immersion however it does not mean that the first language/mother tongue is the language of the emotions and reflexive utterances. Even if for many multilingual people L1 is the language of heart, it does not mean that it is the permanent one (Dewaele, 2013). The fact that L2 or LX can also dominate the emotions as L1 reveals the notion of Central Language.

FUTURE RESEARCH

To identify any individual's central language, it is indispensable to observe her/him in emotion-based events while she/he is producing language. So as to have that kind of observations, social and psychological surveys are required. By the help of social and psychological surveys, enough data can be collected in an experimental way. In addition, in emotion-based situations, scanning the movement of neurons among cortices provides a neurolinguistic approach to the hypothesis of central language. In addition, for further step, the hypothesis of central language will be utilized and studied in the field of consciousness studies.

Central language hypothesis may contribute to the science of psychology in terms of cognition, psychology of language processing and emotions in language. Also it can provide a resource to the field of cognitive science and that way varied aspects may be developed to make new researches and studies.

CONCLUSION

Concept of Central Language has been generated by realizing a specific language which is produced particularly in emotion-based situations by bi/multilingual individuals. Central language hypothesis is an innovative and multidisciplinary study that can be analysed both by neurolinguistic and psycholinguistic surveys. It also brings a new perspective about how human brain dominates languages and emotions and how emotions and language are interconnected. Additionally, it seems that emotions are encoded into some phrases or words by multilingual individuals hence to analyze the unconsciousness; the study of CL would be a convenient step. This is a fact that to be able to analyze human psychology, language and psychological background of language ought to be studied. From this point of view, central language hypothesis has emerged and been studied.

REFERENCES

Abutalebi, J., & Green, D. (2007). Bilingual Language Production: The Neurocognition of Language Representation and Control. *Journal of Neurolinguistics, 20*(3), 242–275. doi:10.1016/j.jneuroling.2006.10.003

Aron, A. R. (2007). The Neural Basis of Inhibition in Cognitive Control. *The Neuroscientist, 13*(3), 214–228. doi:10.1177/1073858407299288 PMID:17519365

Ayçiçeği-Dinn, A., & Caldwell-Harris, C. (2009). *Emotion-memory effects in bilingual speakers: A levels-of-processing approach.* Bilingualism.

Bhatia, T. K. (2006). Author. In T. K. Bhatia & W. C. Ritchie (Eds.), The Handbook of Bilingualism (pp. 5-6). Blackwell.

Birkner, V. (2016). Revisiting Input an Output Hypotheses in Second Language Learning. *Asian Education Studies, 1*(1).

Blakemore, D. (1992). *Understanding Utterances.* Oxford, UK: Blackwell.

Buğa, D. (2016). Central Language Hypothesis in the Decision-Making Process. In B. Christiansen & E. Lechman (Eds.), *Neuroeconomics and Decision-Making Process* (pp. 66–83). Hershey, PA: IGI Global. doi:10.4018/978-1-4666-9989-2.ch004

Chauncey, K., Grainger, J., & Holcomb, P. J. (2008). Code-Switching Effects In Bilingual Word Recognition: A Masked Priming Study with Event-Related Potentials. *Brain and Language, 105*(3), 161–174. doi:10.1016/j.bandl.2007.11.006 PMID:18191445

Cherry, B. J. (2003). Memory, Explicit / Implicit. In H. Withaker (Ed.), *Concise Encyclopedia of Brain and Language* (pp. 332–334). Oxford, UK: Elsevier.

Chomsky, N. (1965). *Aspects Of The Theory Of Syntax.* The M.I.T. Press.

Chomsky, N. (2006). *Language and Mind.* New York: Cambridge University Press. doi:10.1017/CBO9780511791222

Christoffels, I. K., Firk, C., & Schiller, N. O. (2007). Bilingual Language Control: An event-related brain potential study. *Brain Research*, 193. PMID:17391649

Christoffels, I. K., Firk, C., & Schiller, N. O. (2007). Bilingual Language Control: An event-related brain potential study. *Brain Research, 1147*, 192–208. doi:10.1016/j.brainres.2007.01.137 PMID:17391649

Cicogna, P., & Bosinelli, M. (2001). Consciousness During Dreams. *Consciousness and Cognition, 10*(1), 26–41. doi:10.1006/ccog.2000.0471 PMID:11273624

Coello, Y., & Bartolo, A. (2013). *Language and Action in Cognitive Neuroscience.* New York: Psychology Press.

Costa, A., & Pickering, M. J. (2016). Do Bilinguals Automatically Activate Their Native Language When They Are Not Using It? *Cognitive Science.* PMID:27766658

Dawaele, J.-M., & Pavlenko, A. (2001-2003). *Web questionnaire bilingualism and emotions.* University of London.

Dewaele, J.-M. (2006). Expressing Anger in Multiple Languages. In A. Pavlenko (Ed.), *Bilingual Minds: Emotional Experience, Expression and Representation*. Multilingual Matters Ltd.

Dewaele, J.-M. (2008). The emotional weight of "I love you" in multilinguals' languages. *Journal of Pragmatics, 40*(10), 1753–1780. doi:10.1016/j.pragma.2008.03.002

Dewaele, J.-M. (2013). Multilingualism and Emotions. In C. A. Chapelle (Ed.), *The Encyclopedia of Applied Linguistics*. Blackwell Publishing.

Edwards, J. (2006). Foundations of Bilingualism. In T. Bhatia & W. Ritchie (Eds.), *The Handbook of Bilingualism* (pp. 5–29). Oxford, UK: Blackwell. doi:10.1002/9780470756997.ch1

Foster, R. P. (1996). The bilingual self—thoughts from a scientific positivist or pragmatic psychoanalyst? *Psychoanalytic Dialogues*, 142–143.

Gass, S. M., & Selinker, L. (2008). *Second Language Acquisition*. New York: Routledge.

Grosjean, F. (1997). The Bilingual Individual. *Interpreting, 2*(1-2), 163–187. doi:10.1075/intp.2.1-2.07gro

Grosjean, F. (2013). Bilingualism: A Short Introduction. In F. Grosjean & P. Li (Eds.), *The Psycholinguistics of Bilingualism* (pp. 5–25). Wiley-Blackwell.

Harley, T. A. (2008). *The Psychology of Language*. New York: Psychology Press.

Harris, C. L., Gleason, J. B., & Ayçiçeği, A. (2006). When is a First Language More emotional? Psychophysiological Evidence from Bilingual Speakers. In A. Pavlenko (Eds.), Bilingual Minds: Emotional Experience, Expression and Representation (pp. 257-279). Multilingual Matters.

Hernandez, A. (2016). *Bilingual Brain*. Houston, TX: University of Houston.

Houwer, A. D. (2016). Bilingual language input environments, intake, maturity and practice. *Bilingualism: Language and Cognition*.

Ivanova, I., Murillo, M., Montoya, R. I., & Gollan, T. H. (2016). Does Bilingual Language Control Decline in Older Age? *Linguistic Approaches to Bilingualism, 6*(1-2), 86–118. doi:10.1075/lab.15003.iva PMID:28090222

Kecskes, I., & Albertazzi, L. (2007). *Cognitive Aspects of Bilingualism*. Dordrecht: Springer. doi:10.1007/978-1-4020-5935-3

Lee, N., & Schumann, J. H. (2005). The interactional instinct: The evolution and acquisition of language. Congress of the International Association for applied Linguistics, Madison, WI.

Levelt, W. J. (2013). *A History of Psycholinguistics*. Oxford University Press.

Lindquist, K. A., MacCormack, J., & Shablack, H. (2015). The Role of Language in Emotion: Predictions From Psychological Constructionism. *Frontiers in Psychology*, *6*. doi:10.3389/fpsyg.2015.00444 PMID:25926809

Molnar, M., Ibáñez-Molina, A., & Carreiras, M. (2015). Interlocutor Identitiy Affects Language Activation in Bilinguals. *Journal of Memory and Language*, *81*, 91–104. doi:10.1016/j.jml.2015.01.002

Nickels, L., Biedermann, B., Fieder, N., & Schiller, N. O. (2015). The Lexical-Syntactic Representation of Numbers. *Language, Cognition and Neuroscience*, *30*(3), 287–304. doi:10.1080/23273798.2013.879191

Pavlenko, A. (2005). *Emotions and Multilingualism*. New York: Cambridge University Press.

Perlovsky, L. (2009). Language and Cognition. *Neural Networks*, *22*(3), 247–257. doi:10.1016/j.neunet.2009.03.007 PMID:19419838

Perlovsky, L. (2009). Language and Emotions: Emotional Sapir-Whorf Hypothesis. *Neural Networks*, *22*(5-6), 518–526. doi:10.1016/j.neunet.2009.06.034 PMID:19616406

Reinders, H. (2012). *Towards a definition of intake in second language acquisition*. Applied Research in English.

Schrauf, W. R., & Rubin, D. C. (1998). Bilingual Autobiographical Memory in Older Adult Immigrants: A Test of Cognitive Explanations of the Reminiscence Bump. *Journal of Memory and Language*, *39*(3), 437–457. doi:10.1006/jmla.1998.2585

Strijkers, K., & Costa, A. (2016). On Words and Brains: Linking psycholinguistics with neural dynamics in speech production. *Language, Cognition and Neuroscience*, *31*(4), 524–535. doi:10.1080/23273798.2016.1158845

The Anatomy of the Brain. (2015). Retrieved on April 12, 2015, from: http://psychology.about.com/od/biopsychology/ss/brainstructure_2.htm

The Brain and Its Functions. (2015). Retrieved on April 9, 2015, from: http://mybrainonline.ca/?page=3

Traxler, M. J., & Gernsbacher, M. A. (2006). *Handbook of Psycholinguistics*. Oxford, UK: Elsevier.

Wei, L. (2000). *The Bilingual Reader*. London: Routledge. doi:10.4324/9780203461341

Wei, L., & Moyer, M. G. (2008). *The Blackwell Guide to Research Methods in Bilingualism and Multilingualism*. Oxford, UK: Blackwell Publishing. doi:10.1002/9781444301120

Whitaker, H. (2010). *Concise Encyclopedia of Brain and Language*. Oxford, UK: Elsevier.

ADDITIONAL READING

Clement, R., Gardner, R. C., & Smythe, P. C. (1980). Social and individual factors in second language acquisition. *Canadian Journal of Behavioural Science*, *12*(4), 293–302. doi:10.1037/h0081081

Grimshaw, G. M., Adelstein, A., Bryden, M. P., & MacKinnon, G. E. (1998). First-Language Acqusition in Adolescence: Evidence for a Critical Period for Verbal Language Development. *Brain and Language*, *63*(2), 237–255. doi:10.1006/brln.1997.1943 PMID:9654433

Lacan, J. (2006). *Écrits*. New York: W. W. Norton & Company.

VanPatten, B., & Williams, J. (Eds.). (2007). *Theories in second language acquisition: An introduction*. Mahwah, NJ: Lawrence Erlbaum Associates Publishers.

Chapter 2
The Role of Context on Age of Acquisition Effect:
Strategic Control in Word Naming in Turkish

Ilhan Raman
Middlesex University, UK

ABSTRACT

Processes involved in converting print to sound are reported to be flexible and under the strategic control of skilled readers even in transparent orthographies. In this respect, word frequency effect, regularity, and lexicality have been the topic of much research and debate in understanding how context is involved in the emergence of strategies. However, whether age of acquisition (AoA) effects are influenced by context and under the strategic control of readers have yet to be established. A series of single-word naming experiments addresses this issue and examines the role of filler type critically manipulated on lexicality, frequency, and imageability on the size of AoA effect in word naming in an entirely transparent orthography. Overall, results, which are discussed within the current theoretical frameworks, suggest that context plays a significant role on AoA.

INTRODUCTION

It has long been acknowledged that readers can attune their reading strategies in response to task demands as determined by context (e.g. Frederiksen & Kroll, 1976; Baluch & Besner, 1991; Paap & Noel, 1991; Rastle & Coltheart, 1999). An example

DOI: 10.4018/978-1-5225-4009-0.ch002

of this flexibility in selecting the most effective strategy is observed when the effect of word frequency is eliminated when subjects name words and nonwords mixed together in a single block. Historically, this phenomenon reported in English and other orthographies had been explained within the dual-route model of reading (e.g., Baluch & Besner, 1991; Coltheart & Rastle, 1994; Monsell, Patterson, Graham, Hughes, & Milroy, 1992; Raman, Baluch & Sneddon, 1996; Rastle & Coltheart, 1999; Reynolds & Besner, 2005; Tabossi & Laghi, 1992; Zevin & Balota, 2000). According to the dual-route model generation of phonology can take place via two qualitatively distinct routes: namely the lexical and the nonlexical route (e.g. Coltheart, 1978; Coltheart and colleagues, 1993; 1999). What characterizes these two routes is that while the nonlexical phonology can be 'assembled' via rules, assumptions about generating phonology via the lexical route is twofold: One way to generate lexical phonology is assumed to be via the direct orthography-to-phonology, OP, route where words' phonology is directly 'addressed'. A second way of generating lexical phonology is assumed to be via the orthography-to-semantics route where a word's meaning is activated for the purpose of generating phonology. Some dual-route theorists have argued that the dual-route model is in effect a three-route model, whilst, it is generally assumed that the impact of the semantic route on single-word naming in skilled reading is minimal (e.g. Besner, 1999; Besner & Smith, 1992). This is because the general consensus within the dual-route framework (in terms of RTs) is that attaining phonology from print via the semantic route is the slowest of the two routes. It is further assumed that the involvement of the semantic route in computing words' phonology is only facilitated when words' semantic characteristics such as imageability is involved. However, it must be highlighted that systematic investigation of imageability effects in single-word naming is not a widely explored issue in English with the exception of several papers (Strain, Patterson, & Seidenberg, 1995; Hino & Lupker, 1996) and to date just a handful of papers have been reported on other writing systems, e.g. Persian (Baluch & Besner, 2001) and Turkish (Raman & Baluch, 2001). In summary, semantics is assumed to contribute to the computation of phonology from print in orthographies with inconsistent and/or irregular OP representations, such as English and opaque Persian, but not in orthographies with entirely consistent OP representations such as Turkish. It would be naïve to assume that there is no semantic involvement in reading entirely transparent orthographies as semantic information ought to be utilized in order to extract meaning during reading. When OP mappings are entirely transparent, however, the input from semantics in decoding OP mappings that are exception to the rule becomes redundant. Therefore, the claim here is that semantics develops and exerts itself differentially as a function of orthographic transparency across different languages. Indeed, evidence for this claim was presented in Turkish (Raman & Baluch, 2001) and Persian (Baluch & Besner, 2001).

Insofar as strategies are considered, although several positions (e.g. attentional control, de-emphasis of routes) have been proposed to explain the phenomenon of how presenting identical target stimuli in different contexts, i.e. mixed vs pure blocks, has differential influence on RTs and accuracy, the time criterion is the most plausible alternative account thus far (Lupker, Brown & Colombo, 1997; Kinoshita & Lupker 2002; 2007). The proposition is that a time-criterion which is determined by the perceived difficulty of the stimuli to be named is active prior to computing a phonological output. The notion of difficulty is central to time-criterion because it leads to strategically adjusting the generation of an acceptable criterion appropriate for all stimuli to be named which in effect leads to the homogenisation of RTs. Previous work in Turkish explored the role of nonword fillers on word frequency in which single-word naming in Turkish was strongly influenced by the setting of a time-criterion in response to presence of nonwords that lent support to the time-criterion account (Raman, Baluch & Besner, 2004). While the time-criterion account is mute with respect to the issue of the nature of OP representations, the number of routes and which route drives the computation of phonology, one of it's most prominent feature is that readers employ a checking strategy especially under 'slow' conditions such as the irregular English words when computing phonology. This strategy is to ensure that a corresponding phonological code exists in the phonological output lexicon prior to attempting articulation, hence maximising a successful outcome. It is not yet established whether a checking mechanism can be extended to totally transparent orthographies in which OP mappings are one-to-one with very low error rates in pronunciation in which such a mechanism would redeem futile. Equally, it could be argued that the checking mechanism may evolve as an artefact of the writing system.

Traditionally, research on examining strategies in word naming has primarily focused on the influence of context on word frequency and regularity effects, and lexicality, i.e. the use of nonwords (e.g., Baluch & Besner, 1991, Kinoshita & Lupker, 2002; 2007, Lupker, et al, 1997; Raman et al, 1996, Raman et al, 2004, Reynolds & Besner, 2005 amongst others). It is of importance, therefore, to explore whether context will differentially influence and modify another lexical variable that has attracted much research, namely AoA. According to Johnston and Barry (2006) 'AoA effects .. have also been claimed to operate either instead of, or over and above, those of word frequency.'. Understanding the conditions that facilitate or hinder the AoA effects in word naming will be a key addition to the growing body of literature on strategies.

It is widely accepted that the age at which particular words enter into our vocabulary has a long-lasting effect such that early acquired words have been consistently demonstrated to possess an advantage over words that are acquired comparably later on in life (see Juhasz, 2005, and Johnston & Barry, 2006 for comprehensive reviews). This advantage known as the AoA effect has an impact on lexical processing, picture naming and face recognition amongst other tasks. More importantly, AoA is now agreed to be a universal phenomenon in lexical processing irrespective of the linguistic properties of a given language. To date reports exist in alphabetic languages such as English (e.g., Gerhand & Barry, 1999; Morrison & Ellis, 1999; and Morrison & Ellis, 2000; Morrison, Hirsh, Chappell & Ellis, 2002), Spanish (e.g., Cuetos, Ellis & Alvarez, 1999), French (Bonin and colleagues, 2001; 2002), Italian (Barca, Burani & Arduino, 2002; Bates, Burani, D'Amico & Barca, 2001), Greek (e.g., Bogka, Masterson, Druks, Fragkioudaki, Chatziprokopiou & Economou, 2003), Dutch (e.g., Ghyselinck, Custers & Brysbaert, 2004), Turkish (Raman, 2006), German (Brase & Raman, 2009) and non-alphabetic languages such as Japanese (Havelka & Tomita, 2006; and Yamazaki, Ellis, Morrison & Lambon Ralph, 1997) and Chinese (Chen and colleagues, 2007a, 2007b).

The arbitrary mapping hypothesis (Ellis & Lambon Ralph, 2000; Monaghan & Ellis, 2002a; 2002b) and the semantic hypothesis (Brysbaert, Lange & Van Wijnendaele, 2000; Brysbaert, van Wijnendaele & De Deyne, 2000) are two main theoretical views that explain the locus of AoA effects in lexical processing. Whilst OP mappings are central to understanding the AoA effects in the former account, semantics is at centre of the latter view. Therefore, OP mappings together with semantics play a central role in understanding the AoA effects particularly as a function of orthographic transparency. If one assumes that AoA (and imageability) arise at the level of arbitrary mappings and/or semantics then we would not expect reliable effects in writing systems in which OP mappings are totally predictable and one-to-one. This premise is partially supported in that no reliable imageability effects were found in Turkish (Raman & Baluch, 2001) or in transparent Persian (Baluch & Besner, 2001) whilst a robust AoA effect in word naming was reported in Turkish (Raman, 2006). Collectively the findings suggest that in extremely transparent orthographies a) the contribution of semantics is minimal insofar as computation of phonology is concerned (but see point above in the role of semantics in extracting meaning), and b) a reliable AoA effect is perhaps indicative of a lexical locus for AoA, similar to word frequency. Consequently, since reports of AoA effects are so ubiquitous AoA must be a universal and an inherent property of the cognitive architecture (Raman, 2006).

The aim of the series of experiments reported here is twofold: a) first, the aim is to explore the impact of context on AoA to test the claims of the time-criterion account - a limitation in the current literature - in an entirely transparent orthography and b) second, to examine the issue of strategic control in word naming in relation to AoA. If the time-criterion account holds true, then the AoA effect is predicted to vary and to be modified in response to the ease/difficulty of the filler stimuli. More specifically, a significant AoA effect is expected to be maintained when Early and

Late items are presented on their own in Experiments 1 and 6 as well as with High frequency and High imageable filler items in Experiments 2 and 7, respectively. Moreover, AoA effect should be reduced considerably when Early and Late items are presented with nonwords, in Experiments 5 and 10 as well as when presented with Low frequency and Low imageable items in Experiments 4 and 9. The effect of Mid frequency and Mid imageable filler items is expected to considerably reduce the AoA effect.

GENERAL METHOD

Participants

Participation in all experiments was on a voluntary basis from native Turkish speaking undergraduate students at the Eastern Mediterranean University, Cyprus. Each experiment employed a different set of participants who did not take part in any other experiment. Participants were given course accreditation in return of their participation.

Apparatus and Procedure

Participants were instructed to call out each word presented on the computer screen as fast and as accurately as possible. The stimuli were presented one at a time using Superlab experimental software. Each word appeared in the centre of an Acer notepad screen in Times New Roman, black 32-point lowercase font. All test items were mixed at random and presented in two blocks. A block of practice trials with 10 words were presented for naming prior to the main experiment. This allowed the participants to familiarise themselves with the experimental procedure and for the voice key to be adjusted accordingly. Order of presentation for each block of stimuli was counterbalanced for participants. Reaction times were recorded via a voice activated microphone. A 1000ms inter-stimulus interval was followed by the target word which remained on the screen until it was named. Errors were noted by the experimenter.

Materials

The target and filler stimuli used in the experiments came from previously established norms for AoA, imageability and frequency in Turkish (Raman, 2001; 2004; 2006). Word frequency, imageability and AoA counts were obtained for 433 words based on subjective ratings from 50 highly literate, native speakers of Turkish. Frequency norms were obtained by asking participants to indicate the frequency with which they encountered a word on a 7-point rating scale ranging from 1 (most frequent) to 7 (least frequent). Subjective ratings thought to be closely linked with objective norms (Gernsbacher, 1984; Gordon, 1985) were used for frequency, AoA and imageability in the absence of objective word norms in Turkish. Word imageability was also rated on a 7-point scale ranging from 7 (very high imageability) to 1 (no imageability). Word imageability norms in Turkish was previously demonstrated to be reliably correlated with (r = 0.8) with those obtained by Paivio, Yuille and Madigan (1968) in English (see Raman & Baluch, 2001 for details). For example, a high imageable word such as ANNE (*mother*) has a rating of 6.3 in Turkish and a corresponding rating of 6.7 in Paivio et. al.'s scale. Similarly, a low imageable word such as FELEK (*fate*) has a rating of 1.98 in Turkish and 2.3 in English.

The instructions for AoA ratings were adapted from Gilhooly and Logie (1980) in that participants were required to estimate the age they encountered a word for the first time in their language environment - either in spoken or written form. The scale on which they had to indicate the acquisition age ranged from 1 to 7, where 1 = 0-2 years old, 2 = 3-4 years old, 3 = 4-5 years old, 4 = 5-6 years old, 5 = 7-9 years old, 6 = 10-11 years old and 7 = 12 years old or older. For the purpose of the study, a word was selected as being acquired early if it had a mean rating of 2.5 (up to 4yrs of age) or less, and late if it had a mean rating of 6 (over 10yrs of age) or above.

Two target word sets, Early AoA and Late AoA, each with 25 items were created. All words in each of the two sets were high frequency, high Imageable and were matched on initial phoneme, letter and syllable length. The critical variable was AoA with an early acquired word such as GÜNEŞ (*sun*) matched with a late acquired word GÜMÜŞ (*silver*). Early AoA and Late AoA Turkish words and their English equivalents are presented with their corresponding AoA, imageability and frequency ratings in the Appendix. The norms for English translations were obtained from the electronic MRC Psycholinguistic Database.

The filler items were matched to the target stimuli on as many variables particularly on number of letters and initial phoneme as best as possible. In addition, care was taken to match the filler items in Study 1 (High, Mid, and Low Frequency conditions) with Study 2 (High, Mid, and Low Imageable conditions) on AoA, Imageability, Frequency and Letter length in an attempt to control for as many extraneous variables as possible. Summary statistics for Target and Filler items are presented in Table 1. Full details of the filler items including the nonwords used in Experiments 5 and 10 are presented in the Appendix.

Table 1. Summary statistics (Mean and SD) of target and filler items AoA, imageability and frequency ratings together with letter and syllable length

	Target Stimuli		Filler Items Study 1			Filler Items Study 2		
	Early AoA	Late AoA	HF Exp 2	MF Exp 3	LF Exp 4	HI Exp 7	MI Exp 8	LI Exp 9
AoA	1.89 (.31)	4.54 (.64)	3.34 (.82)	4.89 (.91)	4.97 (.64)	3.47 (.86)	4.64 (.87)	4.98 (.65)
Imageability	5.33 (.32)	5.03 (.30)	4.94 (.34)	4.56 (.28)	3.33 (.84)	5.02 (.51)	4.78 (.23)	2.78 (.60)
Frequency	1.78 (.46)	1.96 (.36)	1.77 (.20)	3.78 (.18)	4.63 (.48)	1.93 (.62)	3.05 (.82)	4.01 (1.44)
Letter Length	4.04 (1.17)	4.44 (1.39)	4.54 (.86)	5.62 (1.59)	5.10 (1.17)	5.04 (1.01)	4.98 (1.08)	5.24 (1.08)
Syllable Length	1.76 (.44)	1.76 (.60)	1.84 (.37)	2.24 (.66)	2.08 (.44)	2.02 (.32)	2.02 (.38)	2.18 (.56)

Study 1

Study 1 comprised five single-word naming experiments all utilising the target items (25 Early and 25 Late acquired words) in the presence of filler items manipulated on frequency (high, mid, low) and lexicality (nonwords).

Experiment 1

In a single-word naming task, 33 participants were required to call out 25 early and 25 late acquired target items only. The mean RTs for early acquired words was 519ms compared to 550ms for late acquired words and a planned comparison showed that this difference (31ms) was statistically significant [$t(32)=4.04$ $p<0.0001$]. This finding is in line with earlier reports of a reliable AoA effect in Turkish.

Experiment 2

The results of Experiment 1 re-establish that early acquired words are named significantly faster than late acquired words in Turkish. The aim of Experiment 2 is to examine the impact of filler stimuli, namely High frequency words, on the AoA effect. A different group of 34 participants were asked to read aloud the target items together with 50 High frequency filler words. If reading is under the strategic control of readers as previously reported in Raman et al (2004) we predict that according to the time-criterion account, the AoA effect should prevail because

High-frequency filler items are ‘easy’ items to name. Due to the large proportion (75%) of fast items comprised of Early items (25%) together with High frequency filler items (50%) in the naming task, all RTs irrespective of AoA should be speeded up if homogenisation of RTs occur.

The mean RTs for early acquired items was 499ms and 517ms for late acquired items yielding a difference of 18ms between the two conditions that was significant [$t(33)=4.05$ $p<0.0001$]. Noteworthy is that as predicted both mean RTs for early and late acquired words are faster than in Experiment 1.

Experiment 3

It is clear from the results in Experiment 2 that when a large proportion of stimuli in the naming list are ‘easy/fast’, the RTs for the target stimuli are speeded up. Employing 36 participants, Experiment 3 investigates the role of 50 mid-frequency filler items, presumably ‘slower’ items than high-frequency words, on AoA. Again, if participants modify their RTs in response to the naming list, which is comprised of fast Early items (25%), slow Late items (25%) and mid-speed Mid frequency fillers (50%) one would predict overall RTs to slow down and the AoA to be reduced as a result as homogenisation occurs.

A 15ms difference found between the mean RTs of early acquired words (516ms) and late acquired words (531ms) was significant in the planned comparison [$t(35)=2.3$ $p<0.03$]. It is important to note however that there is a considerable overall slowing down of the RTs compared to Experiment 2.

Experiment 4

As can be seen in Experiment 3, the RTs for each condition have slowed down whereby a significant AoA has been maintained. The aim of Experiment 4 is to investigate the impact of 50 low-frequency items on AoA. Participants were 36 undergraduates. It is predicted that AoA will be eliminated or largely reduced to reflect the influence of a large proportion (75%) of slow items made up of Late items (25%) and Low frequency filler items (50%) on the homogenisation of RTs in the list compared to 25% fast Early items if readers adjust their naming in response to the naming list.

The mean RTs for early acquired words is 524ms and for late acquired words 529ms. The difference of 5ms is non-significant [$t(35)=1.8$ $p>0.05$] in the planned comparison. This finding is in line with the predictions of the time-criterion account.

Experiment 5

The findings from Experiment 4 clearly demonstrate that RTs are slowed down in response to low-frequency filler words such that the AoA effect is eliminated. It is of interest to turn to Experiment 5 in which filler items are matched nonwords, or 'very slow' items. In line with the time criterion account, the outcome is expected to be similar to Experiment 4 will a null effect for AoA as 75% of items are slow compared with 25% that are fast. Thirty-six undergraduate students took part in this task.

The mean RTs for early acquired words was 534ms versus 539ms for late acquired words. The difference between the two conditions (5ms) was non-significant [$t(35)=1.7$ $p>0.05$]. Moreover, in line with previous reports in Turkish a reliable lexicality effect, i.e., the faster naming of words compared to matched nonwords, was observed.

A summary of the results of Study 1 across five experiments can be seen in Table 2. Data from Experiments 2-4 were subjected to a 2 (AoA: Early vs Late) x 3 (Filler type: High, Mid, Low Frequency) factorial ANOVA which demonstrated a main effect for Filler type, $F(2,144)=3.5$ $p<0.03$ and a marginal main effect for AoA, $F(1, 144)=3.77$ $p<0.05$ and no interaction. The gradual elimination of the AoA effect when Early and Late items were presented within an increasingly slower and more difficult context from Experiment 1 to Experiment 5 lends further support

Table 2. Summary results for experiments 1-5 in study 1. Mean RTs in milliseconds and standard deviations (SD in brackets) for early and late acquired words (EA and LA) and frequency filler stimuli; Difference in mean AoA RTs and statistical test

	EA Mean, SD	LA Mean, SD	Filler Item Mean, SD	Difference Between Early and Late; and Statistical Test (EA vs LA)
Exp1 (N=33) Target words	519 (33)	550 (30)	NA	31ms t(32)=4.04 p<0.0001
Exp2 (N=34) Target words + High Frequency fillers	499 (26)	517 (31)	501 (35)	18ms t(33)=4.05 p<0.0001
Exp3 (N= 36) Target words + Mid Frequency fillers	516 (38)	531 (42)	546 (30)	15ms t(35)=2.3 p<0.03
Exp4 (N=36) Target words + Low Frequency fillers	524 (35)	529 (31)	571 (26)	5ms t(35)=1.8 p>0.05 ns
Exp5 (N=36) Target words + Nonword fillers	534 (29)	539 (33)	587 (76)	5ms t(35)=1.7 p>0.05 ns

to the flexibility with which readers generate phonology from print. The findings are in line with the predictions of the time-criterion account and demonstrate the homogenisation of RTs even in an entirely transparent orthography. Noteworthy is that the overall error rates were typically less than 1% therefore excluded in the Table and were not subjected to formal analyses.

Study 2

A subsequent set of five experiments were designed similar to those in Study 1 and the Method, Apparatus and Procedure were the same as before. The major difference was that the filler items were manipulated on word imageability instead of frequency. The rationale for manipulating word imageability as contextual background is motivated by the fact that it is a semantic variable and qualitatively different to word frequency. As discussed previously, the role of imageability in word naming appears to be unique to irregular or opaque orthographies such as English and Persian.

Predictions in Study 2 are similar to those in Study 1 where the AoA effect is predicted to be influenced and finally eliminated with increasing difficulty of the filler items. Two of the experiments in Study 2, namely Experiments 6 and 10, were identical to Experiments 1 and 5 in Study 1, and were conducted to affirm the reliability of the earlier findings. The previous findings in Experiment 1 were indeed confirmed in Experiment 6, with a 35ms difference that was significant for target items only, i.e. Early and Late items, [$t(29)=2.88$ $p<0.007$]. In Experiment 10, a 5ms difference that was nonsignificant [$t(29)=0.89$ $p>0.05$] for target items in the presence of matched nonwords also confirmed the results of Experiment 5 and the predictions of the time-criterion hypothesis. Again a lexicality effect was observed. In Experiments 7-9, participants named the target items when filler items were critically manipulated on imageability (High, Mid, Low).

Experiment 7

Participants (N=30) were asked to name the target stimuli together with 50 high-imageable filler words. It is expected that while the AoA effect persists, homogenisation of RTs should favour the speeding up of both Early and Late items if the effect of high imageable filler items is similar to the one observed for High frequency fillers in Experiment 2. This is because 75% (Early + High imageable) of the items in the naming list are fast compared to 25% which are slow (Late).

A statistically significant 26ms difference between Early (482ms) and Late (508ms) items is found [$t(29)=4.11$ $p<0.0001$]. This finding replicates the results of Experiment 2 indicating that AoA effects are maintained when target items are mixed with fast filler items.

Experiment 8

In this experiment, 30 participants named the target words presented with 50 medium-imageable words. As in Experiment 3, 25% of stimuli were fast, 25% were slow while 50% were mid-speed. It is expected that the RTs will be overall slower with a reduction in the AoA effect. Early items were 21ms faster in comparison to late items (508ms and 529ms respectively) that was reliable [t(29)=1.94 p<0.06]. It is important to note that although RTs have slowed down for both Early and Late items as predicted, the AoA effect is larger than in Experiment 3 (15ms difference).

Experiment 9

In this experiment, participants (N=30) called out the target words mixed with 50 low-imageable filler items. Early items were 9ms faster in comparison to late items (517ms and 526ms respectively) that is not significant [t(29)=1.40 p>0.05] as predicted.

A summary of the results of Study 2 across five experiments can be seen in Table 3. RTs from Experiments 7-9 were subjected to a 2 (AoA: Early, Late) x 3 (Filler type: High, Mid, Low Imageable) factorial ANOVA which showed a main effect for Filler type, F(2, 144)=4.06 p<0.01, and AoA, F(1,144)=4.67 p<0.03 and no significant interaction between the two variables. Error rates were less than 1% and were not subjected to formal analyses.

Table 3. Summary results for experiments 6-10 in study 2. Mean RTs in milliseconds and Standard Deviations (SD in brackets) for Early and Late Acquired words (EA and LA) and filler stimuli; Difference in mean AoA RTs and statistical test

	EA Mean, SD	LA Mean, SD	Filler Item Mean, SD	Difference Between Early and Late; and Statistical Test (EA vs LA)
Exp6 (N=30) Target words	504 (76)	539 (58)	NA	35ms t(29)=2.88 p<0.007
Exp7 (N=30) Target words + High Imageable fillers	482 (45)	508 (55)	496 (39)	26ms t(29)=4.11 p<0.0001
Exp8 (N=30) Target words + Mid Imageable fillers	508 (64)	529 (67)	520 (65)	21ms t(29)=1.94 p<0.06
Exp9 (N= 30) Target words + Low Imageable fillers	517 (75)	526 (73)	537 (63)	9ms t(29)=1.47 p>0.05 ns
Exp10 (N=30) Target words + Nonword fillers	526 (41)	531 (25)	575 (54)	5ms t(29)=0.89 p>0.05 ns

In order to evaluate the impact of filler word type on AoA, data from Experiments 2-4 and 7-9 were combined in a 2 (Filler word type: Frequency, Imageability) x 2 (AoA: Early, Late) factorial ANOVA which showed a significant main effect for AoA [$F(1, 296)=8.12$ $p<0.01$]. No significant main effect for filler word type [$F(1,296)=2.28$ $p>0.05$] or interaction between AoA and filler word type [$F(1,296)= 0.27$ $p>0.05$] was found. These results statistically firmly establish that the modifications in the AoA effect observed for Experiments 2-4 and 7-9 were a direct result of the filler stimuli, i.e. context, not due to the interaction between word frequency, imageability and AoA.

GENERAL DISCUSSION

The current studies sought to experimentally investigate the extent to which AoA effects in word naming can be modified by context in a series of naming experiments by putting the claims of the time-criterion account to the test. The results clearly demonstrate that naming RTs of target words, i.e., Early and Late acquired words, are differentially modified in response to filler items in the naming list. In brief, when filler items are either high frequency or high imageable words, the AoA effect is maintained and when filler items are low frequency or low imageable or nonwords, the AoA effect is eradicated. In the first instance, the findings are in line with the suppositions of the time criterion account which has been tested mainly on word frequency and regularity effects in previous studies (Lupker et al, 1997; Raman et al, 2004; Kinoshita & Lupker, 2002; 2007).

The findings from the current study are important on several accounts: First, they firmly establish the fact that the magnitude of the AoA effect is modified according to the filler words' frequency *and* imageability to the same extent in a transparent orthography. Second, the time criterion account of setting deadlines in response to all stimuli to be named in a naming list holds true for a novel psycholinguistic variable, AoA. In this context, the supposition of the time criterion that readers utilise a global checking mechanism prior to reading aloud in response to the task at hand is verified irrespective of the nature of the reading list (e.g. Chateau & Lupker, 2003; Kinoshita & Lupker, 2002; 2007; Raman et al, 2004). The results of Study 1 and Study 2 are in line with those reported earlier for Turkish (Raman et al., 2004) in which it was demonstrated that contrary to previous findings in the literature, word frequency effect was maintained in the presence of 'easy' nonwords whilst a null effect was found in the presence of 'difficult' nonwords. This further suggests to us that despite the extreme OP transparency readers of transparent orthographies also develop strategies in visual word recognition tasks which is modified accordingly in response to task demands and that this is a universal process.

Because imageability is thought to be a central variable in the semantic system and because the semantic system is thought to contribute to word naming and lexical decision (e.g., Baluch & Besner, 2001; Strain et al., 1995; Zevin & Seidenberg, 2002), its orthogonal impact on AoA reported here is remarkable. This is taken to support previous research in Dutch and English which AoA and imageability are manipulated orthogonally with a null effect for imageability and a reliable AoA effect under controlled conditions (e.g., Brysbaert et al., 2000a, 2000b; Morrison & Ellis, 2000).

Locating the origin of AoA effects has proved to be one of the major theoretical challenges for AoA researchers in the past four decades. This is partly because of the methodological shortcomings of earlier investigations that primarily utilised regression analyses which led to the portrayal of AoA as an artifactual variable that was derived from a combination of sources. In this respect, the locus of the AoA effect was initially thought to be either in the phonological output lexicon or in the mappings between the semantics and the lexical output phonology (e.g., Barry, Hirsch, Johnston & Williams, 2001; Brown & Watson, 1987; Gerhand & Barry, 1999; Morrison & Ellis, 1999). In view of contradictory evidence where reliable AoA effects were reported for tasks that do not require phonological processing (e.g. Brysbaert et al., 2000b; Yamazaki et al., 1997) there has been a shift towards a phonological input rather than a phonological output position in understanding the locus of AoA.

To summarise, the magnitude of the AoA effect in the ten experiments reported here appears to be dependent on the difficulty of the next item in the naming list. The easier the next item (as in Experiments 1, 2, 6 and 7) the larger the AoA effect. One could speculate further by assuming that the linguistic peculiarities of deep orthographies with less predictable OP mappings such as English may stipulate that readers attend to a particular strategy (i.e. lexical or nonlexical) that provides the most efficient and successful phonology early on in the process. Because an extremely transparent orthography such as Turkish is devoid of such linguistic dichotomies, it was previously suggested that the impact of the difficulty of the filler stimuli takes its toll later on in the process of deriving phonology, just prior to articulation (Raman et al., 2004). Based on the evidence reported here, the contribution from the semantic and lexical routes appear to contribute equally to the attuning of the AoA effect when filler items are manipulated on imageability and frequency, respectively. This in line with our earlier speculation that perhaps the contribution from the two routes are more harmonious than in a less transparent orthography since there is never a conflicting OP outcome. It is of interest to pursue the contribution from each route in English and other opaque orthography under similar filler conditions. One could speculate the magnitude of the AoA effect to be larger for example in Experiment 4 under the low frequency filler condition as opposed to the low imageability filler condition in Experiment 9 because it is plausible to expect readers of opaque orthographies to utilise a semantic strategy to compute phonology under more 'difficult' reading conditions.

ACKNOWLEDGMENT

The experiments in the first study were fully funded by the British Academy's Small Projects Grant, SG-45010 (January 2007-January 2008) and the experiments in the second study by the Experimental Psychology Society (July 2008-July 2009) to the author. Part of the findings reported here were presented to the Experimental Psychology Society and BPS Cognitive Section meetings.

REFERENCES

Baluch, B., & Besner, D. (1991). Visual word recognition: Evidence for strategic control of lexical and nonlexical routines in oral reading. *Journal of Experimental Psychology. Learning, Memory, and Cognition*, *17*(4), 644–652. doi:10.1037/0278-7393.17.4.644

Baluch, B., & Besner, D. (2001). Basic processes in reading: Semantics affects speeded naming of high-frequency words in an alphabetic script. *Canadian Journal of Experimental Psychology*, *55*(1), 63–69. doi:10.1037/h0087353 PMID:11301729

Barca, L., Burani, C., & Arduino, L. S. (2002). Word naming times and psycholinguistic norms for Italian nouns. *Behavior Research Methods, Instruments, & Computers*, *34*(3), 424–434. doi:10.3758/BF03195471 PMID:12395559

Barry, C., Hirsch, K. W., Johnston, R. A., & Williams, C. L. (2001). Age of acquisition, word frequency, and the locus of repetition priming of picture naming. *Journal of Memory and Language*, *44*(3), 350–375. doi:10.1006/jmla.2000.2743

Bates, E., Burani, C., D'Amico, S., & Barca, L. (2001). Word reading and picture naming in Italian. *Memory & Cognition*, *29*(7), 986–999. doi:10.3758/BF03195761 PMID:11820758

Besner, D. (1999). Basic processes in reading: Multiple routines in localist and connectionist models. In P. A. McMullen & R. M. Klein (Eds.), *Converging methods for understanding reading and dyslexia*. Cambridge, MA: MIT Press.

Besner, D., & Smith, M. C. (1992). Basic Processes in reading: Is the orthographic depth hypothesis sinking? In R. Frost & L. Katz (Eds.), *Advances in psychology: orthography, phonology, morphology and meaning*. North-Holland. doi:10.1016/S0166-4115(08)62788-0

Bogka, N., Masterson, J., Druks, J., Fragkioudaki, M., Chatziprokopiou, E. S., & Economou, K. (2003). Object and action picture naming in English and Greek. *The European Journal of Cognitive Psychology*, *15*(3), 371–403. doi:10.1080/09541440303607

Bonin, P., Chalard, M., Meot, A., & Fayol, M. (2002). The determinants of spoken and written picture naming latencies. *British Journal of Psychology*, *93*(1), 89–114. doi:10.1348/000712602162463 PMID:11839103

Bonin, P., Fayol, M., & Chalard, M. (2001). Age of acquisition and word frequency in written picture naming. *Quarterly Journal of Experimental Psychology*, *54*(2), 469–489. doi:10.1080/713755968 PMID:11394057

Brase, J., & Raman, I. (2009). The Role of Age of Acquisition in Picture and Word Naming in German. Presented at the Annual Cognitive Section Meeting, BPS, Hertfordshire, UK.

Brown, G. D. A., & Watson, F. L. (1987). First in, first out: Word learning age and spoken word frequency as predictors of word familiarity and word naming latency. *Memory & Cognition*, *15*(3), 208–216. doi:10.3758/BF03197718 PMID:3600260

Brysbaert, M., Lange, M., & Van Wijnendaele, I. (2000). The effects of age-of-acquisition and frequency-of-occurrence in visual word recognition: Further evidence from the Dutch language. *The European Journal of Cognitive Psychology*, *12*(1), 65–85. doi:10.1080/095414400382208

Brysbaert, M., Van Wijnendaele, I., & De Deyne, S. (2000). Age-of-acquisition is a significant variable in semantic tasks. *Acta Psychologica*, *104*, 215–226. doi:10.1016/S0001-6918(00)00021-4 PMID:10900706

Chateau, D., & Lupker, S. J. (2003). Strategic effects in word naming: Examining the route-emphasis versus time-criterion accounts. *Journal of Experimental Psychology. Human Perception and Performance*, *29*(1), 139–151. doi:10.1037/0096-1523.29.1.139 PMID:12669753

Chen, B., You, W., & Zhou, H. (2007a). Age of acquisition effects in reading Chinese: Evidence in favor of the semantic hypothesis. *Acta Psychologica Sinica*, *39*(1), 9–17.

Chen, B., Zhou, H., Dunlap, S., & Perfetti, C. A. (2007b). Age of acquisition effects in reading Chinese: Evidence in favour of the arbitrary mapping hypothesis. *British Journal of Psychology, 98*(3), 499–516. doi:10.1348/000712606X165484 PMID:17705943

Coltheart, M. (1978). Lexical access in simple reading tasks. In G. Underwood (Ed.), *Strategies of information processing*. San Diego, CA: Academic Press.

Coltheart, M., Curtis, B., Atkins, P., & Haller, M. (1993). Models of reading aloud: Dual route and parallel distributed processing approaches. *Psychological Review, 100*(4), 589–608. doi:10.1037/0033-295X.100.4.589

Coltheart, M., & Rastle, K. (1994). Serial processing in Reading aloud: Evidence for Dual-route Models of Reading. *Journal of Experimental Psychology. Human Perception and Performance, 20*(6), 1197–1211. doi:10.1037/0096-1523.20.6.1197

Cuetos, F., Ellis, A. W., & Alvarez, B. (1999). Naming times for the Snodgrass and Vanderwart pictures in Spanish. *Behavior Research Methods, Instruments, & Computers, 31*(4), 650–558. doi:10.3758/BF03200741 PMID:10633980

Ellis, A. W., & Lambon Ralph, M. A. (2000). Age of acquisition effects in adult lexical processing reflect loss of placticity in maturing systems: Insights from connectionist networks. *Journal of Experimental Psychology. Learning, Memory, and Cognition, 26*(5), 1103–1123. doi:10.1037/0278-7393.26.5.1103 PMID:11009247

Frederiksen, J. R., & Kroll, J. F. (1976). Spelling and sound: Approaches to the internal lexicon. *Journal of Experimental Psychology. Human Perception and Performance, 2*(3), 361–379. doi:10.1037/0096-1523.2.3.361

Gerhand, S., & Barry, C. (1999). Age-of-Acquisition and frequency effects in speeded word naming. *Cognition, 73*(2), B27–B36. doi:10.1016/S0010-0277(99)00052-9 PMID:10580164

Gernsbacher, A. M. (1984). Resolving 20 Years of Inconsistent Interactions Between Lexical Familiarity and Orthography, Concreteness and Polysemy. *Journal of Experimental Psychology. General, 113*(2), 256–281. doi:10.1037/0096-3445.113.2.256 PMID:6242753

Ghyselinck, M., Custers, R., & Brysbaert, M. (2004). The Effect of Age of Acquisition in Visual Word Processing: Further Evidence for the Semantic Hypothesis. *Journal of Experimental Psychology. Learning, Memory, and Cognition, 30*(2), 550–554. doi:10.1037/0278-7393.30.2.550 PMID:14979824

Gilhooly, K. J., & Logie, R. H. (1980). Age of acquisition, imagery, concreteness, familiarity and ambiguity measures for 1944 words. *Behavior Research Methods and Instrumentation*, *12*(4), 395–427. doi:10.3758/BF03201693

Gordon, B. (1985). Subjective frequency and the lexical decision latency function: Implications for mechanisms of lexical access. *Journal of Memory and Language*, *24*(6), 631–645. doi:10.1016/0749-596X(85)90050-6

Havelka, J., & Tomita, I. (2006). Age of acquisition in naming Japanese words. *Visual Cognition*, *13*(7/8), 981–991. doi:10.1080/13506280544000156

Hino, Y., & Lupker, S. J. (1996). Effects of Polysemy in Lexical Decision and Naming: An Alternative to Lexical Accounts. *Journal of Experimental Psychology. Human Perception and Performance*, *22*(6), 1331–1356. doi:10.1037/0096-1523.22.6.1331

Johnston, R. A., & Barry, C. (2006). Age of acquisition and lexical processing. *Visual Cognition*, *13*(7-8), 789–845. doi:10.1080/13506280544000066

Juhasz, B. J. (2005). Age-of-Acquisition Effects in Word and Picture Identification. *Psychological Bulletin*, *131*(5), 684–712. doi:10.1037/0033-2909.131.5.684 PMID:16187854

Kinoshita, S., & Lupker, S. J. (2002). Effects of filler type in naming: Change in time-criterion or attentional control pathways? *Memory & Cognition*, *30*(8), 1277–1287. doi:10.3758/BF03213409 PMID:12661858

Kinoshita, S., & Lupker, S. J. (2007). Switch costs when reading aloud words and nonwords. *Psychonomic Bulletin & Review*, *14*(3), 449–454. doi:10.3758/BF03194087 PMID:17874586

Lupker, S. J., Brown, P., & Colombo, L. (1997). Strategic control in a naming task: Changing routes or changing deadlines? *Journal of Experimental Psychology. Learning, Memory, and Cognition*, *23*(3), 570–590. doi:10.1037/0278-7393.23.3.570

Monaghan, J., & Ellis, A. W. (2002a). What exactly interacts with spelling-sound consistency in word naming? *Journal of Experimental Psychology. Learning, Memory, and Cognition*, *28*(1), 183–206. doi:10.1037/0278-7393.28.1.183 PMID:11827080

Monaghan, J., & Ellis, A. W. (2002b). Age of acquisition and the completeness of phonological representations. *Reading and Writing*, *15*(7/8), 759–788. doi:10.1023/A:1020958722472

Monsell, S., Patterson, K. E., Graham, A., Hughes, C. H., & Milroy, R. (1992). Lexical and sublexical translation of spelling to sound: Strategic anticipation of lexical status. *Journal of Experimental Psychology. Learning, Memory, and Cognition*, *18*(3), 452–467. doi:10.1037/0278-7393.18.3.452

Morrison, C. M., & Ellis, A. W. (1999). Age of acquisition, lexical processing and ageing: Changes across the lifespan. In *Proceedings of the 21st Annual Meeting of the Cognitive Science Society*. Mahwah, NJ: Lawrence Erlbaum Associates.

Morrison, C. M., & Ellis, A. W. (2000). Real age of acquisition effects in word naming and lexical decision. *British Journal of Psychology*, *91*(2), 167–180. doi:10.1348/000712600161763 PMID:10832512

Morrison, C. M., Ellis, A. W., & Quinlan, P. T. (1992). Age of acquisition, not word frequency, affects object naming, not object recognition. *Memory & Cognition*, *20*(6), 705–714. doi:10.3758/BF03202720 PMID:1435273

Paap, K. R., & Noel, R. W. (1991). Dual-rote models of print to sound: Still a good horse race. *Psychological Research*, *53*(1), 13–24. doi:10.1007/BF00867328

Paivio, A., Yuille, J. C., & Madigan, S. A. (1968). Concreteness, imagery and meaningfulness values for 925 words. *Journal of Experimental Psychology Monograph*, *76*(3).

Raman, I. (2006). On the Age of Acquisition Effects in Word Naming and Orthographic Transparency: Mapping specific or universal? *Visual Cognition*, *13*(7/8), 1044–1053. doi:10.1080/13506280500153200

Raman, I., & Baluch, B. (2001). Semantic Effects as a Function of Reading Skill in Word Naming of a Transparent Orthography. *Reading and Writing*, *14*(7/8), 599–614. doi:10.1023/A:1012004729180

Raman, I., Baluch, B., & Besner, D. (2004). On the Control of Visual Word Recognition: Changing Routes Versus Changing Deadlines. *Memory & Cognition*, *32*(3), 489–500. doi:10.3758/BF03195841 PMID:15285131

Raman, I., Baluch, B., & Sneddon, P. (1996). What is the cognitive system's preferred route for deriving phonology from print? *European Psychologist*, *1*(3), 221–227. doi:10.1027/1016-9040.1.3.221

Rastle, K., & Coltheart, M. (1999). Serial and strategic effects in reading aloud. *Journal of Experimental Psychology. Human Perception and Performance*, *25*(2), 482–503. doi:10.1037/0096-1523.25.2.482

Reynolds, M., & Besner, D. (2008). Contextual Effects on Reading Aloud: Evidence for Pathway Control. *Journal of Experimental Psychology. Learning, Memory, and Cognition*, *34*(1), 50–64. doi:10.1037/0278-7393.34.1.50 PMID:18194054

Strain, E., Patterson, K., & Seidenberg, M. S. (1995). Semantic effects in single word naming. *Journal of Experimental Psychology. Learning, Memory, and Cognition*, *21*(5), 1140–1154. doi:10.1037/0278-7393.21.5.1140 PMID:8744959

Tabossi, P., & Laghi, L. (1992). Semantic priming in the pronunciation of words in two writing systems: Italian and English. *Memory & Cognition*, *20*(3), 303–313. doi:10.3758/BF03199667 PMID:1508055

Yamazaki, M., Ellis, A. W., Morrison, C. M., & Lambon Ralph, M. (1997). Two age of acquisition effects in the reading of Japanese Kanji. *British Journal of Psychology*, *88*(3), 407–421. doi:10.1111/j.2044-8295.1997.tb02648.x

Zevin, J. D., & Balota, D. A. (2000). Priming and attentional control of lexical and sublexical pathways during naming. *Journal of Experimental Psychology. Learning, Memory, and Cognition*, *26*(1), 121–135. doi:10.1037/0278-7393.26.1.121 PMID:10682293

APPENDIX

Table 4. Early and late acquired Turkish words and AoA, imageability and frequency norms with their corresponding English translations and AoA, imageability and frequency norms

Early Acquired Turkish words N=25	AoA	Imageability	Frequency	English Translation	AoA MRC Database N = 10	Imageability MRC Database N = 25	Kucera Francis Frequency MRC Database N= 25
anne	1.10	5.88	1.54	mother	144	638	216
aç	1.48	5.24	1.73	open/hungry*	*	425	319
göz	1.55	5.50	1.54	eye	167	603	122
kedi	1.67	5.02	2.24	cat	*	617	23
ev	1.66	5.48	1.46	house	*	606	591
bebek	1.74	5.70	2.04	baby/doll	*/161	608/565	62/10
oyun	1.80	5.22	2.10	game	242	521	123
saç	1.63	5.08	1.32	hair	*	580	148
şişman	1.30	5.76	1.35	fat	236	574	60
deniz	2.35	5.28	1.58	sea	*	606	95
süt	1.73	5.46	1.92	milk	*	638	49
kardeş	2.04	5.56	1.54	brother	219	589	73
makas	2.00	5.90	1.47	scissors	*	609	1
güneş	2.02	5.62	1.64	sun	181	639	112
gece	2.12	5.30	1.38	night	222	607	411
kapı	2.08	5.00	1.44	door	214	599	312
uçak	2.24	4.85	2.27	plane	*	556	114
bardak	2.04	5.12	1.76	glass	*	585	99
erkek	2.20	5.10	1.58	man	*	567	1207
ateş	2.20	5.52	2.60	fire	*	634	187
sabah	2.10	5.26	1.26	morning	*	579	211
çocuk	2.00	5.56	1.50	child	*	619	213
balık	2.14	5.12	2.74	fish	*	615	35
yatak	2.16	5.08	1.51	bed	169	635	127
ayı	1.96	4.66	3.00	bear	*	572	57
MEAN	1.89	5.33	1.78		196	593	199
SD	0.31	0.32	0.46		35	45	249
Late Acquired Turkish words N=25	**AoA**	**Imageability**	**Frequency**	**English Translation**	**AoA MRC Database N = 8**	**Imageability MRC Database N = 20**	**Kucera Francis Frequency MRC Database N = 22**
aday	4.88	4.76	2.06	candidate	578	452	34
af	4.37	4.96	2.08	amnesty	*	*	*
göç	4.73	4.92	2.03	migration	*	*	10
katı	4.24	4.35	2.63	solid	*	*	77
et	3.78	5.33	2.18	meat/flesh	*	618/567	45/52
bilim	5.42	5.00	1.69	science	458	423	131
otel	4.80	4.94	1.55	hotel	308	697	126
sap	3.84	5.31	1.57	stem	*	533	29
şafak	4.67	5.16	2.26	dawn	350	586	28
daire	3.88	5.02	1.46	circle	522	556	81
sert	3.47	4.86	1.98	hard	*	460	202
kilit	4.29	4.95	1.68	lock	328	532	23
mantar	3.40	5.55	1.88	mushroom	*	*	2
gümüş	4.14	4.98	2.08	silver	317	582	29
genç	3.63	5.45	1.70	young	*	521	385
kriz	5.26	4.50	2.26	crisis	*	375	82
ulus	5.10	5.15	2.35	nation	425	436	139
boyut	5.42	4.76	1.39	size	*	415	138
esmer	4.02	5.33	1.44	brunette	*	*	*
albay	5.02	5.00	2.38	colonel	*	522	37
sanat	5.06	5.06	2.22	art	*	493	208
çağdaş	5.24	5.10	2.38	modern/new	*	368	198
beygir	5.42	5.06	2.31	nag/horse	*	508/624	*
yaşam	4.56	4.92	1.46	life	*	482	715
ak	4.86	5.36	2.08	white	*	556	365
MEAN	4.54	5.03	1.96		411	512	141
SD	0.64	0.30	0.36		102	87	166

* denotes to missing value in the English norms; *N* number of English translations with normative data

Filler words (N=50) with their corresponding English translations and AoA, Imageability and Frequency ratings, Letter and Syllable length

Table 5. Experiment 2

HF Filler Word	Translation	AoA	Imageability	Frequency	Letter Length	Syllable Length
okul	school	2.37	5.60	1.18	4	2
insan	human	2.63	5.67	1.32	5	2
söz	word	2.92	4.76	1.37	3	1
uyku	sleep	2.33	5.23	1.38	4	2
sınıf	class	3.45	4.92	1.51	5	2
kitap	book	2.45	5.65	1.52	5	2
soğuk	cold	2.49	4.92	1.54	5	2
isim	name	2.35	4.98	1.60	4	2
duygu	feeling	4.47	5.06	1.60	5	2
sevinç	joy	3.88	5.22	1.60	6	2
erken	early	3.27	4.69	1.61	5	2
mavi	blue	2.35	4.75	1.62	4	2
yavaş	slow	3.22	4.60	1.70	5	2
merak	curiosity	3.88	4.75	1.70	5	2
haber	news	3.42	4.86	1.70	5	2
esya	furniture	2.84	4.86	1.71	4	2
özel	private	4.73	4.80	1.72	4	2
dünya	world/earth	2.98	5.71	1.72	5	2
rahat	comfortable	3.98	4.42	1.76	5	2
son	end	3.53	4.66	1.76	3	1
toplum	community	5.02	5.21	1.76	6	2
tek	single/sole	3.10	4.86	1.78	3	1
karar	decision	4.47	4.92	1.78	5	2
defter	exercise-book	2.64	5.16	1.78	6	2
uzun	long	2.73	4.60	1.80	4	2
soru	question	2.76	4.78	1.80	4	2
sabır	patience	4.84	4.94	1.80	5	2
fikir	idea	5.02	5.10	1.82	5	2
sayı	number	2.92	5.32	1.82	4	2
bilgi	information	4.20	4.70	1.84	5	2
giysi	clothing	2.60	5.04	1.84	5	2
suç	crime	3.40	4.72	1.86	3	1
zengin	rich	3.72	4.94	1.86	6	2
resim	picture	2.45	5.08	1.86	5	2
aşk	love	4.14	5.08	1.86	3	1
deli	mad	2.86	4.83	1.88	4	2
doktor	doctor	2.34	5.46	1.88	6	2
kural	rule/regulation	4.20	5.00	1.92	5	2

continued on following page

Table 5. Continued

HF Filler Word	Translation	AoA	Imageability	Frequency	Letter Length	Syllable Length
basit	simple	4.16	4.22	1.96	5	2
inat	stubbornness	3.67	4.76	1.96	4	2
tarak	comb	2.60	4.96	1.96	5	2
can	life/soul	3.38	5.09	1.98	3	1
yazı	writing	2.80	5.25	2.0	4	2
güç	power	3.59	5.02	2.02	3	1
ters	opposite	3.87	4.15	2.04	4	1
tavuk	chicken	2.35	4.65	2.04	5	2
yalan	lie	2.90	4.80	2.04	5	2
umut	hope	4.96	4.85	2.04	4	2
yeşil	green	2.34	5.04	2.04	5	2
salak	idiot	3.51	4.40	2.08	5	2
	MEAN SD	3.34 .82	4.94 .34	1.77 .20	4.54 .86	1.84 .37

Table 6. Experiment 3

MF Filler Word	Translation	AoA	Imageability	Frequency	Letter Length	Syllable Length
ayar	adjustment	5.2	4.27	3.50	4	2
taviz	concession	5.58	4.23	3.52	5	2
kaygan	slippery	4.53	4.44	3.53	6	2
eser	masterpiece	4.98	5.21	3.53	4	2
tekne	boat	3.41	4.44	3.54	5	2
evcil	domesticated	4.44	4.60	3.54	5	2
ihtiras	desire	5.86	4.32	3.55	7	3
dernek	organization	5.52	4.77	3.58	6	2
pul	stamp	3.92	4.88	3.58	3	1
müracaat	application	5.48	4.56	3.59	8	4
miting	meeting	5.58	4.90	3.59	6	2
parmaklık	railings	4.32	4.60	3.60	9	3
evren	universe	5.14	4.92	3.62	5	2
sıfat	adjective	4.92	4.38	3.63	5	2
ilim	science	5.22	4.84	3.63	4	2
kumar	gamble	5.16	4.46	3.64	5	2
oruç	fasting	4.22	5.16	3.64	4	2

continued on following page

Table 6. Continued

MF Filler Word	Translation	AoA	Imageability	Frequency	Letter Length	Syllable Length
kalıtsal	genetic	5.67	4.35	3.65	8	3
antlaşma	agreement	5.27	4.66	3.66	8	3
entrika	intricate	5.98	4.10	3.70	7	3
gereksinme	necessity	6.0	4.44	3.71	10	4
züppe	pretentious	5.46	4.36	3.73	5	2
esnek	flexible	4.88	4.15	3.74	5	2
kale	castle	3.04	4.85	3.75	4	2
denetim	inspection	5.59	4.27	3.78	7	3
tutsak	captive	5.02	4.56	3.78	6	2
bağlaç	conjunction (gram)	5.27	4.08	3.82	6	2
buluş	invention	5.29	4.62	3.82	5	2
uçurtma	kite	2.76	5.00	3.82	7	2
tahrip	destruction	5.82	4.19	3.83	6	2
boru	pipe	3.46	4.00	3.86	4	2
izmarit	cigarette butt	5.02	4.52	3.86	7	3
iman	belief	5.14	4.92	3.88	4	2
tasa	worry	4.96	4.23	3.90	4	2
kasırga	hurricane	5.20	4.45	3.90	7	3
sendika	syndicate	5.78	4.57	3.90	7	3
tüfek	rifle	3.06	5.04	3.90	5	2
fener	torch	3.43	4.58	3.92	5	2
töre	custom	5.46	4.69	3.94	4	2
körfez	gulf	5.02	4.60	3.96	6	2
çapraz	cross	5.02	4.35	3.98	6	2
simge	symbol	5.33	4.50	3.98	5	2
istikrar	power	5.88	4.40	4.0	8	3
örf	custom	5.67	4.62	4.0	3	1
görenek	custom	5.67	4.77	4.02	7	3
çeyiz	trousseau	5.20	4.79	4.02	5	2
sömürge	colony	5.54	4.51	4.04	7	3
tren	train	2.33	4.87	4.04	4	1
küp	cube	4.14	4.53	4.06	3	1
hamam	bath	3.62	4.66	4.24	5	2
	MEAN SD	4.89 .91	4.56 .28	3.78 .18	5.62 1.59	2.24 .66

Table 7. Experiment 4

LF Filler Word	Translation	AoA	Imageability	Frequency	Letter Length	Syllable Length
esir	prisoner of war	4.70	2.65	4.00	4	2
yosun	moss	4.18	3.82	4.06	5	2
baygın	unconscious	4.86	3.14	4.08	6	2
vali	governor	4.84	3.56	4.08	4	2
sanayi	industrial	5.36	4.60	4.08	6	3
tekel	monopoly	5.45	3.91	4.10	5	2
zelzele	earthquake	4.27	2.88	4.16	7	3
çelik	steel	5.20	3.56	4.16	5	2
vefa	loyalty	5.82	2.83	4.18	4	2
ok	arrow	3.12	2.92	4.18	2	1
dikey	perpendicular	5.04	4.23	4.18	5	2
veznedar	cashier	5.45	2.44	4.20	8	3
sürgün	exiled	5.08	1.48	4.22	6	2
inci	pearl	3.78	3.98	4.22	4	2
küme	group	4.50	2.52	4.24	4	2
bellek	memory	5.65	3.41	4.29	6	2
baldır	calf	4.58	4.26	4.29	6	2
verem	tuberculosis	4.88	2.52	4.32	5	2
yetim	orphan	4.68	3.98	4.32	5	2
gevrek	crisp	4.52	4.10	4.39	6	2
tezkere	discharge (army)	5.86	4.52	4.45	7	3
hisse	share	5.90	4.36	4.50	5	2
hilal	crescent	5.02	3.86	4.51	5	2
peri	fairy	3.61	4.24	4.53	4	2
baston	cane	3.38	4.40	4.56	6	2
ilik	bone marrow	4.69	3.73	4.58	4	2
diyar	land	5.28	4.38	4.60	5	2
yazgı	fate	5.77	2.58	4.65	5	2
zurna	oboe	4.33	2.64	4.65	5	2
gelgit	tide	5.54	2.28	4.67	6	2
serüven	adventure	5.54	2.35	4.67	7	3
kuşatma	siege	5.50	4.24	4.70	7	3
yarıçap	circumference	5.40	3.04	4.73	7	3
saçak	eave	5.04	2.12	4.74	5	2

continued on following page

Table 7. Continued

LF Filler Word	Translation	AoA	Imageability	Frequency	Letter Length	Syllable Length
türbe	tomb	4.96	2.56	4.76	5	2
bayır	meadow	5.04	2.43	4.80	5	2
çıban	spot	4.48	4.10	4.80	5	2
fosil	fossil	5.59	4.26	4.98	5	2
çığır	era	5.58	2.80	5.00	5	2
yayla	plateau	4.94	2.65	5.02	5	2
bulgu	result	5.92	3.94	5.02	5	2
benek	spot	4.67	3.88	5.04	5	2
vampir	vampire	4.53	2.42	5.08	6	2
havan	mortar	4.84	2.02	5.37	5	2
gedik	gap	5.46	2.65	5.39	5	2
peçe	veil	5.10	4.54	5.44	4	2
yele	mane	5.02	4.25	5.56	4	2
tunç	bronze	4.98	2.90	5.57	4	1
us	mind	5.81	2.15	5.80	2	1
irin	pus	5.16	3.62	5.80	4	2
	MEAN SD	4.97 .64	3.33 .84	4.63 .48	5.10 1.17	2.08 .44

Table 8. Experiment 6

HI Filler Word	Translation	Frequency	Imageability	AoA	Letter Length	Syllable Length
çirkin	ugly	2.12	4.75	2.82	6	2
ince	thin	2.18	4.69	2.86	4	2
koltuk	armchair	1.18	4.96	2.30	6	2
ayna	mirror	1.18	5.00	2.32	4	2
toprak	soil	1.18	6.33	2.78	6	2
sigara	cigarette	1.20	6.32	3.04	6	3
tepsi	tray	1.38	4.85	3.14	5	2
yaprak	leaf	1.40	5.00	2.52	6	2
dosya	file	1.42	5.04	4.25	5	2
fırın	oven	1.44	4.86	3.0	5	2
zeytin	olive	1.44	6.14	2.39	6	2
rengarenk	colorful	1.50	4.80	3.98	9	3
köy	village	1.52	5.08	2.92	3	1

continued on following page

Table 8. Continued

HI Filler Word	Translation	Frequency	Imageability	AoA	Letter Length	Syllable Length
yurt	homeland	1.66	5.28	4.52	4	1
berber	barber	1.74	4.62	3.24	6	2
balkon	balcony	1.74	5.00	2.58	6	2
uzman	expert	2.74	5.00	5.43	5	2
gitar	guitar	1.76	4.76	3.60	5	2
basın	press	2.76	5.10	5.32	5	2
biber	pepper	1.78	4.75	2.52	5	2
yoksul	poor	1.80	5.20	4.12	6	2
belge	document	1.81	4.82	4.90	5	2
gölge	shadow	1.82	4.96	3.51	5	2
düğme	button	1.84	4.65	2.55	5	2
kutu	box	1.86	4.71	3.06	4	2
deprem	earthquake	2.86	4.86	3.88	6	2
bahçe	garden	1.86	6.30	2.51	5	2
bitkin	tired	2.92	4.69	5.8	6	2
şiir	poem	2.92	4.98	4.33	4	2
altın	gold	1.94	6.20	3.56	5	2
fare	mouse	1.96	4.50	2.51	4	2
sakat	disabled	1.98	4.78	3.76	5	2
damar	vein/artery	1.98	4.98	4.24	5	2
bayrak	flag	1.98	6.56	2.71	6	2
gemi	ship	1.02	4.94	2.43	4	2
tepe	hill	1.04	4.62	3.06	4	2
iğne	needle	1.04	4.78	2.56	4	2
çilek	strawberry	1.10	4.60	2.74	5	2
ipek	silk	2.18	5.06	4.12	4	2
sivri	sharp	2.26	4.73	3.57	5	2
damla	drop	2.26	4.83	3.74	5	2
kare	square	2.40	4.62	3.71	4	2
cadı	witch	3.43	4.69	3.02	4	2
kızıl	scarlet	1.43	4.77	4.78	5	2
nehir	river	2.44	4.87	3.53	5	2
kıyı	shore	2.46	4.73	4.44	4	2
saray	palace	2.10	4.78	3.65	5	2
yiğit	brave	3.31	4.96	4.92	5	2
kule	tower	3.37	4.81	3.39	4	2
	MEAN SD	3.47 .86	5.02 .51	1.93 .62	5.04 1.01	2.02 .32

Table 9. Experiment 7

MI Filler Word	Translation	Frequency	Imageability	AoA	Letter Length	Syllable Length
güzel	pretty/beautiful	1.40	5.10	2.32	5	2
rüya	dream	1.46	4.90	2.98	4	2
heyecan	excitement	1.82	4.65	4.14	7	3
mantık	logic	2.88	4.87	5.21	6	2
güven	security	2.92	4.24	4.65	5	2
tarih	history	2.54	4.86	4.16	5	2
çözüm	solution	2.74	5.00	4.65	5	2
yürek	heart/soul	4.14	5.10	4.29	5	2
yemin	vow	3.20	4.79	4.18	5	2
fakir	poor/needy	2.20	5.06	3.59	5	2
kibar	refined	2.22	4.94	4.0	5	2
eşit	equal	2.24	4.85	4.34	4	2
sarı	yellow	2.28	4.72	2.33	4	2
hüzün	sadness	2.30	4.68	5.33	5	2
kanun	law	2.30	5.00	4.64	5	2
görev	duty	2.30	5.06	4.55	5	2
birey	individual	2.31	5.06	5.42	5	2
işlem	procedure	2.37	4.79	4.75	5	2
şiddet	severity; violence	2.38	4.82	4.69	6	2
öneri	proposal	3.39	4.81	5.22	5	3
burç	bastion	4.43	4.90	4.90	4	1
bulut	cloud	2.47	5.17	2.86	5	2
barış	peace	2.52	4.40	3.86	5	2
güncel	topical	2.53	4.62	5.39	6	2
onur	honour	2.53	5.12	5.41	4	2
müjde	good news	3.90	4.90	4.16	5	2
vicdan	conscience	4.62	5.17	5.45	6	2
bayram	festival	2.62	5.51	2.72	6	2
sevda	love	2.64	4.62	5.22	5	2
gayret	effort	3.66	4.96	4.65	6	2
adil	just	3.78	5.12	5.53	4	2
lisan	language	3.79	5.06	4.96	5	2
kayıt	registration	2.88	4.81	5.14	5	2
ölçü	measurement	3.40	4.68	4.18	4	2
hizmet	service	3.50	5.00	5.37	6	2

continued on following page

Table 9. Continued

MI Filler Word	Translation	Frequency	Imageability	AoA	Letter Length	Syllable Length
şeref	honour	3.64	4.74	5.39	5	2
uygar	civilised	3.80	5.04	5.53	5	2
denge	balance	3.90	4.85	5.12	5	2
anı	memory	3.08	4.36	4.86	3	2
oy	vote	3.12	5.12	4.88	2	1
çerçeve	frame	3.20	4.80	4.24	7	3
azim	willpower	3.20	4.96	5.30	4	2
ahmak	foolish	3.24	4.84	4.02	5	2
yasa	law	3.24	4.90	5.18	4	2
zihin	cognition	3.24	5.12	5.28	5	2
örgüt	association	3.35	4.74	5.78	5	2
gür	plentiful	4.44	4.64	4.69	3	1
kitle	mass	3.47	4.67	5.62	5	2
verim	production	3.48	4.74	5.22	5	2
güngörmüş	wise	5.52	4.66	5.80	9	3
	MEAN SD	4.64 .87	4.78 .23	3.05 .82	4.98 1.08	2.02 .38

Table 10. Experiment 8

LI Filler Word	Translation	Frequency	Imageability	AoA	Letter Length	Syllable Length
hayal	imagination	2.18	2.40	4.51	5	2
eksik	missing	2.50	3.29	3.46	5	2
genel	general	2.62	3.40	4.88	5	2
berbat	terrible	2.26	3.18	4.86	6	2
çeşit	variety	2.78	3.19	4.41	5	2
uygulama	application	3.73	2.58	5.33	8	4
önlem	precaution	2.93	2.42	4.85	5	2
günah	sin	2.85	2.26	4.02	5	2
serseri	tramp	4.50	2.59	4.30	7	3
gönül	heart/mind	2.50	2.65	4.91	5	2
kaba	rude, thick	2.80	3.56	4.16	4	2
kıyaslama	comparison	2.54	2.54	5.56	9	4
dönem	term	2.74	3.34	4.80	5	2
dizi	series	2.54	4.39	3.78	4	2

continued on following page

Table 10. Continued

LI Filler Word	Translation	Frequency	Imageability	AoA	Letter Length	Syllable Length
bela	trouble	2.65	2.20	4.72	4	2
uyarı	warning	2.90	3.54	4.86	5	3
boşluk	emptiness	2.69	2.42	4.29	6	2
rakip	opponent	4.73	2.58	4.84	5	2
tutku	passion	3.74	2.52	5.54	5	2
aşama	level	3.79	2.56	5.76	5	3
uyuz	idle	3.83	3.42	4.57	4	2
kin	hate	3.86	2.44	4.98	3	1
taklit	mimicking	2.90	3.42	4.32	6	2
savunma	defense	2.96	2.64	5.40	7	3
müddet	time	3.02	3.43	5.32	6	2
dargın	cross/upset	3.08	2.43	3.82	6	2
siyasi	political	3.08	2.44	5.58	6	3
biçim	shape/form	3.16	2.63	4.24	5	2
katil	murderer	3.29	4.33	4.22	5	2
bayat	stale	3.30	3.41	3.98	5	2
kavram	concept	3.33	2.02	5.54	6	2
eylem	action	3.44	3.54	5.32	5	2
mağdur	victim	6.49	3.52	6.0	6	2
doyum	satiety	4.50	2.56	5.04	5	2
ihale	auction	5.16	2.29	5.66	5	3
üvey	step-(family members)	4.23	3.54	4.92	4	2
kısır	infertile	4.30	2.04	5.42	5	2
felek	fate/destiny	5.54	2.64	5.41	5	2
evre	universe	5.55	3.15	5.88	4	2
evliya	saint	6.54	2.22	5.20	6	3
külfet	inconvenience	6.34	2.68	5.57	6	2
beniz	colour of the face	5.35	2.62	5.56	5	2
buhran	crisis	6.51	2.30	6.04	6	2
iblis	devil	6.61	2.22	5.35	5	2
tümce	sentence	5.65	2.48	5.24	5	2
gürz	mace	6.87	1.54	5.91	4	1
güdük	short/stunted	6.12	2.54	5.70	5	2
ati	future	6.18	2.10	5.69	3	2
ablak	dull	6.29	2.22	5.17	5	2
	MEAN SD	4.98 .65	2.78 .60	4.01 1.44	5.24 1.08	2.18 .56

Table 11. Experiments 5 and 10

Nonword Fillers	
apuk	oroy
aj	böglö
apran	takef
botkan	abü
berzik	selek
cuto	derkit
çifre	tark
deset	gülç
evsol	sö
fazur	tilme
gaj	aylap
genzit	ölez
hesel	irel
ircin	iratak
kenyip	çorkaz
küç	mektil
merki	kefröz
pepi	gataf
süp	caratlı
tapul	cava
ignör	çiren
gisye	dopul
yumin	evsol
yanoç	firan
yusi	gavar

Chapter 3
Measuring Phonological and Orthographic Similarity:
The Case of Loanwords in Turkish and English

Muhlise Coşgun Ögeyik
Trakya University, Turkey

ABSTRACT

Marked and unmarked language forms can be distinguished with the level of simplicity or complexity denotations of the forms. Unmarked target language forms may create little or no difficulty, even if they do not exist in the native language of the learner, while marked forms can be relatively difficult for language learners. In addition to the notions of markedness/unmarkedness, there has also been an emphasis on similarity and dissimilarity between the items of first (L1) and second languages (L2). Along with similarity or dissimilarity of L1 and L2 forms, the level of difficulty may vary enormously in different language-specific procedures. In this chapter, therefore, it is intended to build an understanding of the recognized pronunciation and orthographic problems of similar loanwords in both Turkish (L1 of the participants) and English (L2).

INTRODUCTION

Knowing two languages means recognizing two ways of speaking, writing, listening, and reading in both L1 and L2. The syntactic, lexical, semantic, or phonetic similarities of two languages, predominantly phonetic similarity, may make language

DOI: 10.4018/978-1-5225-4009-0.ch003

learners be familiar with the linguistic information of the target language skills easily. It may also be presumed that phonetic similarity between languages can promote the pace of learning or acquiring the target language; however, contrary to intuitive expectations, phonetic similarity may raise difficulty in discovering and appreciating the identical sounds in both native language and target language (Gass, 2013). Additionally, orthographic similarity between two languages may also be both promoting and obstructing for L2 learners. In both cases, difficulty may arise from the potential resemblance causing interference from L1 representation, namely cross-linguistic influence.

Considering the similarities and dissimilarities of L1 and L2, this chapter primarily highlights the case of loanwords in Turkish as L1 and English as L2 by taking the Markedness Differential Hypothesis –MDH- and Speech Learning Model–SLM- as references to interpret the issue. For depicting the probable troubles and facilities of loanwords, the outputs of the advanced level language learners of English have been examined. Some sets of the loanwords gathered and evaluated in terms of pronunciation and orthographic rules have been classified and presented in the chapter. The purpose of focusing on the mentioned issue is to raise the awareness of foreign language –FL- practitioners and FL learners.

BACKGROUND

The impact of L1 on L2 and the notion of interference while learning a foreign language have been one of the chief concerns of the scholars in the field of L2 language education. The remarkable views have been the core of discussions, and the field courses to train L2 learners have been designed by taking these views into account. Among such views, cross-linguistic influence (CLI), for illustration, insists that using data from L1 or L2 has a considerable influence on L2 learning. CLI was used by Kellerman and Sharwood (1986) to refer to the phenomena such as language transfer- positive and negative transfer-, interference, and borrowing. Positive transfer is the experience which makes learning easier and may occur when both L1 and L2 have the identical form, whereas negative transfer, known as interference, is the use of L1 pattern or rule which leads to an error or inappropriate form in L2 (Richards & Schmidt, 2002). CLI can be noticed at all linguistic levels, whether phonological, lexical, syntactical, or semantic. By comparing groups of learners with different L1 backgrounds learning English as L2 and by clarifying more complex ways beyond simply formal similarities among individual items, Ringbom (2006) distinguished between different types of cross-linguistic similarity relations which refer to items and systems, form and meaning, L1 and L2 transfers, and perceived or assumed similarities. Depending on such distinguished points, it can be noted that the abundance of similarity among language items may foster promising results in language learning process. Conversely, dissimilar points among languages may lead to obscurity and difficulty in comprehension and production levels. The degree of difficulty in this sense can be explained through marked and unmarked items of any language (Ortega, 2009); and the models offered to describe the occurrence are Markedness Differential Model and Speech Learning Model.

MARKEDNESS DIFFERENTIAL HYPOTHESIS AND SPEECH LEARNING MODEL

The rate of second or foreign language learning is affected by various features of both native language (L1) and target language (L2). Since some linguistic features are simpler or more basic in relation to others, such features are explained with the degree of markedness and unmarkedness. The notion of markedness that is known to interact with L1 influences (Ortega, 2009) derives from Chomsky's theory of Universal Grammar (UG) which distinguishes the rules of a language as core or periphery (Ellis, 2008). While core rules are governed by universal principles, peripheral rules are controlled by parameters which are language specific features. The degree of markedness of a feature can also vary within certain core rules depending on the parameter setting involved (Ellis, 2008). By referring to Eckman's (1977) Markedness Differential Hypothesis (MDH), which is based on phonological theory of markedness, Gass (2013) argues that one way to think of markedness is that an unmarked form, whether phonological or syntactic, is more common, more usual in the world's languages than a marked one. Ellis (2008) restates MDH and explains the degree of difficulty an L2 learner has on the basis of a comparison of L1 and L2 as following (p.386):

1. Those areas of L2 that are different from L1 and are relatively more marked than in L1 will be difficult;
2. The degree of difficulty associated with those aspects of L2 that are different or more marked than in L1 corresponds to the relative degree of markedness associated with those aspects;
3. Those areas of L2 that are different from L1 but are relatively more marked than L1 will not be difficult.

In the above comparison by Ellis (2008), the degree of difficulty between L1 and L2 items is pointed out. In that case, how such difficulty between L1 and L2 is applied to phonology needs to be observed. If language sounds are more common to many languages, they are classified as unmarked ones; but if they are not, they are labeled as marked ones. How does it apply to L2 learning situation? It can be supposed that if the sounds are unmarked, they are learnt before marked ones. Along with the MDH, some other theoretically derived hypotheses such as the Structural Conformity Hypothesis which addresses the role of markedness in terms of marked and unmarked structures (Ellis, 2008), the Similarity Differential Hypothesis which claims dissimilar sounds being acquired faster than similar sounds, and the Ontogeny Phylogeny Hypothesis which is intended to capture phonological relationships between L1 and L2 (Gass, 2013) seek for account of the three general characteristics of L2 phonology. The specific claims are given below (Gut, 2009: 25):

1. The presence of L1 phonological features in the learners' speech
2. The tendency for learners to substitute unmarked forms where the target language requires marked forms
3. The occurrence of unique phonological forms in the learners' L2 production, including those found in L1 acquisition.

These focused characteristics on L1 and L2 phonological features are interrelated with the notion of transfer, either positive or negative.

The similarities between L1 and L2 can facilitate L2 learning, since learners do not look for differences but for similarities as basic cases (Ringbom, 2007). However, according to Speech Learning Model -SLM- proposed by Flege (1995), in addition to the notion of markedness and unmarkedness, the more distant an L2 sound is from L1 sound, the more learnable the L2 sound is. In other words, it is stated that if L2 sounds are similar to L1 sounds, they are not easily perceived by L2 learners; since learners do not classify them as different, they do not set up a contrast theory. Although similarity of the sounds in L1 and L2 can make it easier for learners to comprehend and produce in L2, those similar sounds are categorized as marked sounds. At the lexical level, similarity can be explained in terms of linguistic transfer. In the storage of lexical items, cross-linguistic similarities of both L1 and L2 have influences on learners' perception and production progress (Rignbom, 1987; Gabrys-Barker, 2006; Jarvis & Pavlenko, 2008). Lexical storage by the use of similarities can be reported as positive lexical transfer derived from the availability of translation equivalents in both languages by mapping the existing semantic representations in L1. In other words, if the degree of lexical similarity between L1 and L2 is greater, learners store those words quickly; but if the phonetic similarity of the words is greater, learners face difficulties while producing such words in L2. The implication is that similar sounds between L1 and L2 in production can be evaluated in markedness/unmarkedness category. As a result of the similarity of speech sounds at lexical level, one of the areas of the research interest has been loanwords and their properties in L2 learning process.

CATEGORIES OF LOANWORDS IN TERMS OF MARKEDNESS/ UNMARKEDNESS AND SPEECH LEARNING MODEL

Loanwords are the lexical items borrowed from a foreign language into another language. The literature pertaining to loanwords specifies that phonological and semantic linguistic alterations take place during the process of borrowing (Kay, 1995; Tsujimura, 1996; Major, 2008; Beel & Felder, 2013). Such alterations are attributable to the nature of the differences of sound systems of both languages. In other words, since loanwords might have different sounds from the ones in the phonology of the recipient language, they undergo phonological adaptations to make the lexical item be more native and less foreign because of the impact of similarity and markedness on L2 acquisition (Major, 2008). Despite the linguistic alterations, similarities of loanwords in phonological and semantic aspects help learners discover and learn such words beforehand. Cross-language similarities of loanwords have the facilitative advantages on learners of L2 and they treat loanwords as great sources in language learning (Ringbom, 2007). In this respect, regarding the vocabulary learning in general and loanwords in particular, the question debated is whether the impact of L1 on L2 yields positive results or not: if the transfer is positive, the result is positive; but if negative, the impact causes to erroneous output. On account of the phonological and semantic similarities, loanwords seem to be supportive catalysts for learners during language learning process. When the prior knowledge benefits the learning task, positive transfer occurs by applying the previous performance and knowledge to subsequent learning (Brown, 2007). Hence, corresponding words in L1 and L2 as cognates are effective tools for building vocabulary knowledge. However, as abovementioned, if L2 sounds are similar to L1 sounds or L1 sounds are adapted to loanwords, it is not always easy to perceive those sounds and to classify them as different (Flege, 1995). Accordingly, negative transfer occurs due to habitual manners for the sound system in L1.

Therefore, in this chapter, the purpose is to evaluate the effect of the perceived cross-linguistic phonetic similarity on the case of learning English words that are classified as loanwords in Turkish regarding the theories of markedness/unmarkedness and Speech Learning Model (SLM). SLM deals with how the perception and production of sounds in L2 are influenced by L1. Before presenting the research data, building an understanding of the adaptation of loanwords in Turkish is intended in the following section.

Adaptation of Loanwords in Turkish

Turkish is a language in which many loanwords have been borrowed from other languages. The number of loanwords in Turkish has rapidly increased because of language contact situations such as trade, politics, communication, education, and etc. While adapting the loanwords to the reception language, the phonological features of this language are followed as adaptation strategies. Beel and Felder (2013:5) describe three main strategies when applying a loanword from English to Turkish phonology: substitution, deletion, and epenthesis:

- *Substitution* is the adaption process that a language uses by substituting one phoneme (speech sound) with another more familiar phoneme. For example, the English loanword *mathematics*, which is phonetically written as [mæθmædɪks], is pronounced by native Turkish speakers as *matematik,* phonetically written as [mʌtɛmʌtik]. However, since [θ] does not exist in Turkish phonology, native Turkish speakers will substitute the unfamiliar [θ] with the more familiar [t]. Thus, rather than pronouncing *mathematics* as [mæ*θ*mædɪks], native Turkish speakers will pronounce it as [mʌ*t*ɛmʌtik].
- *Deletion* is the adaptation process of entirely removing a sound that makes a word too difficult to pronounce. Turkish has borrowed the word *apartment* from English, but native Turkish speakers have trouble while pronouncing it correctly due to the consonant cluster *nt* that occurs at the end of the word. By using the process of deletion, Turkish speakers adapt *apartment* from its original pronunciation [əpɑɹtmɛ*nt*] to [ɑpɑɹtmɑ*n*] by completely removing the final [t]. This simple consonant removal allows the elimination of a consonant cluster, thus conforming to the established Turkish syllable structure allowance.
- *Epenthesis* which is the most common loanword coping strategy among Turkish speakers is the process that inserts a vowel to make a word more pronounceable. Like deletion, epenthesis is generally used to break up consonant clusters that give native Turkish speakers extreme difficulty in the word's pronunciation. For example, the Turkish language borrowed the word *graffiti*, phonetically [gɹəfidi], from English. Though English phonology and syllable structure allow English speakers to place consonants [g] and [ɹ] next to each other, Turkish speakers find this combination almost impossible to pronounce without adaptation. Thus, Turkish speakers will modify the pronunciation by inserting a vowel in between the consonant clusters [g] and [ɹ] resulting in the final pronunciation [*gɪɹ*afiti].

The study of Beel and Fedler (2013) reveals that adaptations of loanwords are based on the systematic phonological rule vowel harmony in Turkish. In this perspective, through close adaptation strategies, the loanwords in Turkish still have phonological and semantic similarities with the ones in English; that is, Turkish shares cognates with English. Thus, such sound-meaning correspondences can be evaluated on bases of both positive/negative transfers dichotomy and markedness/ unmarkedness dichotomy within the framework of SLM.

Some research studies carried out to show the effect of cognates in L1 on the process of L2 vocabulary learning concluded that similarity between L1 and L2 makes it easy to learn L2 (August, et al., 2008; Ringbom, 2007). Some other studies focus on the measurable progress in perception and production concluded that perception and production play equal roles in the word-loaning process through adaptation (Chiyuki & Kenstowicz, 2009; Broselow, 2009). In another study by Arabski (2006), it has been concluded that L1 and L2 similarity comes into contact through transfer or borrowing. In a study carried out to verify the types of lexical transfer by Celaya and Torras (2001), it was elucidated that adults and adolescents draw on L1 more than children in language learning process which combines L1 and L2 coinages. Likewise, Major (2008) claimed that advanced learners have more difficulty in producing similar sounds, while beginning learners show difficulty in producing new sounds. Regarding the results of the studies, it can be presupposed that positive transfer from L1 is a constructive catalyst for learning L2 vocabulary, and the perception and production through the similarity of L1 and L2 cognates can be evaluated on unmarkedness dichotomy.

PURPOSE

The analysis in this section to build an understanding of the recognized phonological, semantic, and orthographic circumstances in both oral and written products presents the effect of the perceived cross-linguistic similarity/dissimilarity on the base of the Speech Learning Model (SLM). Based on this purpose, answers have been sought to the following research questions:

1. How does L1 influence the oral performance of Turkish learners of EFL at the phonological level?
2. How does L1 influence the oral performance of Turkish learners of EFL at the semantic level?
3. How does L1 influence the written performance of Turkish learners of EFL at the orthographic level?
4. How does L1 influence the written performance of Turkish learners of EFL at the semantic level?

Method

The research that is descriptive in nature was carried out through classroom observation reports and written products of the participants who were 46 fourth year student teachers attending the English Language Teaching Department (ELT) at a Turkish university. They were exposed to English for twelve years –two years at primary education, six years at secondary education, and four-year intensive courses at BA level. They were between upper-intermediate and advanced linguistic levels. All participants were exposed to consent process wherein they allowed their work to be published.

Data Collection and Analysis

Written products were collected randomly through the exam papers of the curriculum courses for corpus collection. The topic was not concern of the corpus; merely random loanwords used by the participants were recorded. Qualitative analyses were used to evaluate the collected data. One source is the corpus of the oral products recorded during English courses for five weeks. The other source is the corpus collected by the use of hand-written documents taken from various ELT course exam papers of the participants. In both data sets, only the loanwords were sampled.

FINDINGS

The oral and written data of loanwords which were classified according to positive/negative transfer and unmarkedness/markedness dichotomies are displayed in separate tables and evaluated qualitatively.

As displayed in Table 1, the loanwords which have almost equivalent phonetic features in L1 and L2 were transferred from Turkish to English under the influence of positive transfer and were assumed to be unmarked words. But the ones which are classified as marked were influenced negatively from the transfer due to similar L1 correspondences in L2.

As seen in Table 2, no loanwords were exposed to negative transfer and categorized at markedness level regarding the meaning transfer. This situation indicates the positive influence of cross-linguistic features in semantic level. Since all loanwords listed in the table have the same correspondences in L1, the participants did not have any difficulty while they were communicating orally with those words at semantic level.

In Table 3, the loanwords that are classified as marked/unmarked and positive/negative transfer in written products of the participants are listed. The loanwords in Turkish which have close resemblance in English were inscribed in correct form in

Table 1. Similarity of loanwords at phonological level

	Positive Transfer/ Unmarkedness Loanwords and English-Turkish Correspondences		**Negative Transfer/ Markedness Loanwords and English-Turkish Correspondences**	
Oral Performance at Phonological Level	Actor-aktör Actress-aktris Africa-Afrika Alarm-alarm Album albüm America-Amerika Anonym-anonim Archeologist-arkeolog Argot-argo Arena-arena Aristocracy-aristokrasi Arithmetic-aritmetik Artist-artist August-ağustos Bacteria-bakteri Bank-banka Basketball-basketbol Bureaucracy-bürokrasi Cacao-kakao Cactus-kaktüs Calcium-kalsiyum Caricature-karikatür Catalog-katalog Characteristic-karakteristik Chocolate-çikolata Civil-sivil Coffee-kahve Commission-komisyon Complex-kompleks Composition-komposizyon Copy-kopya Corridor-koridor Costume-kostüm Credit-kredi Cristal-kristal Critic-kritik Diplomatic-diplomatik Economy-ekonomi Electronic-elektronik Emperor-imparator Faculty-fakülte Federation-federasyon Feminist-feminist Festival-festival Function-fonksiyon Graphic-grafik Hotel-otel Monologue-monolog Passport-pasaport Picnic-piknik Politics-politika Phonetics-fonetik Physics-fizik Radiation-radyasyon Rational-rasyonel Reception-resepsiyon Reform-reform Refuse-refuze Rehabilitation-rehabilitasyon Restoration-restorasyon Speculation-spekülasyon Stabilization-stabilizasyon	Strategy-strateji Sweater-süeter Symmetry-simetri Tanker-tanker Taxi-taksi Telecommunication-telekomünikasyon Television-televizyon Tennis-tenis Telepathy-telepati Telephone-telefon Terror-terör Terrorism-terörizm Test-test Thermal-termal Toast-tost Tone-ton Transformation-transformasyon Transportation-transportasyon Transit-transit Tropical-tropik Variation-varyasyon Volcanic-volkanik Whisky-viski	Address-adres Agent-acenta Accessory-aksesuar Aquarium-akvaryum Allergy-allerji Alphabet-alfabe Alcohol-alkol Alcoholism-alkolizm Amateur-amatör Analysis-analiz Abnormal-anormal Antique-antik Apartment-apartman Archeology-arkeoloji Assistant-asistan Atmosphere-atmosfer Baggage-bagaj Balcony-balkon Biography-biyografi Biology-biyoloji Cafeteria-kafeterya Capacity-kapasite Capital-kapital Captain-kaptan Carbondioxide-karbondioksit Category-kategori Champion-şampiyon Chimpanzee-şempanze Club-klüp Coalition-koalisyon College-kolej Communism-kominizm Compartment-kompartman Conference-konferans Concert-konser Corner-korner Cousin-kuzen Crisis-kriz Culture-kültür Detective-detektif Decoration-dekorasyon Dynamite-dinamit Dialog-diyalog Dozen-düzine Empathy-empati Encyclopedia-ansiklopedi Energy-enerji Energetic-enerjik Filter-filtre Garage-garaj Gas-gaz Generator-jeneratör Geology-jeoloji Guarantee-garanti Grammar-gramer Hypermarket-hipermarket Icon-ikon Ideal-ideal Idealism-idealizm Ideology-ideoloji Image-imaj Internet-internet Industry-endüstri Inflation-enflasyon	International-enternasyonel Legal-legal Liter-litre Journal-jurnal Material-materyal Mathematics-matematik Medium-medyum Meteorology-meteoroloji Million-milyon Modern-modern Muslim-müslüman Objective-objektif Operation-operasyon Original-orijinal Pajamas-pijama Paragraph-paragraf Parameter-parametre Pedagogy-pedegoji Performance-performans Philology-filoloji Photography-fotoğraf Pizza-pizza Practical-pratik Profile-profil Professor-profesör Psychiatry-psikiyatri Psychology-psikoloji Regime-rejim Restaurant-restoran Romantic-romantik Schizophrenia-şizofreni Semester-sömestr Specific-spesifik Socialist-sosyalist Sociology-sosyoloji Special-spesiyal Speaker-spiker Station-istasyon Statistics-istatistik Style-stil Sultan-sultan Supermarket-süpermarket Surprise-sürpriz Symbol-sembol Sympathy-sempati Symposium-sempozyum Tactic-taktik Technology-teknoloji Telegraph-telgraf Textile-tekstil Theory-teori Tolerance-tolarans Tour-tur Tourism-turizm Traffic-trafik Train-tren Transfer-transfer Uniform-üniforma University-üniversite Vitamin-vitamin Visa-vize Zoology-zooloji

Table 2. Correspondences of loanwords at semantic level in oral performance

	Positive Transfer/ Unmarkedness				**Negative Transfer/ Markedness**	
Oral Performance at Semantic Level	Abnormal Accessory Actor Actress Address Africa Agent Alarm Album Alcohol Alcoholism Allergy Alphabet Amateur America Analysis Anonym Antique Apartment Aquarium Archeologist Archeology Arena Argot Aristocracy Arithmetic Artist Assistant Atmosphere August Bacteria Baggage Balcony Bank Basketball Biography Biology Bureaucracy Cacao Cactus Cafeteria Calcium Capacity Capital Captain Carbondioxide Catalog Category Champion Characteristic Chimpanzee Chocolate Civil Club Coalition	Caricature Coffee College Commission Communism Compartment Complex Composition Concert Conference Copy Corner Corridor Costume Cousin Credit Crisis Cristal Critic Culture Decoration Detective Dialog Diplomatic Dozen Dynamite Economy Electronic Empathy Emperor Encyclopedia Energetic Energy Faculty Federation Feminist Festival Filter Function Garage Gas Generator Geology Grammar Graphic Guarantee Hotel Hypermarket Icon Ideal Idealism Ideology Image Industry Inflation	International Internet Journal Legal Liter Material Mathematics Medium Meteorology Million Modern Monologue Muslim Objective Operation Original Pajamas Paragraph Parameter Passport Pedagogy Performance Philology Phonetic Photography Physic Picnic Pizza Politics Practical Professor Profile Psychiatry Psychology Radiation Rational Reception Reform Refuse Regime Rehabilitation Restaurant Restoration Romantic Schizophrenia Semester Socialist Sociology Speaker Special Specific Speculation Stabilization Station Statistics	Strategy Style Sultan Supermarket Surprise Sweater Symbol Symmetry Sympathy Symposium Tactic Tanker Taxi Technology Telecommunication Telegraph Telepathy Telephone Television Tennis Terror Terrorism Test Textile Theory Thermal Toast Tolerance Tone Tour Tourism Traffic Train Transfer Transformation Transit Transportation Tropical Uniform University Variation Visa Vitamin Volcanic Whisky Zoology	-	-

Table 3. Similarity of loanwords at orthographic level

	Positive Transfer/ Unmarkedness Loanwords and English-Turkish Correspondences		**Negative Transfer/ Markedness Loanwords and English-Turkish Correspondences**	
Written Performance at Orthographic Level	Actor-aktör Africa-Afrika Alarm-alarm Album-albüm America-Amerika Anonym-anonim Argot-argo Arena-arena Arithmetic-aritmetik Artist-artist Bank-banka Basketball-basketbol Cacao-kakao Cactus-kaktüs Cafeteria-kafeterya Calcium-kalsiyum Catalog-katalog Category-kategori Characteristic-karekteristik Chocolate-çikolata Civil-sivil Coffee-kahve Complex-kompleks Composition-komposizyon Copy-kopya Costume-kostüm Credit-kredi Crisis-kriz Cristal-kristal Critic-kritik Diplomatic-diplomatik Economy-ekonomi Electronic-elektronik Energy-enerji Faculty-fakülte Federation-federasyon Feminist-feminist Festival-festival Function-fonksiyon Gas-gaz Hotel-otel International-uluslararası Internet-internet Legal-legal Material-materyal Modern-modern Operation-operasyon Original-orijinal Passport-pasaport Picnic-piknik Pizza-pizza Politics-politika Phonetic-fonetik Radiation-radyasyon Rational-rasyonel Reception-resepsiyon Reform-reform Refuse-refuze Restoration-restorasyon Romantic-romantik Station-istasyon Statistics-istatistik Strategy-strateji Sultan-sultan	Supermarket-süpermarket Tactic-taktik Tanker-tanker Taxi-taksi Telecommunication-telekomünikasyon Television-televizyon Tennis-tenis Telephone-telefon Test-test Thermal-termal Toast-tost Tone-ton Tour-tur Tourism-turizm Traffic-trafik Train-tren Transformation-transformasyon Transportation-transportasyon Transfer-transfer Transit-transit Tropical-tropic University-üniversite Variation-varyasyon Visa-vize Vitamin-vitamin Volcanic-volkanik	Actress-aktris Address-adres Agent-acenta Accessory-aksesuar Allergy-allerji Aquarium-akvaryum Archeologist-arkeolog Aristocracy-aristokrasi Alphabet-alfabe Alcohol-alkol Alcoholism-alkolism Amateur-amatör Analysis-analiz Abnormal-anormal Antique-antik Apartment-apartman Archeology-arkeoloji Assistant-asistan Atmosphere-atmosfer August-Ağustos Bacteria-bakteri Baggage-bagaj Balcony-balkon Biography-biyografi Biology-biyoloji Bureaucracy-bürokrasi Capacity-kapasite Capital-kapital Captain-kaptan Carbondioxide-karbondioksit Caricature-karikatür Champion-şampiyon Chimpanzee-şempanze Club-klüp Coalition-koalisyon College-kolej Commission-komisyon Communism-kominizm Compartment-kompartıman Conference-konferans Concert-konser Corner-korner Corridor-koridor Cousin-kuzen Culture-kültür Detective-detektif Decoration-dekorasyon Dynamite-dinamit Dialog-diyalog Dozen-düzine Empathy-empati Emperor-imparator Encyclopedia-ansiklopedi Energetic-enerjik Filter-filtre Garage-garaj Generator-jeneratör Geology-jeoloji Graphic-grafik Guarantee-garanti Grammar-gramer Hypermarket-hipermarket Icon-ikon	Ideal-ideal Idealism-idealism Ideology-ideoloji Image-imge, imaj Industry-endüstri Inflation-enflasyon Liter-litre Journal-jurnal Mathematics-matematik Medium-medyum Meteorology-meteoroloji Million-milyon Monologue-monolog Muslim-müslüman Objective-objektif Pajamas-pijama Paragraph-paragraf Parameter-parametre Pedagogy-pedegoji Performance-performans Philology-filoloji Photography-fotoğraf Physics-fizik Practical-pratik Profile-profil Professor-profesör Psychiatry-psikiyatri Psychology-psikoloji Regime-rejim Rehabilitation-rehabilitasyon Restaurant-restoran Schizophrenia-şizofreni Semester-sömestr Specific-spesifik Socialist-sosyalist Sociology-sosyoloji Special-spesiyal Speaker-spiker Speculation-spekülasyon Stabilization-stabilizasyon Station-istasyon Statistics-istatistik Style-stil Surprise-sürpriz Sweater-süeter Symmetry-simetri Symbol-sembol Sympathy-sempati Symposium-sempozyum Technology-teknoloji Telegraph-telgraf Telepathy-telepati Terror-terör Terrorism-terörizm Textile-tekstil Theory-teori Tolerance-tolerans Uniform-üniforma Whisky-visky Zoology-zooloji

English. The participants did not assess them as marked; therefore, positive transfer emerged as a result of close orthographic features of the words. However, the more complicated or diverse from Turkish forms the words were, the more marked they were for the participants. Since the participants did not establish new perceptual categories for the loanwords phonetically similar to those in Turkish, they did not process orthographic representation in English. In this respect, the phonetic similarity of loanwords, unless they are very identical to the ones in English, resulted in negative transfer; the participants made spelling mistakes.

As seen in Table 4, no difficulty in written performance at semantic level emerged. In other words, positive transfer is predominant at meaning level. Such an outcome is consistent with the oral production of the participants at semantic level. The positive influence of the similarity of Turkish loanwords was helpful for the participants while performing the written tasks.

In terms of cross-linguistic influence, the corpus displays the predominance of L1 influence on loanword procedure. The distinction can be made between explicit and implicit cross-linguistic influence as a result of the perceived similarity of the loanwords in both Turkish and English. When the loanwords in both languages are pronounced exactly the same, no deviation appeared in the oral productions of the participants; however, when they detected pronunciation similarity between the two language loanwords, those loanwords were exposed to negative transfer and classified in markedness dichotomy. Likewise, in the written productions of the participants, the difficulty appeared at orthographic level. L1 similarity led to negative transfer and was evaluated in markedness dichotomy; still, the loanwords having almost the same orthographic characteristics were evaluated in unmarkedness dichotomy and created no difficulty due to positive transfer. At semantic levels of both oral and written productions, the participants faced no difficulty in terms of adopting the meaning of loanwords to contextual usage; that is, the similarity of the loanwords assisted the participants to use the words appropriately. It is apparent that the semantic relatedness of the loanwords in both Turkish and English prevented them from making semantic errors.

SOLUTIONS AND RECOMMENDATIONS

In this chapter, the research strategy is to predict the probable difficulties the student teachers of English faced while applying pronunciation and orthographic rules of the loanwords in both Turkish and English. The purpose is to question the validity of the theories, Markedness Differential Hypothesis and Speech Learning Model by evaluating the data on the base of these theories.

Table 4. Correspondences of loanwords at semantic level in writing

	Positive Transfer/ Unmarkedness				**Negative Transfer/ Markedness**	
Written Performance at Semantic Level	Abnormal	Caricature	International	Strategy	-	-
	Accessory	Coffee	Internet	Style		
	Actor	College	Journal	Sultan		
	Actress	Commission	Legal	Supermarket		
	Address	Communism	Liter	Surprise		
	Africa	Compartment	Material	Sweater		
	Agent	Complex	Mathematics	Symbol		
	Alarm	Composition	Medium	Symmetry		
	Album	Concert	Meteorology	Sympathy		
	Alcohol	Conference	Million	Symposium		
	Alcoholism	Copy	Modern	Tactic		
	Allergy	Corner	Monologue	Tanker		
	Alphabet	Corridor	Muslim	Taxi		
	Amateur	Costume	Objective	Technology		
	America	Cousin	Operation	Telecommunication		
	Analysis	Credit	Original	Telegraph		
	Anonym	Crisis	Pajamas	Telepathy		
	Antique	Cristal	Paragraph	Telephone		
	Apartment	Critic	Parameter	Television		
	Aquarium	Culture	Passport	Tennis		
	Archeologist	Decoration	Pedagogy	Terror		
	Archeology	Detective	Performance	Terrorism		
	Arena	Dialog	Philology	Test		
	Argot	Diplomatic	Phonetic	Textile		
	Aristocracy	Dozen	Photography	Theory		
	Arithmetic	Dynamite	Physic	Thermal		
	Artist	Economy	Picnic	Toast		
	Assistant	Electronic	Pizza	Tolerance		
	Atmosphere	Empathy	Politics	Tone		
	August	Emperor	Practical	Tour		
	Bacteria	Encyclopedia	Professor	Tourism		
	Baggage	Energetic	Profile	Traffic		
	Balcony	Energy	Psychiatry	Train		
	Bank	Faculty	Psychology	Transfer		
	Basketball	Federation	Radiation	Transformation		
	Biography	Feminist	Rational	Transit		
	Biology	Festival	Reception	Transportation		
	Bureaucracy	Filter	Reform	Tropical		
	Cacao	Function	Refuse	Uniform		
	Cactus	Garage	Regime	University		
	Cafeteria	Gas	Rehabilitation	Variation		
	Calcium	Generator	Restaurant	Visa		
	Capacity	Geology	Restoration	Vitamin		
	Capital	Grammar	Romantic	Volcanic		
	Captain	Graphic	Schizophrenia	Whisky		
	Carbondioxide	Guarantee	Semester	Zoology		
	Catalog	Hotel	Socialist			
	Category	Hypermarket	Sociology			
	Champion	Icon	Speaker			
	Characteristic	Ideal	Special			
	Chimpanzee	Idealism	Specific			
	Chocolate	Ideology	Speculation			
	Civil	Image	Stabilization			
	Club	Industry	Station			
	Coalition	Inflation	Statistics			

Table 5. Relativity of perception and production of loanwords

Classification of Performance levels	The Cross-Linguistic Influence	Evaluation of Cross-Linguistic Similarity on the Base of the Perception and Production of Learners
Oral performance at phonological level	Positive transfer/ Unmarkedness	Learners' perception and classification of L2 sounds as not different from L1 sounds in oral production
	Negative transfer/ Markedness	Learners' perception of L2 sounds as similar as L2sounds and violation of L2 pronunciation in oral production
Oral performance at semantic level	Positive transfer/ Unmarkedness	Learners adopt appropriately the loanwords in L1 that have same semantic components in L2 in oral performance at L2 semantic level
	Negative transfer/ Markedness	No deviation appears from L1 loanwords into L2 as negative transfer and at markedness level
Written performance at orthographic level	Positive transfer/ Unmarkedness	Learners' successful insertion of L1 graphemes almost equivalent to L2 graphemes in written performance
	Negative transfer/ Markedness	Learners' failure in spelling the loanwords in L1 because of similar sounds and graphemes
Written performance at semantic level	Positive transfer/ Unmarkedness	Learners adopt L1 loanwords to L2 effectively at semantic level
	Negative transfer/ Markedness	No deviation from L2 semantic components of loanwords at semantic level

The findings display the competing influences of similar Turkish and English loanwords on learners' oral and written products in terms of phonological and semantic representations. The results indicate that if the similarity of the loanwords is almost equal at phonological level in both Turkish and English, it facilitates the use of their corresponding in English. In written performance, the extent of the similarity also influences learners' transcribing ability in English. Almost equal similarity creates no difficulty and can be treated as effective tools for positive transfer. Conversely, the level of the diverse orthographic forms of the loanwords from English, despite the close orthographic similarity, leads to erroneous transcribing. Another result of the study is that the similarity of the loanwords in Turkish and their correspondences in English facilitates the appropriate use of those words in oral and written communication at semantic level. In this respect, resemblance of the loanwords in L1 and L2 facilitates or obstructs the language usage of learners depending on the degree of similarity.

The results also indicated that the ignorance of the exact dissimilarity and relatively similarity of speech sounds on the surface level leads to negative transfer and results in marked category. However, the convergence in meaning level facilitates appropriate semantic transfer in both oral and written performances of L2 learners. According to Speech Learning Model, the greater the perceived phonetic divergence between L1 and L2 speech sounds, the more likely learners will be able to distinguish the difference between L1 and L2 sounds; but the phonetic convergence of the lexis in the two languages obstructs learners' awareness of the discrepancy of the sounds. The results of the present analysis supports the idea put forward by this model. The results, as consistent with the studies by Chiyuki and Kenstowicz (2009) and Broselow (2009), also suggest that the degree of perception and production of the sounds display significant equal roles while adapting loanwords.

The research report also sought answers to the research questions through building an understanding of the competing differences and similarities between Turkish and English phonological and semantic features of the loanwords. The question "How does L1 influence the oral performance of Turkish learners of EFL at the phonological level?" and "How does L1 influence the oral performance of Turkish learners of EFL at the semantic level?" can be held in two perspectives: positive transfer/unmarkedness perspectives and negative transfer/markedness perspectives. The participants did not perceive and classify the L2 sounds of some loanwords as diverse from their corresponding L1 sounds, since L1 knowledge influenced oral production positively. The participants seem to have recognized those sounds as unmarked ones. As Ringbom (2007) emphasizes learners, consciously or not, do not look for differences, but they look for similarities wherever they can find them. However, in markedness level, the participants perceived the L2 sounds as identical to the L1 sounds and violated the phonological rules in English. On the other hand, at semantic level, the participants adopted the loanwords in the English context appropriately, since those words have the same semantic correspondences in Turkish, and all participants valued them as unmarked. This indicates the constructive influence of positive transfer from L1 in oral performance of the participants. As for the question about the written performance "How does L1 influence the written performance of Turkish learners of EFL at the orthographic level?, the markedness/unmarkedness problem emerges in different ways from oral performances. The loanwords that have similar L2 graphemes were inserted successfully, and positive transfer from L1 encouraged the participants to use them appropriately in their written products. However, the participants failed to spell some loanwords that were more complicated and diverse at orthographic level in L2. Those deviations seem to have been perceived as marked by the participants. They mapped the loanwords into the existing semantic representation of Turkish. The fourth research question on the semantic level in writing performance "How does L1 influence the written performance of Turkish learners of EFL at the semantic level?" sought answers to the question whether the participants faced any difficulty while transferring semantic knowledge from Turkish into English. It was found out that the semantic correspondence of the loanwords both in Turkish and English promoted the participants' performance level and no deviation appeared.

This research report has consistent results with the other studies carried out to indicate the issues that cause to negative transfer of loanwords by introducing the phonological, morphological, semantic changes (Kay, 1995; Simon-Maeda, 1995; Tsujimura, 1996). When marked structure appears in L2, it interacts with negative transfer and results in erroneous forms (Jarvis & Pavlenko, 2008). The studies mostly emphasize the alteration of loanwords from another language in L1 which leads to errors.

As noted in the findings section, the oral performance at phonological level supports the hypothesis of Speech Learning Model which focuses on how the perception and production of sounds in a second language are influenced by L1. The findings from written productions at orthographic level supports Markedness Differential Hypothesis which claims that the differences between L1 and L2 components are more marked and creates difficulty due to negative transfer. In this respect, the results of this research study support the claims of these two models for phonological and orthographic loanword outcomes in L2 which are influenced by L1 similarity. The competing influences of similarity and difference between L1 and L2 sound systems and orthographic systems of loanwords lead to both negative and positive transfer from L1 and are perceived as marked and unmarked. However, the semantic correspondence of the loanwords in L1 and L2 leads to positive transfer and is identified as unmarked in learning process. Considering the influence of L1, both negative and positive transfers of form and merely positive transfer of meaning are likely to occur in description.

CONCLUSION

This descriptive analysis is a sample diagnostic study. The proposed models to distinguish the difficulties in both oral and written productions of L2 learners could be used in L2 educational settings to raise awareness on L1 and L2 similarities and dissimilarities. Based on the findings, it would be possible to conclude that the features of L1 has both facilitative and debilitative effects on L2 language learning process. When two languages share a number of loanwords, it gives learners a start in vocabulary learning by raising their confidence. But in some cases, as in loanword transfer, it is difficult to establish the extent of facilitative and debilitative effects. When loanwords in L1 have similar sounds in the phonology of L2, they undergo both negative and positive transfer. Cross-linguistic influence does not introduce facilitative changes. This occurrence is attributable to dominant negative transfer.

The data in this study show that loanword phonology in L1 does not always conform to L2 phonology. Thus, those elements are perceived as not diverse from L1 and pronounced in the same manner as in L1. In meaning level, they do not create difficulty for L2 learners; instead, due to the universality of meaning, learners easily and positively transfer L1 knowledge. At orthographic level, as a result of different spelling features, learners have difficulty and make negative transfer. Since they do not perceive the loanwords as different, adaptation of loanwords creates difficulties in L2.

FUTURE RESEARCH DIRECTIONS

The focus of this chapter is to display and discuss some controversies emerging from cross-linguistic influence in terms of loanwords. The research process has been limited with Turkish- as L1- and English –as L2-. Thus, the models discussed in this chapter could be used for future research opportunities in different L1 and L2 contexts with different age groups and genders. To have a detailed description of the instances, longitudinal studies are suggested for further studies. In addition, it would be useful to design a treatment process for exploring the reasons of negative transfer and make learners notice their errors attributable to negative transfer. After treatment process, the developmental stages need to be recorded and evaluated. Moreover, as for further research concerns, cross-linguistic influences can be considered beyond phonological and orthographic levels; and innovative studies would be carried out to report decision making processes of language learners while transferring L1 knowledge into L2.

REFERENCES

Arabski, J. (2006). Language transfer in language learning and language contact. In J. Arabski (Ed.), *Cross-linguistic influences in the second language lexicon* (pp. 12–21). Clevedon, UK: Multilingual Matters.

August, D., Carlo, M., Dressler, C., & Snow, C. (2008). The critical role of vocabulary development for English language learners. *Learning Disabilities Research & Practice*, *20*(1), 50–57. doi:10.1111/j.1540-5826.2005.00120.x

Beel, R., & Felder, J. (2013). Phonological adaptations of English loanwords in Turkish. *Other Undergraduate Scholarship*. Retrieved from http://digitalcommons.liberty.edu/eml_undergrad_schol/2

Broselow, E. (2009). Stress adaptation in loanword phonology: Perception and learnability. In Phonology in perception (pp. 191–234). New York: Mouton de Gruyter.

Brown, D. (2007). *Principles of language learning and teaching*. White Plains, NY: Pearson Education.

Celaya, M. L., & Torras, M. R. (2001). L1 influence and EFL vocabulary: do children rely more on L1 than adult learners? In *Proceedings of the 25th AEDEAN Meeting*. University of Granada.

Chiyuki, I., & Kenstowicz, M. (2009). Mandarin loanwords in Yanbian Korean II: Tones. *Language Research*, *45*(1), 85–109.

Ellis, R. (2008). *The study of second language acquisition*. Oxford, UK: Oxford University Press.

Flege, J. (1995). Second-language speech learning: theory, findings and problems. In W. Strange (Ed.), *Speech perception and linguistic experience: issues in cross-language research* (pp. 233–273). Timonium, MD: York Press.

Gabrys-Barker, D. (2006). The interaction of languages in the lexical search of multilingual language users. In J. Arabski (Ed.), *Cross-linguistic influences in the second language lexicon* (pp. 144–166). Clevedon, UK: Multilingual Matters.

Gass, S. M. (2013). *Second language acquisition*. New York: Routledge.

Gut, U. (2009). *Non-native Speech: a corpus-based analysis of phonological and phonetic properties of L2 English and German*. Frankfurt, Germany: Peter Lang. doi:10.3726/978-3-653-01155-5

Jarvis, S., & Pavlenko, A. (2008). *Crosslinguistic influence in language and cognition*. London: Routledge.

Kay, G. (1995). English loanwords in Japanese. *World Englishes*, *14*(1), 67–76. doi:10.1111/j.1467-971X.1995.tb00340.x

Kellerman, E., & Sharwood, S. (1986). *Crosslinguistic influence in second language: an introduction*. Oxford, UK: Pergamon.

Major, R. C. (2008). Transfer in second language phonology. *Phonology and Second Language Acquisition, 36*, 63-94.

Ortega, L. (2009). *Understanding second language acquisition*. London: Hodder Education.

Richards, J. C., & Schmidt, R. (2002). *Longman dictionary of language teaching and applied linguistics* (3rd ed.). London: Longman.

Ringbom, H. (1987). *The role of the first language in foreign language learning*. Clevedon, UK: Multilingual Matters.

Ringbom, H. (2006). The Importance of different types of similarity in transfer studies. In J. Arabski (Ed.), *Cross-linguistic influences in the second language lexicon* (pp. 36–45). Clevedon, UK: Multilingual Matters.

Ringbom, H. (2007). The importance of cross-linguistic similarities. *Language Teaching*, *31*(9), 3–5.

Simon-Maeda, A. (1995). Language awareness: Use/misuse of loan-words in the English language in Japan. *The Internet TESL Journal, 1*(2). Retrieved from http://www.aitech.ac.jp/~iteslj/

Tsujimura, N. (1996). *An introduction to Japanese linguistics*. Oxford, UK: Blackwell publishing.

Chapter 4
The Emotional Aspect in Foreign Language Learning Process:
The Role of Emotional Development in Child's Foreign Language Learning

Işıl Gamze Yıldız
Trakya University, Turkey

ABSTRACT

Language is one of the most essential features of humans. Another basic feature that is common for all mankind is emotions, and expression of emotions is through the use of language whether it is verbally uttered or represented by body language. This interrelated and human-specific nature of language and emotions gains a place in foreign or second language learning process studies as well. However, the emotional aspect in learning a second or foreign language has mostly been neglected, or in other words, it has commonly taken the backseat. From this point forth, this chapter descriptively represents how the emotional development of an individual—specifically the child's—fosters the foreign language learning process. In doing this, learning/acquisition theories and a child's emotional development process—as a foreign language learner—are reviewed and assumptions/suggestions are displayed through a detailed literature review.

INTRODUCTION

A child's development occurs in four basic dimensions which are; cognitive, physical, social and emotional. These dimensions are strictly interrelated and an alteration in one of these influences the others. However, in second language acquisition studies

DOI: 10.4018/978-1-5225-4009-0.ch004

this indivisible structure of developmental dimensions has mostly been neglected or they typically focused on the cognitive dimension assuming learning is in most part related with the cognition (Garret & Young, 2009; Scovel, 1999). It is pleasing that there is a growing interest in taking the other developmental dimensions into consideration in second language acquisition contexts with the help of the studies on motivation and affect (e.g., Arnold, 1999; Dörnyei, 2003, 2005; Gardner & MacIntyre, 1991, 1993).

The focus on emotional aspect started to be seen a key factor in ensuring the individual's socialization in language learning process since human is a social being and could not be thought separate from the environment where s/he is living. In this sense, driven with the idea of sociocultural theory (Vygotsky, 1978), language learner should be utilized in her/his own learning context and her/his very own world of emotions. Learning a foreign or second language also comes true in all learning context with the emotional characteristics the learner has brought with. Moreover, learning another language has its own distinguishing features and context in which the learner is in need of extra attention because of the emotional load s/he is carrying. By the help of educational psychology and its reflection on learning theories in determining the exact developmental stage of the learner to support the emotional development properly, this study descriptively tries to represent how emotional development of a young learner fosters foreign language learning process. Besides, current studies on this subject are presented to form an opinion about the recent research and to keep up with the latest developments. Before explaining the need to put emotions into consideration in foreign language learning, it would be useful to clarify the meaning of emotion briefly.

Reeve (2005: 294) states that emotions are short-lived, feeling-arousal-purposive-expressive phenomena that help us adapt to the opportunities and challenges we face during important life events. For Aragao (2011: 302) emotions represent various ways being in relation to the dynamics of the immediate environment. According to Imai (2010; 279) emotions are not just an individual's private inner workings in response to external stimuli but are socially constructed acts of communication that can mediate one's thinking, behavior, and goals. In short, emotions are feelings that can be either positive or negative in its nature and they shape or are shaped by all the experiences of a living organism including the language learning as well. Thus, emotional development of a learner should also be the concern of the foreign language learning environment. Since this study basically focuses on the young learners, it would be worth mentioning to the current foreign language learning / teaching tendencies in global context to better understand the general trends and necessities for implicating in the emotional aspect.

With the impact of globalization, foreign language teaching has experienced several changes and developments. The growing need to communicate with other countries as a result of mobilization and technological developments increased the need to learn other languages more than ever. According to Johnstone (2002:15) the logic of learning a foreign language in 1990s was to be able to learn the language of the neighbors (border on). However, this idea has changed in the beginning of 2000s and the concept of 'neighbor' is enlarged as covering any of the countries in the world as 'virtual neighbors'.

Relationships among countries are shaped by numerous organizations and unions and these organizations designed and planned language learning policies to communicate effectively by learning the cultures, attitudes, lifestyles of the member communities. Their starting point was to form 'a unity in variability' (Starkey, 2002). The member communities can live among a large political context if only they believe in this idea (Starkey, 2002:7). In this case the term 'communicative competence' is regarded as one of the aims of language learning and teaching (CEF: 2001). Besides, a new concept 'life-long learning' comes to the fore. Thus, learning is not restricted with the compulsory education and limited in a school context; it is a competence that should be continued through the entire life of a learner (Dehmell, 2006:50).

Life-long learning is an enduring process and it should start as early as possible. In this context, learning a foreign language in an early age becomes one of the most essential aims of foreign language learning policies throughout the world (Neuner, 2002: 12). Promoting an early start in learning a foreign language necessitates a detailed analysis of young learner characteristics to construct effective learning environments. This could only be possible by regarding the learner (the child) as a whole. Emotional development of a child is one of the dimensions that should be worthy of notice and it should first be evaluated in a holistic approach to see the whole picture. In the following section of this study, the developmental features of a child and the identity of a child as a learner is discussed in the light of the developmental psychology and second language learning/acquisition theories. Following this, an overview to the current literature is displayed via including suggestions.

BACKGROUND

Basically, human development is a complex process which consists of physical, cognitive, emotional, and social development (İnanç, et. al., 2007:11). Accordingly, so as to understand the nature of the human development, focusing only one of these dimensions is inadequate. The development of an individual should be studied in an attitude which consists of all these dimensions. Besides, the development of child is a small representative of human development. This holistic approach for the developmental dimensions also includes sub-categories such as; moral development, sexual development and etc. (Sroufe et al., 1996: 15-24). However, this study is based on the fact of learning and focused on four main developmental dimensions in general. Driven with the notion of developmental psychology, it is possible to interpret how learning works cooperatively with the developmental process.

According to Piaget, every child experiences the same developmental process throughout his life. Thus, the difference in physical environment or conditions does not have any impact on this development. In this sense, Piaget ignores the environmental factors in development and states that the ability to use the language is closely related with cognitive development (Pinter, 2006:6). In order to understand what a child is able to do in this process it would be helpful to look through the cognitive dimensions that Piaget put forward. There are four main dimensions in cognitive development as; sensory-motor (birth-2 years), pre-operational stage (2-7 years), concrete operational (7-11 years) and abstract operational period (11+) (Brown 2000; Cameron 2001, Pinter 2006). The focus of this study is covering the ages between 7-11 thus only the concrete operational stage will be explained. Concrete operational stage is regarded as a key point because the child starts to think logically similar to adults and at the same time logical questioning is observed. However, this ability is limited with the current (concrete) context which means that they cannot generalize the comprehension effectively. In this sense, abstract thought is not possible yet (Bacanlı, 2011; Pinter, 2006). Piaget's point of view in acquiring the first language has become a matter of debate. The theories claiming that Piaget's theory is limited and inadequate have aroused. In this sense, Cameron (2001) indicates that researchers supporting Piaget's view are ignoring the child's further abilities and the role of social interaction. It is true that Piaget's view is limited both in understanding the real nature of the child as a whole by categorizing the children into specific segments and in indicating that they all experience the same process at the same time and ignoring the social factor in a child's life (Pinter, 2006). However, his cognitive developmental theory is still an important basis to understand the nature of L1 and L2 acquisition.

Another considerable theorist who leads the researchers and theorists to understand the child development is Vygotsky. He put forward the socio-cultural theory in order to explain the operation of human mind. According to this theory, he claimed that language is acquired through social interaction. Thus, so as to comprehend the language acquisition, the interaction between the child and his environment is important. Although it is supposed that Vygotsky's view is mainly constructed upon social and modern developments, he had never ignored the individual and his cognitive development (Cameron, 2001). With the term zone of proximal development (ZPD), Vygotsky added meaning to the concept of intelligence. ZPD refers to the child's abilities with a guided help from others. In other words, ZPD is a sign of understanding what a child can do with the help of an adult (Lightbown & Spada, 1999; Scarcella & Oxford, 1992). Vygotsky, similar to Piaget, believes in the idea that there are common features in the language development of a child however, he mentions to the significance of environment in the socialization of the child (Brewster, Ellis & Girard, 2002; Scarcella & Oxford, 1992).

Likewise Piaget and Vygotsky, Bruner also followed up a cognitive approach in explaining how children think and learn. According to Bruner, language is the most important tool for cognitive development. The term 'scaffolding' is specific to Bruner. According to this, a child might be unsuccessful in keeping in mind the communicative goal if he focuses on a specific part of a task. At this point, he needs an adult who will guide and help him in remembering the main task. One of the elements of scaffolding is the use of routines which symbolizes that a child needs sustained repetition in order to understand the new knowledge easily. Bruner also supports the idea that language is central for cognitive development. Bruner, by placing a great emphasis on scaffolding seems to resemble Piaget in many aspects, since scaffolding and ZPD could be regarded as similar concepts (Brewster, 1991).

All of the theories on cognitive development have also found their reflections in second language acquisition studies (Brewster, Ellis & Girard, 2002; Cameron, 2001; Halliwell, 1992; Foley & Thompson, 2003;) and will continue to be guide for researchers, theorists and educators in understanding the nature of development and its impact on learning foreign or second language/s.

From the deductions on the cognitive development of child, it is also possible to make interpretations about other developmental features; in addition, the theories based on cognitive development even indicates the emotional situation of the child by expressing their affective mood through specific age groups.

CHILD DEVELOPMENT AND EMOTIONS

Emotions are the central features of human-beings. In other words, human is a total of all her/his emotions and these emotions affects her/his whole world. For example; an unhappy child (whatever the reason is) would not be content in her/his relations with others too. This could be the reason of being unsuccessful both in educational settings or interaction with others. This structure of emotions affecting other experiences is a sign to the parents, educators, and teachers to design contexts and contents supporting the child's emotional development. Thus, supporting the development of emotional dimension would also be helpful for the entire life of the child together with her/his academic success. That is to say, "the communicative activity of users/ learners is affected not only by their knowledge, understanding and skills, but also by selfhood factors connected with their individual personalities, characterized by the attitudes, motivations, values, beliefs, cognitive styles and personality types which contribute to their personal identity" (CEF, 2001:105). This definition refers to the term 'existential competence'. According to the existential competence, all of these factors listed above affects the language learning process since they include all the components in a person's life from the values to the personal factors. Individuals bring their own characteristics into the language learning contexts. It is possible to suggest that existential competence stresses the role of emotional development in language learning too as Platon states "every learning has an emotional basis". These personality factors are mostly acquired biologically while some of them might possibly be acquired later on with the experiences. In this context, to promote positive personality factors, emotional development –like other developmental dimensions-should be supported. For the most part, factors such as self-esteem, self-knowledge are strictly related with the emotional development. These factors are also listed in Common European Framework for Languages (2001:160) as "the learner's different competences are closely related to individual characteristics of a cognitive, affective and linguistic nature which need to be taken into account in establishing the potential difficulty of a given task for a particular learner". In this statement, affective factors are seen as one of the most essential learner competences in learning a second language. In the same source, affective factors are listed as: self-esteem (a positive self-image), involvement and motivation (full involvement/ intrinsic or extrinsic motivation), state (learner's physical and emotional state), and attitude (learner's degree of willingness) (CEF,2001: 161).

Similarly Ellis (1994:483) states that learner's affective factors are obviously of crucial importance in accounting for individual differences in learning outcomes. Whereas learner's beliefs about language learning are likely to be fairly stable, their affective states tend to be volatile affecting not only overall progress but responses to particular learning activities on a day-by- day and even moment-by-moment basis.

For the most part, attitudes and personality factors greatly affect not only the language users' roles in communicative acts but also their ability to learn. Hence the focus of this study is limited to young learners of English as a foreign language, specific features related with their attitudes and emotional characteristics will be examined. Scott and Ytreberg (1997:4-5) indicate that children between the ages of 8 to 10 have strict ideas on what they love to make, they develop a sense of justice about what is happening in the classroom, and they start questioning the decisions of the teacher. With regard to this statement, designing a classroom atmosphere and selection of the content should be well organized to support the motivation and self-esteem in language learning.

Similarly Harmer (2007:83) lists some items related with the characteristics of children in this age group. One of these items is closely related with the emotional development. Children of this age group (8-11) are in need of attention and acceptance from their teachers, they like to talk about themselves and are willing to learn subjects they would like, they have a great desire in learning and curious about what is happening in the world they are living. The expectation of attention and acceptance should be met in the classroom. Otherwise, they would be sad and lose their motivation and self-esteem, resulting with the extinction of desire to learn. To prevent this, designing course contents enabling students to express their own feelings and thoughts would be favorable.

Children of this age group belong to the concrete operational stage and they start to socialize in real context. In other words, real interaction starts with other individuals. Through this process of socialization, emotions are of great concern since children like to be part of a community, share their thoughts and learn about the thoughts of others. For this reason, it is obvious that the child would be content to interact effectively with the others. Likewise, Senemoğlu (2011:59) points out that "teachers should not rule out the social aspect in learning. Interaction of students with their teachers and peers help them to develop social, emotional and cognitive features. It helps them to explain their own ideas while learning about the others' and to discuss these ideas". Every component supporting the social development is closely related with the emotional development. Hence, social and emotional development are given together in various studies (Bernard, 2006; Hallam, 2009; Hromek & Roffey, 2009; Joseph & Strain, 2003; Norris, 2003; Zeidner, et.al., 2002; Zins, et.al., 2003). In addition to these studies, recent studies are briefly summarized in the discussion part, and a table displaying the young learners' general features depending on their emotional development and its reflections on foreign language teaching are also represented.

SOLUTIONS AND RECOMMENDATIONS: STUDIES ON EMOTIONAL ASPECTS OF EFL LEARNERS

From the literature review given above, it is obvious that most of the studies in the field of foreign language teaching are focusing on the social competence rather than the emotional or has a tendency to discuss them together. These studies generally make reference to the traditional structure of the school, and make suggestions on the value of social and emotional development in the education that will be presented. According to this belief, schools should support social and emotional development of the child as well as cognitive development to raise healthy generations (Durlak, et.al., 2011:406). In other words, preparing students for life necessitates a balanced education which supports them in being academically successful and responsible adults.

Although social and emotional developments are interrelated features, every developmental feature should also be taken into consideration separately. While social development focusing on a qualified interaction between the learners, emotional development focuses on the emotional expectations convenient to a specific age group, indicates every emotional factor possibly affecting the foreign language learning, and finds out how learning occurs best in the process of foreign language learning. Dörnyei (2005) urges upon specific learner characteristics which could be listed as; anxiety, creativity, willingness to communicate, self-esteem, and learner beliefs. If these characteristics are supported learner would automatically be motivated and willing to learn.

From now on, some studies just focusing on the emotional development are listed in the thought that it would be a loadstar for researchers to learn about the contemporary studies on emotional development enabling them to conduct several studies or it would be a guide for the teachers who are willing to design effective language classes by supporting the emotional development of their students.

In their study titled "Emotions and their effects in a language learning Mexican context", Lopez and Cardenas (2014) display the results of the research on the expression of emotions in a second language in a Mexican context. In other words, to understand the impact of students' emotional experiences on their motivation, the participants were required to write an emotional journal. The study was carried out in the form of qualitative research via using narratives, journals and semi-structured interviews with the students. The study was conducted at the ELT department of a state university. It is stated that students were starting their second year of the program, and most of the students were from low socio-economic level. It's supposed that the economic level of the students might lead them to experience unpleasant events throughout their lives or they could be stronger in coping with negative experiences. The purpose of the research was presented to the students and 18 students of 24 enrolled in the class agreed to participate in the study. The ages of the participants ranged from 18 to 24. Consent was obtained from students and they were asked to choose a pseudonym to use through the whole study. A total of 250 journal entries and 18 interviews were analyzed. The results of the study indicated that there were seven different motivational sources for the students and the students were able to transform negative emotions into motivational energy. The study also displayed that the presence of interpersonal interactional support is a key in managing emotions in a language learning environment. The most striking point of the study is summarized by the researchers as "negative emotions might be considered unfavorable to language learning motivation, the research findings in this study seem to show that negative emotions are not always detrimental, at least for those students who decide to take obstacles as challenges to be met" (Lopez & Cardenas, 2014: 305). This qualitative study is highly successful in displaying effects of the emotional experiences on students' learning motivation in a specific context.

It might be a guide to the researchers working on the same field. By the help of the study, other instruments could be conducted specific to the young learners, since this study includes secondary year students at a university.

A similar study was conducted by Aragao (2011) titled "Beliefs and emotions in foreign language learning". This study is aimed to reflect the relationship between emotions and beliefs in foreign language learning by presenting the results of a qualitative research which was also a part of a doctoral thesis study. The participants of the study were chosen from the students at the beginning of the semester of an EFL programme named UFMG the language teacher education course. Out of 24 students who were enrolled in the class, seven were volunteered to participate in the research. Multiple procedures were used in gathering the data such as; a written language learning narrative, videotaped scenes from 19 classes, notes from students' language learning journals, transcribed semi-structured interviews, notes from informal conversations, notes from the participant observation, a visual representation of students' emotional dynamics and a questionnaire evaluating the participation in the research project. The results of the study indicated that 'speaking' was one of the most challenging skills of all. Findings revealed that students' beliefs about their speech, classmates and teacher influenced their feelings of embarrassment, shyness and class inhibition. This interplay in turn, modulated the way they behaved in class" (Aragao, 2011: 306). From the findings of the gathered data with multiple procedures it was of the opinion that there was a close relationship between beliefs and emotions in foreign language learning. According to Aragao (2011) there is a tight relationship between beliefs and emotions in foreign language learning. Observing and researching this interplay is important for understanding students' actions in class. In the following sections of the study extra suggestions on some pedagogical reflections for teachers were also included. These reflections are significant for teachers and researchers in developing similar or enlarged studies or classes supporting the emotional development of learners. They are also important to display the basic features for supporting the emotional development of the young learners and coherent with the background knowledge presented in this study.

In the article "Emotions in SLA: New insights from collaborative learning for an EFL classroom" Imai (2010) discusses the role and meaning of emotions in the second language learning process, and focuses on how learners' emotions manifest in their verbal communication over the course of a semester-long joint task (pp. 278). In this study, Imai conducted two case studies including two different groups of Japanese university EFL students, which lasted for 3 months. In these studies, Imai used multiple data collection procedures as in the study of Aragao (2011). These were videotaping, emotion logs, emotional temperature questionnaires, and stimulated recall interviews. The findings revealed that emotions supposedly detrimental to an individual's learning, such as boredom and frustration, could become a psychological resource for development, depending on how individuals participating in a given learning activity make sense of and appropriate (or ignore) these emotions interactionally (Imai, 2010: 288). According to Imai, emotions are mediators between cognitive demands and subsequent learning behavior allowing the learner to being a part of a given language learning activity. It is also suggested that there is a need for a more holistic approach bringing all types of emotions (whether verbal or not) related with learning in order to make a better analysis on the development of emotions.

Another study was conducted by Ma (2012), "A study of the shaping of the 'emotion and attitude' domain in the new English language curriculum of China through an EFL textbook". The study displays English language curriculum in China which was revised with the modernization movement in 1970s. In doing so, it had become an obligation and necessity to include the features emotion and attitude both to this curriculum and textbooks. Thus, Ma designed a study on analyzing a textbook named PEP Primary English 6A which was designed accordingly with English language syllabus to find out whether these features were met. Through this case study, the textbook was analyzed from three perspectives. Firstly, the perspective of affective learning' as reflected through the types of activities which aim to develop positive affect in students; secondly, the perspective of pedagogy as reflected through the affective teaching strategies recommended in the teachers' guide; and thirdly, the perspective of affective expression as reflected through the language forms and meaning presented (Ma, 2012: pp., 237). Moreover 4 strategies were used in analyzing the textbook. First strategy included respecting individuals, encouraging endeavor, safeguarding self-esteem and positive attitude while second strategy was designing co-operative learning activities, fostering collaborative learning, peer help, joint achievement and co-operative spirit. Third strategy was special attention to introvert students or those with learning difficulties. The last strategy was on establishing a harmonious, democratic channel of communication between teachers and students. The analysis of the textbook displayed that the writer of the book is aware of the emotion and attitude features, the lesson plans in the teachers' guide were developed accordingly however, small percentage of words related with emotions are presented in the textbook. Ma concludes the findings of the study with a statement taken from the work of Dewaele (2005) many of the foreign language textbooks are 'emotion-free' and do not prepare learners to become proficient foreign language users capable of identifying and expressing emotions crucial to human mental and social life (pp., 245).

In another study "The effects of affective factors in SLA and pedagogical implications" (2012) Ni focuses on the growing interest in the analysis of the effect of affective factors and their implications in English language teaching. The objective of the study was to improve the methods in English language teaching and figure out a basic alternative for students. By focusing on the research questions "how do the English majors evaluate their English on the whole?", "what are the effects of the affective factors (motivation, self-confidence and anxiety) on their language learning?", and "what are the attitudes of students toward their teachers' feedback?", a questionnaire was administered to 50 English majors who were enrolled foreign languages department of Heze University. The findings indicated that the affective factors decide the proportion of language learners' input and intake. The excellent students usually have high motivation, much self-confidence and a low level of anxiety and they receive and they take in plenty of language input. It is a pity that there are still some students who learn language with low motivation, little self-confidence and a high level of anxiety, to which teachers should give correct guidance on their affective factors (Ni, 2012: 1512). This study gives the researchers an evidence representing the degree of success is important in the emotional situation of an individual. In this sense, alternative studies can be conducted to obtain how a teacher could change this situation.

Zhao (2015) in the article titled "The influence of learners' motivation and attitudes on second language teaching", tries to reveal the co-relation between motivation and attitude of language learners and the second language teaching, and intends to improve the teaching effect by means of exploring the influences that a learner's motivation and attitude bring to foreign language teaching. A self-administered questionnaire was conducted by Zhao to find out the impact that learners' motivation and attitude have on students' learning process. The students were Mongolian and majors in clinical medicine in Inner Mongola University for the Nationalities. The study concluded that over half of the students participated in the research took a positive attitude toward English learning, the type of a teacher and the course content also had an effect on learning English. Although this study is presenting the general tendency of the students who are learning a second or foreign language it would even be a guide to the researchers in displaying a different context. In addition Zhao (2015) lists some of the teaching tips on learning attitude that would be useful for the teachers and researchers in the following part of the study.

In the article "Contribution to language teaching and learning: a review of emotional intelligence" Sucaromana (2012) introduces the importance of emotional intelligence and the extent to which emotional intelligence could be implemented and used to improve language teaching and learning. It is a descriptive study that could be a guide to educators and teachers in understanding the nature of emotions in the process of language learning. The author specifically stresses on the significance of emotional intelligence in learning languages and displays a two faceted context including students and the teachers.

Zhou (2016) in "The roles of social anxiety, autonomy, and learning orientation in second language learning: a structural equation modeling analysis", examined a model of second language learning in which performance depends not only students' motivation and emotion, but also on classroom learning orientation. A questionnaire was designed on social anxiety, autonomy, and collaborative learning orientation and self-reported English scores to a group of 303 fifth-grade students in China. The results of the study indicated that students who experienced social anxiety in language learning (in particular, a fear of public speaking) felt less autonomous, held weaker orientations of collaborative learning, and were less successful in their English learning. The results also showed that students' autonomy had both a direct and indirect effect (via collaborative learning orientation) on language learning (pp., 89).

Denham, Bassett and Zinsser's theoretical review (2012) titled "Early childhood teachers as socializers of young children's emotional competence", focuses on the possible teacher roles in the development of young children's emotional competence through presenting the findings taken from the research on parental socialization of emotion. Although this article stresses the pre-school children's emotional competence, it is still a good guide in displaying the significance of emotional development. This study would be a good reference for researchers and educators studying on very young learners and young learners as well since it focuses on the characteristics of young children.

Kim (2011) analyzed Korean elementary school students' decreased motivation for English learning by designing a questionnaire in the study titled "Korean elementary school students' English learning demotivation: a comparative survey study". The data were collected through questionnaires in a major city in Korea. The participants were 6301 elementary school students in grades 3 to 6. The findings revealed that the students' motivation and their satisfaction with their progress and their expectations for following success displayed a decrease as the students got advanced. For the part of the motivation, both instrumental and integrative motivations were strong; however, intrinsic and extrinsic motivations were weaker. Kim's study results showed a gradual decrease in English learning motivation among the respondents. The students' expectation of ultimate success in English learning and their satisfaction with English learning for both public and private education showed a decreasing trend (pp., 6). The causes of decreased motivation, and possible solutions for this decrease could be the subject of another study.

A distinctive study of all given above is conducted by Liu (2016), "The emotional geographies of language teaching" since this study is about an immigrant background English as a second language teacher's emotional experience in a teacher professional community in England. The data were gathered from emotion dairies and interviews. Findings indicated several reasons causing the emotional load for the teacher. Emotional geographies included these dimensions; physical geography, moral geography, sociocultural geography, professional geography, and political geography. Although this study is not relevant to the subject matter of this present study it is presented here to show what kind of obstacles a learner could confront with as an immigrant to the context of foreign language learning. Similarly by quoting Meyer (2011, pp. 76), Liu (2016) states that the findings of the paper bear significant implications for teachers and administrators alike. In transnational migration contexts, being new, foreign, young, and a non-native speaker of English can pose multiple challenges for immigrant background teachers. In order to survive, they need to establish close bonds with other members of the community, and create working conditions to enable 'emotional understanding' of self and others (pp., 493).

Regarding summaries of the abovementioned contemporary studies on emotional development, it is clear that the studies related to the emotional development of young learners in learning English as a foreign language are very limited. However, these studies that were discussed so far also shed light upon the studies that would be conducted in the foreign language teaching to young learners. In addition, these studies are also serve as a model for further studies which would be adapted to the relevant field.

With regard to the background and literature review of this study, the theoretical background of emotional development of young learners in the context of foreign language is summarized. As it has been mentioned before, the terms in teaching foreign languages to learners such as schema, zone of proximal development (ZPD), use of routines, and scaffolding are the main keys in developing emotional feature of the learner. According to ZPD, the child needs to be assisted by a group or a teacher in the process of learning. When this help is given, the child feels safe and encouraged to learn. Besides, child interacts with the people (whether with the teacher or parents), and this leads to the development of self-esteem by socializing since language learning requires social interaction (Verga & Kotz, 2013). The child who could not get the help s/he needed to become unhappy and these results in reluctance in terms of learning. Moreover, this assistance should be related with the developmental stage of the child. Thus, if this assistance is far beyond the level of the child, there would be anxiety causing the decrease in willingness during learning process. For this reason, the new knowledge should be presented incrementally and supported with the questions impelling the child to think (schema). In addition, the success of the child should be appreciated in order to motivate her/him. The last point is that the new knowledge that will be presented should be pertinent to the previous one in order to facilitate the adaptation. By the use of routines, the child would adapt to new learning more easily and feel safe in the new contexts.

FUTURE RESEARCH DIRECTIONS

It is possible to make deduction from the literature review on emotional development of children between the ages of 8-11 who are learning a foreign language. Table 1 displays the summary of such deduction.

This table is presented in order to help the researchers who are interested in the studies about young learners' emotional development. These features given above could also be used as a check list for analyzing the task or activity types that will be designed to support the emotional competence of the young learners.

CONCLUSION

This descriptive study is driven with the notion of stressing the significance of emotional development especially for young learners who are learning English as a foreign or second language. Regarding the literature on emotional development, emotional feature or affective feature -or whatever the theorists called- in language learning, it is obvious that there is a growing tendency among researchers that promoting positive affective variables is vital in the process of language learning (Arnold, 1999). However, research into affect-related teaching in the English as a foreign language classroom or the related pedagogic resources is limited (Ma, 2012: 236). Despite this limitation, it is still possible to design studies on emotional development which is based on educational psychology and specific to human.

Table 1. General features of children and suggestions for teaching

General Features	Deductions for Foreign Language Teaching
Learning cannot occur independently of emotions. Personal characteristics of children affect learning	Learning contents and context that they can express themselves should be designed
Children can learn easily if they like what they are doing for example; they like to talk about themselves	• They should learn while entertaining • Activities and tasks should be designed proper to their area of interest • Moreover tasks should also include contents that students can represent their own personal characteristics
Child is in need of attention and acceptance. For this reason, he needs support and motivation. Anxiety should be reduced. Moreover he needs to develop self-esteem.	• Motivating activities should be designed • Efforts of the students in the classroom should be reinforced and supported • Students success in a task should also be appreciated.
Child needs to communicate with others.	Task types in the classroom should permit to communicate with the peers

As mentioned above, second language acquisition or learning theories have been generated from the principles of educational psychology. In other words, all the developmental process that a child gets through is also valid for learning a second language. The limits of what a child can do in a specific age are also similar to what s/he can do in learning a topic. If the child is in pre-operational stage it is impossible to teach him how to read in English. Therefore lessons should include proper topics and contents to the developmental process of the child. Moreover learning should be supported by placing emphasis on the emotional development of the child as much as his cognitive development since human cannot exist without his feelings. Imai (2010:281) states that it is important to understand the synthesis of an individual's cognition, emotion, and behavior within social interaction and with their environments, in addition to viewing these phenomena as discrete components of an individual's inner properties. In addition to the literature review, a sample is given in the study which is formed by deducting the knowledge on developmental psychology and foreign language learning theories related with young learners between the ages of 8 to 11. In doing so, it is aimed to be a guide for the researchers studying on the emotional development of young learners and for the teachers who know the significance of emotions in learning a foreign language context, and willing to design appropriate courses.

REFERENCES

Aragao, R. (2011). Beliefs and emotions in foreign language learning. *System*, *39*(3), 302–313. doi:10.1016/j.system.2011.07.003

Arnold, J. (1999). *Affect in language learning*. Cambridge, UK: Cambridge University Press.

Bernard, M. E. (2006). It's Time We Teach Social-Emotional Competence as well as We Teach Academic Competence. *Reading & Writing Quarterly*, *22*(2), 103–119. doi:10.1080/10573560500242184

Brewster, J. (1991). What is Good Primary Practice? In C. Brumfit, J. Moon, & R. Tongue (Eds.), Teaching English to Children-From Practice to Principle. London: Longman.

Brewster, J., Ellis, G., & Girard, D. (2002). *The Primary English Teacher's Guide*. London: Pearson Education Limited.

Brown, H. D. (2000). *Principles of Language Learning and Teaching*. NewYork: Longman.

Cameron, L. (2001). *Teaching Languages to Young Learners*. Cambridge, UK: Cambridge University Press. doi:10.1017/CBO9780511733109

Common European Framework for Languages. (2001). Strasbourg, France: Academic Press.

Dehmell, A. (2006). Making a European area of lifelong learning a reality? Some critical reflections on the European Union's lifelong learning policies. *Comparative Education*, *42*(1), 49–62. doi:10.1080/03050060500515744

Denham, S. A., Bassett, H. H., & Zinssen, K. (2012). Early childhood teachers as socializers of young children's emotional competence. *Early Childhood Education*, *40*(3), 137–143. doi:10.1007/s10643-012-0504-2

Dörnyei, Z. (2003). Attitudes, orientations, and motivations in language learning: Advances in theory, research, and applications. *Language Learning*, *53*(S1), 3–32. doi:10.1111/1467-9922.53222

Dörnyei, Z. (2005). The psychology of the language learner: Individual differences in second language acquisition. Mahwah, NJ: Erlbaum.

Durlak, J. A., Weissberg, R. P., Dymnicki, A. B., Taylor, R. D., & Schellinger, K. B. (2011). The impact of enhancing students' social and emotional learning: A meta-analysis of school-based universal interventions. *Child Development*, *82*(1), 405–432. doi:10.1111/j.1467-8624.2010.01564.x PMID:21291449

Ellis, R. (1994). *The Study of Second Language Acquisition*. Shangai: Shangai Foreign Language Education Press.

Foley, J., & Thompson, L. (2003). *Language Learning: A lifelong process*. London: Arnold Hodder Healine Group.

Gardner, R. C., & MacIntyre, P. D. (1991). An instrumental motivation in language study: Who says it isn't effective? *Studies in Second Language Acquisition*, *13*(01), 57–72. doi:10.1017/S0272263100009724

Gardner, R. C., & MacIntyre, P. D. (1993). On the measurement of affective variables in second language learning. *Language Learning*, *43*(2), 157–194. doi:10.1111/j.1467-1770.1992.tb00714.x

Garret, P., & Young, R. F. (2009). Theorizing affect in foreign language learning: An analysis of one learner's response to a communicative Portuguese course. *Modern Language Journal*, *93*(2), 209–226. doi:10.1111/j.1540-4781.2009.00857.x

Hallam, S. (2009). An Evaluation of the Social and Emotional Aspects of Learning (SEAL) Programme: Promoting Positive Behaviour, Effective Learning and Well-being in Primary School Children. *Oxford Review of Education*, *35*(3), 313–330. doi:10.1080/03054980902934597

Halliwell, S. (1992). *Teaching English in the Primary Classroom*. London: Longman.

Harmer, J. (2007). *The Practice of English Language Teaching*. Pearson Longman.

Hromek, R., & Roffey, S. (2009). Promoting Social and Emotional Learning With Games: It's Fun and We Learn Things. *Simulation & Gaming*, *20*(10), 1–18.

Imai, Y. (2010). Emotions in SLA: New insights from collaborative learning for an EFL classroom. *Modern Language Journal*, *94*(2), 278–292. doi:10.1111/j.1540-4781.2010.01021.x

İnanç, B. Y., Bilgin, M., & Atıcı, M. K. (2007). *Gelişim Psikolojisi: Çocuk ve Ergen Gelişimi*. Ankara: PegemA Yayıncılık.

Johnstone, R. (2002). *Addressing the age factor: Some implications for languages policy*. Strasburg: Council of Europe.

Joseph, E. G., & Strain, P. S. (2003). Comprehensive Evidence-Based Social-Emotional Curricula for Young Children: An Analysis of Efficacious Adoption Potential. *TECSE*, *23*(2), 65–76.

Kim, T. (2011). Korean elementary school students' English learning demotivation: A comparative survey study. *Asia Pacific Education Review*, *12*(1), 1–11. doi:10.1007/s12564-010-9113-1

Lightbown, P., & Spada, N. (1999). *How Languages are Learned*. Oxford, UK: Oxford University Press.

Liu, Y. (2016). The emotional geographies of language teaching. *Teacher Development*, *20*(4), 482–497. doi:10.1080/13664530.2016.1161660

Lopez, M. N., & Cardenas, M. A. F. (2014). Emotions and their effects in a language learning Mexican context. *System*, *42*, 298–307. doi:10.1016/j.system.2013.12.006

Ma, A. (2012). A study of the shaping of the 'emotion and attitude' domain in the new English language curriculum of China through an EFL textbook. *Pedagogy, Culture & Society*, *20*(2), 231–250. doi:10.1080/14681366.2012.688764

Neuner, G. (2002). *Policy Approaches to English. Language Policies*. Council of Europe.

Ni, H. (2012). The effects of affective factors in SLA and pedagogical implications. *Theory and Practice in Language Studies*, *2*(7), 1508–1513. doi:10.4304/tpls.2.7.1508-1513

Norris, A. J. (2003). Looking at clasrrom management through a social and emotional learning lens. *Theory into Practice*, *42*(4), 313–318. doi:10.1207/s15430421tip4204_8

Pinter, A. (2006). *Teaching Young Language Learners*. Oxford, UK: Oxford University Press.

Reeve, J. M. (2005). *Understanding motivation and emotion*. Hoboken, NJ: John Wiley & Sons.

Scarcella, R. C., & Oxford, R. L. (1992). *The Tapestry of Language Learning: The Individual in the Communicative Classroom*. Heinle & Heinle.

Scott, W. A., & Ytreberg, L. H. (1997). *Teaching English to Children*. London: Longman.

Scovel, T. (1999). The younger the better myth and bilingual education. In R. Gonzales (Ed.), *Language Ideologies. Critical Perspectives on the English only Movement*. Urbana, IL: National Council of Teachers of English.

Senemoğlu, N. (2011). *Gelişim, Öğrenme ve Öğretim: Kuramdan Uygulamaya*. Ankara: Pegem Akademi.

Sroufe, A., Cooper, R., & Marshall, M. (1996). *Child Development: It's Nature and Course*. New York: McGraw-Hill, Inc.

Starkey, H. (2002). Guide for the development of language education policies in Europe, from linguistic diversity to plurilingual education In *Reference Study in Democratic Citizenship, Languages, Diversity and Human Rights*. Council of Europe. Retrieved August 9, 2010, from http://www.coe.int/t/dg4/linguistics/Source/StarkeyEN.pdf

Sucaromana, U. (2012). Contribution to language teaching and learning: A review of emotional intelligence. *English Language Teaching*, *5*(9), 54–57. doi:10.5539/elt.v5n9p54

Verga, L., & Kotz, S. A. (2013). How relevant is social interaction in second language learning? *Frontiers in Human Neuroscience*, *7*, 550–560. doi:10.3389/fnhum.2013.00550 PMID:24027521

Vygotsky, L. S. (1978). *Mind in society: The development of higher psychological processes*. Cambridge, MA: Harvard University Press.

Zeidner, M., Roberts, R. D., & Matthews, G. (2002). Can Emotional Intelligence be Schooled? A Critical Review. *Educational Psychologist*, *37*(4), 215–231. doi:10.1207/S15326985EP3704_2

Zhao, L. (2015). The influence of learners' motivation and attitıdes on second language teaching. *Theory and Practice in Language Studies*, *5*(11), 2333–2339. doi:10.17507/tpls.0511.18

Chapter 5
Semantic Priming in Monolingual Russian and Bilingual Russian (L1)-English (L2) Speakers in a Single Word Naming Task:
Semantic Priming in Russian

Evgenia Volkovyskaya
Middlesex University, UK

Ilhan Raman
Middlesex University, UK

Bahman Baluch
Middlesex University, UK

ABSTRACT

Identifying and exploring factors that influence bilingual language processing has been the topic of much psycholinguistic research. Semantic priming is typically used to examine semantic processing and refers to the phenomenon in which semantically related items (doctor-nurse) are processed faster and more accurately than semantically unrelated items (doctor-butter). The aim of the chapter is to address two key questions: 1) how the two languages of a bilingual are organised or stored and 2) how the two languages are processed. A review of the literature shows that there are currently no theoretical frameworks that explain Russian monolingual or

DOI: 10.4018/978-1-5225-4009-0.ch005

Russian (L1)-English (L2) bilingual storage or processing. Monolingual Russian speakers and bilingual Russian (L1)-English (L2) speaking university students were asked to name target words under related or unrelated conditions. The results show that the magnitude of the semantic priming effect was determined by L2 proficiency. The implications for these findings is discussed within the current bilingual theoretical models.

BILINGUALISM AND L2 PROFICIENCY

The ability to use spoken language to communicate with one another is a unique, inherent human characteristic that infants acquire without much effort. The additional ability to speak more than one language, i.e. *bilingualism*, because of contact with other communities, immigration and trade has been reported since antique times dating back to the Sumerians (Woods, 2006). In this respect, a widely accepted definition of bilingualism is '*both regular use and communicative competence*' in L1 (first language, native language, mother tongue) and L2 (second language) (Francis, 1999, p. 194). This very human behaviour has attracted much attention from philosophers to physicians throughout history and from psychologists in modern times.

From an evolutionary perspective, bilingualism can be perceived as a complex and a multifaceted process that involves the interaction of cultures, expression of social experience, and history of a particular people as well as the mechanism of interaction of languages (Roberts, 2013). Bilingualism makes contact with others possible, provides socialisation, forms tolerant attitude towards other cultures while it enhances cognitive abilities. At the same time, it is a prerequisite for the formation and perception of ethnic and social identity (Shi, 2007).

One aspect that has preoccupied researchers in the area of bilingual studies is the difficulties faced by a comprehensive classification of bilingualism that accurately defines an individual's skills in different modalities such as literacy and speech, performance and proficiency on the two languages they speak. The most common perception of a bilingual is someone who is almost equally fluent in two languages or at least proficient enough in their L2.

Various classification systems have been offered to explain the variation in fluency, competence, and order of acquisition for bilingual language use. For example, the degree of knowledge of languages has been labelled as either subordinate (when a bilingual speaks one language better than the other) and coordinate (or "pure", when a person speaks two languages in equal measure) (Grosjean, 1997). In addition, bilingualism has been described according to frequency of usage as either active (where both languages are used on a regular basis) and passive (the frequency of the use of one language dominates the other).

The degree of proficiency of the second language has also been used to classify bilinguals as receptive, reproductive, or productive where receptive bilingualism is defined as the ability to understand the subject of a non-native language (L2). Reproductive bilingualism involves the ability to competently reproduce spoken language in L2 and productive bilingualism is the ability to competently express thoughts and speech in L1 and L2 (Grosjean, 1997).

According to Bialystok and Hakuta (1994), a further definition of bilingualism depends on when L2 was acquired in relation to L1 leading to: 1) Simultaneous bilingualism when L1 and L2 were acquired in the same time (from speaking no languages directly to speaking two languages); 2) Early sequential bilingualism - L2 was learnt later than L1 in early childhood which represents a growing group of speakers worldwide; 3) Late bilingualism - L2 was acquired in adolescence or later.

One further aspect of bilingualism that has preoccupied researchers is the proficiency with which a bilingual speaks their second language (L2). This is because L2 proficiency could range from very basic communication to L1 level fluency; hence, it is a very important and an equally difficult factor to control for in bilingual studies. Additionally, bilingualism can be classified by levels of proficiency on production and reception (Bialystock, 2001). Productive bilinguals can speak and understand L2. Receptive bilinguals can understand both languages, but their abilities to produce L2 are limited.

A main objective of the current research is to understand lexico-semantic processes in bilingual Russian (L1) - English (L2) speakers in view of their L2 proficiency by using an objective measure; namely, the Schonell Reading Test (Schonell, 1971). However, it is difficult to find clear types of bilinguals, but rather a combination of types, which depends on particular features of language acquisition. In this respect, Grosjean (1997) considers that the bilingual mind is not a simple combination of two monolingual language systems, but a unique communication system that can use both languages or switch from one language to another depending on the subject and situation, and that bilinguals differ from monolinguals in terms of language reception and production. L2 proficiency therefore ought to be a central tenet in any psycholinguistic theoretical perspective that attempts to explain bilingual language processing.

The ability of the human cognitive system to store and organise language, and knowledge about words (phonological, semantic and orthographic representations) and to be able to retrieve those representations require multifaceted, interlinked, and complex mental processes. In the case of bilingualism, these processes are assumed to be even more complex as they are required to be executed for two languages. Of particular interest are two key questions raised within the bilingual literature context and related to the current chapter:

1. How the two languages of a bilingual are organised or stored; that is, whether each language is stored in one or more locations in bilingual memory
2. How the two languages are processed (i.e., what mental capacities are required to process each language)

Models of Bilingual Language Processing

A critical question that was raised in this respect during the 1980s was whether the two languages of a bilingual were stored in one or two memory stores. According to the separate store model (Potter et al., 1984), two separate lexicons for each language exist while according to the common store model (Paivio, Clark, & Lambert, 1988), only one memory store exists for both languages. Kroll and Stewart's (1994) Revised Hierarchical Model (RHM) integrated both accounts; that is, word association and concept mediation models, and proposed that both L1 and L2 words share conceptual representations (one store) as opposed to the word association model by Potter et al (1984) who suggest that L1 and L2 have separate representations for words (two stores) one for each language.

The RHM was primarily developed to explain the discrepancy in backward/forward translation findings in late bilinguals taking proficiency into account (Kroll & Stewart, 1994). When bilingual speakers translate words from L1 to L2 (forward translation) they are assumed to use conceptual mediation via direct access to the word meaning. While translating backwards from L2 to L1, one must have access to the word meaning via lexical representations, which is by word association. Backward translation is usually faster than forward translation (e.g., Kroll & Stewart, 1994; Sholl, Sankaranarayanan, & Kroll, 1995).

A further assumption is that there is a large overlap in meaning between words in L1 and L2, especially in concrete words as they share more features compared to abstract words. Meanwhile, language-specific words and abstract words are not assumed to share representations in the bilingual mind. The more features in common L1 and L2 have, the easier the translation (Brysbaert et al., 2014). Schoonbaert, Duyck, Brysbaert, and Hartsuiker (2009) assumed that semantic priming can be understood by observing the overlaps L1 and L2 have in forward and backward translation.

The aim of the current research was to place the assumptions of the RHM in relation to lexical and conceptual links to the test an application to language processing in monolingual and Russian (L1) - English (L2) bilinguals.

Methods of Investigation

Historically, the bilingual version of the Stroop test attracted attention from early researchers when the focus shifted from case studies to experimental paradigms, (e.g., Preston & Lambert, 1969). In the traditional Stroop test (1935, Experiment 1) participants were asked to read words in black versus incongruent colour (e.g., GREEN printed in red ink as GREEN), and the participant is required to ignore reading the word out as 'green' and name the colour of the ink as 'red'. The aim was to examine the interference of activation of nontarget information on the target and a highly significant interference from incongruent words in naming colours supported this.

Variations of the Stroop task became popular to investigate the semantic relationship between bilingual's first (L1) and second language (L2) (e.g., Bril & Green, 2013; Marian et al., 2013; Roelofs, 2009; Rosselli et al., 2002; Sumiya & Healy, 2004). It is important to note the level of language proficiency can significantly influence interference. For instance, with proficient bilinguals language interference was greater in within-language colour naming than in between-language (e.g., Chen & Ho, 1986; Preston & Lambert, 1969; Dyer, 1971; Tzelgov et al., 1990).

Overall, between-language Stroop task has become a popular method to evaluate selective lexical processing when both L1 and L2 are activated simultaneously regardless language situation. However, one can argue that language interference measured by Stroop test alone is an artificial effect, when, under natural circumstances (reading) between-language interference may not happen (see MacLeod, 1991, for a review).

The lexical decision task in which participants are presented with a string of letters (words or nonwords) displayed on the computer screen and they must decide whether the letter string is a word or nonword by pressing a key is also widely used in bilingual research. Reaction time and the number of errors are measured. Evidence from lexical decision tasks with bilinguals also suggest that bilinguals activate words from both of their languages when making lexical decisions (DeGroot, Delmaar, & Lupker, 2000; Dijkstra, Van Jaarsveld & Ten Brinke, 1998).

However, in a study with English-Spanish bilinguals, Scarborough, Gerard and Cortese (1984) reported that the participants rejected English words as quickly as nonwords derived from English words (e.g., edan) and both were rejected more quickly than nonwords derived from Spanish. It was concluded that the participants only activated the target language. One criticism of the lexical decision task is that the reading process cannot be simplified to the by the choice between words and nonwords and hence this task is not fully reflects the reading process (Seidenberg & McClelland, 1989).

Another popular research method is the naming task which assumed to better reflect the natural reading. Naming tasks attempt to identify processes used in generating sound (phonology) from print (orthography), therefore directly activating orthographic (spelling), phonological (sound) and semantic (meaning) representations in the lexicon (Coltheart, 1978; Morton, 1969). One interesting research question in naming tasks is whether bilinguals activate phonological representations in the nontarget language during word naming.

In order to address this question, Jared and Kroll (2001) tested English-French and French-English bilinguals. Findings showed that phonological representations were simultaneously activated in both languages. However, this was dependent on several factors as follows: a) whether bilinguals were naming words in their dominant or less dominant language b) participants' fluency and c) experience with French d) whether English target words were named before or after the French distracters words (Jared & Kroll, 2001).

During the 1970s and 1980's, there was a surge of research that aimed to identify cognitive processes involved in semantic priming in order to establish a theoretical understanding of this robust phenomenon using different experimental paradigms such as lexical decision and naming tasks. In the classic semantic priming task, participants are presented with either semantically related word pairs (e.g., DOCTOR-NURSE) or unrelated pairs (e.g., DOCTOR–BUTTER), typically comprised of a prime-target and asked to name or make a word/non-word judgement of the second word (target) as quickly as possible.

A reliable finding is that naming or making judgments on the target word is faster and more accurate when the prime is related (DOCTOR-NURSE) than unrelated (DOCTOR–BUTTER). This phenomenon is called semantic priming (Meyer & Schvaneveldt, 1971). Semantic priming was of special interest because it provides an opportunity to manipulate the semantic associations between words in order to address two key questions that dominate bilingual research: i) how the two languages of a bilingual are organised or stored; that is, whether each language is stored in one or more locations in bilingual memory and ii) how the two languages are processed (i.e. what mental capacities are required to process each language).

The model of spreading activation is useful in explaining semantic priming. that is, the faster and more accurate retrieval of information (i.e., the target), from memory if related information (i.e., the prime, has been presented a short time before). According to Neely and Kahan (2001), spreading activation principle assumes that words in a given network are activated automatically; that is, the process is fast, occurs without intention, is involuntary, and can occur without conscious awareness. This is because semantically related concepts are assumed to form stronger links or may be stored closer together than those concepts that are unrelated (Neely, 1991).

When one node is activated, activation spreads along the network to other concept nodes that are located nearby. The semantic-priming effect is argued to arise because the activation of a semantically related prime word leads to shorter response times to the target word, since the distance between related a prime-target pair (e.g., drink-taste) is shorter than an unrelated prime-target pair (e.g. drink-swallow).

Monolingual studies under different semantic priming manipulations have shown a robust effect (for reviews, see McNamara & Holbrook, 2003; Neely, 1991), yet between-language semantic experiments show ambivalent results (see Altarriba & Basnight-Brown, 2007 for a review). Proficiency in L2 has been considered an extraneous variable which influences the outcome of bilingual research on semantic priming. The general assumption is that bilinguals who are proficient in both languages would show a larger semantic priming effect than those who are not (Basnight-Brown & Altarriba, 2007).

For the purpose of this research, semantic priming was employed in a series of monolingual Russian and bilingual Russian (L1) – English (L2) experiments. The semantic in semantic priming means that priming is caused by true relations of the meaning. Hence, the particular interest induces the exploration of semantic effects in a bilingual context. Semantic priming is traditionally the most common type of priming in psycholinguistic experiments, particularly in word naming tasks (Harley, 2013).

Russian Orthography and Psycholinguistic Research

Modern Russian is a widely spoken East Slavic language which belongs to the Indo-European family of languages. Estimates of the number of people who speak Russian as either a first or second language vary from 285 million speakers (Weber, 1997) to 455 million (Crystal, 2008). Russian is one of the six official languages of the United Nations.

The modern Russian alphabet is based on the Cyrillic alphabet and consists of 33 letters; 21 consonants, 10 vowels, and two silent letters (Iliev, 2013). Details of the alphabet together with letters, their names and approximate sounds in English are reported below in Table 1. The relationship between the letters of the alphabet and pronunciation in modern Russian is not phonological. Both derivational and inflectional morphologies are extremely rich. Derivation occurs primarily by means of prefixation and suffixation.

Historically there have been several attempts to change the orthography which was originally based on the ancient Greek alphabet where the aim was to translate religious Greek texts into the Slavic language. By the order of the Byzantine Emperor Michael III at around 863 AD, brothers Cyril and Methodius from Thessaloniki created a new script called Glagolitic that originally contained 24 letters of Greek

Table 1. Russian Cyrillic alphabet

Letter	Name	Letter Sound	Approximate English Sound in Bold	Russian Example, Romanization, Meaning
Аа	а [a]	/a/	**fa**ther	**ананас** – "**a**n**a**n**a**s" - pineapple
Бб	бэ [bɛ]	/b/ or /bʲ/	**b**ig	**б**елка – "**b**elka" – squirrel
Вв	вэ [vɛ]	/v/ or /vʲ/	**v**ase	**в**ода – "**v**oda" - water
Гг	гэ [gɛ]	/g/	**g**et	**г**де – "**g**de" - where
Дд	дэ [dɛ]	/d/ or /dʲ/	**d**og	**д**ень – "**d**en'"-day
Ее	е [je]	/je/, / ʲe/or /e/	**ye**llow	н**е**бо – "n**e**bo" - sky
Ёё	ё [jo]	/jo/ or/ ʲɵ/	**yo**ghurt	**ё**ж – "**yo**zh" – hedgehog
Жж	жэ [ʐɛ]	/ʐ/	trea**s**ure	**ж**ена – "**zh**ena" – wife
Зз	зэ [zɛ]	/z/ or /zʲ/	**z**one	**з**има – "**z**ima" - winter
Ии	и [i]	/i/ or / ʲi/	h**e**	**и**кра – "**i**kra" - caviar
Йй	и краткое [i ˈkratkəɪ]	/j/	bo**y**	сво**й** - "swo**i**" - my
Кк	ка [ka]	/k/ or /kʲ/	**k**eep	**к**амера – "**k**amera" - camera
Лл	эл or эль [ɛl] or [ɛlʲ]	/l/ or /lʲ/	**l**oose	**л**и**л**ия – "**l**i**l**iya" – lilly
Мм	эм [ɛm]	/m/ or/mʲ/	**m**irror	**м**есто – "**m**esto" - place
Нн	эн [ɛn]	/n/ or /ɲ/	**n**ight	**н**ебо – "**n**ebo" - sky
Оо	о [o]	/o/	c**o**re	**о**н**о** – "**o**n**o**" - it
Пп	пэ [pɛ]	/p/ or /pʲ/	**p**arrot	**п**е**п**ел – "**p**e**p**el" - ash
Рр	эр [ɛr]	/r/ or /rʲ/	rolled **r** **r**iver	**р**ыба – "**r**yba" - fish
Сс	эс [ɛs]	/s/ or /sʲ/	**s**un	**с**ело – "**s**elo" - village
Тт	тэ [tɛ]	/t/ or /tʲ/	**t**rea**t**	**т**у**т** – "**t**oo**t**" - here
Уу	у [u]	/u/	s**oo**n	**у**ж – "**u**zh" - adder
Фф	эф [ɛf]	/f/ or /fʲ/	**f**inger	**ф**он – "**f**on" – background
Хх	ха [xa]	/x/	**h**at	**х**леб – "**h**leb" - bread
Цц	це [tsɛ]	/t͡s/	**c**elsius	**ц**апля – "**ts**aplya" – heron
Чч	че [tɕe]	/t͡ɕ/	**ch**air	**ч**ас – "**ch**as" - hour
Шш	ша [ʂa]	/ʂ/	**sh**ark	**ш**елк – "**sh**elk" - silk
Щщ	ща [ɕɕж]	/ɕɕ/	**sh**eer	**щ**ека – "**sch**eka" - cheek
Ъъ	твёрдый знак [ˈtv'ɵrdij znak]	-	Silent	объект – "ob**'**ekt" - object
Ыы	ы [ɨ]	[ɨ]	Roses	**ты** – "*ty*" – you
Ьь	мягкий знак [ˈm'yagkɪj znak]	-	Silent	семь – "sem**'**" - seven
Ээ	э [ɛ]	/ɛ/	s**e**t	**э**кран – "**e**kran" - screen
Юю	ю [ju]	/ju/ or/ ʲʉ/	**u**nited	**ю**ла – "**yu**la" - whirligig
Яя	я [ja]	/ja/ or/ ʲж/	**ya**rd	**я**блоко – "**ya**bloko" - apple

alphabet and 19 letters specific to the Slavic language (Iliev, 2013). Thus, the modern Russian alphabet is derived from the Old Slavic Cyrillic alphabet, which was borrowed from the Bulgarian Cyrillic and became widespread in ancient Russia. At that time, Russian alphabet consisted of 43 letters. Later, four new letters were added, and 14 letters were at different times excluded as unnecessary (Barhudarov & Dosicheva, 1940; Iliev, 2013).

According to Kerek and Niemi, (2009a) the structure of the Russian orthography is complicated by exceptions and hierarchy of system of rules. The complexity of the language lies in its morphology. One of the main features of the grammatical structure of the Russian language is a mandatory change in the form of words according to the gender, number and other factors, and in the formation of phrases and sentences these words has to be coordinated accordingly. The primary means of producing synthetic forms of words in the Russian language is the ending. Endings are formed by means of the form of nouns, adjectives, numerals, pronouns. In most cases, the endings turn out to be syncretic; that is expressing more than one grammatical meaning.

Despite the complex orthography, Russia had one of the highest levels of adult literacy in the world in 2009 (Huebler & Lu, 2013). There are a number of features of Russian orthography and morphology that affect the process of literacy acquisition (Cubberley, 2002; Kornev, Rakhlin, & Grigorenko, 2010). This is partly attributed to the Russian letter-sound correspondences which involve a small number of context-dependent rules which can be difficult for beginner readers.

For example, the two auxiliary signs, the "soft" and "hard" signs which make the letters in words to be read in the different ways depend on the position of "soft" and "hard" signs in the word.

Moreover, a number of words contain the "jotated vowels" е (je), я (ja), ю (ju), and ё (jo). These vowels [j] correspond with other letters ([e], [a], [u] and [o] respectively) after the consonants and can change palatalization of consonants and the quality of the vowel. Russian approach to reading pedagogy helps accommodate these complexities with syllable-based approach to reading (Kornev, 1995, 2003; Egorov, 2006). Russian orthography is reported to be more phonemic in comparison to English (Grigorenko, 2012) and is morphologically very complex. Phonetic modifications, consonants and a number of irregularities prevent readers to perceive a morpheme as a distinct unit (Kerek & Niemi, 2009b).

Diversity of languages provides a platform from which their properties and characteristics of specific features can be examined in bilingual research. This has led to a large body of research in different language pairs (e.g., Italian (L1) - English (L2), (Tabossi and Laghi, 1992); Russian (L1) - English (L2), (Abu-Rabia, 2001); Spanish (L1) - English (L2), (Rosselli, Ardila, Santisi, Arecco, Salvatierra, & Conde,

2002); Greek (L1) - French (L2), (Voga & Grainger, 2007); Greek (L1) - English (L2), (Niolaki, Masterson, & Terzopoulos, 2014).

The Russian language is one of the most widely used languages, but research based on the study of the Russian language is relatively small (Kerek & Niemi, 2009b). Language features that combine the complexity and regularity is what makes the Russian writing system important for between-language research, particularly with English as there are shared features between Russian (Cyrillic and Roman) and English (Roman) orthographies. As can be seen in Table 2, Modern Russian alphabet is a mixture of Cyrillic and Roman orthographies and consist of 33 letters: six letters are orthographically and phonologically shared with the English (Roman) writing system; seven letters are orthographically shared, but phonologically unique; a total of 14 letters are orthographically unique, but phonologically shared, and six Cyrillic letters are orthographically and phonologically unique.

The increased world-wide use of Russian along with the wave of immigration of the Russian-speaking population in the last 20 years makes it essential to understand the processes of being a Russian (L1) - English (L2) bilingual speaker. One of the few psycholinguistic studies on Russian bilingual language processing is reported by Abu-Rabia (2001) where the relationship between Russian and English orthographies was tested. Participants were bilingual Russian (L1) - English (L2) speakers. They were tested on working memory, spelling, visual and phonological conditions, orthographic skills, word attack and word identification. Orthographic skills showed correlation within-languages, but not between-languages. Additionally, phonological and spelling skills in Russian (L1) seem to be predictors of word identification in English (L2).

In another study, Brill and Green (2011) recruited bilingual English (L1) – Russian (L2) speakers to test whether in a Stroop test bilingual speakers ignore one language when they switch to the other language. English (L1) speakers who formally studied Russian as L2 were presented with a within-language English Stroop test and a between-language Russian Stroop test. The results showed a bigger interference effect for English (L1) than for Russian (L2), while bilingual speakers demonstrated equally large interference effect for both English (L1) and Russian (L2). These results were taken as evidence to support the assumption that bilinguals access both their languages simultaneously.

Recent developments saw the emergence of the first normative data in Russian. Tsaparina, Bonin and Meot (2011) used the colour version of the Snodgrass and Vanderwart (1980) pictures (Rossion & Pourtois, 2004). This set of pictures has been normed and used for research in different languages, such as Turkish (Raman, Raman, & Mertan, 2014), Spanish (Sanfeliù & Fernandez, 1996), British English (Barry, Morrison, & Ellis, 1997), French (Alario & Ferrand, 1999), Icelandic (Pind, Jónsdóttir, Tryggvadóttir, & Jónsson, 2000), Italian (Nisi, Longoni, & Snodgrass,

2000), Japanese (Nishimoto, et al., 2005), Chinese (Weekes et al., 2007), and Modern Greek (Dimitropoulou et al., 2009), and others.

The colour version was successfully used in a number of psycholinguistic studies: picture-naming study in Chinese (Weekes et al., 2007); picture naming in English (Therriault, Yaxley, & Zwaan, 2009); norms for name agreement, AoA, and visual complexity were collected in Modern Greek (Dimitropoulou et al., 2009) and in a free-recall task in Turkish (Raman et al., under review). Tsaparina and colleagues (2011) reported norms for name agreement, image agreement, conceptual familiarity, imageability, and age of acquisition in Russian. The role of AoA on monolingual Russian and bilingual Russian (L1) – English (L2) free-recall were also recently reported (Volkovyskaya, Raman and Baluch, under review).

Current Study

Given the general lack of literature on lexico-semantic processes in Russian speakers, the attention first turned to monolingual Russian speakers in order to gather evidence and to establish a theoretical framework of lexico-semantic processes in Russian.

Experiment 1

Design

In a repeated measures design, monolingual Russian participants were required to name target words under related and unrelated prime-target experimental conditions. The naming RTs (ms) and errors were recorded.

Participants

A total of 20 adult, monolingual Russian speaking students from St. Petersburg State Paediatric Medical University in St. Petersburg, Russia took part in Experiment 1. All the participants were monolingual Russian speakers with normal or corrected to normal vision.

Materials

Care was taken to use only very common or frequent words because a variation in word frequency has been reported to influence the semantic priming outcomes (see Lemhöfer et al., 2008 for a review); therefore, word frequencies were taken from the Word Frequencies Dictionary of modern Russian language which was based on a collection of texts of the Russian National Corpus, representing the modern Russian language for the period of 1950-2007 (Lyashevskaya & Sharov, 2009).

Materials comprised of either 21 semantically related pairs [врач - медсестра (nurse)] and [собака (dog)-кошка (cat)] or 21 unrelated pairs [врач (doctor) – кошка(cat)] which were presented using SuperLab software.

Procedure

A practice trial of four primes and four targets were run to familiarize participants with the procedure and the equipment. The participants were tested one at a time in a quiet laboratory at St. Petersburg State Paediatric Medical University and were seated approximately 60 centimeters from a computer screen and instructed to name the target words as quickly and as accurately as possible.

SuperLab experiment generator was used to present the stimuli and to record naming RTs via an SV-voicebox. First, a fixation point was presented on the computer for 500ms, followed by a 250ms blank, and then by the prime word in black font size 18 against white background in the middle of the screen for the next 500ms. The target followed the prime on the screen and disappeared after a response was made or after a 1000ms deadline to respond before the next trial began.

If participants did not name the target within the deadline, this was recorded as NR (no response). Finally, the related and unrelated conditions were counterbalanced to prevent order effects. The participants' number of errors was recorded by the experimenter.

Results

Data were analysed using descriptive statistics (see Table 2) and a repeated measures t-test. The SD values similar indicating homogeneity of variance. A difference of 25ms between related and unrelated conditions was found to be statistically significant. The results showed a significant semantic priming effect for monolingual Russian speakers, $t(19) = 2.6$, $p<0.01$. The error rates were less than 1% and therefore were not entered into analyses.

Table 2. Descriptive statistics showing naming RTs in milliseconds and SD in related and unrelated prime-target conditions in Experiment 1 for Russian monolinguals

Experimental Condition in Russian	Mean RTs	SD
Related	515	49
Unrelated	540	44
Magnitude of semantic priming	25	

Interim Discussion

The aim of Experiment 1 was to establish the existence of semantic priming effects in native Russian speakers in a naming task. As can be seen from the results reported above, a significant semantic priming effect is reported here for the first time in Russian adds to the body of literature in different languages. This was predicted by automatic spread of semantic network activation (Collins & Quillian, 1969) hypothesis and is taken to further support the universality of this phenomenon in the human mind irrespective of language.

Armed with this result, the focus turns to Experiments 2 and 3 in an attempt to examine within-language semantic priming in Russian (L1) - English (L2) bilinguals. This query is in line with the current trends in bilingual research as discussed under discussion.

Experiment 2

Method

Experiment 2 was a replication of Experiment 1 in which 20 bilingual Russian (L1) - English (L2) speaking university students were recruited from Middlesex University, London, in the United Kingdom. The participants were required to respond to the same stimuli as in Experiment 1 in Russian (L1) and were tested one at the time in a laboratory setting at Middlesex University using SupeLab software. Naming RTs and errors were recoded the same way. None of participants were enrolled in the English-as-a-Second-Language program or in intensive English courses.

Three possible outcomes were predicted: i) semantic priming effect will be the same for monolingual Russian (L1) and Russian (L1)-English (L2) bilinguals; ii) semantic priming effect will be smaller for Russian (L1)-English (L2) bilinguals compared to monolingual Russian (L1); and iii) semantic priming effect will be larger for Russian (L1)-English (L2) bilinguals compared to monolingual Russian (L1).

It therefore follows that if i) the size of semantic priming effect is the same for monolingual Russian (L1) and bilingual Russian (L1)-English (L2) speakers, it will be taken to indicate that having semantic networks (Collins & Quillian, 1969) in two different languages does not influence spreading activation (Collins & Loftus, 1975). If ii), then it will be assumed that nontarget language L2 is activated which has a negative influence on the semantic priming effect in the target language L1. If iii), this will be taken to indicate that although nontarget language L2 is activated, it has a positive or facilitatory effect on L1 semantic priming effect.

Evidence for (i) would support a two-store model where L1 and L2 are stored in semantic networks independent of each other (e.g., Potter et al., 1984). Evidence for (ii) and (iii) will be taken to indicate a common store (Paivio et al., 1988) as depicted in the RHM by Kroll and Stewart (1994), one memory store for concepts for both languages.

A major methodological and theoretical consideration in Experiment 2, is therefore the measure of objective proficiency of the Russian (L1)-English (L2) bilinguals in their L2 (e.g., in English), using the Schonell reading test (1971). As discussed previously, according to the RHM direct access to meaning in L2 strengthens with proficiency. Therefore, the more proficient a bilingual is the more reliant they become on their direct L2 conceptual link for accessing meaning according to the RHM (Kroll & Stewart, 1994).

A highly proficient bilingual would therefore show comparable semantic priming effects in both L1 and L2, whereas a less proficient bilingual would show a smaller or null effect for semantic priming in L2. The procedure was the same as in Experiment 1 with the addition of the English (L2) language proficiency test using the Schonell Reading Test in English (Schonell, 1971).

The present study took objective proficiency measures into account for the first time to ascertain fluency in the two languages of the participants. Participants were asked to read words given in the test paper from left to right, from top to bottom as accurate as possible. If participants had difficulties with a pronunciation of a particular word he or she was asked to sound it out anyway. When participants were not able to say the word they were asked to go on to the next one. One mark was given for the each word correctly pronounced, even if the reader self-corrected.

The researcher did not correct participants and did not suggest a pronunciation. The number of errors was measured and the test was stopped if eight consecutive errors are made. This test had no time limit. The number of correct words and errors were compared with a normative table given in the test. Those participants who read correctly 75% of the words and above were taken to be proficient enough in English (L2). It is important to note that all the participants who took part in Experiment 2 were proficient in their L2.

Results

Data were analysed using descriptive statistics as can be seen in Table 3 and a repeated measures t-test which showed a statistically significant priming effect, i.e. statistically significant difference between related and unrelated target words in Russian (L1) for bilingual Russian (L1) - English (L2) speakers, $t(19)=4.04$ $p<0.001$. Error rates were less than 1% and therefore were not the subject of analyses.

The naming RTs from Experiments 1 and 2 were further analysed using a t-test as the descriptive statistics showed a large difference between monolingual (25ms) and bilingual (50ms) semantic priming effects in Russian (L1). The results confirmed that this difference was statistically significant $t\ (19) = 2.2,\ p<0.04$.

Table 3. Descriptive statistics showing naming RTs in milliseconds and SD in related and unrelated Russian prime-target conditions in Experiment 2 for Russian (L1) - English (L2) bilinguals

Experimental Condition in Russian (L1)	Mean RTs	SD
Related	522	57
Unrelated	572	85
Magnitude of semantic priming	50	

Interim Discussion

The findings in Experiment 2 show a magnified semantic priming effect for bilingual Russian (L1) - English (L2) speakers compared to monolingual Russian speakers and are taken to indicate that semantic activation occurs automatically where activation of both L1 and L2 in bilinguals increases the priming effect. Furthermore, this effect can only come about if the two languages are activated from a single store (Altarriba & Basnight-Brown, 2007). It is also important to note that monolingual RTs to experimental conditions in Experiment 1 were notably faster to those in Experiment 2 although in both experiments participants responded to L1 prime-L1 target conditions.

Experiment 3

The aim of Experiment 3 is to examine semantic priming in English (L2) in Russian (L1) - English (L2) bilinguals.

Method

The experimental conditions were within-language in English (L2); that is, related and unrelated prime-target pairs were presented in English (L2) (e.g., doctor-cat and dog-nurse, respectively.) Naming RTs to target words were recorded together with errors.

Participants

The same Russian (L1) - English (L2) bilingual participants from Experiment 2 were recruited for the purpose of this experiment.

Materials and Procedure

A total of 42 trials were presented in English using SuperLab; 21 semantically related pairs (doctor-nurse, dog-cat); 21 unrelated pairs were formed by re-pairing the stimuli in the related cases (e.g., doctor-cat, dog-nurse). Word frequencies in English were taken from the Celex Lexical Database (Baayen, Piepenbrock, & Van Rijn, 1993) using the combined written and spoken frequency measures of the word. The procedure was the same as in Experiment 2.

Results

As can be seen from Table 4, a difference of 46ms is observed between related and unrelated prime-targets when participants name targets in English (L2). Formal analysis of data showed a significant semantic priming effect [$t(19)=2.7$, $p<0.01$] in English (L2) for bilingual Russian (L1) - English (L2) speakers. Error rates were recorded but were too small for analyses (less than 1%).

Combined Analyses for Experiments 2 and 3 and Interim Discussion

Data from Experiments 2 and 3 were collapsed for analyses in order to examine the issue of storage in the bilingual memory. As highlighted previously, proficiency of bilinguals has been reported to influence the outcome of semantic priming effects (Kroll & Stewart, 1994). The Schonell Reading Test (1971) was employed to the Russian (L1) - English (L2) bilingual participants who took part in both Experiments 2 and 3.

It was found that proficiency in English (L2) had a significant positive correlation with the magnitude of the semantic priming effect in Russian (L1) only, $r(20)=.57$ $p< 0.009$. The correlation between proficiency in L2 and semantic priming in L2 was nonsignificant ($p>0.05$).

As can be seen in Figure 1, despite showing a parallel and comparable semantic priming effect size in Russian (L1) and English (L2), Russian (L1) - English (L2) bilinguals are nevertheless slower in naming RTs in their second language English (L2) than their native language, Russian (L1). Moreover, a significant correlation was reported between proficiency in English (L2) and semantic priming effect size

Table 4. Descriptive statistics showing naming RTs in milliseconds and SD in related and unrelated English prime-target conditions in Experiment 3 for Russian (L1) - English (L2) bilinguals

Experimental Condition in English (L2)	Mean RTs	SD
Related	602	74
Unrelated	648	59
Magnitude of semantic priming	46	

Figure 1. Naming RTs under related and unrelated conditions for Russian (L1) - English (L2) bilinguals in Experiments 2 and 3

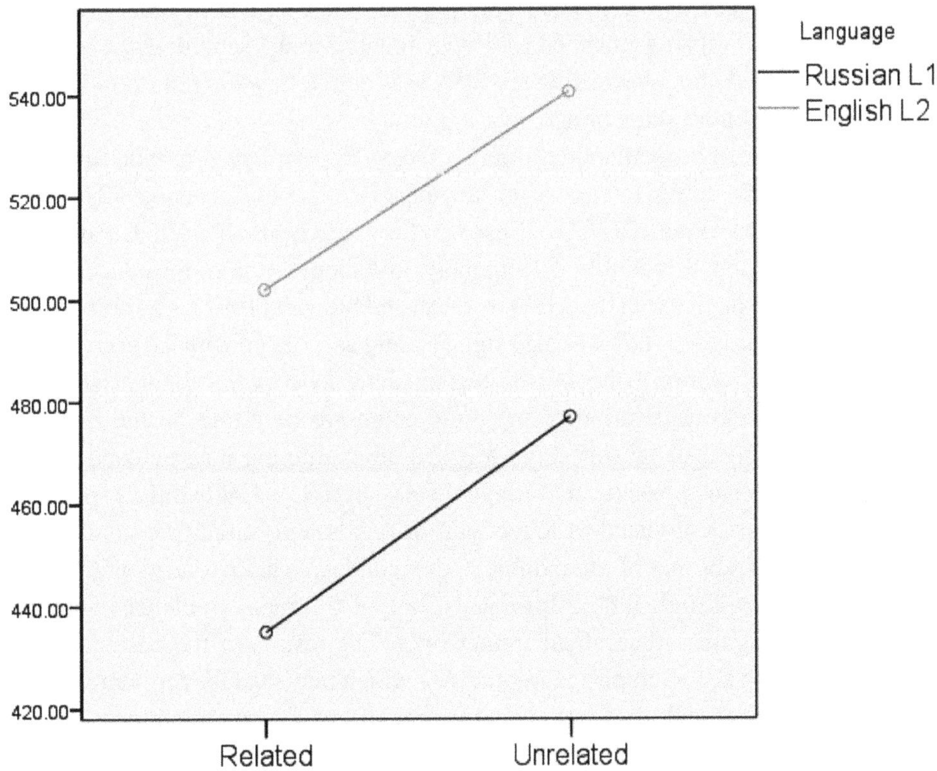

only in Russian (L1). This is taken as an indication of a) shared store for the two languages and b) the spreading activation where L1 and L2 are simultaneously and automatically activated thus benefiting the already strong links between L1 and their concepts according to the RHM (Kroll & Stewart, 1994).

In conclusion, the current set of experiments reported here provide evidence to support the claims of the bilingual RHM in that within-language effects were found for Russian (L1) - English (L2) bilingual participants in both their languages. Most importantly, the magnitude of the priming effect was found to be affected by proficiency in L2 indicating that the two languages are interconnected and affect each other's processes and activation. This is in line with current findings from other languages (for an overview see Lemhofer et al., 2008). It thus follows that if each of the bilinguals' languages were stored independent of each other none of these effects would have been reported.

The RHM (Kroll & Stewart, 1994) not only addresses the issue of organisation and storage of two representational systems, but it also takes into account the proficiency of the second language (L2). This is an important factor as discussed in detail because it has implications on both the organisation and the processing of the two languages. An important note here is that all Russian (L1) - English (L2) bilingual participants recruited for Experiments 2 and 3 scored a high level of proficiency on the Schonell Reading test (1974) although they did not start learning English (L2) until nine years of age on average.

The magnitude of the semantic priming effect in Experiment 1 for monolinguals was smaller (25ms) compared to within-language (L1-L1) in Experiment 2 (50ms) and (L2-L2) in Experiment 3 (46ms). Based on the predictions above, these findings are in strong support of position (iii); namely, one memory store for concepts for both languages as depicted in the RHM by Kroll and Stewart (1994). The significant priming effect in English (L2) was also significantly associated with L2 proficiency confirming its contribution to the activation of semantic networks in bilingual memory.

With a careful consideration of the quite extensive literature on the topic of lexico-semantic processing, this study focused on examining how evidence from monolingual Russian speakers and bilingual Russian (L1) – English (L2) speakers could inform theories of visual word recognition and lexico-semantic organisation. However, given the absence of comparable studies conducted in Russian monolinguals and Russian (L1) – English (L2) bilinguals, one of the main challenges was the lack of psycholinguistic theoretical frameworks. The results of the current study have both theoretical and empirical importance which may lead for further research endeavours and practical implications in the area of lexico-semantic processing in monolingual and bilingual normative and clinical Russian speaking population.

In conclusion, semantic priming in naming is a universal phenomenon across the range of languages including Russian. This finding is in line with the predictions of the semantic activation hypothesis and is reported in single word naming in Russian for the first time. Furthermore, the notion that two languages of bilingual speakers are activated automatically via semantic activation was confirmed by finding that the magnitude of semantic priming effect in Russian bilinguals is larger than in monolinguals. Hence, the assumption can be made that bilingualism positively contributes to lexico-semantic processing.

REFERENCES

Abu-Rabia, S. (2001). Testing the interdependence hypothesis among native adult bilingual Russian-English students. *Journal of Psycholinguistic Research*, *30*(4), 437–455. doi:10.1023/A:1010425825251 PMID:11529524

Alario, F.-X., & Ferrand, L. (1999). A set of 400 pictures standardized for French: Norms for name agreement, image agreement, familiarity, visual complexity, image variability, and age of acquisition. *Behavior Research Methods, Instruments, & Computers*, *31*(3), 531–552. doi:10.3758/BF03200732 PMID:10502875

Altarriba, J., & Basnight-Brown, D. M. (2007). Methodological considerations in performing semantic-and translation-priming experiments across languages. *Behavior Research Methods*, *39*(1), 1–18. doi:10.3758/BF03192839 PMID:17552467

Baayen, H., Piepenbrock, R., & van Rijn, H. (1993). *The CELEX database on CD-ROM*. Philadelphia: Linguistic Data Consortium.

Barhudarov, S. E., & Dosycheva, E. I. (1940). *Грамматика русского языка. Часть первая. Фонетика и морфология* [Russian grammar. Part one. Phonetics and morphology]. Moscow, Russia: State Educational and Pedagogical Publishing.

Barry, C., Morrison, C. M., & Ellis, A. W. (1997). Naming the Snodgrass and Vanderwart pictures: Effects of age of acquisition, frequency, and name agreement. *The Quarterly Journal of Experimental Psychology: Section A*, *50*(3), 560–585. doi:10.1080/783663595

Basnight-Brown, D. M., & Altarriba, J. (2007). *Methodological considerations in performing semantic-and translation-priming experiments across languages*. Academic Press.

Bialystok, E. (2001). Metalinguistic aspects of bilingual processing. *Annual Review of Applied Linguistics*, *21*, 169–181. doi:10.1017/S0267190501000101

Bialystok, E., & Hakuta, K. (1994). *In other words: The science and psychology of second-language acquisition*. New York: Basic Books.

Bril, A., & Green, R. (2013). Bilingual Stroop in English Speakers with Russian as a Second Language: Exploring the Model of the Bilingual Mind. *FIVE: The Claremont Colleges Journal of Undergraduate Academic Writing*, *2*(1), 3. doi:10.5642/five.20130201.03

Brysbaert, M., Ameel, E., & Storms, G. (2014). Bilingual Semantic Memory: A New Hypothesis. In *Foundations of Bilingual Memory* (pp. 133–146). New York: Springer. doi:10.1007/978-1-4614-9218-4_7

Chen, H. C., & Ho, C. (1986). Development of stroop interference in Chinese-English bilinguals. *Journal of Experimental Psychology. Learning, Memory, and Cognition*, *12*(3), 397–401. doi:10.1037/0278-7393.12.3.397

Collins, A. M., & Loftus, E. F. (1975). A spreading-activation theory of semantic processing. *Psychological Review*, *82*(6), 407–428. doi:10.1037/0033-295X.82.6.407

Collins, A. M., & Quillian, M. R. (1969). Retrieval time from semantic memory. *Journal of Verbal Learning and Verbal Behavior*, *8*(2), 240–247. doi:10.1016/S0022-5371(69)80069-1

Coltheart, M. (1978). Lexical access in simple reading tasks. Strategies of Information Processing, 151-216.

Crystal, D. (2008). Two thousand million? *English Today*, *24*(01), 3–6. doi:10.1017/S0266078408000023

Cubberley, P. (2002). *Russian: A linguistic introduction*. Cambridge, MA: Cambridge University Press.

de Groot, A. M., Delmaar, P., & Lupker, S. J. (2000). The processing of interlexical homographs in translation recognition and lexical decision: Support for non-selective access to bilingual memory. *The Quarterly Journal of Experimental Psychology: Section A*, *53*(2), 397–428. doi:10.1080/713755891 PMID:10881612

Dijkstra, T., Van Jaarsveld, H., & Brinke, S. T. (1998). Interlingual homograph recognition: Effects of task demands and language intermixing. *Bilingualism: Language and Cognition*, *1*(01), 51–66. doi:10.1017/S1366728998000121

Dimitropoulou, M., Duñabeitia, J. A., Blitsas, P., & Carreiras, M. (2009). A standardized set of 260 pictures for Modern Greek: Norms for name agreement, age of acquisition, and visual complexity. *Behavior Research Methods*, *41*(2), 584–589. doi:10.3758/BRM.41.2.584 PMID:19363201

Dyer, F. (1971). Color-naming interference in monolinguals and bilinguals. *Journal of Verbal Learning and Verbal Behavior*, *10*(3), 297–302. doi:10.1016/S0022-5371(71)80057-9

Egorov, T. G. (2006). *Психология овладения навыком чтения* [The psychology of reading acquisition]. St. Petersburg, Russia: KARO.

Francis, W. S. (1999). Cognitive integration of language and memory in bilinguals: Semantic representation. *Psychological Bulletin*, *125*(2), 193–222. doi:10.1037/0033-2909.125.2.193 PMID:10087936

Grigorenko, E. L. (2010). *Report on the Russian Language for the world dyslexia forum*. Yale University, Columbia University, and Moscow State University, Russia.

Grosjean, F. (1997). The bilingual individual. *Interpreting*, *2*(1-2), 163–187. doi:10.1075/intp.2.1-2.07gro

Harley, T. A. (2013). *The psychology of language: From data to theory*. New York: Psychology Press.

Huebler, F., & Lu, W. (2013). *Adult and Youth Literacy: National, Regional and Global Trends, 1985-2015*. Academic Press.

Hutchison, K. A. (2003). Is semantic priming due to association strength or feature overlap? A microanalytic review. *Psychonomic Bulletin & Review*, *10*(4), 785–813. doi:10.3758/BF03196544 PMID:15000531

Iliev, I. G. (2013). Short History of the Cyrillic Alphabet. *International Journal of Russian Studies*, *2*(2), 1–65.

Jared, D., & Kroll, J.F. (2001). Do bilinguals activate phonological representations in one or both of their languages when naming words? *Journal of Memory and Language, 44*, 2-31.

Kerek, E., & Niemi, P. (2009a). Russian orthography and learning to read. *Reading in a Foreign Language*, *21*(1), 1–21.

Kerek E., & Niemi P. (2009b). Learning to read in Russian: effects of orthographic complexity. *Journal of Research in Reading, Volume, 32*(2), 157–179. DOI: 10.1111/j.1467-9817.2008.01390.x

Kornev, A. N. (1995). *Дислексия и дисграфия у детей* [Dyslexia and dysgraphia in children]. St. Petersburg, Russia: MiM.

Kornev, A. N. (2003). *Нарушения чтения и письма у детей* [Difficulties in reading and writing in children]. St. Petersburg, Russia: Rech.

Kornev, A. N., Rakhlin, N., & Grigorenko, E. L. (2010). Dyslexia From a Cross-Linguistic and Cross-Cultural Perspective: The Case of Russian and Russia. *Learning Disabilities (Weston, Mass.)*, *8*(1), 41–69.

Kroll, J. F., & Stewart, E. (1994). Category interference in translation and picture naming: Evidence for asymmetric connections between bilingual memory representations. *Journal of Memory and Language*, *33*(2), 149–174. doi:10.1006/jmla.1994.1008

Lemhöfer, K., Dijkstra, T., Schriefers, H., Baayen, R. H., Grainger, J., & Zwitserlood, P. (2008). Native language influences on word recognition in a second language: A megastudy. *Journal of Experimental Psychology. Learning, Memory, and Cognition*, *34*(1), 12–31. doi:10.1037/0278-7393.34.1.12 PMID:18194052

Lyashevskaya, O., & Sharov, S. (2009). *The frequency dictionary of modern Russian language*. Moscow, Russia: Azbukovnik.

MacLeod, C. M. (1991). Half a century of research on the Stroop effect: An integrative review. *Psychological Bulletin, 109*(2), 163–203. doi:10.1037/0033-2909.109.2.163 PMID:2034749

Marian, V., Blumenfeld, H. K., Mizrahi, E., Kania, U., & Cordes, A.-K. (2013). Multilingual Stroop performance: Effects of trilingualism and proficiency on inhibitory control. *International Journal of Multilingualism, 10*(1), 82–104. doi:10.1080/14790718.2012.708037 PMID:24039546

McNamara, T. P., & Holbrook, J. B. (2003). *Semantic memory and priming*. Handbook of psychology. doi:10.1002/0471264385.wei0416

Meyer, D. E., & Schvaneveldt, R. W. (1971). Facilitation in recognizing pairs of words: Evidence of a dependence between retrieval operations. *Journal of Experimental Psychology, 90*(2), 227–234. doi:10.1037/h0031564 PMID:5134329

Morton, J. (1969). Interaction of information in word recognition. *Psychological Review, 76*(2), 165–178. doi:10.1037/h0027366

Neely, J. H. (1977). Semantic priming and retrieval from lexical memory: Roles of inhibitionless spreading activation and limited-capacity attention. *Journal of Experimental Psychology. General, 106*(3), 226–254. doi:10.1037/0096-3445.106.3.226

Neely, J. H. (1991). Semantic priming effects in visual word recognition: A selective review of current findings and theories. *Basic Processes in Reading: Visual Word Recognition, 11*, 264-336.

Neely, J. H., & Kahan, T. A. (2001). Is semantic activation automatic? A critical re-evaluation. In H. L. Roediger III, J. S. Nairne, I. Neath, & A. M. Surprenant (Eds.), *Science conference series. The nature of remembering: Essays in honor of Robert G. Crowder* (pp. 69–93). Academic Press. doi:10.1037/10394-005

Niolaki, G. Z., Masterson, J., & Terzopoulos, A. R. (2014). Spelling improvement through letter-sound and whole-word training in two multilingual Greek-and English-speaking children. *Multilingual Education, 4*(1), 1–23. doi:10.1186/s13616-014-0020-3

Nishimoto, T., Miyawaki, K., Ueda, T., Une, Y., & Takahashi, M. (2005). Japanese normative set of 359 pictures. *Behavior Research Methods, 37*(3), 398–416. doi:10.3758/BF03192709 PMID:16405135

Nisi, M., Longoni, A. M., & Snodgrass, J. G. (2000). Italian measurement on the relation of name, familiarity, and acquisition age for the 260 figures of Snodgrass and Vanderwart. *Giornale Italiano di Psicologia, 27*, 205–218.

Paivio, A., Clark, J. M., & Lambert, W. E. (1988). Bilingual dual-coding theory and semantic repetition effects on recall. *Journal of Experimental Psychology. Learning, Memory, and Cognition, 14*(1), 163–172. doi:10.1037/0278-7393.14.1.163

Pind, J., Jónsdóttir, H., Tryggvadóttir, H. B., & Jónsson, F. (2000). Icelandic norms for the Snodgrass and Vanderwart (1980) pictures: Name and image agreement, familiarity, and age of acquisition. *Scandinavian Journal of Psychology, 41*(1), 41–48. doi:10.1111/1467-9450.00169 PMID:10731842

Potter, M. C., So, K. F., Von Eckardt, B., & Feldman, L. B. (1984). Lexical and conceptual representation in beginning and proficient bilinguals. *Journal of Verbal Learning and Verbal Behavior, 23*(1), 23–38. doi:10.1016/S0022-5371(84)90489-4

Potter, M. C., So, K. F., Von Eckardt, B., & Feldman, L. B. (1984). Lexical and conceptual representation in beginning and proficient bilinguals. *Journal of Verbal Learning and Verbal Behavior, 23*(1), 23–38. doi:10.1016/S0022-5371(84)90489-4

Preston, M. S., & Lambert, W. E. (1969). Interlingual interference in a bilingual version of the Stroop color-word task. *Journal of Verbal Learning and Verbal Behavior, 8*(2), 295–301. doi:10.1016/S0022-5371(69)80079-4

Raman, I., Raman, E., Ikier, S., Kilecioglu, E., Uzun, D., & Zeyveli, S. (under review). Differential Effects of Age of Acquisition and Frequency on Memory. *Evidence from Free Recall of Pictures and Words in Turkish.*

Raman, I., Raman, E., & Mertan, B. (2014). A standardised set of 260 pictures for Turkish: Norms of name and image agreement, age of acquisition, visual complexity and conceptual familiarity. *Behavior Research Methods, 46*(2), 588–595. doi:10.3758/s13428-013-0376-4 PMID:23943583

Roberts, S. G. (2013). *Evolutionary approach to bilingualism* (PhD thesis). University of Edinburgh, United Kingdom.

Roelofs, A. (2009). Attention and Facilitation: Converging Information Versus Inadvertent Reading in Stroop Task Performance. *Journal of Experimental Psychology. Learning, Memory, and Cognition, 36*(2), 411–422. doi:10.1037/a0018523 PMID:20192539

Rosselli, M., Ardila, A., Santisi, M. N., Arecco, M. D. R., Salvatierra, J., Conde, A., & Lenis, B. O. N. I. E. (2002). Stroop effect in Spanish–English bilinguals. *Journal of the International Neuropsychological Society*, *8*(06), 819–827. doi:10.1017/S1355617702860106 PMID:12240746

Rossion, B., & Pourtois, G. (2004). Revisiting Snodgrass and Vanderwart's object pictorial set: The role of surface detail in basic-level object recognition. *Perception*, *33*(2), 217–236. doi:10.1068/p5117 PMID:15109163

Sanfeliù, M. C., & Fernandez, A. (1996). A set of 254 Snodgrass–Vanderwart pictures standardized for Spanish: Norms for name agreement, image agreement, familiarity, and visual complexity. *Behavior Research Methods, Instruments, & Computers*, *28*(4), 537–555. doi:10.3758/BF03200541

Scarborough, D. L., Gerard, L., & Cortese, C. (1984). Independence of lexical access in bilingual word recognition. *Journal of Verbal Learning and Verbal Behavior*, *23*(1), 84–99. doi:10.1016/S0022-5371(84)90519-X

Schonell, F. J. (1971). *Reading and Spelling Tests*. Edinburgh, UK: Oliver and Boyd.

Schoonbaert, S., Duyck, W., Brysbaert, M., & Hartsuiker, R. J. (2009). Semantic and translation priming from a first language to a second and back: Making sense of the findings. *Memory & Cognition*, *37*(5), 569–586. doi:10.3758/MC.37.5.569 PMID:19487749

Seidenberg, M. S., & McClelland, J. L. (1989). A distributed, developmental model of word recognition and naming. *Psychological Review*, *96*(4), 523–568. doi:10.1037/0033-295X.96.4.523 PMID:2798649

Shi, X. (2007). Intercultural Language Socialization: Theory and Methodology. *Intercultural Communication Studies*, *16*(1), 230.

Sholl, A., Sankaranarayanan, A., & Kroll, J. F. (1995). Transfer between picture naming and translation: A test of asymmetries in bilingual memory. *Psychological Science*, *6*(1), 45–49. doi:10.1111/j.1467-9280.1995.tb00303.x

Snodgrass, J. G., & Vanderwart, M. (1980). A standardized set of 260 pictures: Norms for name agreement, image agreement, familiarity, and visual complexity. *Journal of Experimental Psychology. Human Learning and Memory*, *6*(2), 174–215. doi:10.1037/0278-7393.6.2.174 PMID:7373248

Stroop, J. R. (1935). Studies in interference in serial verbal reactions. *Journal of Experimental Psychology*, *18*(6), 643–661. doi:10.1037/h0054651

Sumiya, H., & Healy, A. F. (2004). Phonology in the bilingual Stroop effect. *Memory & Cognition*, *32*(5), 752–758. doi:10.3758/BF03195865 PMID:15552352

Tabossi, P., & Laghi, L. (1992). Semantic priming in the pronunciation of words in two writing systems: Italian and English. *Memory & Cognition*, *20*(3), 303–313. doi:10.3758/BF03199667 PMID:1508055

Therriault, D. J., Yaxley, R. H., & Zwaan, R. A. (2009). The role of color diagnosticity in object recognition and representation. *Cognitive Processing*, *10*(4), 335–342. doi:10.1007/s10339-009-0260-4 PMID:19471986

Tsaparina, D., Bonin, P., & Méot, A. (2011). Russian norms for name agreement, image agreement for the colorized version of the Snodgrass and Vanderwart pictures and age of acquisition, conceptual familiarity, and imageability scores for modal object names. *Behavior Research Methods*, *43*(4), 1085–1099. doi:10.3758/s13428-011-0121-9 PMID:21717267

Tzelgov, J., Henik, A., & Leiser, D. (1990). Controlling Stroop interference: Evidence from a bilingual task. *Journal of Experimental Psychology*, *16*, 760–771.

Voga, M., & Grainger, J. (2007). Cognate status and cross-script translation priming. *Memory & Cognition*, *35*(5), 938–952. doi:10.3758/BF03193467 PMID:17910178

Volkovyskaya, E., Raman, I., & Baluch, B. (under review). Age of Acquisition (AoA) effect in monolingual Russian speakers and bilingual Russian (L1) - English (L2) speakers in a free recall task. *Writing Systems Research Journal*.

Weber, G. (1997). Top Language. *Language Monthly*, (3).

Weekes, B. S., Shu, H., Hao, M., Liu, Y., & Tan, L. H. (2007). Predictors of timed picture naming in Chinese. *Behavior Research Methods*, *39*(2), 335–342. doi:10.3758/BF03193165 PMID:17695362

Woods, C. (2006). Bilingualism, Scribal Learning, and the Death of Sumerian. In S. L. Sanders (Ed.), Margins of Writing, Origins of Culture (pp. 91–120). Chicago: Academic Press.

Chapter 6
The Impact of Grammatical Aspects on Cognition Level in Foreign Language Learning Process

Nur Cebeci
Trakya University, Turkey

ABSTRACT

Linguistics as the study of the nature of languages has a visible impact on various fields such as education, language teaching, philosophy, computer science, and anthropology. However, the nature of language is a broad idea, which makes it hard to give a clear, simple definition. One of the most fundamental assumptions is the rule-governed feature of the human language interrelated with pronunciation, word formation, and grammatical construction. The aim of this chapter is to discuss how the rules of the language have an impact on foreign language learning process and how it affects foreign language learners' storing and processing the language in the brain. In doing so, some predetermined samples of lexical items and formal structures of language are analyzed in terms of the foreign language learners' cognition as prospective teachers of English in the teacher training process.

INTRODUCTION

The main concern of linguistics is to understand how language itself is structured and how it functions. The more the human language is understood, the more the process of human thought is recognized. In this view, the study of language is

DOI: 10.4018/978-1-5225-4009-0.ch006

eventually the study of the human mind. Chomsky (1975) expressed that language is the reflection of thought like a mirror of mind in deep and important sense. Yet, it is a broad term focusing on how languages are structured and used. Therefore, it is better to break down the broad definition into categories such as morphology, phonology, syntax and semantics which are all interrelated. It has a constant relation to language variation, change, psychology of language, and the brain as well. In this sense, various assumptions have been proclaimed to take the attention to the different aspects of the language. Of the assumptions, the most striking one is that human language at all levels is rule-governed together with pronunciation, word formation, and grammatical construction (Akmajian, et al 2001).

Each language has its own systematic rules in order to govern its components in lexical and syntactic levels. The message through these regular linguistic rules is conveyed to the receiver in order to create both communication and interaction. However, some important generalizations regulate the use of language to communicate as well. At this point, two different types of rules such as prescriptive and descriptive ones need to be clarified in order to have a better understanding of the generalizations obeyed. Prescriptive rules in general, prescriptive grammar in particular, are taught to the speaker of the language in order to produce the language correctly, whereas descriptive rules along with descriptive grammar express generalizations and regularities about various aspects of the language. While prescriptive grammar tries to focus on how languages should be used correctly, descriptive grammar is only interested in what languages are and how they are used by their speakers (Çelik, 2007). Namely, prescriptive grammar overlooks changes and popular usages that occur as time passes, whereas descriptive grammar deals with the recent usage. In this regard, when linguists analyze language, they do not refer to prescriptive rules from grammar books; instead, they try to formulate descriptive rules that describe the actual language of some group of speakers (Akmajian, et al 2001). Garret (1986) claims that explicit grammar knowledge cannot be used by students in their efforts at natural communication. He states that students are often unable to use a given grammar point correctly even after frequent explanations, illustrations, repeated drills, and apparent success on the tests. Therefore, the purpose of this chapter is to discuss how the rules of a language have an impact on foreign language learning process and how they affect foreign language learners' storing and processing language in the brain. In the chapter, some predetermined samples of lexical items and formal structures of language are analyzed in order to describe the foreign language learners' written or oral output in teacher training context.

BACKGROUND

The human brain has a complicated role in language learning process while acquiring and storing the mental lexicon and grammar and retrieving that linguistic storehouse to speak and understand in real life situation. Understanding the notions how knowledge is stored and how linguistic competence is shaped which are complex procedural processes has been the core of linguistic discussions. Fromkin (2003) claims that memorizing a stored string with its meaning is not possible because of the language creativity. In this aspect, it is proclaimed that language learners do not learn language by memorizing and storing sentences, but by composing grammatical sentences. Thus, in comprehending and producing the language, first of all, the learner accesses lexicon to find the words, and then uses the rules of grammar to make original sentences and to produce the sounds that express the message tried to be delivered. The learner, as the speaker and receiver, relates linguistic units to each other during comprehension and production stages.

It is stressed that there are several mechanisms that enable speaker to comprehend and produce meaningful sounds and speech, pull words from the mental lexicon, and construct phrase structure exemplification of the retrieve words (Fromkin, 2003). Comprehending or producing sentences in one's own native language may not usually be difficult since it is a natural process of unconscious awareness. In other words, even in the native language, language users may have experience making errors or mostly slip of tongue, or misunderstanding of an accurate sentence or interpreting ungrammatical sentences. Although such complexities seem to happen in second language learning process, they may occur in both second language and native language since languages share a similar level of complexities. In addition to the complexities of each language, all languages share some similarities and dissimilarities as well. Chomsky (1995) expresses the common similarities and dissimilarities of languages as principles and parameters of languages; all languages have sentences made up of smaller phrasal units, words, and sounds. All of these units of human languages indicate that languages share similar structural units. Beneath the surface variation, languages are similar in form and function and conform to certain universal principles (Akmajian et al, 2001). All languages also share some common features for asking questions, making requests, getting permission, and etc. Certain similar expressions in different languages can be found as well. Therefore, one can experience problems while learning a second language because of being influenced by native language and may transfer some units from first language to the second language. Parker and Riley (2005) discuss that the learner creates a rule-governed interlanguage between the first language and second language. Interlanguage arises from several different sources besides language transfer. These sources are seen on the forms from the native language imposed on the second language.

The Impact of Native Language on Second Language

Crystal (1997) defines interlanguage as the reflection of the learner's evolving system of rules and states that it results from a variety of processes, including the influence of the first language ('transfer'), contrastive interference from the target language, and the overgeneralization of newly encountered rules. Children sometimes produce certain types of ungrammatical forms when they are acquiring their first language. Thus, it is natural for a second language learner to produce similar forms at certain stages. Yule (2014) gives the example of *womens* as a type of overgeneralization (of - s as the plural marker) made by the learners based on the common way of making plural forms in English. Besides, language learners make negative transfer which is also known as interference in which some property of the first language hinders acquisition of the second language. They may also exhibit positive transfer which is also known as facilitation in which some property of the first language supports the acquisition of the second language (Parker&Riley, 2005). Likewise, Odlin (1989) defines the term transfer as the influence resulting from the similarities and differences between the target language and any other language that has been previously acquired. Brown (2007) classifies sources of error into interlingual transfer, that is the negative influence of the mother tongue of learner, intralingual transfer, that is the negative transfer of items within the target language; context of learning, which overlaps both types of transfer; and communication strategies, that is the conscious employment of verbal mechanisms for communicating an idea when linguistic forms are not available to the learner for some reasons. For intralingual transfer, the use of "the" article by Turkish learners is a common example. Since Turkish does not have any article rule, the Turkish learners of English overgeneralize the use of article "the" and produce ungrammatical sentences.

Nemati and Taghizadeh (2013) and similarly Houmanfar, Hayes, and Herbst (2005) insist that first language has significant role in second language learning process and an important component for learning L2 properties. Macaro (2001) claims that second language learners are affected by the language through which they think. Lee and Macaro (2013) evaluates such effects of L1 on L2 learning process as an advantage for learners, since they become sentimentally ready for production.

Wang (2015) mentions five categories of errors caused by negative transfer. They are underused attributive clauses including avoidance strategy, redundant pronoun or antecedent, omission preposition, underused, misplaced or redundant relative words. Tarone (2006) suggests that there is a crucial and central psycholinguistic difference between child NL acquisition and adult second language (L2) acquisition: children always succeed in completely acquiring their native language, but adults only very rarely succeed in completely acquiring a second language.

Harmer (2001: 38-40) also emphasized the age factor in designing the way of teaching in classroom. He describes leaners as young learners, adolescent and adult learners.

As displayed in Table 1, learners at different age levels share different characteristics. Each student is considered as an individual having different learning styles and life experiences in learning process. This frame of learners' characteristics regarding their age enables teachers to decide on how to design their route to teach to each group. An individual teacher, thus, may draw on different principles at different times depending on the type of the learners to whom s/he is teaching (Richard & Rodgers, 2001).

MAIN FOCUS OF THE CHAPTER

In this chapter, the data sets of prepositions produced by Turkish adult learners of English are examined and the possible causes are discussed. To highlight the possible causes of the erroneous productions of the adult learners, answers are sought to the following research questions:

1. What types of errors do 3rd year students of English Language Teaching (ELT) department make in their written and oral classroom production?
2. Why do 3rd year students ELT department make such linguistic errors?

The participants of the study were 90 3rd year students at the ELT department at a Turkish university. The data were gathered by the researcher via written and

Table 1. Learner groups as young learners, adolescents and teenagers and adult

Young Children	Adolescent and Teenagers	Adults
Ages up to ten or eleven, Respond to meaning even if they do not understand individual work, Often learn indirectly, Understanding comes not just from explanation but also from what they experience, Display an enthusiasm for learning and curiosity about the world, and in need for individual attention from the teacher, Keen to talk about themselves as well as responding to others, Have a limited attention span.	in search for individual identity, peer approval may considerable, be more important than the attention of the teacher, they may provoke from being disruptive, can cause discipline problems, may push teachers to limit, but they are much happier if that challenge is met, if they are engaged, they have a great capacity to learn, a great potential for creativity, must be encouraged to respond to texts and situations with their own thoughts and experiences	engage with abstract thought, have a whole range of life experiences to draw on, have expectations about the learning process, tend to be more disciplined than some teenagers, are often prepared to struggle on despite boredom. come into classroom with a rich range of experiences have a clear understanding of their own learning

oral classroom products of the 3rd year students in the courses "Teaching English to Young Learners I" and "Teaching English to Young Learners II". The researcher was the lecturer of these courses as well. The study covered two academic terms. Since the students were teacher trainees, they had to prepare lesson plans within the course content. First term, their lesson plans and classroom instructions were analyzed in order to outline the corpus of the study.

Findings

The most common sets of errors determined were the misusage of the prepositions of "to" with the verb 'listen' and 'want'. Besides, the researcher found that they misused subject and verb agreement, particularly 3rd singular person –s ending. During the course, in order to create awareness, the lecturer gave some feedback about both teaching experience and linguistic errors. Some of them used the preposition correctly in the lesson plan, yet they did not use it in their speech while giving classroom instructions. Some of them did not write on their lesson plans correctly and as a consequence they did not produce correctly during their micro teaching. More interestingly, some of them did not write the correct procedure of preposition in the lesson plan; however, they used it correctly in their micro-teaching presentations. The raw data of some of the participants' products are listed in Table 2.

Table 2 indicates that some teacher trainees sometimes wrote the correct usage of preposition of "to" with the verb 'listen' and 'want' in their lesson plan and

Table 2. Erroneous preposition data sets

Subjects	Erroneous Items	Written Products	Oral Products
1	listen (to)	OK kids, liste*n t*he song carefully	OK kids, liste*n t*he song.
2	listen (to)	Yes, children. Liste*n* again and fill in the blanks.	Yes, children. Liste*n* again and fill in the blanks.
3	listen (to)	Are you ready for listening activity? Liste*n to* the song and do the actions.	Are you ready for listening? Liste*n t*he song and do the actions.
4	listen (to)	Class! Be quiet. Liste*n a*nd watch the video.	Class! Be quiet. Liste*n a*nd watch the video.
5	listen (to)	Look! I'm going to tell you a story about a lion. Liste*n to* me and try to understand	Look! I'm going to tell you a story about a lion. Liste*n me* and do the actions.
6	listen (to)	Yes, kids. Liste*n me* and repeat the words.	Yes, kids. Liste*n to* me and repeat the words
7	listen (to)	Ok everybody, are you ready for the song. Now, liste*n to*…	Ok everybody, are you ready for the song. Now, liste*n to* …
8	want (to)	Yes, I *want you to* find the correct picture on the board.	Yes, I *want that you should find* the correct picture on the board.
9	want (to)	Do you *want me to play* the CD player again?	Do *you want I play* the CD player again?
10	want (to)	I'*d like you to give* the card when you find it on the ground.	I *want to you to give* me card when you find it on the ground.

produced correctly while giving instructions to the students during micro-teaching presentations. For instance, S2 used the sentence "Listen_again and fill in the blanks." in which the verb 'listen' does not require the use of the preposition "to". On the other hand, S1, S4, S7 did not use preposition "to" appropriately, and as a result, they did not produce the phrase correctly while giving instructions since they were influenced by the written sentences in the lesson plan. More interestingly, S7 used the preposition "to" when there was no necessity to use it since it was a bare imperative command. This may be due to overgeneralization or may be the result of the over feedback by the lecturer that might have caused an addition instead of omission. S6 also did not write the use of preposition correctly, yet he produced correctly while giving the instructions to the students. The reason could be the teacher trainee's lack of attention to the word processing and not checking the grammar points before sending the lesson plan to the lecturer of the course. This simply indicates that the written misusage cannot be regarded as errors without checking the reasons or the factors of occurrence. S3, S5, S8, S9 and S10 wrote the correct use of the preposition "to" in the written products; however, they were not correct in oral production. The reasons may vary: anxiety factors, first language inference, and not knowing the correct form.

Table 3 displays that S1, S2, S3, S7, S8 misused subject and verb agreement in written products, particularly 3rd singular person –s ending; however, in oral products they did not misuse since the sentences were mostly composed of the imperative forms which necessitate bare form. When written product of the S4 was analyzed, it was found that she did not use –s ending with the verb "ask" although the subject is teacher who can be addressed as he or she in terms of gender. S5 used correct

Table 3. Erroneous 3rd singular person –s ending data sets

Erroneous Items	Subjects	Written Products	Oral Products
3rd singular person "s"	1	Teacher tell the story	"I tell the story."
	2	Teacher play the CD player and ask students listen to the song	"Now, I play the CD player and listen to the song."
	3	Students plays the BINGO game	"Play the BINGO game"
	4	Teacher ask the students how the weather is.	"How is the weather?"
	5	Teacher repeats the words.	"'An apple' repeat after me please. An apple!"
	6	Students come together and do pair work activity	"Come together and do pair work activity"
	7	One of the students come to the board and mime the actions.	"One of you will come to the board and mime the actions."
	8	Only one child stand up when he hears the words in his hand.	"You will stand up when you hear the word you hear."

subject and verb agreement on 3rd singular – s ending. S6 used correct subject and verb agreement as well, hence the agreement was on plural subject. The reason for this correct use could be the reason of positive transfer since in Turkish syntactic rule there is no use of 3rd singular –s ending or similar changes for specifically for 3rd singular person. "He come*s*" means "O gelir" whereas "They come" means "Onlar gelir(ler)" in Turkish. As seen in the sample sentences, without using –ler which makes the predicative plural because of onlar- they, the sentence is accepted as a correct sentence grammatically as well. Therefore, it is more likely for Turkish students to produce present time expressions in plural person more accurately than in 3rd singular person.

By the end of the first semester, the researcher examined the lesson plans and after creating the corpus of the study, she asked the students why they did such errors in their lesson plans and classroom practices. In order to collect data, she used an open-ended questionnaire. The causes of their errors and the possible factors that have impacts on the participants' erroneous products are evaluated and classified in five categories which are the impact of L1, prior knowledge, previous teachers, input channels, and affective factors. The list of the participants' raw statements is presented below:

1. The impact of L1 - Interlingual errors:
   "There is no equivalent for "to" in Turkish."
   "We do not have such preposition in Turkish."
   "I think we think in L1 and we speak in L2"
   "It has been a slip of tongue which we can call a mistake rather than an error"
   "It's common linguistic mistake."
2. Lack of good knowledge of grammar in English -Intralingual errors:
   "I think we know the rule but we forget to use it while speaking"
   "I think my teachers taught me the rules not the use of it"
   "I studied multiple choice questions a lot before coming to the university. I did not know how to compose my own sentences"
   "I was shocked when you warned me. I did not know that I was saying listen the song.
   "We learned the prepositions in rule not in context"
   "Since the phrasal verb 'lis*t*en *t*o *t*he song' has three –t letter which sounds consonant and it is hard to pronounce.."
   "We have a limited amount of chance to speak. We just speak from micro-teaching to microteaching. The more chance should we given…"
   "I prepared lesson plan before the presentation. I used listen without "to" and during the presentation I looked at the plan and misused. When the teacher warned me I realized my mistake and I was surprised."

"Giving simple instruction is hard for us."

3. Previous teachers and prior knowledge:
   "My English teacher in high school used "listen me" so received the input from him and I think I acquired it. Now, it is difficult for me change. But I try"
   "I received the input from my previous teacher. She used 'listen' without 'to'"
   "I was not given any feedback till now"
   "No one warned me"
   "Students imitate their teachers. My teachers did not use either"
   "My teacher corrected me when I was going to high school."
   "our teacher perhaps did same mistake and we heard it from them. It is fossilized."
4. Input channels:
   "I received the input from my previous teacher. She used 'listen' without 'to'"
   "We got used to use what we've heard. I'm loving in ads. We're exposed to this language and start to use"
   "I watch Tv series aand pick up the daily language use."
   "Songs break the rules of the language and I listen to any kind of music. I hear it from the songs."
   "I got used to using daily nongrammatical English."
5. Affective factors:
   "I feel anxious while speaking"
   "I do not feel comfortable in front of the class being observed by my teacher and criticized. This feeling forces me to do more mistakes."
   "I lose my self monitoring in front of an audience."
   "we use unconsciously, I think we do not pay attention"
   "During the presentation, I want to be quick and finish the micro-teaching presentation. So, 'listen song' is easier."
   "I feel nervous in presentations so I make mistakes"
   "phrasal verbs are always difficult"
   "I'm serious about it and I use -listen to"
   "I was afraid of making a mistake"
   "We are excited when we are on the board. It may be a situational mistake although we know the true from"
   "I did not care about prepositions"
   "I feel overconfident and do not care about minor mistakes."

SOLUTIONS AND RECOMMENDATIONS

The data sets which are displayed in the tables display that the Turkish learners of English misuse preposition "to" and 3rd singular person "s" mostly because of the negative transfer from their first language, Turkish, since Turkish does not have such rules. The reasons why students at that level do such errors can be grouped as:

The Impact of L1 (Interlingual)

There is a mismatch problem between English and other languages regarding some language (Celce-Murcia, 1991). One of such mismatch between Turkish and English appears while using "listen to". In this sample statement "They can *listen* _ a song or watch a video", the participants omit the preposition "to". The cause of the omission in this statement is most probably arise from Turkish language. In Turkish, such statement is used as "*Şarkı dinleyebilirler* ya da *video* izleyebilirler" without any preposition. Likewise, omitting third person singular "s" can also be evaluated as the impact of L1 on L2, or negative transfer, or interlingual error. In Turkish, there is no distinction for using "s" with third person singular in present form. Although Yule (2014) claims that negative transfer is more common in the early stages of second language learning and often decreases as the learner develops greater familiarity with the second language, the findings of this study shows that most of the ELT students are still under the effect of negative transfer.

Lack of Good Knowledge of Grammar in English (Intralingual)

Another reason may be due to lack of grammar knowledge in English. Thus, intralingual error may appear due to the forms of other verbs which does no necessitate preposition. For instance, read, write, come, go, take, drink, etc. In such instances, learners may overgeneralize the linguistic rules of English which leads to intralingual errors. However, omission of third person singular "s" cannot be evaluated as an intralingual error.

The Role of Previous Teachers and Prior Knowledge

In some language classroom settings, teachers may prefer using L1 alongside English while teaching (Butler, 2012; Meadows & Muramatsu, 2007; Park & Abelmann, 2004). In the questionnaire, the participants reflected that their previous teachers also misused the verb "listen to" by omitting "to". Such experiences from their previous teachers may have a strong influence on their erroneous products. Green (2016) in his study declares that teaching methods might also have an influence on students' products; whether the L2 is supplied to students by their teachers as something that should be consciously memorized, like historical dates, or something that is learnt through repetition may affect their learning behavior positively or negatively. In addition, the previous experience of acquiring L1, the comprehension of structures and linguistic devices, and even the accumulation of knowledge about how these are deployed in social settings can become genuine barriers to successful L2 learning (Castello, 2015)

Input Channels

Input channel in the classroom environment is the other important factor for acquiring or learning languages. How teachers give the input, how they pay attention to form and structure of utterances, and how they give feedback to students are also among the input channels. The participants in this study declared that they received the input from various sources such as TV series, songs, advertisements, etc. For instance, one of the participants declared that he heard "*I'm loving*" in one of the ads, so he used this chunk habitually because of being exposed to this chunk in this way.

Affective Factors

Understanding how human beings feel and respond, believe, and value is an exceedingly important aspect of a theory of language learning and acquisition (Brown, 2007). The degree of self-esteem, inhibition, risk taking, anxiety, and motivation are among the affective factors on students' learning behavior. For instance, the participants mostly declare that they make errors when they feel anxious and not comfortable. Some feel that being criticized by the teacher and classmates makes them nervous. On the other hand, they declare that they feel themselves overconfident about the linguistic rules; that's why they are not aware of their errors. In other words, adults' learning may be problematic in some cases, particularly when they experience failure or criticism at school which makes them anxious and under-confident about learning a language (Harmer, 2001).

The results which are classified in five categories in this chapter display that there are various influential factors on students' cognition while learning and producing the target language. Although errors are not tolerable in language learning process, Yule (2014) states that one essential feature of the most communicative approaches is the acceptance of "errors" produced by students, since this toleration of learners' errors is a kind of shift from traditional view and encourages students to produce language without being corrected by their teachers. But in language teacher training process, it is expected that a language teacher should have a good command of the target language. For training qualified language teachers, some renovations and corrections need to be implemented.

Cook (2013) suggests that teachers should avoid explicit discussion of grammar, and grammar rules could be demonstrated within in the context. There is no guarantee that conscious understanding will help the learner use it correctly. On the other hand,

Table 4. Table of error types, the number of the participants and sample sets

Type of usage	Type of error: Sample	Written Product Number of participants (out of 120)	Oral Product Number of Participants (out of 120)
Correct usage of the verb 'listen to'	No error: Liste*n to* the song and do the actions.	76	87
Usage of the verb 'listen' without 'to'	Omission: OK kids, listen the song carefully	42	31
Usage of the verb 'listen' with the preposition 'to' when not necessary	Addition: Now, liste*n to.*	2	2

some explicit instruction and declarative-learning can be beneficial in the early stages of learning an L2 (Morgan-Short et al. 2014), and implicit-learning of L2 alone may not effective (Andringa & Rebuschat 2015, Boers et al. 2014, Kirschner et al. 2006).

When the participants were questioned about the reasons of their errors, they offered some recommendations: One of the students suggested that for a better linguistic competence, students should be given more auditory input during the teaching procedure. In Krashen's Input Hypothesis, it is stressed that speaking is a result of acquisition and the cause. Speech cannot be taught directly but emerges on its own as a result of building competence via comprehension input (Selinker, 2008). Another student recommended that such verbs need to be taught as chunks but not separately. This recommendation of the student is noteworthy for teaching chunks within a context, since chunks that are repeated across learning experiences also become better remembered (Doughty & Long, 2005).

While the participants were making recommendations about their own failures in using appropriate prepositions, it was noticed that they consciously used suitable terms to reflect their situations. This may be due to the fact that in teacher training process they were trained on teaching methodology issues in various courses such as Second Language Acquisition, English Language Teaching Methodology Courses. This indicates that they had good command of teaching principles as prospective teachers for future occupation, and the courses raised their awareness on how to teach.

FUTURE RESEARCH DIRECTIONS

By taking all data sets into account, it is noticed that, as Parker and Riley (2005) discuss, the learner creates a rule-governed interlanguage between the first language and second language. In addition, the previous learning experience of the learner is also influential on learning process. For instance, the participants declared that they studied multiple choice questions before coming to the university; that's why they did not know how to compose their own sentences. Besides, they insisted that their previous teachers did not take their attention to the erroneous items completely; thus, such items became fossilized. The causes of such errors may increase in number and vary in different educational settings. To notice the erroneous items, to record them, to give feedback to students for self-correction, to treat the mismatches should be among the chief concerns of teachers in order to avoid fossilization. Additionally, if learners are adult and also prospective teachers of English like the participants of this study, as Fromkin, Rodman, and Hymas (2003) suggested, metalinguistic awareness which refers to a speaker's conscious awareness about language and the use of language should be increased to use contextually appropriate language. Future research may also focus on larger group studies by investigating gender differences. In this study, the focus is merely on describing the existing problem and determining the possible reasons; there is a need for further studies to reach more detailed outcomes.

CONCLUSION

Classroom learning is more syntactic in nature than L1 acquisition, and requires a more conscious and sustained effort (Castello, 2015). In classroom learning, learners are exposed to various mechanisms for comprehending, internalizing, and producing knowledge in L2. The learners may be exposed to L2 input, but L1 transfer or interference may be found out more effective on L2 performance. The conclusions drawn so far indicate that the main causes and possible factors of the erroneous L2 preposition usage also result from previous teachers, prior knowledge, input channels, and affective factors. It can be admitted that human brains that are coded to learn are all admirable at learning languages. Therefore, teachers may make the human brains excellent through appropriate teaching methods and suitable input channels. Thus, learners can clearly realize that they do not know how to use linguistic items appropriately in the target language (Gass & Selinker, 2008). This study is of great importance to teachers and teacher trainers for making the subject matter noteworthy, since prospective teachers who are also language learners as the rings of education chain will shape the future of the next generation in language learning.

REFERENCES

Akmajian, A., Demers, R., Farmer, A., & Harnish, R. (2001). *An Introduction to Language and Communication.* Library of Congress Cataloging-in-Publication Data.

Brown, H. D. (2007). *Principles of Language Learning and Teaching.* Prentice Hall Regents.

Butler, Y. G. (2012). What Level of English Proficiency Do Elementary School Teachers Need to Attain to Teach EFL? Case Studies from Korea, Taiwan, and Japan. *TESOL Quarterly*, *38*(2), 245–278. doi:10.2307/3588380

Castello, D. (2015). *First Language Acquisition and Classroom Language Learning: Similarities and Differences* (Master's thesis). University of Birmingham.

Celce-Murcia, M. (1991). *Teaching English as a Second or Foreign Language.* Boston: Heinle & Heinle Publishers.

Çelik, M. (2007). *Linguistics for Students of English Book I.* EDM Publishing.

Chomsky, N. (1975). *Reflections on Language.* New York: Pantheon Books.

Cook, V. (2013). *Second Language Learning and Language Teaching.* New York: Routledge.

Crystal, D. (1997). *The Cambridge Encyclopedia of Language.* Cambridge, UK: Cambridge University Press.

Doughty, C. J., & Long, M. H. (2005). *The Handbook of Second Language Acquisition.2003.* Blackwell Publishing. doi:10.1111/b.9781405132817.2005.x

Fromkin, V., Rodman, R., & Hyamas, N. (2003). *An Introduction to Language.* Heinle.

Garret, N. (1986). The problem with grammar: what kind can the language learner use? *Modern Language Journal, 70*, 133–149.

Green, K. (2016). The Human Brain Does Not Need High Levels of Motivation to Learn a Foreign Language: Motivation Has Had its Day. *Advances in Language and Literary Studies*¸ *7*(5).

Harmer, J. (2001). *The Practice of English Language Teaching.* Longman.

Houmanfar, R., Hayes, L. J., & Herbst, S. A. (2005). An Analog study of first language dominance and interference over second language. *Analysis of Verbal Behavior*, *21*(1), 75–98. doi:10.1007/BF03393011 PMID:22477315

Lee, J. H., & Macaro, E. (2013). Investigating Age in the Use of L1 or English-Only Instruction: Vocabulary Acquisition by Korean EFL Learners. *Modern Language Journal*, *97*(4), 887–901. doi:10.1111/j.1540-4781.2013.12044.x

Macaro, E. (2001). *Learning Strategies in Foreign and Second Language Classrooms*. London: Continuum.

Meadows, B., & Marumatsu, Y. (2007). Native speaker or non-native speaker teacher? a report of student preferences in four different foreign language classrooms. *Arizona Working Papers in SLA & Testing*, (14), 95-109.

Nemati, M., & Taghizadeh, M. (2013). Exploring Similarities and Differences between L1 and L2. *International Research Journal of Applied and Basic Sciences*, *4*(9), 2477–2483.

Odlin, T. (1989). *Language Transfer*. Cambridge, UK: Cambridge University Press. doi:10.1017/CBO9781139524537

Park, S. J., & Abelmann, N. (2004). Class and Cosmopolitan Striving: Mothers' Management of English Education in South Korea. *Anthropological Quarterly*, *77*(4), 645–672. doi:10.1353/anq.2004.0063

Parker, F., & Riley, K. (2005). *Linguistics for Non-Linguists*. Pearson.

Richard, J. C., & Rodgers, T. S. (2001). Approaches and Methods in Language Teaching. United States of America. Cambridge. doi:10.1017/CBO9780511667305

Schmidt, R. (1995). *Attention and Awareness in Foreign Language Learning*. Second Language Teaching & Curriculum Center University of Hawaii.

Susan, G., & Selinker, L. (2008). *Second Language Acquisition*. Routledge.

Tarone, E. (2006). Interlanguage. Elsevier Ltd.

Wang, Y. (2015). *Negative Transfer of Mother Language in English Compositions by Jiujiang University Students*. Academic Press. doi:10.1051/shsconf/20151401008

Yule, G. (2014). The Study of Language. Cambridge University Press.

Chapter 7
Complex Structures in the Child-Directed Speech of Native and Nonnative Speakers

Aslı Altan
Okan International University, USA

Erika Hoff
Florida Atlantic University, USA

ABSTRACT

Children in bilingual communities are frequently exposed to speech from nonnative speakers, but little research has described how that input might differ from the input of native speakers. There is evidence that input from nonnative speakers might be less useful to language learning children, but little research has asked why. This chapter analyzes the frequency of complex structures in the child-directed speech of 30 native English speakers and 36 nonnative speakers who were late learners of English, all speaking English to their two-and-a-half-year-old children. All instances of nine categories of complex structures were coded in transcripts of mother-child interaction. The frequency of all but one category was greater in the speech of native speakers. These findings suggest that input provided by native speakers provides more frequent models of complex structures than nonnative input.

INTRODUCTION

It is well established in the literature on monolingual development that children's language skills reflect the quantity and quality of their language experience. This is no less true of bilingual children (Hoff & Core, 2013). One feature of the language

DOI: 10.4018/978-1-5225-4009-0.ch007

experience of many bilingual children is exposure to nonnative speakers. In immigrant bilingual populations, parents often speak with their children in a late-acquired second language. Studies of Spanish-English bilingual children in immigrant families in the U.S. have found that the majority of many children's English exposure comes from nonnative English speakers (Place & Hoff, 2011; 2015), and several sources of evidence suggest that the input provided by native speakers is more supportive of children's language development than the input provided by nonnative speakers.

The debate about native skills (NS) versus non-native skills (NNS) and the different input they provide has always been a topic for debate. Several studies of second language acquisition (SLA) and use have focused on native speaker/non-native speaker (NS-NNS) conversation and its role in the acquisition process (Long, 1983). Even speakers who may be considered "fluent" in a second language due to their mastery of the grammar and vocabulary of that language may still lack pragmatic competence; in other words, they may still be unable to produce language that is socially and culturally appropriate (Tanck, 2002).

In the present paper, we focus on the frequency and types of complex structures in non-native child-directed speech (CDS) for two reasons. One, previous research found that the frequency and diversity of syntactic structures in children's input predicts children's vocabulary and syntactic development (Naigles & Huttenlocher, Waterfall, Vasilyeva, Vevea & Hedges, 2010; Valian, 2013). Two, we hypothesize that non-native speakers may show reduced use of complex sentences compared to native speakers. The structures to be analyzed are relative clauses, embedded clauses, and other grammatically complex structures. The aim is to ask if their use and frequency in child-directed speech differs between the native English and non-native English of native Spanish bilingual mothers.

PREVIOUS STUDIES

The Role of Complex Syntax in Children's Input

The frequency of complex structures in input is positively related to children's lexical and grammatical development. Marchman et al. (2016) worked on caregiver talk to young Spanish-English bilinguals and they reported a critical role of verbal engagement between caregivers and children in shaping children's early language outcomes in both of the languages they were learning. Huttenlocher et al. (2010) found, in a study of caregiver input and language growth between 14-46 months, caregiver clausal diversity and number of caregiver uses of complex clauses both predicted children's clausal diversity. More generally, it has been argued that the human language processor is sensitive to frequency (Bybee & Hopper, 2001; Ellis,

2002; Gennari & MacDonalds, 2008; Wells et al., 2009), and thus the frequency with which particular structures appear is likely to be a relevant feature of children's input. Consistent with that argument, Valian (2013) found, in a study with children between 2;6 and 3;2, that children who heard auxiliary structures more produced more auxiliary sentences than a control group who had less auxiliary exposure. Relatedly, Altınkamış et al. (2013) studied the use of relative clauses in child-directed speech in Turkish and concluded that lack of input frequency should also be regarded as a contributor to monolingual Turkish children's late emergence and rare use of relative clauses.

Differences Between Native and Nonnative Input

Several findings suggest native and nonnative input differ in the degree to which they provide children the information that supports language acquisition. That evidence includes findings from Canada that English use at home by immigrant parents did not predict immigrant children's English skill but exposure to English from native speakers outside the home was a positive predictor (Paradis, 2011), findings from the U.S. that the proportion of children's English input provided by native speakers was a unique positive predictor of the children's English skill (Place & Hoff, 2011, 2015) and findings, also from the U.S., that English use at home was a significant predictor of children's English skills for bilingual children who had one native English speaking parent but not for children for whom both parents were nonnative English speakers (Hoff, Rumiche, Burridge, Ribot, & Welsh, 2014). A reason for these findings is suggested in previous research that used automated, CLAN-produced measures of speech (MacWhinney, 2000) and found that the child-directed speech of native speakers made use of a richer vocabulary and longer utterances than the child-directed speech of nonnative speakers (Shanks & Hoff, 2015). The use of complex structures, which must be coded by hand, has not been investigated.

Complex Syntax in Bilingual Children's Speech

The potential relevance of the frequency of complex structures in native and nonnative child-directed speech is suggested by findings that English-German bilingual children lag behind English monolingual children on four dimensions of relative clause use: their adverbial constructions were shorter, less often integrated into a complex sentential structure (used as a simple clause), and when they were integrated, they were less often placed in sentence-initial position (Wiechmann, Steinfeld & Kerz, 2013). Furthermore, bilingual productions exhibited a greater frequency of violations of the semantic usage conditions of adverbial subordinators. Overall, this work indicates that bilinguals around age five have not caught up on their monolinguals peers in the domain of complex sentences and suggests the hypothesis that the nonnative input characteristics that bilinguals experience may not aid the acquisition of these structures as much as native input does.

AIM OF THE PRESENT STUDY

In the present study we analyzed the English addressed to their 2 ½ year old children by mothers who were U.S. born native speakers of English and by mothers who were native speakers of Spanish, born in a Spanish-speaking country, and currently living in the U.S. We asked whether the frequency with mothers used a range of complex structures in their child-directed speech differs as a function of native speaker status.

DATA

Participants

The participants were 30 monolingual native English-speakers and 36 Spanish-English bilinguals who were native Spanish speakers and late learners of English. All participants lived in the U.S. at the time of the study. The native English speakers were U.S. born; the native Spanish speakers were born in Spanish-speaking countries in South America and the Caribbean. The mean age of immigration for the native Spanish speakers was 23.62 years (SD = 5.89), the range of age of arrival was from 17 to 35 years. All participants were mothers of 2 ½ year old children. The native Spanish speakers all reported that they regularly interacted with their children in English. The children of the native English speakers were typically-developing monolingual English speakers (16 girls and 14 boys) with a mean age of 30.55 months (SD = .41). The children of the native Spanish speakers were also typically-developing children (19 girls and 17 boys) with a mean age of 30.39 months (SD = .38), who were exposed to and were acquiring both English and Spanish.

Among the native English speakers, 28 were college graduates, 2 were high school but not college graduates; among the native Spanish speakers, 17 were college graduates, 15 were high school but not college graduates, and 4 had less than a high school education. Of the nonnative speakers, 10 reported that they received English education and 26 reported that they had not received any education in English. In a self-reported proficiency assessment, the non-native English mothers rated themselves as proficient (25 out of 36 mothers); a smaller number (9 among 36) rated themselves as having somewhat limited proficiency, and 2 rated themselves as not proficient, while still using English in speech to their children.

Procedure

The data were collected as part of a larger study of language development in children from monolingual English homes and children from bilingual Spanish-English speaking homes. During a visit to the participants' homes (or in 18 cases a university laboratory playroom) the mothers and children were provided with two toy sets (toy animals, pretend food), and with books each for 10 minutes. They were asked to play and look at books as they normally would. The video-recordings were transcribed according to the conventions of the CHILDES system (MacWhinney, 2000) by trained research assistants.

The mean duration of the recordings of native speaker-child interaction was 28.73 minutes (SD= 3.25), and the mean for non-native speakers was 28.80 minutes (SD= 4.17). The mean number of utterances for native caregivers was 674.13 (SD= 155.08) and for non-native caregivers the mean number of utterances was 657.97 (SD= 194.63). Neither difference approached statistical significance.

The transcripts were coded by the first author as not complex or as instances of one of the 9 categories listed in Table 1 below. Categories 1 through 7 were defined by Diessel (2004), and categories 8 and 9 were added to more fully capture all the complex utterances in the mothers' speech. Interrater reliability was calculated with a second coder who coded all the maternal speech in 3 transcripts from native speakers and 3 transcripts from nonnative speakers. Among these 6 transcripts there were only 5 utterances that were categorized differently by the two coders.

RESULTS

Frequency of Complex Structures in Native and Non-Native CDS

The frequency with mothers produced complex structures in their child-directed speech was calculated first for five categories of structures as follows: subject control structures (two verbs with the same subject), coordinate clauses, embedded structures (all relative clauses and complement clauses), adverbial clauses and double embeddings (combination of two embedded structures)[1]. Frequencies of each type for each group are plotted in Figure 1. Because the distributions of the frequencies were skewed, the non-parametric Mann- Whitney U Test was used to compare groups. Native mothers used significantly more subject control structures, (M=60.73, SD= 25.23) than non-native mothers (M=42.89, SD=22.61), $U = 110, p < .001$. The number of coordinate clauses was also found to be significantly different between two groups, native English-speaking mothers used more coordinate clauses

Table 1. Categories of complex structures with examples from child-directed speech

1. **Finite complement (COMP) clause** I think the deer likes grass. I think he's in here. I know you like these. 2. **Non-finite complement (COMP) clause** You want me to put it together? Want mommy to read it? 3. **Finite relative (REL) clause** What do you see in the sky that's yellow? Who's your girlfriend that we go to the zoo with? Let's put everything that goes on land in there. 4. **Non-finite relative (REL) clause** We don't have a baby to give the booty to. Do you want something to drink? 5. **Finite adverbial (ADV) clause** You know when we take a walk. There's a story about where trains get stuck in the mud. 6. **Non-finite adverbial (ADV) clause** Let's see what Rosario brought you to play with. Can I have something to drink? 7. **Coordinate clause** So let's put the fence there. That's a plate so we can put the food. The fence is broken but it'll be ok. 8. **Double embeddings** (utterances which included two or more of the categories above) Well then we're not going to be able to see what's in that black bag. Do you know what that is? I don't know what that guy is. I thought you said you like the green grapes better. I think there's something in here you might like. Cows like grass but I don't think we have a cow. 9. **Subject control clauses** (constructions that include more than one verb with the same subject and the second verb [infinite or gerund] is not conjugated for tense) I wanna go. I need to eat. You want to sing.

(adapted from O'Grady, 2011)

(M=6.40, SD=4.40) than non-native mothers (M=2.22, SD=3.44), U = 182, $p <$ .001. Native mothers also used more single embedded structures (M=14, SD=8.49) than non-native mothers (M=6.3, SD=4.81), U = 110, $p < .001$. Also, native mothers used significantly more adverbial sentences (M=1.8, SD=1.7) when compared to non-native mothers (M=0.3, SD=0.8), U = 200.5, $p < .001$. The number of double embedded clauses were also significantly different between the two groups, native mothers used more double embedded clauses (M=11.87, SD=8.23) than non-native mothers (M=3.00, SD= 3.42), U = 115, $p < .001$.

The second analysis compared the frequencies of the more narrowly-defined types of structures in native and non-native child-directed speech. Means are presented in

Figure 1. The frequency of five categories of complex structures of mother-child interaction in English for mothers who were native and non-native speakers of English

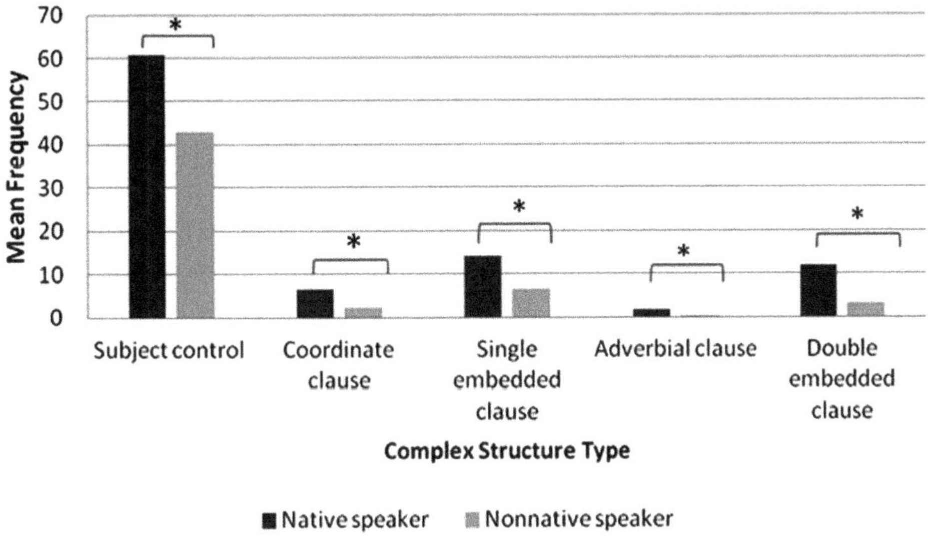

Table 2 along with the outcome of comparisons using the Mann- Whitney U Test. For all categories except non-finite COMP clauses, native speakers produced the structure significant more frequently than non-native speakers.

Table 2. Means (and standard deviations) for the frequency of nine (fine-grained) complex structure types in the child-directed speech of native and nonnative caregivers

	Native	**Non-Native**	**U**	*p*
	Mean (SD)	Mean (SD)		
Subject control structures	60.73 (25.23)	42.89 (22.61)	$U = 346$	$p = .012$
Finite COMP clause	8.77 (5.84)	3.36 (3.57)	$U = 235$	$p < .001$
Non-finite COMP clause	3.27 (2.65)	2.58 (2.59)	$U = 434$	P= .169
Finite REL	1.60 (2.06)	.36 (.86)	$U = 313$	$p = .001$
Non-finite REL	.37 (.66)	.08 (36)	$U = 411$	$p = .010$
Finite ADV	1.53 (1.59)	.33 (.89)	$U = 220$	$p < .001$
Non-finite ADV	.30 (.59)	.03 (.16)	$U = 428$	$p = .011$
Coordinate	6.40 (4.40)	2.22 (3.44)	$U = 182$	$p < .001$
Double embedding	11.87 (8.23)	3.00 (3.42)	$U = 115$	$p < .001$

Ungrammatical Structures in Non-Native CDS

In addition to using fewer complex structures, the non-native English speakers also produced ungrammatical structures, which the native speakers did not. This clearly illustrates that most of the non-native mothers in our data set had difficulty using complex structures in unplanned speech. The reasons for ungrammaticality are mostly the lack of subject-verb agreement, failure to do inversion in questions, lack of subject-verb agreement as can be observed with examples from data below. It should be noted here that these types of errors only occurred in complex structures, that is non-native mothers did not do such errors (subject-verb agreement errors and word-order errors) in simple structures.

Non-native input/ Ungrammatical examples, (*) used for ungrammaticality:

1. Word order (failure to do inversion in questions)
   MOT: *I don't know what's this. (non-native)
   MOT: *tell me what is this animal. (non-native)
   MOT: *do you remember where is the giraffe. (non-native)
   MOT: *Is it do you think a sheep? (non-native)
   MOT: *you know what is this? (non-native)
   MOT: *tell me what do you have there. (non-native)
   MOT: *do you know where do they live? (non-native)
   MOT: *show me where is the egg. (non-native)
   MOT: *do you know how this call it. (non-native)
2. The failure to use 'to' to join two verbs/ using 'to' when not necessary
   MOT: *I know you have eat this. (non-native)
   MOT: *we're gonna pretend that open it. (non-native)
   MOT: *help me to do the clean up. (non-native)
   MOT: *help me to find the fruits. (non-native)
   MOT: *let's give to me all the yellow. (non-native)
3. The lack of subject-verb agreement
   MOT: Tell me does the horsey has any hair. (non-native)
4. Other ungrammatical structures:
   MOT: *Let's play that you're gonna go to bed. (non-native)
   MOT: *Don't forget the tete to put it in here. (non-native)
   MOT: *you want some cheese for eat? (non-native)

There are many instances in the data, where the mother appears to use two simple clauses and avoid using a RC. Also, more avoidance strategies have been employed by non-native mothers where they prefer to use two sentences instead of a single clause joined by a relative clause.

MOT: Because we don't eat that part. That part grows from the ground. (non-native)
MOT: you remember? (non-native)
MOT: the panda in the movie?
MOT: remember? (non-native)
MOT: the other animal in panda movie?

DISCUSSION AND CONCLUSION

The primary aim of the present study was to ask how the child-directed speech of native speakers differs from the child-directed speech of nonnative speakers in the use of complex structures. The study thus investigates two questions of relevance to the study of bilingualism and bilingual development: (1) it examines an unstudied domain of bilinguals' use of their second language—speech to children, and (2) it explores a frequent source of language input to bilingually developing children—nonnative adult speakers.

The examination of the adults' speech revealed substantial differences in the frequency with which native and nonnative speakers of English produced complex sentences when talking to children. The difference was significant for each of five different types of complex structure: finite and non-finite complement clauses, relative clauses, adverbial clauses, coordinate structures, and infinitive verb structures as well. Differences were also significant comparing the frequency of 9 finer-grained categories, with the exception of non-finite complement clause structures.

There are limitations to the conclusions that can be drawn from the present study. In the present sample, the native English speakers had, on average, higher levels of education than the nonnative speakers, suggesting the hypothesis that these differences reflect education level rather than native speaker status. However, there were no differences between the groups in how much they talked to their children in these spontaneous speech samples, which is the most salient difference in child-directed speech associated with parent education (Hoff, 2006). The difference was in the syntactic complexity of their speech. It may very well be that the difference in the syntactic complexity of the English spoken by native and nonnative speakers arises from differences attributable to their educational experience in English. Most certainly, the nonnative speakers are not a monolithic group, and explaining variance among nonnative speakers is an important topic for future research. Another limitation in the conclusions that can be drawn from the present study arises from the fact that we did not pursue the consequences of these differences for the children's language growth. We suggest that these observed differences between native and nonnative speakers in the syntactic complexity of their child-directed speech are the explanation for previous findings that that native input is more supportive of language growth than nonnative input, but we do not have direct evidence.

These limitations notwithstanding, the finding of differences between native and nonnative speakers in the present study does have two implications: (1) that talk to children demands a high level of language proficiency, and (2) that children of nonnative speakers hear less complex speech than children of native speakers. With respect to the demands of talk to children, one might think that talking to a 2-year-old would place fairly low demands on a speaker's syntactic competence and that this task would not be sensitive to differences between native and nonnative speakers in proficiency, but this turns out not to be the case. Even among nonnative speakers who for the most part rate themselves as proficient in English and who all use English in talking to their children on a regular basis, the speech they address to their children is syntactically less complex than the speech of native speakers. Previous analyses of native and nonnative child-directed speech, from some but not all of these same caregivers, have found differences in the vocabulary richness and utterance length (Hoff et al., 2016). These results also support the findings of Paradis & Jia (2016) whose study showed that language environment factors such as the amount of input, quality of input and frequency and complexity of linguistic structures shape not only early-stage but also late-stage bilingual development. The present findings add important detail to that picture of native and nonnative input to children. With respect to the implications for children, one might think that so long as the adult is more advanced than the child, the adult is providing useful input. However, research with monolingual children acquiring English has found that children's vocabulary and syntactic development are related to the variety and complexity of structures in the child's speech (Naigles & Hoff-Ginsberg, 1998; Huttenlocher et al., 2010). Thus, while children do learn from nonnative input, they may not learn as much as from native input. That conclusion is consistent with a variety of findings that native input more supportive of language development than input is from nonnative speakers.

ACKNOWLEDGMENT

Preparation of this article was supported by grant HD068421 from the Eunice Kennedy Shriver National Institute of Child Health and Human Development to Erika Hoff, Principal Investigator. We thank Feyza Altınkamış for her help in establishing interrater reliability.

REFERENCES

Altınkamış, F., Altan, A., & Sofu, H. 2013. Properties of relative clauses in child directed speech [İlgi Tümceciklerinin Çocuğa Yöneltilmiş Konuşmadaki Özellikleri]. *Proceedings of the 27th National Linguistics Conference*, 51-60.

Bybee, J. L., & Hopper, P. J. (2001). *Frequency and the emergence of linguistic structure*. John Benjamins Publishing. doi:10.1075/tsl.45

Ellis, N. C. (2002). Frequency Effects in language processing. *Studies in Second Language Acquisition*, 143–188.

Gennari, S. P., & MacDonalds, M. C. (2008). Semantic indeterminacy in object relative clauses. *Journal of Memory and Language*, *58*(2), 161–187. doi:10.1016/j.jml.2007.07.004 PMID:19724662

Hoff, E. (2006). How social contexts support and shape language development. *Developmental Review*, *26*(1), 55–88. doi:10.1016/j.dr.2005.11.002

Hoff, E., Coard, W., & Senor, M. (2013). *Bilingual Parent's Child-directed Speech in two languages: Do native and non-native input differ?* Poster presented at Society for Research in Child Development Biennial Meeting, Seattle, WA.

Hoff, E., & Core, C. (2013). Input and Language development in bilingually developing children. *Seminars in Speech and Language, 34*, 215-226. DOI: 10.1055/S-OO33-1353448

Hoff, E., Core, C., Place, S., Rumiche, R., Señor, M., & Parra, M. (2012). Dual language exposure and early bilingual development. *Journal of Child Language*, *39*(01), 1–27. doi:10.1017/S0305000910000759 PMID:21418730

Hoff, E., Welsh, S., Place, S., & Ribot, K. M. (2014). Bilingual environments, bilingual input, and bilingual development. In T. Grüter & J. Paradis (Eds.), *Input and Experience in Bilingual Development.* Amsterdam, The Netherlands: John Benjamins Publishing Company.

Huttenlocher, J., Waterfall, H. R., Vasilyeva, M., Vevea, J., & Hedges, L. (2010). Sources of variability in children's language growth. *Cognitive Psychology*, *61*(4), 343–365. doi:10.1016/j.cogpsych.2010.08.002 PMID:20832781

Long, M. H. (1983). Native speaker/non-native speaker conversation in the second language classroom. *Working Papers in English as a Second Language*.

MacWhinney, B. (2000). *The CHILDES project: Tools for analyzing talk* (3rd ed.). Mahwah, NJ: Erlbaum.

Marchman, V. A., Martinez, L. Z., Hurtado, N., Grüter, T., & Fernald, A. (2016). Caregiver talk to young Spanish-English bilinguals: Comparing direct observation and parent-report measures of dual-language exposure. *Developmental Science*, 1–13. PMID:27197746

Naigles, L. R., & Hoff-Ginsberg, E. (1998). Why are some verbs learned before other verbs-Effects of input frequency and structure on children's early verb use. *Journal of Child Language*, *25*(1), 95–120. doi:10.1017/S0305000997003358 PMID:9604570

O'Grady, W. (2011). Relative Clauses: Processing and acquisition. In E. Kidd (Ed.), *The Acquisition of Relative Clauses: Processing, Typology and function*. John Benjamins Publishing Company. doi:10.1075/tilar.8.03gra

Paradis, J. (2011). Individual differences in child English second language acquisition: Comparing child-Internal and child-external factors. *Linguistic Approaches to Bilingualism*, *1*(3), 213–237. doi:10.1075/lab.1.3.01par

Paradis, J., & Jia, R. (2016). Bilingual children's long-term outcomes in English as a second language: Language environment factors shape individual differences in catching up with monolinguals. *Developmental Science*, 1–15. PMID:27320539

Place, S., & Hoff, E. (2011). Properties of dual language exposure that influence 2-year-olds' bilingual proficiency. *Child Development*, *82*(6), 1834–1849. doi:10.1111/j.1467-8624.2011.01660.x PMID:22004372

Place, S. & Hoff, E. (2015). Effects and non-effects of input in bilingual environments on dual language skills in 2 1/2-year-olds. *Bilingualism: Language and Cognition*.

Shanks, K., & Hoff, E. (2015). *Qualities of Mothers' Native and Non-native Child-directed Speech in Spanish- English Bilingual Households*. Poster presented at BUCLD.

Tanck, S. (2002). Speech act sets of refusal and complaint: A comparison of native and non-native English speakers' production. Studies in Second Language Acquisition.

Valian, V., & Lyman, C. (2013). Young children's acquisition of wh-questions: The role of structured input. *Journal of Child Language*, *30*(1), 117–143. doi:10.1017/S0305000902005457 PMID:12718295

Wells, J. B., Christiansen, M. H., Race, D. S., Acheson, D. J., & MacDonals, M. C. (2009). Experience and sentence processing: Statistical learning and relative clause comprehension. *Cognitive Psychology*, *58*(2), 250–271. doi:10.1016/j.cogpsych.2008.08.002 PMID:18922516

Wiechmann, D., Steinfeld, J., & Kerz, E. 2013. Modeling bilingual children's acquisition of complex sentences in German. In M. Knauff, M. Pauen, N. Sebanz, & I. Wachsmuth (eds.), *Proceedings of the 35th Annual Conference of the Cognitive Science Society* (pp. 3753-3758). Austin, TX: Cognitive Science Society.

ENDNOTE

1 There was no evidence that these properties of mothers' child directed speech varied because mothers were accommodating their children's age or language level. The children were all the same age, and correlations calculated between the frequency of these structures and children's scores on a measure of expressive vocabulary were all non-significant.

Chapter 8
Context Effects in Bilingual Language Processing

Sugandha Kaur
Indian Institute of Technology Guwahati, India

Bidisha Som
Indian Institute of Technology Guwahati, India

ABSTRACT

Previous studies show that the presence of a context word in picture naming either facilitates or interferes with the naming. Although there has been extensive research in this area, there are many conflicting findings, making it difficult to reach firm conclusions. This chapter aims to delve into the dynamics of such processing and understand the nuances involved in experimental manipulations that may influence the pattern of results and be responsible for differences in outcomes. The series of experiments reported in this chapter was aimed at refining our understanding of mechanisms in the way bilinguals process language production by examining two different paradigms—primed picture naming and picture-word interference. This was investigated by manipulating both the type of visual context words presented with the picture and the time interval between the presentation of context word and picture. The results are interpreted within the context of current models of lexical access.

INTRODUCTION

Psycholinguistics has greatly enriched the field of bilingualism research by providing insights into the bilingual mind in order to better understand the cognitive basis of bilingualism and the logic of experimental and formal approaches to language

DOI: 10.4018/978-1-5225-4009-0.ch008

science. A fundamental question which has dominated bilingual psycholinguistic research in terms of language processing is whether bilingual individuals activate or access lexical representations selectively or non-selectively. In order to determine language selectivity in bilinguals, a pivotal investigation has been using words that are similar across languages. In both bilingual word recognition and production research, a substantial part has been dedicated to investigate how cognates and non-cognates are represented and processed. Previous research shows that regardless of what languages or bilingual populations are used, cognate words are likely to be recognized faster than non-cognate words, and this may influence the results. This general finding in the psycholinguistic literature is known as *the cognate facilitation effect* which indicates the activation of lexical items in both languages, simultaneously. Moreover, the way bilinguals can vary as a result of their Second Language (L2) Age of Acquisition (AoA) and proficiency can also influence the co-activation of languages. The majority of the studies in the past have investigated bilinguals differing in their L2 AoA and over the years, numerous studies which have made use of different tasks and paradigms have demonstrated differences in processing as a function of L2 AoA. For example, Kim et al., (1997), Weber-Fox & Neville (1999) and Wuillemin & Richardson (1994) have shown contrasts between early and late bilinguals. Several studies investigating the degree of co-activation and interaction between the two languages of a bilingual have observed that variation in L2 proficiency also differentially affects cross-language interactions at various levels. For example, studies employing cross-language semantic priming and translation priming paradigms have observed that differences in proficiency affect semantic and translation priming effects (Frenck and Pynte, 1987). The fact that AoA and proficiency are highly intertwined complicates the situation even more. For example, the influence of both factors has been observed in Silverberg and Samuel's (2004) study. Further, studies addressing the role of script in either bilingual word recognition or production generally assume that script is nothing but a normal orthographic difference which bypasses redundant search of both lexicons and helps in guiding the lexical search to the lexicon appropriate for the task. However, this assumption is not supported by enough experimental evidence as numerous studies have examined lexical processing in same-script bilinguals, but the number of published studies examining these questions in different-script bilinguals is few. Overall, the evidence in support of non-selective access is substantial, and much stronger than for selective access.

Multifarious models have evolved over time depicting the representation of words in dual languages and the inherent inter-connectivity between them. Models of lexical access in bilingual speech production are generally categorized into two theoretical camps: selective/language-specific vs. non-selective/language-non-specific. As per the assumptions of the selective view, lexical access in bilingual word production is fundamentally a selective process. With respect to language, selection occurs at the conceptual level, activating lemmas only in the intended language. On the other hand, as per the assumptions of the non-selective view, lexical access in bilingual word production is fundamentally a non-selective process. In this case, language selection does not occur at the conceptual level and thus, lemmas from both languages get activated simultaneously. Although, research on bilingual word production, in terms of lexical activation mainly supports the non-selective view, the manner of lexical selection is still under debate. The manner of lexical selection has been further divided into two theoretical camps: language-specific selection and language-non-specific selection. According to the language-specific view, when a bilingual intends to speak in a language, lexical candidates from both languages become active. However, lexical candidates from the non-response language do not interfere in the process of selection, and thus, only the candidates in the response language are finally considered for selection (e.g., Costa et al., 1999). In contrast to the language-specific view, the language-non-specific view assumes that, in addition to lexical candidates in both the response and non-response languages being simultaneously active, lexical candidates from both languages also compete for selection (e.g., Hermans et al., 1998). Thus, influence of the non-response language is evident in the selection process which has to go through further processes like inhibition of the non-response language or higher-level activation of the response language, in order for the intended language to be spoken.

Furthermore, in recent literature, there has been a debate concerning the manner of language selection and the evidence that supports each alternative model. Some studies suggest that, alternative candidates from both languages are active at the lemma level but only candidates from the intended language are encoded phonologically (e.g., Hermans et al., 1998). On this view, language selection occurs at the lemma level. Others demonstrate that alternative candidates from both languages are active all the way to the phonological level and language is selected at the phonological level (e.g., Colomé, 2001; Costa et al., 2000).

BACKGROUND

In recent years, experimental research on language production has started to make increasing use of the context effects to investigate how manipulations of content at different levels of representation influence word production. Studies on context effects in naming tasks have been the focus of two distinct research fields: (i) the priming research of the early seventies, and (ii) research on the Stroop phenomenon and picture-word interference paradigm. Research on these two distinct fields has produced different results but unfortunately, very few attempts have been made to reconcile the results obtained within both fields (La Heij et al., 1990). Previous research has shown that the manipulation of both the type of context words presented with the picture and the time interval between the presentation of context word and picture can have a significant effect on the outcome. For example, a context word can have either facilitative or inhibitive effects on picture naming depending on the type of relationship it shares with the picture. Moreover, interaction between Stimulus Onset Asynchrony (SOA) and type of context words can have a significant effect. Previous research shows that in priming experiments, when a context word shares semantic relation with a target picture, naming of the picture is facilitated. However, in picture-word interference experiments, such a relation hampers the naming of the picture. Similarly, when participants are presented with a context word that is identical to a target picture, they are typically able to name the picture faster than when the context word is unrelated to the target picture (Glaser & Dungelhoff, 1984; Rosinski et al., 1975; Rosinski, 1977; Smith & Magee, 1980). This facilitative effect is robust and has been observed at a variety of SOAs (Biggs & Marmurek, 1990). Moreover, even when other items intervene between the context word and the target word, robust facilitative effect has been observed (Durso & Johnson, 1979). In contrast to the facilitative effects described above, the presence of a context word which is semantically related (versus unrelated) to the target picture have produced mixed results. Although some studies differing in their use of SOAs have shown semantic facilitation effect, these studies varied widely in terms of the size of the semantic facilitation effect. For example, in studies by Bajo (1988) and Carr et al., (1982), substantial semantic facilitation effects have been found; in the study of Sperber et al., (1979), only a small but significant effect has been observed; and in the study by Irwin and Lupker (1983), the effect did not even reach significance. The results of these studies indicate that the size of the SOA used cannot cause the inconsistency in the facilitative effect because semantic facilitation was obtained both with SOA values as small as approximately 200 ms (Carr et al., 1982) and with SOA values larger than 1000 ms (e.g. Bajo, 1988). Moreover, although the amount of processing of the prime word has been indicative of the respective priming effect as indicated by the results of a number of studies (e.g. Irwin & Lupker, 1983), a large facilitation effect has also been observed in the study by Bajo (1988) in a condition in which no reaction to the prime was required. Nor do the instructions concerning the processing of the prime word seem crucial. Furthermore, some studies using the naming procedure with masked priming and electrophysiological recordings also observed that the relationship between the prime word and the target picture affected the picture naming latencies (Blackford et al., 2012; Chauncey et al., 2009).

Picture-word interference paradigm, a modified version of the Stroop task, is one of the most frequently used methods in experimental psycholinguistic research on language production. Similar to the Stroop task, this phenomenon is strongly influenced by the nature of the superimposed word (Lupker, 1982). For example, naming a picture of a cat together with the word "dog" takes longer than naming the same picture without the word. The PWI task was first used by Rosinski et al., (1975) to study automatic reading skills of children. Some other monolingual PWI studies, investigated the exact levels in the bilingual production system where co-activation of the non-target language occurred, by manipulating both the type of distracter words presented with the picture and the time interval between the presentation of distracter and picture. These studies showed that in comparison to neutral or unrelated distracters, semantic distracters slowed down the picture-naming response (e.g., Bajo et al., 2003; Levelt et al., 1999; Roelofs, 1992; Schriefers et al., 1990; Starreveld & La Heij, 1995, 1996). Interestingly, phonological distracters showed facilitative rather than inhibitive effect. Moreover, these studies showed that the occurrence of these effects depend on the time relation between picture and distracter (Schriefers et al., 1990). In general, these effects hinted the competition between lemmas, therefore, provided evidence in support of language non-selective activation.

Following the footsteps of within-language production studies, many between-language production studies have also used the picture-word interference paradigm. In these studies, bilinguals name a picture in one language while ignoring a visually or auditorily presented distracter word in the same or other language. Ehri and Ryan (1980) showed that English–Spanish bilinguals named pictures more slowly, in both of their languages, when a word from the non-target language was superimposed over the picture than when a neutral distracter stimulus (a series of Xs) was superimposed. In a further study, Mägiste, 1984b (see also Mägiste, 1985), testing German–Swedish bilinguals at various levels of proficiency in their L2, obtained this same interference effect and showed that its size depended on the learners' relative proficiency in the two languages—the stronger the non-target language, the larger the interference effect. Both these studies thus hinted at the occurrence of language non-selective activation in bilingual word production. More recent bilingual picture-naming studies, using both the distracter methodology (Costa & Caramazza, 1999; Costa et al., 2000; Hermans et al., 1998, Hoshino, 2006) and versions of the task in which pictures are presented without distracters (Colomé, 2001; Costa et al., 2000; Gollan & Acenas, 2004; Kroll et al., 2000; Rodriguez-Fornelss et al., 2005), focused on various aspects of the theoretical contrasts introduced earlier. However, with regard to the manner of language selection, there exists different interpretation in the literature. To illustrate, Hermans and his colleagues (1998) interpreted the findings of their study as support for a language non-specific model of bilingual production. Contrary to the interpretation of Hermans et al. (1998), Costa and his colleagues considered an alternative to language non-selective (or "language non-specific") selection, in which the selection mechanism ignores the activation in the non-target language (Costa et al., 1999; Costa & Caramazza, 1999; Costa et al., 2003).

To summarize, despite the frequent use of the primed picture naming and picture-word interference paradigm, it is important to note that there has been criticism task. Although cross-language identity and semantic effects have been investigated in cross-language experiments, they do not allow strong conclusions since contrasting results were obtained across these studies. Moreover, all of this past research, except one (Hoshino, 2006) have examined bilingual performance for bilinguals whose languages are orthographically similar. Therefore, the issue of whether facilitation or inhibition is found with different-script bilinguals remains unresolved. The presented work in this chapter follows the same line of research, but it intended to bridge this gap by exploring the nature of bilingual language production in a previously unexamined different-script language pair, i.e., Bodo–Assamese. The study aims to delve into the bilingual's cognition aspect in order to gain an insight into the interaction between different languages in his/her mind. The study was largely based on the premise of languages mutually affecting each other, the premise against which models relating to bilingual language processing were to be evaluated.

THE PRESENT STUDY

The present study discusses context effects in picture naming by examining two different paradigms—primed picture naming (Experiment 1, 2 and 3) and picture-word interference (Experiment 3, 4, and 5). The authors used a cross-representational paradigm in combination with behavioral measures in order to examine the time-course of facilitation and inhibition during picture naming task. The primary goal of the study was to examine the time course of prime and distracter effects as a way of identifying the activity of the non-target language during each stage of production (i.e., at the conceptual, lemma, and phonological levels). Given the interpretation of cross-language facilitation and interference effects in previous studies discussed above, it was expected that naming times would be shorter to picture targets preceded by words that were identical (versus unrelated) to the picture's name. This would indicate facilitation by overlapping activation from the prime or distracter word at multiple levels of representation – conceptual, lemma and phonological. Of most interest was the pattern of naming times to the picture targets preceded by semantically related words. Based on previously reported behavioral findings, the authors expected to see a semantic interference effect on naming times, i.e. it was expected that naming times of picture targets preceded by semantically related words to be longer than those preceded by semantically unrelated words.

Experiment 1: Blocked Picture Naming in L2

Method

Participants

Fifty-three Bodo–Assamese bilingual speakers (38 male and 15 female). Participants ranged in age from 21 to 45 years (mean age = 38 years, *SD* = 9.9). All participants were native speakers of Bodo and used Assamese as their L2. Each participant completed a language background questionnaire which included questions on their language history and usage. Self-report measures relating to AoA was used to divide the participants into Early L2 learners (learning of L2 before 7 years) and Late L2 learners (learning of L2 after 7 years). The ratings showed that early bilinguals began to learn Assamese at a mean age of 2.6 years, whereas the late learning groups began to learn Assamese at a mean age of 8.7 years. The questionnaire also included a 7 point self-assessment scale to map the proficiency of the participants in speaking, reading, writing and comprehension in respect to both languages, in order to further divide the Late L2 learners into high and low proficient groups, relating to their L2 proficiency, The results of the self-report ratings show that the Bodo ratings of the three groups of bilinguals on all four proficiency measures are similar. However, the Assamese ratings on all four proficiency measures are higher for the high proficient groups than for the low proficient group.

In order to further assess the proficiency levels of the bilinguals, all participants also took part in an objective naming test. The results of the objective naming test show that the average L1 score for all three bilingual groups is similar. In case of L2, the average score for the Late High Proficient group matches the average score for the Early High Proficient group (48.1 vs. 47.2 respectively) and the scores do not yield a significant difference [$t(50) = 1.09$, $p = .412$]. This indicates that the proficiency level of the two groups is similar. However, the average score of the Late High Proficient group is noticeably higher than the average score of the Late Low Proficient group (48.1 vs. 36.3) and the scores yielded a significant difference [$t(48) = 11.53$, $p = .000$]. Based on the survey responses, three bilingual groups, namely (i.e., Early High Proficient, Late High Proficient, and Late Low Proficient) were created.

Stimuli

The stimuli used in this experiment consisted of twenty pictures as targets. Half of the picture targets were cognates and the other half were non-cognates. Each picture in this set of twenty pictures was paired with a word prime to construct word-picture pairs. These pairs had one of three types of relationship: identity semantically related and unrelated. Identity pairs consisted of a context word that corresponded to the name of the picture, semantically related pairs consisted of words and target pictures that were both co-category exemplars, and unrelated pairs consisted of words and target pictures that were not related to each other. Moreover, each picture was paired with both Assamese word primes (same-language) and their Bodo counterparts (different-language). There was no significant difference in number of letters, or number of syllables of the names of target pictures across the three types of primes.

Procedure

Participants were tested individually in a quiet room. Verbal and written instructions were administered in Assamese. Participants were informed that they would see words followed by pictures and were asked to ignore the words and name the picture as fast and as accurately as possible in Assamese. Each trial had the following structure. First, a fixation point (a plus sign) was shown in the center of the screen for 500 ms, followed by a blank interval of 200 ms. Then the prime word was presented for 250 ms followed by the target picture for a maximum of 2,000 ms. If a response was not provided within 2,000 ms, the next trial started automatically. Response latencies were measured from the onset of the stimulus to the beginning of the naming response. Before the experiment proper, the participants performed a training block of fifteen trials.

Results

A mixed-effects analysis was run separately on the reaction time data and error data. The results of the reaction time analysis did not reveal a main effect of Relatedness [$F < 1$]. A significant main effect of Cognate Status was observed [$F(1,107) = 9.491$, $p = .003$]. Pictures with cognate names were responded to 61 ms faster than non-cognates. The main effect of Bilingual Group approached significance [$F(2,49) = 8.264$, $p = .001$]. The main effect of Prime Type was also significant [$F(2,107) = 40.643$, $p = .000$], with the shortest latencies in the identity condition (831 ms), followed by the unrelated condition (967 ms) and the longest naming latencies was observed in the semantically related condition (1046 ms). There was also a significant main effect of Prime Language [$F(1,107) = 67.124$, $p = .000$]. Of most interest, however, there was a significant interaction between Prime Type and Prime Language [$F(2,107) = 10.354$, $p = .000$]. The two-way interaction between Cognate Status and Bilingual Group approached significance [$F(2,5215) = 27.626$, $p = .000$]. The Prime Type and Prime Language interaction was found to be significant [$F(2,107) = 10.354$, $p = .000$]. The Prime Type and Bilingual Group approached significance [$F(4,5210) = 44.199$, $p = .000$]. A significant interaction was observed between Prime Language and Bilingual Group [$F(2,5205) = 35.201, p = .000$]. The Relatedness and Bilingual Group interaction also approached significance [$F(2,5199) = 8.210, p = .000$]. The three-way interaction between Cognate Status, Prime Type and Bilingual Group was found to be significant [$F(4,5204) = 11.224, p = .000$]. The Prime Type, Prime Language and Bilingual Group interaction approached significance [$F(4,5205) = 25.030, p = .000$]. The Relatedness, Prime Language and Bilingual Group interaction approached significance [$F(2,5198) = 38.239, p = .000$]. Finally, the Relatedness, Cognate Status and Bilingual Group interaction was also found to be significant [$F(2,5198) = 6.981, p = .001$]. Planned comparisons were conducted to examine the individual differences of the three groups of bilinguals (see Table 1). The results revealed that the overall reaction times of the Late High Proficient bilinguals (906 ms) were faster than the Early High Proficient (946 ms) and Late Low Proficient (991 ms) bilinguals. The pattern of results of this study is different from the results of the blocked picture-word interference experiments in which the Late Low Proficient bilinguals produced the fastest naming latencies.

The analyses of the error data did not show a main effect of Relatedness [$F < 1$]. The main effect of Cognate Status was marginal [$F(1,107) = 3.491, p = .003$]. Participants made greater errors in cognate targets than non-cognate targets. Moreover the main effect of Prime Type reached significance [$F(2,107) = 9.643, p = .000$]. Errors were numerous more in the semantic primes than the identity and unrelated primes. The main effect of Distracter Language was not significant [$F < 1$]. However, the main effect of Bilingual Group approached significance [$F(2,49) = 8.264, p = .001$]. Greater errors were observed in the low proficient group than the high proficient groups. All other comparisons were not significant (all Fs < 1). In the next experiment, the goal was to further explore how primes which share different relationship with the target picture affect the performance of Bodo–Assamese bilinguals when naming in their dominant language Bodo.

Experiment 2: Blocked Picture Naming in L1

The participants, stimuli and procedure remained the same as in Experiment 1. However, since participants had to name picture targets in Bodo, verbal and written instructions were provided in Bodo.

Results

Similar to Experiment 1, a mixed-effects analysis was run on the reaction time and error data of Experiment 2. The results of the reaction time data revealed a significant main effect of Prime Type [$F(2,107) = 26.798, p = .000$]. The main effect of Prime Language was not significant [$F < 1$]. The main effect of Bilingual Group reached

Table 1. Mean RTs (ms) and percentage of errors for cognate and non-cognate targets for all three bilingual groups as a function of Prime Type and Prime Language in Experiment 1

	Prime Language/Bilingual Group					
	Bodo			**Assamese**		
	Early	**Late High**	**Late Low**	**Early**	**Late High**	**Late Low**
Prime Type	**RT (Error %)**	**RT (Error %)**	**RT (Error %)**	**RT (Error %)**	**RT (Error %)**	**RT (Error %)**
Cognate						
Identical	936 (4.2)	880 (11.1)	934 (22.2)	759 (2.9)	491 (11.1)	751 (11.1)
Semantically related	1032 (13)	996 (11.1)	1041 (22.2)	1006 (20.3)	947 (11.1)	1016 (38.9)
Unrelated	1004 (10.1)	936 (0)	1101 (38.9)	904 (10.1)	879 (11.1)	906 (33.3)
Identity effect (unrelated–identical)	**68**	**56**	**167**	**145**	**388**	**155**
Semantic effect (unrelated–semantically related)	**–28**	**–60**	**60**	**–102**	**–68**	**–110**
Non-cognate						
Identical	987 (12.7)	1004 (9)	1104 (22.7)	761 (5.5)	551 (0)	813 (9)
Semantically related	1067 (14.5)	1274 (18.2)	1114 (22.7)	1008 (27.3)	1054 (9)	995 (9)
Unrelated	973 (9)	969 (0)	1163 (22.7)	921 (1.8)	893 (0)	960 (27.2)
Identity effect (unrelated–identical)	**–14**	**–35**	**59**	**160**	**342**	**147**
Semantic effect (unrelated–semantically related)	**–94**	**–305**	**49**	**–87**	**–161**	**–35**

significance [$F(2,50) = 8.104, p = .001$]. The interaction between Prime Type and Bilingual Group approached significance [$F(4,5830) = 20.772, p = .000$]. The Relatedness and Bilingual Group interaction was significant [$F(2,5835) = 29.063, p = .000$]. The three-way interaction between Relatedness, Prime Language and Bilingual Group approached significance [$F(2,5835) = 24.246, p = .000$]. There was another significant interaction between Prime Type, Prime Language and Bilingual Group [$F(4,5829) = 32.229$, $p = .000$]. The Cognate Status, Prime Language and Bilingual Group interaction also approached significance [$F(2,5831) = 28.473$, $p = .000$]. As in the previous experiments, planned comparisons were conducted to examine individual differences of the three groups of bilinguals (see Table 2). The overall results revealed shorter naming latencies for Early High Proficient (846 ms)

Table 2. Mean RTs (ms) and percentage of errors for cognate and non-cognate targets for all three bilingual groups as a function of Prime Type and Prime Language in Experiment 2

	Prime Language/Bilingual Group					
	Bodo			**Assamese**		
	Early	**Late High**	**Late Low**	**Early**	**Late High**	**Late Low**
Prime Type	**RT (Error %)**	**RT (Error %)**	**RT (Error %)**	**RT (Error %)**	**RT (Error %)**	**RT (Error %)**
Cognate						
Identical	728 (2.8)	802 (0)	864 (0)	703 (1.4)	689 (0)	828 (5.6)
Semantically related	895 (4.3)	903 (0)	1014 (5.6)	860 (4.3)	894 (0)	885 (5.6)
Unrelated	884 (2.9)	961 (0)	936 (5.6)	888 (2.9)	801 (11.1)	847 (5.6)
Identity effect (unrelated–identical)	**156**	**159**	**72**	**185**	**112**	**19**
Semantic effect (unrelated–semantically related)	**−11**	**58**	**−78**	**28**	**−93**	**−38**
Non-cognate						
Identical	744 (0)	622 (0)	739 (0)	722 (1.9)	823 (0)	949 (27.3)
Semantically related	977 (9)	967 (18.2)	1110 (13.6)	941 (0)	955 (9)	943 (18.2)
Unrelated	913 (0)	911 (0)	918 (9)	895 (3.6)	851 (0)	916 (13.6)
Identity effect (unrelated-identical)	**169**	**289**	**179**	**173**	**28**	**−33**
Semantic effect (unrelated-semantically related)	**−64**	**−56**	**−192**	**−46**	**−104**	**−27**

and Late High Proficient (848 ms) bilinguals than Late Low Proficient (912 ms) bilinguals.

In the error analyses, no main effect of Relatedness was observed [$F < 1$]. The main effect of Cognate Status was marginal [$F(1,107) = 2.638, p = .002$]. Participants made greater errors to non-cognate targets than to cognate targets. The main effect of Prime Type was significant [$F(2,107) = 7.734, p = .000$]. Errors were numerous more in the semantic and unrelated primes than the identity primes. However, the main effect of Prime Language was not significant. The percentage of errors was similar in primes from both languages. The main effect of Bilingual Group was significant [$F(2,50) = 9.216$, $p = .001$]. Moreover, the interaction between Prime Type and Bilingual Group approached significance [$F(4,5830) = 6.524$, $p = .000$]. All other comparisons were not significant (all Fs < 1). The overall pattern of results of the Experiment 1 and 2 suggest that bilingual language production is non-selective in nature. However, the blocked naming task might have allowed participants to focus their lexical search on the target language only. To further test the issue of language selectivity, the authors investigated primed picture naming in a mixed context.

Experiment 3: Mixed Picture Naming in L1 and L2

The participants and stimuli used in Experiment 1 and 2 were used in this experiment as well. However, the authors introduced the following changes to the procedure: (1) the primes of both languages appeared simultaneously, (2) a colored (red or blue) dot was used as fixation point to cue the response language (*red* for Bodo and *blue* for Assamese); (3) participants named the experimental pictures in both Bodo and Assamese depending on the language cue. Each trial began with a brief fixation point of 500 ms, which was followed by a blank of 200 ms. The language cue (a red or blue dot) then appeared on the screen for 250 ms. Next two strings of letters in Bodo and Assamese appeared simultaneously, one above the other followed by the target picture for a maximum of 2,000 ms.

Results

A mixed-effects analysis on the reaction time data revealed a significant main effect of Cognate Status [$F(1,54) = 6.643$, $p = .013$]. Cognate pictures (1027 ms) were named faster than non-cognate pictures (1092 ms). A reliable effect of Prime Type was observed [$F(2,54) = 4.997, p = .010$]. The main effect of Target Language approached significance [$F(1,5283) = 25.097, p = .000$]. The main effect of Bilingual Group was also found to be significant [$F(2,51) = 30.761$, $p = .000$]. The two-way interaction between Cognate Status and Target Language approached significance [$F(1,5280) = 43.393$, $p = .000$]. The Cognate Status and Bilingual Group interaction approached significance [$F(2,5275) = 10.844, p = .000$]. The interaction between Prime Type and Target Language was also found to be significant [$F(2,5280) = 45.603, p = .000$]. The Prime Type and Bilingual Group interaction approached significance [$F(4,5268) = 18.970, p = .000$]. Another significant two-way interaction was observed between Target Language and Bilingual Group [$F(2,5265) = 49.163, p = .000$]. The three-way interaction between Cognate Status, Prime Type and Bilingual Group approached significance [$F(4,5269) = 22.761, p = .000$]. The Cognate Status, Prime Type and Target Language interaction approached significance [$F(2,5280) = 36.561, p = .000$]. Another significant interaction was observed between Cognate Status, Target Language and Bilingual Group [$F(2,5262) = 6.925$), $p = .001$]. Finally, the Prime Type, Target Language and Bilingual Group also approached significance [$F(4,5262) = 9.145, p = .000$]. Planned comparisons were conducted to examine the individual differences of the three groups of bilinguals (see Table 3). The results revealed a pattern different than the blocked picture naming experiments. The overall naming latencies of Early High Proficient (1022 ms) and Late Low Proficient bilinguals (1020 ms) were shorter than Late High Proficient bilinguals (1135 ms).

A mixed-effects analysis of the error data did not show a main effect of Relatedness [$F < 1$]. The main effect of Cognate Status did not reach significance [$F < 1$]. Participants made similar number of errors to cognate targets and non-cognate targets. The main effect of Prime Type was not significant [$F < 1$]. The main effect of Target Language also did not reach significant [$F < 1$]. However, the main effect of Bilingual Group approached significance [$F(2,51) = 11.761, p = .000$]. Errors were numerous more for the low proficient group than the high proficient groups. Moreover, the interaction between Prime Type and Target Language was also found to be significant [$F(2,5280) = 8.034, p = .000$]. All other comparisons were not significant (all Fs < 1).

Discussion

In Experiment 1, when pictures were preceded by words that were identical to their names, reaction times of the participants were faster for both same-language and different-language pairs. That is, identity priming was found for both same-language and different-language pairs when pictures were preceded by words that were identical (versus unrelated) to their names. However, facilitation effect was larger for same-language pairs. On the other hand, participants showed longer reaction times when pictures were preceded by semantically related (versus unrelated) words. Experiment 2 showed results similar to Experiment 1, i.e., facilitation for identity primes and inhibition for semantic primes. Experiment 3, showed that when the primes appeared simultaneously and when the task was not blocked by the language

Table 3. Mean RTs (ms) and percentage of errors for cognate and non-cognate targets for all three bilingual groups as a function of Prime Type and Target Language in Experiment 3

	Target Language					
	Bodo			Assamese		
	Early	Late High	Late Low	Early	Late High	Late Low
Prime Type	RT (Error %)	RT (Error %)	RT (Error %)	RT (Error %)	RT (Error %)	RT (Error %)
Cognate						
Identical	971 (7.4)	1033 (15)	896 (17.5)	1030 (8.6)	1032 (5)	1019 (25)
Semantically related	991 (8.6)	1066 (20)	875 (17.5)	1048 (7.2)	1149 (20)	1074 (22.5)
Unrelated	989 (6.5)	1148 (20)	922 (30)	1025 (7.2)	1107 (10)	1102 (22.5)
Identity effect (unrelated–identical)	**18**	**115**	**26**	**−5**	**75**	**83**
Semantic effect (unrelated–semantically related)	**−2**	**82**	**117**	**−23**	**−42**	**28**
Non-cognate						
Identical	1062 (5.5)	1304 (0)	998 (22.7)	1003 (10.6)	932 (9)	913 (31.8)
Semantically related	969 (10.6)	1394 (18.2)	1150 (22.7)	1095 (6)	1268 (18.2)	1263 (27.3)
Unrelated	1041 (7.6)	1028 (27.3)	924 (36.4)	1042 (9)	1154 (9)	1104 (22.7)
Identity effect (unrelated–identical)	**−21**	**−276**	**−74**	**39**	**222**	**191**
Semantic effect (unrelated–semantically related)	**72**	**−366**	**−226**	**−53**	**−114**	**−159**

of response, more cross-language interaction was observed. However, although an overall identity effect was observed, it was not consistent in all conditions. Moreover, it was surprising that the semantic effect was found to be modulated by the cognate status of the pictures—facilitation was observed for cognate pictures, whereas, inhibition was found for non-cognate pictures.

Another interesting observation of the study was that the size of the facilitation or interference effects was found to be modulated by the AoA and proficiency of the bilinguals. Results can be interpreted in terms of production models. The facilitation for the identity primes, when the prime was the name of the picture in both same- and different-language pairs can be interpreted within a lexical model that assumes that words of both the target and non-target language are considered for lexical selection and can, therefore, compete for selection. Moreover, the interference effect which was observed for semantically related primes in the same-language vs. different-language conditions can also be interpreted with a model that supports language non-selective access. However, the results of the mixed condition were complex which makes it difficult to ascertain at this point. The interpretation of the data emerging from the experiments is complex as well and equivocal at times. At this point, it is difficult to ascertain precisely how the different factors interact. The authors further investigate this issue in the next series of experiments, where Bodo–Assamese bilinguals were asked to name a set of pictures presented with a superimposed word.

Experiment 4: Blocked Picture Naming in L2

Method

Participants

Fifty-five Bodo–Assamese bilingual speakers with an average age 29.7 ($SD = 4.3$) years participated in this experiment. Analyses of the self-report data and scores of the objective naming show results similar to the results of the participants in Experiment 1, 2 and 3.

Stimuli

The stimuli remained the same.

Procedure

Each trial had the following structure. First, a fixation point (a plus sign) was shown in the center of the screen for 500 ms, followed by a blank interval of 200 ms. Then the picture and the word were presented for 2,000 ms. If a response was not provided within 2,000 ms, the next trial started automatically.

Results

A mixed-effects analysis of the reaction time data showed the following effects: A significant effect of Relatedness was observed [$F(1,110) = 19.193$, $p = .000$]. Participants named related distracters (1088 ms) slowly than unrelated distracters (980 ms). The main effect of Distracter Type was significant [$F(2,107) = 10.286$, $p = .000$]. There was also a significant main effect of Distracter Language [$F(1,107) = 9.655$, $p = .002$]. Naming latencies to same-language Assamese distracters (1017 ms) were faster than different-language Bodo distracters (1087 ms). No significant effects were observed for the variables Cognate Status and Bilingual Group [Fs < 1]. Table 5.25 shows the mean reaction times and percentage of errors as a function of Cognate Status, Distracter Type, and Distracter Language. Of crucial interest in this experiment is the interaction between Relatedness and Bilingual Group. This interaction was significant [$F(2,4804) = 52.675$, $p = .000$]. Another significant interaction was between Distracter Type and Bilingual Group [$F(4,4789) = 28.456$, $p = .000$]. There was a marginally significant interaction between Distracter Type and Distracter Language [$F(2,107) = 4.558$, $p = .013$] and between Distracter Language and Bilingual Group [$F(2,4794) = 4.406$, $p = .012$]. Apart from the significant two-way interactions, the result of the present study also revealed some significant three-way interactions. The Relatedness, Distracter Language and Bilingual Group interaction was significant [$F(2,4799) = 17.528$, $p = .000$]. The interaction between Relatedness, Cognate Status and Bilingual Group approached significance [$F(2,4797) = 14.692$, $p = .000$]. The Distracter, Distracter Language and Bilingual Group interaction was also significant [$F(4,4796) = 12.510$, $p = .000$]. Finally, another significant interaction was observed between Cognate Status, Distracter Type and Bilingual Group [$F(4,4794) = 9.998$, $p = .000$]. Planned comparisons were conducted to examine the individual differences of the three groups of bilinguals (see Table 4). The results revealed that the overall naming latencies of Late Low Proficient bilinguals (1017 ms) were shorter than Early High Proficient (1056 ms) and Late High Proficient bilinguals (1083 ms).

The analysis of error data did not show a main effect of Relatedness [$F < 1$]. The main effect of Cognate Status was marginal [$F(1,107) = 2.115$, $p = .032$]. Participants made greater errors in cognate targets than non-cognate targets. Moreover errors were numerous more for the different-language distracters than the same-language distracters. The main effect of Bilingual Group was not significant [$F < 1$]. There was no difference in errors among the bilingual groups. All other comparisons were non-significant (all Fs < 1). The goal of the next experiment was to explore lexical retrieval processes when Bodo–Assamese bilinguals performed a picture-word interference task in their native language, Bodo.

Table 4. Mean RTs (ms) and percentage of errors for cognate and non-cognate targets for all three bilingual groups as a function of Distracter Type and Distracter Language in Experiment 4

	Distracter Language/Bilingual Group					
	Bodo			**Assamese**		
	Early	**Late High**	**Late Low**	**Early**	**Late High**	**Late Low**
Distracter Type	**RT (Error %)**	**RT (Error %)**	**RT (Error %)**	**RT (Error %)**	**RT (Error %)**	**RT (Error %)**
Cognate						
Identical	1147 (22.2)	1198 (28.9)	1116 (16.7)	968 (33.3)	1050 (11.1)	974 (0)
Semantically related	1061 (44.4)	1194 (37.8)	1032 (27.8)	1076 (33.3)	1109 (28.9)	1139 (27.8)
Unrelated	1031 (25.9)	987 (24.4)	1034 (5.6)	1060 (33.3)	992 (26.7)	852 (5.6)
Identity effect (unrelated–identical)	**–116**	**–211**	**–82**	**92**	**–58**	**–122**
Semantic effect (unrelated–semantically related)	**–30**	**–207**	**2**	**–16**	**–117**	**–287**
Non-cognate						
Identical	1124 (18.2)	1177 (36.4)	1201 (22.7)	972 (36.4)	988 (7.3)	1006 (0)
Semantically related	1092 (33.3)	1187 (21.8)	1061 (22.7)	1057 (30.3)	1101 (29)	1077 (13.6)
Unrelated	1045 (18.2)	1035 (7.3)	867 (9)	1055 (15.2)	979 (12.7)	840 (9)
Identity effect (unrelated–identical)	**–79**	**–142**	**–334**	**83**	**–9**	**–166**
Semantic effect (unrelated–semantically related)	**–47**	**–152**	**–194**	**–2**	**–122**	**–237**

Experiment 5: Blocked Picture Naming in L1

The method used in Experiment 4 was used in this experiment as well.

Table 5. Mean RTs (ms) and percentage of errors for cognate and non-cognate targets for all three bilingual groups as a function of Distracter Type and Distracter Language in Experiment 5

	Distracter Language/Bilingual Group					
	Bodo			**Assamese**		
	Early	**Late High**	**Late Low**	**Early**	**Late High**	**Late Low**
Distracter Type	**RT (Error %)**	**RT (Error %)**	**RT (Error %)**	**RT (Error %)**	**RT (Error %)**	**RT (Error %)**
Cognate						
Identical	909 (14.8)	1022 (15.6)	992 (5.6)	923 (14.8)	938 (17.8)	914 (11.1)
Semantically related	1122 (25.9)	1039 (28.9)	925 (11.1)	949 (29.6)	986 (15.6)	842 (11.1)
Unrelated	1014 (33.3)	1011 (22.2)	955 (11.1)	987 (22.2)	904 (13.3)	760 (5.6)
Identity effect (unrelated–identical)	**105**	**−11**	**−37**	**64**	**−34**	**−154**
Semantic effect (unrelated–semantically related)	**−108**	**−28**	**30**	**38**	**−82**	**−82**
Non-cognate						
Identical	841 (0)	991 (12.7)	1014 (13.6)	997 (9)	950 (16.4)	1070 (9)
Semantically related	1046 (27.3)	975 (12.7)	1059 (9)	1055 (24.2)	954 (10.9)	997 (13.6)
Unrelated	1056 (12.1)	1012 (9)	886 (13.6)	954 (21.2)	931 (10.9)	938 (13.6)
Identity effect (unrelated–identical)	**215**	**21**	**−128**	**−43**	**−19**	**−132**
Semantic effect (unrelated–semantically related)	**10**	**37**	**−173**	**−101**	**−23**	**−59**

Results

A mixed-effects analysis was run on the reaction time data which did not reveal a main effect of Relatedness [$F < 1$]. No main effects of Cognate Status, Distracter Type and Bilingual Group were observed [Fs < 1]. However, a marginal effect of Distracter Language was observed [$F(1,105) = 4.026$, $p = .023$]. The interaction between Distracter Type and Bilingual Group approached significance [$F(4,4789) = 50.234$, $p = .000$]. The Cognate Status and Bilingual Group interaction approached significance [$F(2,5335) = 41.176$, $p = .000$]. The interaction between Distracter Language and Bilingual Group was also significant [$F(2,5331) = 6.629$, $p = .001$]. The three-way interaction between Distracter Type, Distracter Language and Bilingual Group approached significance [$F(4,5332) = 10.762$, $p = .000$]. The Cognate Status, Distracter Language and Bilingual Group interaction was significant [$F(2,5332) = 7.755$, $p = .000$]. Finally, a significant interaction was observed between Cognate Status, Distracter Type and Bilingual Group [$F(4,5331) = 5.841$, $p = .000$]. Planned comparisons were conducted to examine the individual differences of the three groups of bilinguals (see Table 5). The results revealed that the overall reaction times of the Late Low Proficient bilinguals (946 ms) were faster than the Late High Proficient (976 ms) and Early High Proficient bilinguals (988 ms).

A mixed-effects analysis of error data did not show a main effect of Relatedness [$F < 1$]. The main effect of Cognate Status was marginal [$F(1,107) = 2.734$, $p = .018$]. Participants made greater errors in cognate targets than non-cognate targets. The main effect of Distracter Type was significant [$F(2,107) = 8.2472$, $p = .000$]. Greater errors were observed in semantic distracters than identity and unrelated distracters. Moreover, errors were numerous more for the different-language distracters than the same-language distracters. This effect of Distracter Language was significant. The main effect of Bilingual Group was not significant [$F < 1$], indicating that there was no difference among three bilingual groups. All other comparisons were non-significant (all Fs < 1). In the next experiment, the authors assess whether the blocked task might have allowed participants to focus their lexical search on one language and minimize the interfering effect of competing lexical nodes in the non-response lexicon by investigating the performance of the participants in a mixed task.

Experiment 6: Mixed Picture Naming in L1 And L2

Participants and stimuli used in Experiment 4 and 5 were used in this experiment as well. The procedure of the mixed-language picture naming task was identical to that of Experiment 3 with the exception that in this task the distracter words were superimposed with the pictures.

Results

A mixed-effects analysis was run on the reaction time data which revealed a significant main effect of Target Language [$F(1,5100) = 30.895$, $p = .000$]. The main effect of Cognate Status approached significance [$F(1,53) = 13.575$, $p = .001$]. There was significant main effect of Bilingual Group [$F(2,51) = 10.836$,

p = .000]. The interaction between Distracter Type and Bilingual Group reached significance [$F(4,5101)$ = 5.895, p = .000].The Target Language and Bilingual Group interaction was also found to be significant [$F(2,5097)$ = 7.285, p = .001]. The three-way interaction among Cognate Status, Distracter Type and Target Language approached significance [$F(2,5098)$ = 13.686, p = .000]. The Distracter Type, Target Language and Bilingual Group were found to be significant [$F(4,5094)$ = 12.920, p = .000]. Finally, another significant interaction was observed among Cognate Status, Distracter Language and Bilingual Group [$F(4,5100)$ = 6.796, p = .000]. Planned comparisons were conducted to examine the individual differences of the three groups of bilinguals (see Table 6). As in the previous experiments, the results revealed that the overall reaction times of the Late Low Proficient bilinguals (984 ms) were faster than the Late High Proficient (1018 ms) and Early High Proficient bilinguals (1103 ms).

The analysis of the error data did not show a main effect of Relatedness [$F < 1$]. The main effect of Cognate Status did not reach significance [$F < 1$]. Participants made similar number of errors in cognate targets and non-cognate targets. The main effect of Distracter Type was not significant [$F < 1$]. However, errors were numerous in Bodo targets than Assamese targets. This effect of Target Language was significant [$F(1,5100)$ = 10.783, p = .000]. Moreover, the main effect of Bilingual Group was significant [$F(2,51)$ = 9.836, p = .001]. Errors were numerous in the high proficient groups than the low proficient group. The interaction between Cognate Status and Bilingual Group approached significance [$F(2,5102)$ = 13.496, p = .000]. All other comparisons were not significant (all Fs < 1).

Discussion

The identity distracters exhibited different results for the blocked and mixed conditions. No facilitation was found in the Experiment 4 when the target language was the L2 with one exception. Only the Early High Proficient group showed significant facilitation in the same-language distracter condition. In Experiment 5, facilitation was found for only same-language identity distracters. Only Early High Proficient group exhibited significant facilitation for both cognate and non-cognate pictures. The results of Experiment 6 produced facilitative effect for identity distracters in both response languages. The identity effect was observed only with Early High Proficient group which suggests that different types of bilinguals employ different processing mechanisms. The results of the semantic distracters demonstrated similar results in all three experiments. Semantic interference was obtained for both same-language and different-language distracters, replicating previous studies using high proficient bilinguals (e.g., Ehri & Ryan, 1980; Mägiste, 1984b). These effects are robust, having been replicated in the three experiments in a variety of conditions (e.g., blocked

Table 6. Mean RTs (ms) and percentage of errors for cognate and non-cognate targets for all three bilingual groups as function of Distracter Type and Target Language in Experiment 6

	Target Language					
	Bodo			**Assamese**		
Distracter Type	**Early**	**Late High**	**Late Low**	**Early**	**Late High**	**Late Low**
	RT (Error %)	**RT (Error %)**	**RT (Error %)**	**RT (Error %)**	**RT (Error %)**	**RT (Error %)**
Cognate						
Identical	1049 (14.8)	1058 (20)	890 (11.1)	1032 (7.4)	986 (20)	887 (11.1)
Semantically related	1094 (33.3)	949 (28.9)	905 (11.1)	1184 (25.9)	996 (17.8)	877 (5.6)
Unrelated	1030 (25.9)	1022 (22.2)	936 (16.7)	1108 (22.2)	1006 (15.6)	871 (5.6)
Identity effect (unrelated–identical)	**−19**	**−38**	**46**	**76**	**20**	**−16**
Semantic effect (unrelated–semantically related)	**−64**	**73**	**31**	**−76**	**10**	**−6**
Non-cognate						
Identical	1085 (12.1)	1001 (23.6)	982 (13.6)	1145 (24.2)	1039 (16.4)	1149 (18.2)
Semantically related	1100 (24.2)	1008 (20)	1102 (9)	1154 (30.3)	1104 (16.4)	978 (22.7)
Unrelated	1056 (30.3)	983 (25.5)	1059 (13.6)	1196 (21.2)	1061 (16.4)	1170 (22.7)
Identity effect (unrelated–identical)	**−29**	**−18**	**77**	**51**	**22**	**21**
Semantic effect (unrelated–semantically related)	**−44**	**−25**	**−43**	**42**	**−43**	**192**

vs. mixed language naming) and both response languages (Bodo and Assamese). However, two differences were observed in the same and different-language pairs. The facilitation effect was *larger* in same-language pairs than different-language pairs. Furthermore, the results of the study demonstrate that the relative proficiency in the two languages influences the size of the facilitative or inhibitive effects, in accordance with the findings of Mägiste (1984b). The stronger non-target language, the larger chance it will permeate in processing the target language.

The results can be discussed in terms of three types of production models introduced in the Introduction section. The results of the identity effect can be explained by the language non-specific selection hypothesis. To illustrate, the Bodo–Assamese pair मोसौ 'cow'–গ'ৰু '*cow*' can be taken as example. In the identity condition, the picture *cow* will highly activate Assamese lexical node 'গ'ৰু', which would interfere with the selection of the target 'मोसौ' in the Bodo lexicon. The lexical node 'গ'ৰু' is highly activated because, it receives activation from the picture *cow* and the written stimulus 'গ'ৰু', which results in interference. The semantic interference effect which was found in bilingual picture–word naming tasks would seem to indicate that the lexical entries of two languages would compete for selection and therefore, can also be explained by the language non-selective hypothesis. An example of this type of stimuli is given by the Bodo–Assamese pair मोसौ 'cow'–ম'হ 'buffalo'. In the semantic distracter condition, the picture of *cow* will activate its semantic representation and its associated lexical nodes in both languages ('मोसौ' and 'গ'ৰু'). Some activation is also sent to semantically related lexical nodes in the two languages ('मैसो' and 'ম'হ'). In the same way, the distracter word ম'হ also activates its semantic representation and its associated lexical and semantically related nodes in both languages. Thus, the lexical node 'ম'হ' in the Assamese lexicon is highly activated. If lexical nodes in both Bodo and Assamese lexicons compete for selection, ম'হ would interfere with the selection of the Bodo response "मोसौ." Therefore, the finding of identity facilitation and semantic inhibition is consistent with the hypothesis of *language non-specific selection.*

FUTURE RESEARCH DIRECTIONS

The present study has added to theory by providing not only a more detailed explanation of how language processing in bilinguals happens but has also attempted to explain the discrepancy in the results of the previous studies by controlling various experimental manipulations. However, the authors have only considered the question of how a bilingual's languages are processed at word and meaning levels. In the future, research focusing on the syntactical aspect of being a bilingual will be able to answer whether language non-selective access generalizes more contextualized language use, for example when words are part of meaningful sentences or when words are spoken aloud and so it reveals information about the word's language.

CONCLUSION

The primary goal of the study was to determine whether lexical access is language-selective or language-non-selective and what factors determine the activation and selectivity of languages. The study investigated how manipulations of content at different levels of representation influence word production by measuring naming latencies to pictures preceded by words primes and pictures superimposed with words. Several behavioural experiments were designed to examine the nature of bilingual lexical processing in a previously unexamined different-script language pair (Bodo–Assamese). The broad hypothesis was that lexical representations from the first language (L1) are accessed during processing of words from L2 and vice versa. The findings of the study provide evidence for language non-selective activation. However, the evidence does not indicate whether only lemma selection or also phonological encoding is language non-selective. The authors obtained semantic interference-effect not only when the semantic prime preceded the picture but also when the semantic distracter coincided with the picture. Interestingly, the same two studies showed completely different results for identity condition. The effect of the identity prime was facilitative when it preceded the picture. On the other hand, the effect of the identity distracter which was superimposed with the picture was inhibitive rather that facilitative. For example, it slowed down the picture naming response. Thus, the interaction between SOA and the type of prime or distracter can be understood if various processing stages and their order are considered in both tasks in which two processes operate in parallel—processing the context word and naming the picture. Taken together, although the results of the present study provides evidence in support of language non-selective lexical access, the findings suggest that there are complex interactions among L2 AoA and proficiency level, form similarity across languages (i.e. cognate status), and relationship between words.

REFERENCES

Bajo, M.-T. (1988). Semantic facilitation with picture and words. *Journal of Experimental Psychology. Learning, Memory, and Cognition*, *14*(4), 579–589. doi:10.1037/0278-7393.14.4.579 PMID:2972797

Bajo, M. T., Puerta-Melguizo, M. C., & Macizo, P. (2003). The locus of semantic interference in picture naming. *Psicológica (Valencia)*, *24*, 31–55. doi:10.1037/a0033745

Biggs, T. C., & Marmurek, H. H. (1990). Picture and word naming: Is facilitation due to processing overlap? *The American Journal of Psychology, 103*(1), 81–110. doi:10.2307/1423260

Blackford, T., Holcomb, P. J., Grainger, J., & Kuperberg, G. R. (2012). A funny thing happened on the way to articulation: N400 attenuation despite behavioral interference in picture naming. *Cognition, 123*(1), 84–99. doi:10.1016/j.cognition.2011.12.007 PMID:22245030

Carr, T. H., McCauley, C., Sperber, R. D., & Parmelee, C. M. (1982). Words, pictures, and priming: On semantic activation, conscious identification, and the automaticity of nformation processing. *Journal of Experimental Psychology. Human Perception and Performance, 8*(6), 757–777. doi:10.1037/0096-1523.8.6.757 PMID:6218234

Chauncey, K., Holcomb, P. J., & Grainger, J. (2009). Primed picture naming within and across languages: An ERP investigation. *Cognitive, Affective & Behavioral Neuroscience, 3*(3), 286–303. doi:10.3758/CABN.9.3.286 PMID:19679764

Colomé, A. (2001). Lexical activation in bilinguals' speech production: Language-specific or language-independent? *Journal of Memory and Language, 45*(4), 721–736. doi:10.1006/jmla.2001.2793

Costa, A., & Caramazza, A. (1999). Is lexical selection in bilingual speech production language-specific? Further evidence from Spanish–English and English–Spanish bilinguals. *Bilingualism: Language and Cognition, 2*(3), 231–244. doi:10.1017/S1366728999000334

Costa, A., Caramazza, A., & Sebastián-Gallés, N. (2000). The cognate facilitation effect: Implications for models of lexical access. *Journal of Experimental Psychology: Learning, Memory, and Cognition, 26*, 1283–1296. doi: 1037TO278-7393.26.5.1283

Costa, A., Colomé, A., Gómez, O., & Sebastián–Gallés, N. (2003). Another look at cross-language competition in bilingual speech production: Lexical and phonological factors. *Bilingualism: Language and Cognition, 6*(3), 167–179. doi:10.1017/S1366728903001111

Costa, A., Miozzo, M., & Caramazza, A. (1999). Lexical selection in bilinguals: Do words in the bilingual's two lexicons compete for selection? *Journal of Memory and Language, 41*(3), 365–397. doi:10.1006/jmla.1999.2651

Durso, F. T., & Johnson, M. K. (1979). Facilitation in naming and categorizing repeated pictures and words. *Journal of Experimental Psychology. Human Learning and Memory, 5*(5), 449–459. doi:10.1037/0278-7393.5.5.449

Ehri, L. C., & Ryan, E. B. (1980). Performance of bilinguals in a picture-word interference task. *Journal of Psycholinguistic Research*, *9*(3), 285–302. doi:10.1007/BF01067243 PMID:7391998

Frenck, C., & Pynte, J. (1987). Semantic representations and surface forms: A look at across-language priming in bilinguals. *Journal of Psycholinguistic Research*, *16*(4), 383–396. doi:10.1007/BF01069290

Glaser, W. R., & Dungelhoff, F. J. (1984). The time course of picture-word interference. *Journal of Experimental Psychology. Human Perception and Performance*, *10*(5), 640–654. doi:10.1037/0096-1523.10.5.640 PMID:6238124

Gollan, T. H., & Acenas, L. A. (2004). What is TOT? Cognate and translation effects on tip-of-the-tongue states in Spanish–English and Tagalog–English bilinguals. *Journal of Experimental Psychology. Learning, Memory, and Cognition*, *30*(1), 246–269. doi:10.1037/0278-7393.30.1.246 PMID:14736310

Hermans, D., Bongaerts, T., De Bot, K., & Schreuder, R. (1998). Producing words in a foreign language: Can speakers prevent interference from their first language? *Bilingualism: Language and Cognition*, *1*(3), 213–229. doi:10.1017/S1366728998000364

Hoshino, N. (2006). *A psycholinguistic study of native language constraints on speaking words in a second language* (Doctoral dissertation). Pennsylvania State University. Retrieved from https://etda.libraries.psu.edu/paper/7316/

Irwin, D. I., & Lupker, S. J. (1983). Semantic priming of pictures and words: A levels of processing approach. *Journal of Verbal Learning and Verbal Behavior*, *22*(1), 45–60. doi:10.1016/S0022-5371(83)80005-X

Kaur, S. (2016). *Lexical representation and processing in Bodo–Assamese bilinguals* (Unpublished doctoral thesis). Indian Institute of Technology Guwahati, India.

Kim, K. H., Relkin, N. R., Lee, K.-M., & Hirch, J. (1997). Distinct cortical areas associated with native and second languages. *Nature*, *388*(6638), 171–174. doi:10.1038/40623 PMID:9217156

Kroll, J. F., Dijkstra, A., Janssen, N., & Schreifers, H. (2000). *Selecting the language in which to speak: Experiments on lexical access in bilingual production*. Paper presented at the 41st Annual meeting on the Psychonomic Society, New Orleans, LA.

La Heij, W., Dirkx, J., & Kramer, J. (1990). Categorical interference and associative priming in picture naming. *British Journal of Psychology*, *81*(4), 511–525. doi:10.1111/j.2044-8295.1990.tb02376.x

Levelt, W. J., Roelofs, A., & Meyer, A. S. (1999). A theory of lexical access in speech production. *Behavioral and Brain Sciences*, *22*(01), 1–75. doi:10.1017/S0140525X99001776 PMID:11301520

Lupker, S. J. (1982). The role of phonetic and orthographic similarity in picture-word interference. *Canadian Journal of Psychology*, *36*(3), 349–367. doi:10.1037/h0080652 PMID:7172126

Mägiste, E. (1984b). Stroop tasks and dichotic translation: The development of interference patterns in bilinguals. *Journal of Experimental Psychology. Learning, Memory, and Cognition*, *10*, 304–315. doi:10.1037/0278-7393.10.2.304

Mägiste, E. (1985). Development of intra- and interlingual interference in bilinguals. *Journal of Psycholinguistic Research*, *14*, 137–154. doi:10.1007/BF01067626

Rodriguez-Fornelss, A., Van der Lugt, A., Rotte, M., Britti, B., Heinze, H. J., & Münte, T. F. (2005). Second language interferes with word production in fluent bilinguals: Brain potential and functional imaging evidence. *Journal of Cognitive Neuroscience*, *17*(3), 422–433. doi:10.1162/0898929053279559 PMID:15814002

Roelofs, A. (1992). A spreading-activation theory of lemma retrieval in speaking: Modeling attentional control in the Stroop task. *Psychological Review*, *110*, 88–125. doi:10.1037/0033-295X.110.1.88 PMID:12529058

Rosinski, R. R. (1977). Picture-word interference is semantically based. *Child Development*, *48*(2), 643–647. doi:10.2307/1128667

Rosinski, R. R., Golinkoff, R. M., & Kukish, K. S. (1975). Automatic semantic processing in a picture-word interference task. *Child Development*, *46*(1), 247–253. doi:10.2307/1128859

Schriefers, H., Meyer, A. S., & Levelt, W. J. (1990). Exploring the time course of lexical access in language production: Picture-word interference studies. *Journal of Memory and Language*, *29*(1), 86–102. doi:10.1016/0749-596X(90)90011-N

Silverberg, S., & Samuel, A. G. (2004). The effect of age of second language acquisition on the representation and processing of second language words. *Journal of Memory and Language*, *51*(3), 381–398. doi:10.1016/j.jml.2004.05.003

Smith, M. C., & Magee, L. E. (1980). Tracing the time course of picture-word processing. *Journal of Experimental Psychology. General*, *4*(4), 373–392. doi:10.1037/0096-3445.109.4.373 PMID:6449530

Sperber, R. D., McCauley, C., Ragain, R. D., & Weil, C. M. (1979). Semantic priming effects on picture and word processing. *Memory & Cognition*, *7*(5), 339–345. doi:10.3758/BF03196937

Starreveld, P. A., & La Heij, W. (1995). Semantic interference, orthographic facilitation, and their interaction in naming tasks. *Journal of Experimental Psychology. Learning, Memory, and Cognition*, *21*(3), 686–698. doi:10.1037/0278-7393.21.3.686

Starreveld, P. A., & La Heij, W. (1996). Time-course analysis of semantic and orthographic context effects in picture naming. *Journal of Experimental Psychology. Learning, Memory, and Cognition*, *22*(4), 896–918. doi:10.1037/0278-7393.22.4.896

Weber-Fox, C. M., & Neville, H. J. (1999). Functional neural subsystems are differentially affected by delays in second-language immersion: ERP and behavioral evidence in bilingual speakers. In D. Birdsong (Ed.), *New perspectives on the critical period for second language acquisition*. Mahwah, NJ: Lawrence Erlbaum.

Wuillemin, D., Richardson, B., & Lynch, J. (1994). Right hemisphere involvement in processing later-learned languages in multilinguals. *Brain and Language*, *46*(4), 620–636. doi:10.1006/brln.1994.1034 PMID:8044679

KEY TERMS AND DEFINITIONS

Bilingual: People who need and use two (or more) languages in their everyday lives.

Cognate: Translation equivalents similar in meaning and form.

Critical Period Hypothesis: The hypothesis that after a certain age the ability to acquire an L2 is greatly diminished or lost.

Non-Cognate: Translation equivalents similar in meaning only.

Non-Target Language: The language not in use in a specific setting.

Stimulus Onset Asynchrony (SOA): The time lapse between the presentation of prime and the presentation of target.

Target Language: The language to use in a specific setting.

APPENDIX 1

Table 7. Cognate picture targets and corresponding distracters and primes used in Experiment 1, 2, 3, 4, 5, and 6

	Identity			Semantically related			Control		
Picture	**Bodo**	**Assames e**	**Meanin g**	**Bodo**	**Assames e**	**Meanin g**	**Bodo**	**Assamese**	**Meanin g**
	गाद'	গাধ	*'donkey'*	गराय	ঘোঁৰা	*'horse'*	सिफुं	বাঁহী	*'flute'*
	ताला	তলা	*'lock'*	साबि	চাবি	*'key'*	दैहु	কলহ	*'pitcher'*
	फेसा	ফেঁচা	*'owl'*	बादामालि	বাদুলী	*'bat'*	रुवा	কুঠাৰ	*'axe'*
	गिटार	গীটাৰ	*'guitar'*	सिटार	চেতাৰ	*'sitar'*	बिबार	ফুল	*'flower'*
	खोलोम	কলম	*'pen'*	पेन्सिल	পেঞ্চিল	'pencil'	मुफुर	ভালুক	*'bear'*
	सिंह	সিংহ	*'lion'*	मोसा	বাঘ	*'tiger'*	संखि	নিমখ	*'salt'*
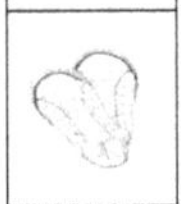	जुथा	জুতা	*'shoe'*	चेनडाल	চেণ্ডেল	*'sandal'*	गिसिब	বিছনী	*'fan'*
	गाजर	গাজৰ	*'carrot'*	मुला	মূলা	*'radish'*	अमा	গাহৰি	*'pig'*
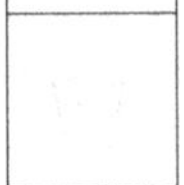	गिलाच	গিলাচ	*'glass'*	काप	কাপ	*'cup'*	सैमा	কুকুৰ	*'dog'*
	हांसो	হাঁহ	'duck'	दावजो	মুৰ্গী	*'hen'*	दिरु	ৰছী	*'rope'*

APPENDIX 2

Table 8. Non-cognate picture targets and corresponding distracters and primes used in Experiment 1, 2, 3, 4, 5, and 6

	Identity			Semantically related			Control		
Picture	Bodo	Assamese	Meaning	Bodo	Assamese	Meaning	Bodo	Assamese	Meaning
	आखाइ	হাত	*'hand'*	आसि	আঙুলী	*'finger'*	दै	পানী	*'water'*
	सान	সূৰ্য্য	*'sun'*	अखाफोर	চন্দ্ৰ	*'moon'*	हा	মাটি	*'soil'*
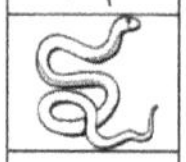	जिबौ	সাপ	*'snake'*	अजगर	অজগৰ	*'cobra'*	फानथाव	বেঙেনা	*'aubergine'*
	दाव	চৰাই	*'bird'*	गां	পাখি	*'wing'*	गइ	তামোল	*'betel nut'*
	मोसौ	গ'ৰু	*'cow'*	मैसो	ম'হ	*'buffalo'*	खुरै	বাতি	*'bowl'*
	बिजाब	কিতাপ	*'book'*	लेखा	বহী	*'copy'*	थै	তেজ	*'blood'*
	बिफां	গছ	*'tree'*	बिलाइ	পাত	*'leaf'*	लानजाइ	নেজ	*'tail'*
	दाबा	কটাৰী	*'knife'*	सिखा	দা	*'broadsword'*	हाजो	পাহাৰ	*'mountain'*
	मोख्रा	বান্দৰ	*'monkey'*	गरिला	গৰিলা	*'gorilla'*	अख्रां	আকাশ	*'sky'*
	न'	ঘৰ	*'house'*	देरा	কুটীৰ	*'cottage'*	बेगर	গুটি	*'seed'*

Chapter 9
Inclusion in Linguistic Education:
Neurolinguistics, Language, and Subject

Dionéla Motta Monte-Serrat
Universidade de Ribeirão Preto, Brazil

ABSTRACT

Education norms have been altered over the years; however, marginalization problems in linguistic education have not changed. A contemporary approach to linguistic education is taken in which individuals with brain injury or dysfunction are not observed isolatedly from the operations that structure them. This chapter is a study on the signification processes that are constituted during enunciation by subjects who, due to brain dysfunction, appropriate reality and produce conscience of themselves in a particular fashion. Linguistic monitoring articulated with neurolinguistics is suggested in order to promote rhythmic, lexical, and syntactic modifications in such subjects' discourse so as to place the significant chain in order as regards its oral or written production. Hence, subjects with brain dysfunction can develop authorship characteristics as concerns both language appropriation and the subjective aspect, thus showing unicity under the form of coherence: such subjects' creative imagination is imposed, ordinating and coordinating the content expressed.

INTRODUCTION

There is a concern in education about the fact that its regulatory norms are altered and that, in spite of such alterations, marginalization problems in linguistic education have not changed over the years. In this chapter, knowledge resulting from years of

DOI: 10.4018/978-1-5225-4009-0.ch009

research on social inclusion and, more recently, inclusion-related issues concerning language learning by children and youngsters with brain injury have been brought together. These are the reasons that have led to the articulation between the theoretical knowledge from neurolinguistics, the Theory of Discourse (Pêcheux, 1988) and the Theory of Literacy (Tfouni, 1992, 2005). The complexity of such articulation is focused on proposing that the concept of authorship can serve as a basis for building a contemporary view of linguistic education so that such view will become more responsive to the difficulties surrounding the topic.

This complex and interdisciplinary theoretical articulation is necessary to deconstruct the systematic look of bureaucratic educational evaluation processes that do not play their political role in society and are not involved with marginalized subjects. All this complexity is due to the presence of elements and forces of such processes that are linked in time and space and need to be evaluated under different perspectives. Trewhella (2016) says that interdisciplinary research can attain the "kind of predictive capability that could inform policy makers". The author states:

Policies that govern the hiring, promotion and allocation of resources often work against interdisciplinary research. If interdisciplinary research is to flourish in academia, then its reward systems have to recognize the different paces at which interdisciplinary research may proceed as well as the fact that it is often a team rather than an individual accomplishment. There is also a need for flexible organizational structures that can operate across discipline-focused departments (Trewhella: 2016).

In this chapter, we need the flexibility of the interdisciplinary because, in this investigation, we have different paces from those in most of the research conducted in this field. We are concerned about real linguistic inclusion that can improve the quality of life of the studied subjects.

The questions pursued in this study began with the investigation on the reason why less literate subjects are marginalized when they participate in literate events held by public institutions (Monte-Serrat, 2013). In later research, the social marginalization of children and youngsters with brain injury (hydrocephalus) who were awaiting surgery or had been operated on at a public hospital (University of São Paulo Medical School, FMRP-USP) was investigated. It was observed that the study on these children's physical limitations based only on the bias of neuroscience would be restricted to a materialistic perspective whose object rests on mechanistic conceptions of mental events.

Such restricted study perspective moves away from phenomena related to the subject that is defined as "self", and to a conscience, which must not be ignored in scientific investigation. An example that such materialistic perspective would bring frustrating results would be the fact that it is applied to the evaluation of children with hydrocephalus, who, due to their brain injury, are not able to develop mathematical thinking or logical reasoning. Baloyannisstates that, in spite of

experimental work and much speculation emphasizing the importance of connections between thalamic nuclei and the cortex of the brain's hemispheres and the developed thalamocortical recurrency, there is not a conclusive explanation of consciousness at the level of neural mechanisms, not even when analysing and tracing the interactions between nerve cells and the neurotransmitters associated with them (Baloyannis, [2009]2017, p. 1).

In Neurolinguistics, information processing and the sensory coding system are usually studied under the aspect of how vivid sensory experience arises in the sensory cortex of the brain or by "accepting the mechanisms of habituation, sensitization and classical conditioning, which has an obvious mechanistic profile" (Baloyannis [2009]2017, p. 1). One must not accommodate to predictable, "evidence-based studies which support a radical neuron doctrine and, in spite of the concept of neuronal plasticity, is materialistic rather than naturalistic" (op. cit.). With this regard, there would be social exclusion and, as stated by Baloyannis (op. cit.), it "leaves a substantial number of problems unsolved, particularly those concerning the inner life, the emotions [...] of human beings".

In this study, the longitudinal follow-up of a subject with hydrocephalus, under the observational participation method and for a period of a slightly longer period than two years, has brought the challenge of attempting to work around the language damage caused by brain injury (Monte-Serrat, 2014, 2015). Language, according to the Discourse Analysis Theory (Pêcheux, 1988), is the place where the "self" is constituted. During the period of collaborative research at IEL-UNICAMP, aspects of linguistic education were studied with attention to the particularities caused by brain injury.

Due to their learning difficulty, these individuals are located at one end of the discursive continuum (which goes from the first contact with writing to the sophisticated form of syllogistic reasoning) (Tfouni, 2005): the end of the least literate. Their position in the discursive chain prevents them from taking positions of a subject in society as such positions are reserved to more literate subjects.

The course of investigation pursued allowed for considering that the subjects of language or thought, whether showing brain injury/dysfunction or not, should not be observed in a systematic fashion, in isolation from the operations that structure them. It is also taken into account that, in each individual, previous processes and relations are developed differently. Such processes and relations are necessary for linguistic acquisition and are not confused with it. These processes constitute translinguistic practices in which language and the subject will configure only moments.

All pre-sign and pre-syntactical processes and relations studied by Neurolinguistics must not be disregarded in a study on language; hence, the importance of interdisciplinary work. They are mixed in a continuum related to the subject's constitution (the "self" who speaks); they operate in a synchronous fashion within the subject's signification process. These processes, which are different for each subject, are driven within the social practice field, in which the body is regarded as part of the process: different types of impulses are indistinctively combined in the practice that involves signification.

The study of these elements described along with the linguistic practices (oral and written discourse) of children with hydrocephalus leads us to consider that writing and speaking outline the way how these children perceive reality. Due to their condition, they are affected in their ability of comprehension and expression and, in this study, suggestions are given in order to minimize such phenomenon.

According to what has been pointed out so far, it can be stated that a comprehensive evaluation in the field of linguistic education must include all individuals, even those with brain injury. How can they all be included? Social inclusion is a practice that reaches beyond what is usually proposed by public policies (Monte Serrat, 2013), since the latter perform evaluations that are based on idealized subjects and discard those that do not fit into a pattern. In this chapter, we seek to use and expand concepts of the discourse theory (Pêcheux, 1988; Foucault:1967, [1963]1969, 1995, 1996, 2004) to address this issue differently from the traditional practice because it is understood that, according to Silva (2001), alphabetic writing is a culturally instituting place of the subject's discursive functions.

Instead of a quantitative approach to data or of tests based on an ideal standardized individual, which cannot possibly correspond to reality, observation of the subject is proposed by going even further: subjects whose bodies bear the condition of hydrocephalus are observed and, therefore, are not idealized bodies. These subjects with damaged brains feel, think, and have emotions, which are elements that can and must be considered in the research and evaluation of linguistic education. The discursive approach to the data in this study, in addition to not hygienizing the observed subjects' ways and desires, supports pluralities: this practice leaves behind that dead quantitative assessment and becomes an effective social work. This perspective, called "fourth-generation qualitative assessment" (Campos & Furtado, 2011), reinforces the

importance of thinking about evaluations as acts of world transformation, practices involved in discovering in order to transform, thus refuting shelf studies due to their cooling, silencing and paralyzing sense to individuals and organizations (Patton: 1997 apudSilva&Brandão: 2011, 143).

There is a consensus (Tfouni, 1992; Pêcheux, 1988) that the writing practice involves an important contemporary political struggle and, according to a UNICEF report (EBC, 2013), the fact that children with alterations in their bodies and in their body functions and structures have less access to resources and services is worrying. In that case, their basic rights of access to education and health are undermined. This report notes that the deprivations faced by these children perpetuate their condition of non-inclusion and prevent adequate public policies from being developed: writing for these children "has to do with being able to survive" (Haraway, 2014, p. 86).

The Discourse Theory to Observe the Subject and Not the Individual

Subject and individual are not considered to be synonymous in this work. The expression "individual" is used to refer to someone in an institutionalized context in order to play a role that is related to the functioning of the State. The individual is the one whose activities are permeated by law, which dictates a power/non-power according to an everyday interpretation of the Law. The individual is one who participates in a supposedly free and equal social relation in the capitalist mode of production. There is an "atomization", an ideological representation of society as a set of separate and free individuals (Miaille 1979, p. 111, emphasis added). This evidence that individuals are free and equal results from an ideological effect (Althusser, 1999; Haroche, 1992).

In this chapter, we work with the concept of subject as conceived by the theories of Discourse Analysis (Pêcheux, 1988; Foucault, 1967, [1963], 1969, 1995, 1996, 2004) and Literacy (Tfouni, 1992, 2005), thus dissolving the supposed equality embedded in the concept of individual. The work with the concept of subject as conceived according to discourse theory directs the study to an articulation with language, with oral or written discourse, with history and with ideology.

The discursive subject is not something predictable, measurable, and submissive to a universal and supposedly transparent language (the latter is presupposed in quantitative research). Pêcheux (1988) supports the concept of subject as a social place constituted by history and influenced by ideology, which will determine what can and what should be said. To Pêcheux, "individuals are 'interpellated' in speaking subjects"; they occupy their subject positions according to the social formation and discursive formations in which they participate (Pêcheux, 1988, p. 161), without realizing this process of interpellation.

The discursive perspective (Pêcheux: 1988) under study is very important because it admits that the subject is constituted and affected by language. It can be understood that he is not born ready, but is constituted the field of language (Elia, 2004). Thus, Discourse Analysis distances itself from the notion of a Cartesian subject who is the master of his actions and free will in order to work with the conception of a cleaved subject that is subjected, submitted to the unconscious and to social-historical conditions (Pêcheux, 1988, 2002; Tfouni, 2005). Finally, it works with a subject that is constituted along with meaning.

It is also pointed out that Discourse Analysis (DA) also deals with the unconscious, accepting concepts derived from psychoanalysis for the understanding of language. DA is considered to be a science because it encompasses three regions of knowledge, according to its general epistemological framework, postulated by Pêcheux and Fuchs (1997):

In our view, it [the epistemological framework] lies in the articulation of three regions of scientific knowledge:

1. Historical materialism, as a theory of social formations and their transformations, therein understood as the theory of ideologies;
2. Linguistics, as a theory of the syntactic mechanisms and of the enunciation process at the same time;
3. The discourse theory, as historical determination of the semantic processes.
4. It is also necessary to explain that these three regions are, in a sense, crossed and articulated by a theory of subjectivity (of a psychoanalytic nature) (Pêcheux& Fuchs:[1975] 1997,163-164, emphasis added).

In this chart, it is observed that DA is permeated by the psychoanalytic theory and, therefore, it does not concentrate only on the objective aspects of language. By focusing attention on the subjectivity that is expressed in language, the DA theory approaches Lacan's concepts, in the sense of distancing itself from the concept of language as being only a system through which the human being communicates his ideas, or as a human capacity to acquire and use complex communication systems. To Lacan ([1953] 1998), language is related to a body, and that body cannot be reduced only to the biological aspect. Language, according to Lacan, interferes in the formation of the self as a function of imagoes withdrawn from the other or from projective identifications (Roudinesco, 1998, p. 194).

Such structure of the self has its own psychological efficiency (Gaufey, 1998, p. 63), which will make the connection between the psychic and the biological (Gaufey, 1998, p. 74). Although the body, language and subject are factors of heterogeneous domains, it cannot be denied that there is a "psychic operation, by which the human being is constituted in an identification with his fellow beings" (Roudinesco, 1998, p. 194) under an unconscious process. The separation between the body and the being is structural, and this leads to the need for an organization or a construction that can function as a remedy by tying them in an illusorily organized space (Rivera, 2009, p. 1). It is believed that such organized space is language.

Linguistic Education for Social Inclusion: Subject and Meaning in the Discourse of Children With Learning Difficulties

The discourse study in this research evaluates the signification processes that are constituted during enunciation by subjects who, due to brain dysfunction, have difficulty in making arrangements that select and combine words. When such subjects' saying is observed, the particular way by which they produce signification, how they appropriate reality and produce conscience of themselves, of their place in the world and of their relationships with others are also observed.

Since the discourse theory emphasizes the socio-historical context in meaning production and, consequently, in the subject's constitution, it gives this study on hydrocephalic children a very peculiar character. Therefore, some conditions that are objects of study of neurolinguistics are considered in the evaluations on these children's language learning. Such conditions are, for instance: the fact that hydrocephalic children do not develop abstract thought, do not have motor coordination, are not capable of evaluating the course of time etc. Discussion on those children's learning goes beyond biological symptoms as well as beyond the processing of information and the sensory coding system. According to the discourse theory, discussion on the possibility of symbolization by the subject is required, since learning is interpreting, producing forms of signification, forms of conceiving the world, things and people; learning is entering symbolic reality (Padilha, 2000).

What has been so far observed is the prevalence of neurolinguistics research which, in the field of learning disabilities, follow a "know-how", that is, a model associated with the methodical anticipation of a project that aims to create an elaborate technical achievement. The results of such research have moved towards marginalization in the school context; at times that marginalization can be verified, but at others, the paradox of inclusion of the excluded arises (Guimarães, 2002).

Such "know-how" as a method for linguistic teaching is based on the logic of reason; it operates in the form of understanding things by establishing proportions, schemes and development phases. It is the prescriptive learning perspective, which excludes that which is personal and leads the researcher's look to lie strictly on what is measurable and verifiable, putting him to observe only behaviors and performances. In this case, particular ways of meaning production are discarded.

The DA theory by Pêcheux (1988) emphasizes that such research position creates a discontinuity in the "knowledge" developed under continuity (Pêcheux & Fichant: 1971, pp. 9-10) and provides a new "perfected" space for problems which is free of immeasurable issues. In this hygienized process of Neurolinguistics, which is disarticulated from problems and from the socio-historical context of the evaluated person, an idealized result is reached, which does not correspond to the reality of the difficulties faced by the subject during learning.

The evaluations performed in this study, in which Neurolinguistics allies with the Discourse Analysis theory, it was possible to observe subjects (and not individuals) with brain injury due to hydrocephalus, that is, someone was observed in his/her own context where there is a body with an affection. The adoption of this evaluation procedure in alignment with the discourse theory considers that language is not an instinct based on genetically transmitted knowledge by means of a language organ (Lieberman, 2002), but it depends on a context, which is considered together with the body that carries the affection.

Language is considered to be an acquired skill which is based on a functional linguistic system located in several areas of the human brain. It is the brain that regulates the comprehension and production of oral language. Therefore, language cannot be considered as something that is isolated from the body. If there is brain damage, that linguistic system will suffer the consequences, and among such consequences, those following below can be enumerated as examples. It is also noted that, although brain lesions have different causes, the consequences of such lesions are similar:

1. Brain damage causes cognitive and communication problems which vary from person to person, according to an individual's personality and abilities and to damage severity. As for cognitive problems, they can be verified by asking: How much does he know? What can he do? When executive functions are achieved, the individual is not able to take care of himself satisfactorily, perform paid work, or maintain normal social relations. Cognitive dysfunctions usually involve specific functions or functional areas; lesions in executive functions affect behavioural aspects;
2. Certain types of brain damage cause long-term difficulties and, in this case, other areas of the brain assume the function of damaged areas. The brains of children show more flexibility than the brains of adults, and in that case, they progress better than adults with similar damage;
3. Some cognitive deficiencies lead to problems of concentration, organization of thought and learning of new information. There may be an inability to interpret the actions of others, thus generating problems in social relationships, inability in decision-making, planning and judgment;
4. Language problems may include difficulty finding words, forming sentences, making descriptions and giving explanations. There may be no understanding of a word and difficulty in understanding the meaning of a joke, sarcasm, adage or a figurative expression;
5. There may be no awareness of mistakes made. Reading and writing skills are often greater than the ability to speak and understand spoken words. Simple and complex mathematical skills are often affected;

6. The speech produced by an individual with brain injury may be slow, difficult, or impossible to understand if the areas of the brain that control the muscles of that discursive mechanism are damaged; there may be difficulty in swallowing food.

Linguistic Evaluation for Social Inclusion: A Joint View Between Neurolinguistics, Language, and the Subject

How can a single group of subjects including individuals with and without brain injury be evaluated? According to DA theories (Pêcheux, 1988) and Literacy (Tfouni, 1992, 2005), it is proposed that researchers' observation has originated from the perspective of "make-know" instead of "know-how". Researchers' observation under such "make-know" perspective causes the connection of various knowledge types in a conjoint view for discussion.

Therefore, rather than simply describing or quantifying symptoms of linguistic learning difficulties, the researcher focuses on the subject, one by one, during the latter's enunciation. This can tell a lot more about the subject in his relation to language: at this time, it is possible to observe the subject author that is being constituted in the discursive chain.

The discursive perspective provides competent work on the language of children with learning disabilities: on one hand, it allows for understanding that changes in language cause changes in the subject, in his relation with his body, with his peers, with objects; on the other, it is capable of considering brain injuries or dysfunctions as factors that cause linguistic learning difficulties to that very subject.

Such interrelation occurs due to the articulation between the process of signification (which involves the body), external materiality and language itself. The lack of attentive care for the language of individuals with dysfunction causes the body to be led to a displacement which, in turn, causes blockades and even the paralysation of functions. The investment in the linguistic education of individuals with hydrocephalus can be observed in the data collected: if for these children, who are at the maximum level of linguistic learning disability due to brain injury, there is success at learning how to write, such success can be extended to all who have shown difficulty in linguistic education.

Why is neurolinguistics recommended in order to discuss linguistic education? Neurolinguistics cannot be ignored in this process precisely because it comprehends the pre-sign relations in which language and the subject constitute only moments. The body should be understood as part of the linguistic education process: it is in it(whether dysfunction is present or not) that impulses of distinct orders combine indistinctly in a practice that involves signification.

Thus, mechanical aspects of language, sensory experience arising in the sensory cortex of the brain and mechanisms of habituation, sensitization and classical conditioning (Baloyannis, [2009]2017) must be evaluated together with physical symptoms (vomiting, irritability, incapacity to understand abstract concepts, etc.) and psychological symptoms (antisocial behaviour and language learning difficulties). None of these elements should be disregarded from the linguistic education theme.

In the study of linguistic education, the subject's interrelation with language and the body allows for the observation of non-idealized individuals with brain disorders or even brain damage. These individuals are then observed not with regard to their "errors" or "success" in abstract tests, but to the articulation that they establish between the signification process that is constituted in them (which involves the body with dysfunction), external materiality and language itself. The lack of attention from parents, caregivers, educators and researchers to aspects of linguistic dysfunction can cause these individuals' bodies to be led to a displacement that will result in blockages or paralyzed functions.

These harmful consequences arise because something in the individual's reality (and, here, the body that carries dysfunctions is referred to) interferes in his development. Thus, particularities of the subject and his context cannot be ignored in linguistic education.

The problem of an ideal methodology ("know-how") for linguistic learning is that, in case the subject suffers from cerebral dysfunction, he will not reach the functionality of the letter, thus being prevented from recognizing himself in the mirror offered by it (the letter) (Biarnès, 1998). In this case, the strategy that the individual will utilize to "connect graphemes, phonemes and meanings" cannot be predicted (Biarnès, 1998, p. 11). As teachers or trainers, we must resign ourselves to not knowing how the student learns; our task is to create learning spaces, in the function of mediators: it is the world of words that will create the world of things for these subjects (Lacan, [1953] 1998).

The Literacy Theory to Achieve Social Inclusion

Public educational policies are focused on the literacy imposed under universal parameters and generic evaluations on the use of oral or written language in order to place everyone under a situation of supposed equality. This practice reinforces the marginalization of those who do not achieve the imposed goals, thus implanting heterogeneity rather than equality.

The adoption of the Literacy Theory (Tfouni, 1992, 2005) makes it possible to observe that the writing activity leads to inequality in the individual sphere and makes power relations natural (Tfouni & Monte-Serrat, p. 2010). There is an ideological work of meanings in the writing activity that is difficult to identify. When performing a comparative study on writing which is not in accordance with the literacy model adopted by schools, Signorini (2001, p. 110) states that the notions of "right" and "wrong", in an evaluation of texts with oral-language characteristics, "are justified in function of a hierarchization [...] that is constituted out of language [...] and that is reflected in writing as a mark on a measuring instrument".

The author (op. cit., 112) says that "objective" writing is now linked "to the psycho-socio-cognitive development of subjects and to the social and technological development of communities", and that such linkage has "an ideological nature [...] between performance in writing a text and the development of individual capacities". She also shows that texts by "agents with different socio-cultural positions" present a mixture of spoken and written language at different degrees, and that such hybridism has neither legitimacy nor visibility within the "socio-pragmatic and political struggle" (Signorini, 2001, p. 101).

The author states that educational policies advocate the "purity of writing style that is not confused with speaking" and the idea of "removing from writing what is perceived as the residue or 'interference' of orality" (Signorini, 2001, p. 114). Thus, the author concludes (op. cit., 124) that the decomposition of writing in levels is "incompatible with the principles of unicity, autonomy and intrinsic rationality of written communication" and eventually suggests that the concept of literacy must be "anchored on the [concept] of social practice" (ibid., 124). Language must, therefore, be evaluated by taking into account the subject's socio-historical context.

It is the concern about the inclusion of marginalized subjects that directs this research towards seeking a criterion of language evaluation which includes literate and illiterate subjects: the concept of authorship (Foucault, [1969] 1983; Tfouni, 2005).

Authorship: Finding a Way for the Viability of Being

In linguistic learning, the connection of phonemes, graphemes and meanings, performed in metaphoric and metonymic processes, does not refer to an autonomous movement of language on itself, but rather to a subject that emerges in the signifying chain. Language has the function to capture the subject (Lemos, [2002] 2012). It is with this regard that the discursive functioning of the metaphoric and metonymic axes of language is understoodas a place of constitution of the subject, allowing him to signify something else beyond what he signified [signified him].

It is in this place of constitution of the subject that indicates the existence of a process of authorship, according to which the observation of the linguistic education of subjects with brain dysfunction is proposed. While the latter may face learning difficulty, attention can be paid to the subject that is constituted and not to what he did "correctly" or "wrongly". This form of observation goes against what we regularly do in terms of research, since the latter departs from a subject as the cause and the origin of the written or oral articulation of an enunciation.

The discursive perspective herein used causes the subject to be discarded as the cause (the place that gives something meaning) and leads to the observation of the subject's enunciative function, which is apprehended in his relation to the body that carries a dysfunction and to a field of objects. This perspective, according to Foucault ([1969]1983), opens a set of possible subjective positions (authorship), instead of establishing its limits.

According to the evaluation criterion by means of authorship, it is possible to observe that enunciations carry a singular value of the subject who has enunciated, such as a signature, which brings the unicity and coherence of its creator (Foucault, [1969]1983).

Based on such criterion, a text (Figure 1) was analyzed. It had been written as a school assignment by R., a 13-year-old girl with malformation of the corpus callosum and hydrocephalus. R. had learned how to read and write at CCAzinho, IEL-UNICAMP and has been tutored together with other younger children at a regular school.

Figure 1.

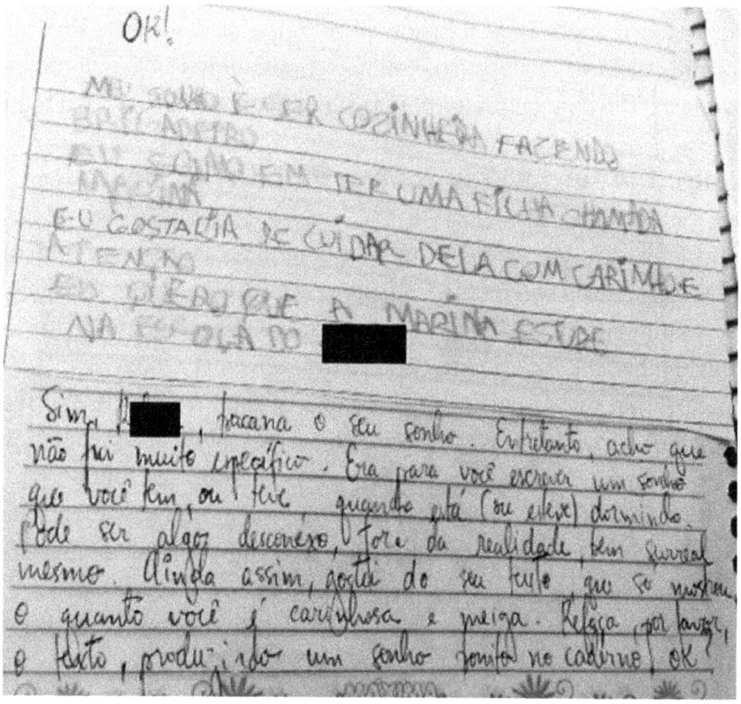

The excerpt analyzed belongs to a corpus that was collected during the longitudinal follow-up of R's writing by these researchers over two years. The transcription of the abovementioned text follows below (see Figure 1):

(teacher) OK!

(R.): "My dream is to be a cook and make truffle. I dream of having a daughter named Marina. I would like to take care of her with love and attention. I want Marina to go to the same school as _________."

(teacher): "Yes, R. Your dream is nice. However, I think that I was not very specific. You were supposed to write about a dream that you have (or had) when you are (or were) sleeping. It can be something scrappy, out of reality, very surreal in fact. Even so, I like your text, which showed how affectionate and sweet you are. Please, redo your text, producing a beautiful dream in your notebook, OK?

(CCA, IEL-UNICAMP, 2015)

In this text, R. writes about the topic requested by the teacher at the school which she attends. The task is that the student should write about her dream. It can be observed in the image (see Figure 1) that the teacher writes "OK" at the beginning of the text and adds a phrase saying "Your dream is nice."However, she tells R. to redo the task based on a supposed transparency of the word "dream", which would refer to a dream that we have when we sleep. R.'s enunciation is related to the dream as a wish, to what one longs for in the sense of feeling included, dreaming of what children her age would dream of. Evaluated according to the criterion of an idealized subject, R. must redo the task. Why not evaluate her according to the criterion of authorship, in which parcelled enunciations form a network and produce meaning?

Tfouni (1994, p. 61) notes that cultural "domination is primarily based on the 'force', 'power' and 'authority' of writing practices. It can be observed, in the analysed excerpt, that there is the presupposition of an authority that imposes the meaning of the word "dream" to be produced, thus making such meaning monological, which does not admit multiple readings (Tfouni, 1992, p. 35). According to Tfouni & Carreira (2007, p. 155), the official language creates a "linguistic barrier" in which the order "equalling for better domination" is hidden.

It is seen, in the excerpt, that the production of meanings from the teacher's perspective is motivated by the belief that there is a homogeneous and universal language which would equal all. It is also perceived that the person responsible for introducing such perspective is the teacher, who occupies the position of a subject of authority and who has specific literate knowledge.

Miaille (1979, p. 170) explains that, in using the set of rules governing a language and when studying a phrase such as "the sky is blue", grammarians are not concerned about the color of the sky, but they examine whether the statement of that phrase is fair; they control only the "formal correction of the phrase (subject, verb, complement or attribute, nature of the terms used, verb tense, etc.)". The author states (op. cit.) that it can be "said that grammar abstracts completely from the content of language and takes nothing into account but its form" and adds that knowledge obeys a "formal logic [which] operates in a similar way", because it is "constituted by the set of rules that define the terms and the ways of using such terms so that thought is coherent" (Miaille, 1979, p. 170).

Such reasoning is utilized in the use of writing. In it, syllogistic reasoning abstracts from the content of language and takes only form into account, thus distancing itself from context. In turn, discursive functioning, from the point of view of Literacy (Tfouni, 1992, 2005), does not attach much importance to the set of grammatical rules, but takes into account the social and historical context of the subject who enunciates.

Miaille (1979, p. 170, emphasis added) adds that logical reasoning goes beyond grammar, since the latter encodes the uses of language and the former "is constitutive of thought" by imposing abstraction and constructing "a certain number of concepts that eliminate the concrete and real content to which, nevertheless, they refer". Thus, the logical reasoning imposed by writing brings forth things that are isolated from their context, putting together and classifying terms and using them within a coherent system (Miaille, 1979, p. 171). This is how the writing system, in Miaille's words (op. cit.) "works for its own unicity", "for a unicity that tries to exclude contradictions".

This process of exclusion of contradictions, which is controlled by a dominant ideology, produces a homogeneous social voice and gives priority to a supposedly transparent, one-way language, thus leading "discourses to become monologizing, totalizing, 'scientific' and 'decentralized'" (Tfouni, 1992, p. 100). According to Tfouni, this use occurs within social practices and institutions where there is imposition of meaning and where it materializes in discursive practices that, in turn, will determine the positions of subject and discursive positions that are not available to all:

The complexity of the social (and discursive) formations produced by writing determines, in the same measure, a complexity of roles to be assumed by the subject [...] In a highly literate society, this non-homogeneous social distribution of knowledge and of social practices organized by literacy, on one hand, guarantees the effective participation of the subjects that master them, and, on the other, marginalizes those who do not have access to such knowledge (Tfouni:1992,104-105).

According to Tfouni (2005), when the process of authorship is valued, the illusion of language transparency is lost. That author (op. cit.) states that there authorship in cases in which the subject who enunciates is capable of controlling the dispersion and drifting of meanings. The author can install new meanings when making a cut out of the flow of signifiers in other places than those predicted by language rules. In the excerpt above, R. understood dream as desire and not as something that happens during sleep. R. demonstrated authorship by controlling the meaning of her writing. What would the reason be for continuing to understand that R. is "wrong" and that she should redo her text? According to the discourse theory (Foucault: 1967, [1963]1969, 1995, 1996, 2004; Pêcheux, 1988) and the theory of literacy (Tfouni, 1992, 2005), the reason for R. to redo her text lies in the imposition of a dominant meaning by means of ideology.

The literacy theory (Tfouni, 1988, 1992, 1994, 2005) opens avenues so that educators can work with an

alternative discourse to the scientific discourse, and offers a space in which illiterate individuals [can] bring their personal experience, values and worldviews to the interaction. In other words, there is the possibility of installation of subjectivity. The production of narratives can be considered as a movement of resistance in discourse in relation to the estrangement that the illiterate feel when faced with highly literate logical discourses. Narratives appear to them as a place where they can look at a phenomenon from a particular, subjective perspective. This perspective brings to the oral and writing scenario the process of learning from what is marginalized by logical reasoning: subjectivity. It is from this perspective that one can "perceive" other knowledge, other meanings and other reasoning than the syllogistic. While logical reasoning excludes other possibilities of interpreting by silencing them, opportunities for enunciation open up and denounce a struggle for a discursive place from which the subject can enunciate and make marginalized knowledge visible. (Tfouni; Carvalho; Monte-Serrat: 2017,11).

FUTURE RESEARCH DIRECTIONS

Issues related to the application of the Brazilian Law on the Inclusion of Persons with Disabilities, which was promulgated on July 6, 2015, are investigated. The challenges of inclusive education in Brazilian educational institutions are surveyed. We seek answers to questions about the challenges of inclusive education to education and health care professionals in relation to the concepts of literacy, writing and structuration of the subject are sought. It discusses the inclusive and interdisciplinary educational context in Brazilian schools are discussed.

CONCLUSION

Linguistic education cannot be evaluated only by means of abstract tests. It must include the relationship of language with the functioning of the nervous system interacting with a body that is not reduced to the biological aspect, since language is also a body (Lacan, [1953]1998).

Language materializes and makes the process by which an individual organizes signifiers and interprets the surrounding world observable. Even if such individual shows brain dysfunction and difficulties in using language, he must not be marginalized. Investment in linguistic education must be made, which will prevent that individual from "shattering".

Linguistic monitoring under the articulation of neurolinguistics with the discourse theory will be capable of promoting rhythmic, lexical, and syntactic changes so as to place the signifying chain in order in the oral or written production of individuals with brain dysfunction. Since successful linguistic interaction acts on the structuration of subjectivity, discursive functioning is stimulated, which, in turn, will trigger a protective function in relation to pathologies.

The attention paid to the neurolinguistic aspects of children with brain dysfunction will reflect on the functioning of the signification process, so that they can develop authoring features, both in relation to language appropriation (writing and speaking according to rules) and to the subjective aspect (writing and speaking without dispersion or drifting, once children understand themselves as a subject in the contexts in which they operate). Hence, there can be unicity of the subject that speaks (Foucault, [(1969) 1983]), in the form of coherence and not of a mere evaluation of language rules: it is the subject's creative imagination that is imposed, ordering and coordinating the content expressed without dispersing on rules imposed from outside. In this process, the subject condenses meanings that are part of his/her experience, in a movement which blends categories that are part of sensitivity (Ostrower, 2013).

REFERENCES

Althusser, L. (1999). *Ideologia e Aparelhos Ideológicos do Estado. In Um mapa da ideologia* (pp. 105–142). Rio de Janeiro: Contraponto.

Baloyannis, S. J. (2009). Neuroscience and Philosophy. *Encephalos, 46*(1), 5-20. Retrieved on January 25, 2017, from: file:///C:/Users/Dion%C3%A9ia/Downloads/Philosophy%20and%20Neurosciencesl%20(1).pdf

Biarnès, J. (1998). O ser e as letras: da voz à letra, um caminho que construímos todos. Revista da Faculdade de Educação-USP, 24(2).

Campos, R., & Furtado, J. (2011). *Desafios da avaliação de programas e serviços em saúde*. EBC, Empresa Brasil de Comunicação. Retrieved on June 28, 2018, from: http://www.ebc.com.br/noticias/internacional/2013/06/relatorio-do-unicef-aponta-exclusao-da-crianca-com-deficiencia

Foucault, M. (1967). *As palavras e as coisas, tradução de Antônio Ramos Rosa*. Lisboa: Portugália Editora.

Foucault, M. (1969). *Qu'est-cequ'unauteur? conferência pronunciada na Sociedade Francesa de Filosofia em 22 de fevereiro de 1969, Littoral, n. 9, Márcia Gatto e Clarice Gato (trad.)*. Paris: Eres. (Original work published 1963)

Foucault, M. (1995). *Arqueologia do saber, Luiz Felipe Baeta Neves (trad.)*. Rio de Janeiro: Ed. Forense Universitária.

Foucault, M. (1996). *A ordem do discurso, Laura Fraga de Almeida Sampaio (trad.)*. São Paulo: Loyola.

Foucault, M. (2004). *A hermenêutica do sujeito, Márcio Alves Fonseca e Salma TannusMuchail (trad.)*. São Paulo: Martins Fontes.

Gaufey, G. (1998). *El lazo especular. Unestudiotraversero de launidad imaginaria, trad.* Graciela Leguizamón, Argentina: Edelp SA.

Guimarães, E. (2002). *Semântica do acontecimento: um estudo enunciativo da designação*. Campinas, SP: Pontes.

Haraway, D., & Kunzru, H. (2014). *A cyborg manifesto: science, technology, and socialist-feminism in the late twentieth century. Antropologia do ciborgue: as vertigens do pós-humano, Tadeu, T., (organização e tradução). Acesso em 23 de janeiro de 2014*. Retrieved from http://mairakubik.files.wordpress.com/2012/06/86532011-haraway-donna-kunzru-hari-antropologia-do-ciborgue-as-vertigens-do-pos-humano-org-tomaz-tadeu.pdf

Haroche, C. (1992). *Fazer dizer, querer dizer*. São Paulo: Hucitec.

Headinjury. (2015). Retrieved on February 3, 2015, from: http://www.headinjury.com/rehabcognitive.html

Lacan, J. (1998). Formulações sobre a causalidade psíquica. In Escritos (pp. 152-194). Rio de Janeiro: Jorge Zahar.

Lacan, J. (1998). *O estádio do espelho como formador da função do eu, Escritos, Vera Ribeiro (trad.)*. Rio de Janeiro: Jorge Zahar. (Original work published 1949)

Lacan, J. (1998). *Função e campo da fala e da linguagem em psicanálise, Escritos*. Rio de Janeiro: Jorge Zahar. (Original work published 1953)

Lemos, C. (2002). Das vicissitudes da fala da criança e de sua investigação. *Cadernos de Estudos Linguísticos, 42*. Retrieved on October 13, 2012, from: http://www.iel.unicamp.br/revista/index.php/cel/article/view/1599/1178

Lieberman, P. (2002). Human Language and Our Reptilian Brain: The Subcortical Bases of Speech, Syntax and Thought *Language in Society*, *31*(4), 609–612.

Miaille, M. (1979). *Uma Introdução Crítica ao Direito* (A. Prata, Trans.). Lisboa: Moraes Editores.

Monte-Serrat, D. (2013). *Letramento e discurso jurídico, Tese defendida no Departamento de Psicologia da Faculdade de Filosofia, Ciências e Letras da Universidade de São Paulo, Campus Ribeirão Preto, FFCLRP-USP, em junho de. Orientadora Profa. Dra. Leda VerdianiTfouni*. Disponível na Biblioteca Digital de Teses e Dissertações da Universidade de São Paulo: http://www.teses.usp.br/teses/disponiveis/59/59137/tde-14032013-104350/

Monte-Serrat, D. (2015). *Relatório de pesquisa como Pesquisadora Colaboradora em Linguística, do Instituto de Estudos da Linguagem da Universidade Estadual de Campinas - IEL-UNICAMP, supervisora Profa. Dra. Maria Irma HadlerCoudry*. Não publicado.

Ostrower, F. (2013). *Acasos e criação artística*. Campinas: Ed. Unicamp.

Padilha, A. M. (2000). *Bianca. O ser simbólico: para além dos limites da deficiência mental*. Tese de Doutorado, Faculdade de Educação, UNICAMP, 2000. Retrieved on March 3, 2014, from: http://www.vigotski.net/ditebras/padilha.pdf

Patton, M. (1997). *Utilizaton-focused evaluation: the new century text* (3rd ed.). Thousand Oaks, CA: Sage Publications.

Pêcheux, M. (1998). *Semântica e Discurso: uma crítica à afirmação do óbvio*. Campinas: Ed. Unicamp.

Pêcheux, M. (2002). *O Discurso: estrutura ou acontecimento?* (3rd ed.). Campinas, SP: Pontes.

Pêcheux, M., & Fichant, M. (1971). *Sur l'histoire des sciences*. Paris: Maspero.

Pêcheux, M., & Fuchs, C. (1997). *A propósito da análise automática do discurso: atualização e perspectivas. In Por uma análise automática do discurso - uma introdução à obra de Michel Pêcheux*. Campinas: UNICAMP. (Original work published 1975)

Rivera, T. (2009). *Ensaio sobre o espaço e o sujeito. Lygia Clark e a psicanálise*. Retrieved on August 3, 2009, from: http://www.scielo.br/scielo.php?pid=S1516-14982008000200004&script=sci_arttcxt

Roudinesco, E. (1998). *Dicionário de psicanálise, trad.* Vera Ribeiro, Brazil: Jorge Zahar.

Signorini, I. (2001). Construindo com a escrita "outras cenas de fala". In *Signorini (org.), Investigando a relação oral/escrito e as teorias do letramento* (pp. 97–134). Campinas: Mercado das Letras.

Silva, M. (2001). *Alfabetização, escrita e colonização, InHistória das ideias linguísticas*. Ed. Unemat.

Silva, R., & Brandão, D. (2011). Nas rodas da avaliação educadora. In R. Campos & J. Furtado (Eds.), Desafios da avaliação de programas e serviços em saúde. Unicamp.

Tfouni, L. (1992). *Letramento e analfabetismo, Tese de Livre-Docência*. Ribeirão Preto: FFCLRP-USP.

Tfouni, L. (2005). *Letramento e alfabetização*. São Paulo: Ed. Cortez.

Tfouni, L., & Carreira. (2010, July). O sujeito submetido à linguagem. *Revista Investigações da Universidade Federal de Pernambuco, 20*(2).

Tfouni, L., Carvalho, & Monte-Serrat, D. (2017). *A prática da oralidade como lugar de resistência*. Submetido à RevistaEducaçãoemFoco UEMG.

Tfouni, L., & Monte-Serrat, D. (2010). Letramento e Discurso Jurídico. In *Virgínia Colares*. Recife: Ed universitária da UFPE.

Trewhella, J. (2016). *The challenges and opportunities for multidisciplinary research in a world of complex interdependent systems*. Retrieved on September 16, 2016, from: https://globalhighered.wordpress.com/2009/06/26/multidisciplinary-research-an-essential-driver-for-innovation/

Chapter 10
An Investigation of the Relationship Between Preschool Teachers' Picture Story Book Reading Activities and Children's Language Development

Gülüzar Şule Tepetaş Cengiz
Abant İzzet Baysal University, Turkey

Mübeccel Gönen
Hacettepe University, Turkey

ABSTRACT

This chapter examines the relationship between teachers' picture story book reading activities and 48- to 60-month-old children's language development and to identify the effect of different variables on this relationship. The study sample was composed of 208 children in classrooms for 48- to 60-month-old children and 10 teachers in five independent pre-schools in the province of Kırşehir. The data obtained in the study were analyzed by using appropriate statistical methods. Based on the study results, a significant relationship was identified between pre-school teachers' picture story book reading activities during their daily programs and language development of children. The result of the study presents the importance of picture story book reading activities for language development. Longitudinal studies that will investigate teachers' and parents' involvement in picture story book reading activities in detail and development of programs that will support children's language development are suggested in the chapter.

DOI: 10.4018/978-1-5225-4009-0.ch010

INTRODUCTION

Children like and examine books starting in their infancy. Language development advances the most during early childhood and therefore new concepts and words are added to the sentence structure with language acquisition in this period. Picture story books are considered primarily in terms of supporting language development. Many studies have tested the correlation between language development and reading activities (Dickinson, McCabe, &Anatasopoulos, 2002; Justice, Mashburn, Hamre & Pianta, 2008; Zucker, Justice, Piasta &Kadaravek, 2010; Pentimonti, Zucker, Justice, Petscher, Piasta & Kaderavek, 2012). These studies report that picture story book reading activities with children or time spent alone with books are significant for the acquisition of future reading habits (Dickinson & Smith, 1994; Çakmak & Yılmaz, 2009).

Relationship Between Language Development and Abstract Thinking

Abstract thinking skills include sense-making, recall and hypothesis building (Bowerman and Lavinson, 2001; Öztan Ulusoy, 2012; Senemoğlu, 2012). Tsao (2002) states that children's thinking styles and their skills in adapting these styles to new situations and conditions are possible with abstract thinking skills. Tsao (2002) also presents that playing and classroom interactions highly support and develop this skill.

Since drama, picture story book reading and games create opportunities to explore past experiences, they have a significant place in developing children's abstract thinking skills. Children assign tasks to symbols in symbolic games and play abstract games; they talk to themselves and engage in monologues. They think during these monologues and generate ideas. They share what they have learned with their peers and continue learning from one another. Additionally, pinpointing their shortcomings, presenting similarities, problem solving through reasoning and explaining causes and results and how events operate are the activities frequently used by children during picture story book reading activities. Pictures and texts in picture story books are significant materials prepared for teachers to generate key questions. A creative adult can only support children's development by thinking in the abstract and in a versatile manner (Justice & Ezell, 1999; Menyuk & Brisk, 2005a; Demircan, 2006; Aydın, 2012; Adıgüzel, 2012; Hanbay, 2013; Öztürk, 2013).

Relationship Between Language Development and Elaboration/Phonology

In general, "phonology" is using the sounds in a conscious manner by children and being aware of differences in the array and characteristics of sounds during daily dialogues or text reading. The child who is aware of the fact that sounds come together to make a word has gained phonological awareness (Chomsky, 1957; Beck & McKeown, 2007; Maybin & Watson, 2009; Lundberg, Larsman & Strid, 2012; Robert & Owens, 2012).

Children with phonological awareness also start to take notice of rhymes, make rhyming words on their own, match similar words by taking the sounds at the beginning or end of words and realize that words are made up of syllables (Ball & Blachman, 1991; Crain-Thoresan & Dale, 1992; Crawford, 1995; Justice & Ezell, 2002; Girolametto, Weitzman, Lefabure & Greenberg, 2007). Phonological awareness increases children's skills to recognize letters and examine words in detail. In their study, Roth, Troia, Wortington and Handy (2006) reported that phonological awareness developed during preschool period provides children with reading readiness (Crain-Thoresan & Dale, 1992; Crawford, 1995; Girolametto, Weitzman, Lefabvre & Greenberg, 2007).

In another sense, phonological awareness is a process of elaborating words for children. Children start to observe sounds more carefully and focus on details. Visual recognition and recall skills are included in the concept of phonology (Ball & Balchman, 1991).

Development of children's interest for picture story books and reading is explained by Schickedanz (1999) in the following statements:

- Children believe that words in a story come from pictures. Hence, they may ask for "reading" when a page has only pictures with no text.
- Children become aware of the text in the second phase and realize that the story is made up of text. They start to become aware of the text and compare them with another. They begin to notice the details in words and match the similarities in them.
- In the third phase, children memorize the text of the story. They can take the story book and recreate the story from the pictures without an adult. They are careful to hold the book and turn the pages like an adult. They try to use the same gestures, mimics and intonations used by the adult who read the story to them.
- In the fourth phase, children begin to map the picture story book. They try to find the memorized text in the book. They struggle to mimic reading on

the words and syllables they see in the book. They try to form connections between what they see and what they pronounce. They mimic reading by tracing the words and matching them with their fingers

All these phases allow the formation of emotional ties between children and books (Pentimonti & Justice, 2010; Neaum, 2010).

Relationship Between Language Development and Classroom Environment/Atmosphere

Creating a positive classroom environment is an important step for teachers in supporting children's language development. Children who feel comfortable and at ease are more concentrated and motivated to learn. Therefore, it becomes easier for teachers to take children to the point where they need to focus their attention (La Paro, Pianta & Schulman, 2004).

Classroom atmosphere should be assessed in terms of group psychology in preschool education because most of the activities are planned and implemented as large group activities. For instance, teachers generally prefer large groups during picture story book reading activities. In order to support language development of each child, it is imperative to make efficient use of classroom management strategies and have a positive classroom atmosphere (Reese & Cox, 1999; Zucker & Landry, 2010; Benson, 2013).

Just like in all classroom activities, the way to create an effective and good classroom atmosphere is to ensure their participation in a manner that will support their development. First of all, cooperation among children should be supported and the language used in the classroom should be well modulated to ensure positive communication (Ezell & Justice, 1998). Clear and concrete use of language should be maintained when the story is explained or told and use of inexplicit expressions should be avoided (Demircan, 2006). Tone of voice and intonation are as important as the words used in communication since they assign different meanings to words. Positive language should be used during activities and accusatory, "connotative" and prohibitive expressions should be avoided. Teachers should correct errors and misinformation but teachers should never humiliate students while correcting them. It is necessary to find polite and non-offending ways to understand whether the accurate information is received by all students. It should be ensured that not some but all children communicate with the teacher and children should be encouraged for this type of communication (Gest, Freeman, Domitrovich & Welsh, 2004; Deretarla Gül, 2013).

This study mainly intended to predict the relationship between pre-school teachers' picture story book activities and children's language development.

It is necessary in Turkey for teachers employed in pre-school institutions to organize daily picture story book reading activities. Turkish language activities have a significant place in 2013 Pre-School Education Program in Turkey as well and teachers are expected to organize and practice activities that support children's language development by creating book centers (MoNE, 2013). Quality picture story book reading activities provided by pre-school teachers are important for children to acquire and sustain good reading habits in the future, to prepare for reading and writing and to develop language skills.

Problem Statement:

1. Is there a relationship between pre-school teachers daily picture story book reading activities and children's language development?

Sub Problems:

1. Is there a relationship between pre-school teachers' skill levels related to usage of language and language development levels of 48-60 month children?
2. Is there a relationship between abstract thinking skills supported by pre-school teachers during picture story book reading activities and language development levels of 48-60 month children?
3. Is there a relationship between elaboration skills supported by pre-school teachers during picture story book reading activities and language development levels of 48-60 month children?
4. Is there a relationship between phonological skills supported by pre-school teachers during picture story book reading activities and language development levels of 48-60 month children?
5. Is there a relationship between pre-school teachers' skills in preparing the classroom atmosphere during picture story book reading activities and language development levels of 48-60 month children?
6. What is the mean score obtained by 48-60 month children for language development levels?
7. Is there a relationship between the socio-economic status of 48-60 month children and their language development levels?
8. Is there a relationship between pre-school teachers' seniority and children's language development levels?
9. Is there a relationship between the type of higher education institution that school pre-school teachers graduated from and children's language development levels?
10. Is there a relationship between the gender of 48-60 month children and their language development levels?

METHOD

Participants

The universe of the study was composed of 48-60-month-old children attending preschools in Kırşehir established under the Ministry of Education. Stratified sampling method was used in the study to determine the sample that would represent the universe. The main criterion used in stratified sampling method was socio-economic status of the school. First of all, preschools were determined in Kırşehir city centre and later categories related to income levels, number of teachers and number of students in these schools and neighbourhoods were examined to select participating schools.

Study sample was composed of 208 children in classrooms for 48-60-month-old children and 10 teachers in five independent pre-schools in the province of Kırşehir.

For children, participation criteria were identified as:

- To be attending 48-60-month groups as registered students in the preschools in Kırşehir established under the Ministry of Education
- To be chronologically 48-60 months old at the time when research data were collected

For teachers, participation criteria were identified as:

- To be teaching 48-60-month groups in the preschools in Kırşehir established under the Ministry of Education
- To be voluntary and willing to participate

Exclusion criteria were identified as:

- To have any disabilities (for children),
- Not to receive parental permit for participation (for children),
- To be unwilling to participate in the study (for teachers).

Design

This study aimed to examine the relationship between teachers' picture story book reading activities and 48-60-month-old children's language development and to identify the different variables (teachers' education levels, age, professional experience) that may have an effect on this relationship. Hence, a mixed method design was used in the study. Qualitative research methods were used in the part of the study which utilized the Systematic Assessment of Book Reading Scale (SABR). Survey method, a quantitative research method, was used to collect data via Peabody Picture Vocabulary Test IV. Cross-sectional research method was selected from survey studies as the most appropriate method for this study.

Teacher Data Form

Teacher Data Form was developed by the researcher to collect information on teachers and students regarding the variables whose impacts were examined in the framework of the study.

"Teacher Data Form" includes questions about the age and gender of the teachers, level of education, period of professional experience, number of students in the classroom and approximate level of income for students' parents. This form was given to teachers by the researcher to be filled.

Peabody Picture Vocabulary Test IV Scale

Peabody Picture Vocabulary Test IV was adapted to Turkish by Kılınç (2014). In this context, Kuder-Richardson (KR-20) and Spearman Brown Split-Halves Test Correlation were calculated in order to determine the internal consistency of the scale. While two halves were identified in the measurement scales in which the questions were listed from easy to hard, odd and even split-halves test correlation was calculated since the use of odd/even criterion was suggested. Internal consistency coefficient for reliability was found as KR-20 = 0.79 and Spearman Brown Split-HalvesTest Correlation was 0.84.

Age was considered as external criterion in the analyses for criterion referenced validity. Accordingly, scores obtained from the scale by 36-47-month, 48-60-month and 61-72-month children were compared and the results presented below were obtained.

Examination of the Table 1 presents significant differences in the language development of 36-47 month, 48-60 month and 61-72 month children [$F_{(2\text{-}321)}=10,868$, $p<.01$]. Receptive language development levels were found to change significantly based on age. In the light of these findings, Peabody Picture Vocabulary Test IV was accepted as a reliable and valid measurement tool. Reliability coefficient of Peabody Picture Vocabulary Test was calculated with Cronbach's Alpha in this study and alpha value was found as 0,793.

Table 1. Differences in the language development of 36-47 month, 48-60 month and 61-72 month children

AGE	N	$\overline{X}$	F	p
36-47 month	48	19,56	10,868	,000*
48-60 month	134	22,45		
61-72 month	142	25,95		
TOTAL	324	23,55		

*p<.01

Systematic Assessment of Book Reading Scale

Systematic Assessment of Book Reading (SABR) was used to observe the characteristics of teachers' book reading activities. Turkish adaptation of the scale for Turkish children was undertaken in the framework of the present study. Systematic Assessment of Book Reading (SABR) was developed by Ohio University Early Childhood Language Development and Preschool Language and Literacy Research Lab.

Justice, Zucker and Sofka (2010) examined teachers' picture story book reading activities in SABR in five subdimensions: Language Development, Abstract Thinking, Elaborations, Print/Phonological Skills, Session Climate:

- **Language Development:** According to SABR, during picture story book reading activities, teachers should support children's language development skills by describing the events in the story via making use of pictures. They also need to ask questions related to problems, solutions and events included in the story book in order to support their comprehension skills (such as "What are they doing? What happens in this picture? What instrument are the children playing in this picture?" etc.).
- **Abstract Thinking:** According to SABR, teachers are expected to help children make comparisons with daily life so that they can support children's abstract thinking skills. Teachers should guide students to have them transfer the events in the picture story book to daily life and compare and contrast them (Such as "What are the differences between cats and lions? Are these frogs the same? Are these garden tools used for the same thing? Have you ever tried this before with your friends?" etc.).
- **Elaboration:** Assessment of elaboration skills are done with SABR by taking various steps into consideration. First of all, teachers are expected to

make use of drama to support children's elaboration skills. It is important that teachers use dramatizations for explanations and sense-making to provide opportunities for children to try this option as well. Hence, children should be motivated and given chances to explain events through role plays (Such as "Can you show/make me an angry face? Can you shake as if you are frightened? Can you show us how we look when we are sleeping?" etc.).

- **Writing/Phonologic Skills**: That section in the scale includes statements related to how teachers hold up the picture story book, show the direction of writing, talk about the illustrator and the author and focus children's attention to punctuation through gests and mimics. In addition to these statements, this section includes pointing to the cover, back and front of the book, where to start reading and read/pretend to read by following with one's finger.
- **Session Atmosphere/Environment**: It is expected that teachers create the suitable atmosphere for reading by ensuring that the classroom environment is prepared for reading activities. In order to sustain such positive environments, teachers should answer children's questions warmly and quickly, behave politely and respectfully towards children, to show care and interest by gests and mimics and to provide positive and motivating feedback and encouragement. It is important to make children active participants in the story by being fair and just to children. In addition, it is expected that children sit in a manner that they can comfortably see the picture story book and feel comfortable during reading. It is imperative that children are given opportunities to touch and examine the book. Teachers should support and encourage children to do this. In order to continue the session atmosphere in a suitable manner, it is necessary to pay individual interest to children by creating opportunities for them to discover the direction of reading, notice lower and upper case letters, see the letters and the numbers on the page and turn pages.

During SABR applications, it is necessary to videotape teachers to evaluate the quality of picture story book reading activities. Videotaped sessions should include pre-reading activities such as preparations for the picture story book reading activity, during-reading activity process and post-reading activities such as discussions and question and answer.

Since there were quantitative scales to ensure the predictions related to reliability and validity of sub scales obtained during scale development process and to ensure parallel form reliability, it was deemed necessary to obtain a total score from the qualitative data collected by the researchers. Hence, a total score obtained form SABR was targeted and the codlings were used to obtain a total score.

SABR addresses the behaviors displayed in the context of sub scales and evaluates tem by questioning whether they are presented or not. There are a total of 21 behaviors that should be displayed categorized as follows: 5 in language development dimension, 4 in abstract thinking dimension, 5 in elaboration dimension, 4 in writing/phonological skills and 3 in session environment/atmosphere. Whether the teacher displays these behaviors or how many times the teacher is involved with these behaviors are marked in the coding key in the scale by the researcher via periodical observations (every five minutes, every three minutes). Assessment regarding the quality of the activity and important points to consider are also noted in the comments section by the researcher by using personal notes and teachers' statements as references. Scores for sub scales and the total score were obtained by observing the statements and behaviors of teachers related to sub scales and steps in picture story book reading activities determined by SABR.

Adaptation of SABR Scale to Turkish, Its Reliability and Validity

Turkish standardization of SABR was realized in a 3-phase process. The scale was translated from its original language (English) to Turkish by three separate language experts to ensure language and concept equality. The test retranslated to English from Turkish was checked by three separate Turkish language experts for congruity to Turkish grammar rules before it was finalized. The scale was examined by five field experts (preschool, child development and children's literature) to obtain their views on the suitability of the subscales and the items included in the subscales to Turkish culture and to the field of preschool education. Changes and arrangements were finalized based on the views of the field experts and the first phase of the standardization was completed after a final check by Turkish language experts. In this phase, experts in the field of qualitative research methods were consulted to review the scale to develop a suitable measurement tool that is in line with qualitative research design.

The second phase in standardization of SABR, included pilot testing with five teachers. Voluntary and willing teachers employed in independent preschools working with 48-60-month-old children were selected for pilot tests implemented during 2013-2014 Spring term. Teachers selected from schools with high, medium and low socio-economic status were video recorded during picture story book reading activities. Video recordings were examined and coded according to subscales and steps included in SABR. Pilot testing was undertaken without any problems and no change was deemed necessary in scale items.

In the last phase, MedCalc program was used in this study to evaluate reliability among implementers in SABR scale and weighted Kappa coefficient was calculated. Values related to the implementation are presented below:

According to Kappa coefficient values found in Table 2; it can be argued that there was a "very good intercoder agreement". SABR data obtained from the 10 teachers who participated in the study and total scores obtained from teachers in the reliability test were used to calculate Cronbach's Alpha value for this study which was found as 0,766.

Coding

Peabody Picture Vocabulary Test IV was implemented for each child individually by the researcher. Children were separately taken to a quiet environment where they would not be distracted (counseling and guidance room, psychologist's room, room of the administrator, interview room etc.), and at first, they were engaged in a conversation. The implementation started when it was determined that the child was no longer excitable. Trial pages were used first to accustom the child to the test. It takes an average of 15 minutes to individually implement Peabody Picture Vocabulary Test- IV for each child. Based on children's levels, sometimes it took 20 minutes to implement the test. Answers provided by children were marked on their individual forms. The errors and blanks were also marked to calculate net scores.

Systematic Assessment of Book Reading Scale examines teachers' picture story book reading activities. Teachers selected the picture story books themselves and implemented the reading activities with the methods they preferred. Teachers were informed beforehand that their sessions would be video recorded and trial recordings were done in different days to accustom the teachers and the children before the actual recording. Various different activities in which the children were involved were also recorded for a few weeks so that children would not be affected by the camera and the natural atmosphere would not be changed. The video camera was set in a corner of the classroom and children became used to its existence. Teachers were first individually interviewed to inquire about volunteering and willingness and volunteer and willing teachers were selected for the study. It was explained both to teachers and parents that video recordings would be confidential and necessary parental permits were acquired for the use of camera as a data collection tool. When

Table 2. Findings Related to Kappa Coefficient for the Implementation of Systematic Assessment of Book Reading (SABR)

SABR Implementation Inter-Rater Weighted Kappa Coefficient Values	
Weighted Kappa	0,853
Standard Error	0,043
95% Cl	0,768 to 0,938

teachers' actual recordings were done, codes for SABR scale were not done in the classroom environment. Unusual circumstances or situations that warranted taking notes were written on the comments section included in the coding key. Actual codes were determined by the researcher after watching the videos repeatedly who paused the videos at an interval of every 15 seconds. Every 15 seconds, it was coded whether teachers implemented the behaviors included in the sub scales. The coding keys were filled in this manner to determine the frequency of implementing the desired behaviors during picture story book reading activities.

Video recordings also included the arrangements in the classroom environment done by teachers before starting picture story book reading activities based on SABR. Data included in the observation notes were used in coding these. Preparations and classroom arrangements done by teachers were examined.

Data Processing and Analysis

SPSS IBM 22 package program and MedCalc program were used in analyzing the data obtained in relation to problem statement and sub problems. "Correlation" analysis was undertaken to test the relationship between characteristics of teachers' picture story book reading activities obtained by SABR and children's language development levels identified with the help of Peabody Picture Vocabulary Test IV. "Kruskall-Wallis H Test" was utilized to test the relationship between the data obtained via Teacher Data Form and children's language development. "Mann Whitney U Test" was used in order to test the relationship between the scores obtained in relation to characteristics of teachers' picture story book reading activities obtained by SABR and its sub scales and teachers' demographic characteristics. Statistical significance level was set as .05 in statistical comparisons and significance of differences were sought and examined.

RESULTS

Table 3 shows that increases in language development skills used by preschool teachers during picture story book reading activities generate increases in children's language development levels (p=0,0001<0,05 r=0,348, SABR min=5, SABR max=23, PPVT-4 min=46, PPVT-4 max=145).

Table 4 presents that increases in abstract thinking skills used by preschool teachers during picture story book reading activities generate increases in children's language development levels (p=0,0001<0,05 r=0,570, SABR min=6, SABR max=26, PPVT-4 min=46, PPVT-4 max=145).

Table 3. Correlation values for identifying the relationship between language development skills supported by preschool teachers during picture story book reading activities based on SABR and children's language development levels

		Correlation
		SABR Language Development TOTAL
PPVT- 4 (Net Score)	r	0,348
	p	0,000
	N	208

*p<0,05

Table 4. Correlation values for identifying the relationship between abstract thinking skills supported by preschool teachers during picture story book reading activities based on SABR and children's language development levels

		Correlation
		SABR Abstract Thinking TOTAL
PPVT- 4 (Net Score)	r	0,570
	p	0,000
	N	208

*p<0,05

Table 5 presents that increases in elaboration skills used by preschool teachers during picture story book reading activities generate increases in children's language development levels (p=0,0001<0,05 r=0,519, SABR min=1, SABR max=27, PPVT-4 min=46, PPVT-4 max=145).

Table 6 shows that preschool teachers did not generally implement any activities in print/phonological skills dimension. Therefore, the planned correlation analysis for this sub scale was not undertaken.

Table 7 shows that increases in skills in terms of motivating and enriching the session atmosphere used by preschool teachers during picture story book reading activities generate increases in children's language development (p=0,0001<0,05 r=0,542, SABR min=6, SABR max=32, PPVT-4 min=46, PPVT-4 max=145).

Table 8 presents that the highest score obtained from Peabody Picture Vocabulary Test IV by 48-60-month-old children in this study was 145 and the lowest score was 46 with a mean score of 85,80.

Table 5. Correlation values for identifying the relationship between elaboration skills supported by preschool teachers during picture story book reading activities based on SABR and children's language development levels

		Correlation
		SABR Elaboration TOTAL
PPVT- 4 (Net Score)	r	0,519
	p	0,000
	N	208

*p<0,05

Table 6. Mean values for identifying the relationship between print/phonological skills supported by preschool teachers during picture story book reading activities based on SABR and children's language development levels

	Teacher	n	Mean	Median	Min.	Max.	sd
SABR Print/phonological skills TOTAL	1	20	0	0	0	0	0
	2	23	0	0	0	0	0
	3	21	1	1	1	1	0
	4	20	0	0	0	0	0
	5	21	0	0	0	0	0
	6	22	0	0	0	0	0
	7	17	0	0	0	0	0
	8	20	0	0	0	0	0
	9	24	0	0	0	0	0
	10	20	0	0	0	0	0
	Total	208	0	0	0	1	0

Table 9 presents the numbers of 48-60-month-old children based on months and the mean scores they obtained from PPVT-4 based on month. According to Table 9, children between 97,7 and 51 month received the highest scores. The lowest scores were obtained by 76,6-56-month-old children.

Table 10 displays that increases in children's socio economic statuses generate significant increases in their language development (p=0,0001 p<0,05, H=47,1).

Table 7. Correlation values for identifying the relationship between teachers' skills related to session climate/atmosphere management supported by preschool teachers during picture story book reading activities based on SABR and children's language development levels

		Correlation
		SABR Session Climate/Atmosphere TOTAL
PPVT – 4 (Net Score)	r	0,542
	p	0,000
	N	208

*p<0,05

Table 8. Values in identifying language development levels of 48-60-month-old children

	n	Mean	Median	Minimum	Maximum	sd
Net Score	208	85,80	80,50	46,00	145,00	21,87

Table 9. Values in identifying the relationship between language development levels and numbers of 48-60-month-old children based on month

Month	f	%	PPVT-4 Mean Score
48,00	3	1,4	87
49,00	13	6,3	77
50,00	19	9,1	85,4
51,00	11	5,3	97,7
52,00	17	8,2	83,5
53,00	17	8,2	85,2
54,00	25	12,0	86,4
55,00	24	11,5	86,8
56,00	25	12,0	76,6
57,00	9	4,3	84,7
58,00	14	6,7	89,2
59,00	13	6,3	85,6
60,00	18	8,7	95,7
Total	208	100,0	85,80

Table 10. Kruskall Wallis H test values for identifying the relationship between language development levels and socio-economic statuses of 48-60 month children

	SES	n	Mean	Median	Min.	Max.	sd	Kruskall-Wallis H test Mean Rank	H	p	Paired Comparison
PPVT-4	Low SES	62	72,0	74,5	46,0	111,0	15,1	66,3	47,1	0,0001	1-2 1-3 2-3
	Medium SES	89	86,5	81,0	47,0	145,0	21,3	107,3			
	High SES	57	99,7	102,0	63,0	140,0	20,0	141,8			
	Total	208	85,8	80,5	46,0	145,0	21,9				

*p<0,05

Table 11 shows a statistically significant difference between language development levels of 48-60 month children and their teachers' professional seniority (*p*=0,000 *p*<0,05, z=88,88).

Table 12 presents no statistically significant differences between children's gender and their language development levels (*p*= 0,190 *p*>0,05 z= -1,31). However, although there was no statistically significant difference, it was identified that language development levels of male students in the sample were higher than those of female children.

Table 11. Kruskall Wallis H test values for identifying the relationship between language development levels of 48-60 month children and their teachers' professional seniority

		PPVT - 4 n	Mean	Median	Min	Max	sd	Kruskal Wallis Test Mean Rank	z	p	Paired Comparison
Professional Seniority	2-5 years	62	72,0	74,5	46	111	15,1	66,3	88,88	0,000*	1-2 1-4 2-3 3-4
	6-10 years	61	99,4	100	63	145	20,0	141,6			
	11-15 years	45	72,1	71	47	112	13,9	66,5			
	21 years &more	40	102,0	103	72	134	16,4	149,9			
	Total	208	85,8	80,5	46	145	21,9				

*p<0,05

Table 12. Mann Whitney U Test values for identifying the relationship between language development levels of 48-60 month children and children's gender

		Gender						Mann Whitney U Test		
		n	Mean	Median	Minimum	Maximum	sd	Mean Rank	z	p
PPVT – 4	Female	101	83,6	79	47	145	20,0	98,9	-1,31	0,190
	Male	107	87,9	83	46	140	23,4	109,8		
	Total	208	85,8	80,5	46	145	21,9			

*p<0,05

DISCUSSION

It was determined that a positive significant relationship exists between children's language development levels and teacher support in children's language development skills. Practices in preschool education institutions are usually based on the use of language and since there are a high number of individuals in children's environment to whom they can talk; children have the opportunity to listen and talk to others in preschool classrooms (Nelson, 1973; Maviş, 2005). This allows the generation of environments where teachers can support children's language skills. Additionally, native tongue activities included in preschool programs are periods where children spend time with their teachers to learn their mother tongues. By using poetry, rhymes, riddles, finger games, storytelling and follow up activities, teachers develop children's receptive and expressive language skills (Robert and Owens, 2012).

In their study, Erdoğan, Şimşek Bekir and Erdoğan Aras (2005) examined that factors that affected language development of 5-6-year-old children that attended preschool. They reported that time spent in preschool institutions and teachers' effective use of language had impact on children's language development. Aydoğan and Koçak (2003) also found in their study that quality time supported by language activities in preschool environments increased their achievements in language development. In their study that focused the significance of preschool education, Koçak, Ergin and Yalçın (2014) stated that children's language development was related to factors such as taking teachers as role models and time spent at the school.

It is necessary for preschool teachers to use language correctly and support and enhance children's language development with different activities. In their study, Gönen, Ünüvar, Bıçakçı, Koçyiğit, Yazıcı, Orçan, Aslan, Güven and Özyürek (2010) identified that most of the preschool teachers allocated an average of half hour to language activities during daily routine activities. The authors reported that teachers recognized the importance of language development and therefore they implemented pre-reading, while reading and post-reading activities. Similarly, Çocuk, Yanpar Yelken, Emsal Aslantürk and Güçlü (2013) reported that teachers preferred using children's literature for language activities and they used activities to allow them to express themselves and enhance their creativity to support language development.

Present study identified that teachers sometimes had difficulty to find creative ways in developing children's language skills. It was observed that almost all teachers followed the order of pre-reading, while reading and post-reading activities while reading picture story books. It was found that teachers frequently preferred the same finger games with students and generally used picture story books to tell stories. It was observed that the majority of teachers was more interested in the text of the story and did not spend much time on the pictures. As identified by Gönen et. al. (2010), teachers mostly benefited from poems, rhymes, riddles and finger games prior to story reading. These activities used to develop children's language skills usually ended with reading the picture story book and teachers preferred only drama for post-reading activities.

Mashburn, Downer, Hamre, Justice and Pianta (2010) stated that teachers play an important role in enhancing children's language skills. Therefore, they reported that it is necessary for teachers to prefer creative spaces and use different ways of storytelling frequently while reading picture story books. Their study presented that teachers' use of language skills and encouraging students with different methods (questions, discussions, conversations) to use language skills significantly increased children's language development scores. Dickinson (2011) stated the importance of teachers' professional development for reading activities and significance of effective reading activities in the study which presented the finding that preschool institutions and teachers were the most important factors on children's language development. Similarly, the present study found that increases in teachers' use of language skills increased children's language development. A positive and significant relationship was found between teacher support and reinforcement for children's abstract thinking skills and children's language development. Blank and Solomon (2007) underlined that teachers had a significant role in the development of abstract thinking skills. However, they stated that abstract thinking cannot only be assessed with teacher factor environmental factors and a well-structured program should also be taken into consideration to develop abstract thinking skills.

Abstract thinking is associated with various different areas of activity. Although picture story book reading is an activity on its own in preschool education, it can also be integrated with different areas. Preschool teachers allow visualization of story texts by using the pictures in the story. It was found in this study that the observed teachers were more interested in the story line and they had a tendency to miss the outstanding elements in the events since they read the story rapidly. It was identified that they did not discuss the qualities of characters, emotions in the story and the spaces included in the story with students and they tended to show students the pictures and continued to read/tell the story. Oers and Poland (2007) reported that schemas are important to develop children's abstract thinking skills. With the help of schemas, children make associations with their prior knowledge, become aware of similarities and discover the differences. After this phase, children begin to create new schemas by thinking in the abstract. According to SABR, teachers should ensure that students make associations between picture story books and their past experiences. Children who make connections between the text and real life are expected to present the differences and similarities between events in the book and real life. Teachers try to support students by asking questions in order to guide students in lie with this purpose.

Smith, Wigboldus and Dijksterhuis (2008) remarked that abstract thinking skills continue to develop in children along with the development of thinking skills. The stronger a child's emotions and thinking powers are the stronger their development in abstract perceptions of events will be. Thinking on picture story books, pictures and events, generating ideas, questioning and presenting new ideas are indicators that their thinking skills are developing. It is necessary for teachers to focus on children's interpretations, comments and feelings to deepen and enhance these thinking skills.

Zucker, Cabell, Justice, Pentimonti and Kadavek (2013) examined the effect of preschool interactive large group reading activities on children's language development and abstract thinking skills. They reported the finding that children's early literacy skills developed and abstract thinking skills were enhanced in parallel when they were supported by picture story books. Pentimonti, Zucker and Justice (2011) presented that picture story books selected by teachers were important and development of many skills were based on book selection. They emphasized the fact that quality reading materials supported children's abstract thinking, language development, early literacy skills and personality development and underlined the importance of selecting the right books. Hindman, Wasik and Erhart (2012) stressed the fact that the most important point in interactive book reading activities is the book based discussions which is instrumental in supporting abstract thinking. All these findings present the contributions of picture story book reading activities to children's abstract thinking skills. However, it is emphasized that the biggest responsibility lies with the teacher.

It was identified that teacher support for children's elaboration skills positively contributes to children's language development. For preschool children, learning by fun generates permanent learning. They do not forget the information they have obtained when they have fun and recall them longer. Hence, dramas and games are activities in which children use their bodies, relax and learn by having fun. Correll (2008) examined the important factors in the development of vocabulary of four-year-old children and later devised a program for this purpose. Correll (2008) identified that the most important factor in children's language development is recall and found that children do not forget the words when they learn them with interesting learning tools and they try to use them in daily life. Picture story books are materials that develop children's vocabulary (Justice, Bowles, Pence and Gosse, 2010).

Elaboration increases along with children's vocabulary and creativity. Expressing the self better and using words correctly are indicators of the development of elaboration skills (Lee, Skarakis-Doyle, Dempsey, 2011). Moreover, observing the events of daily life and explaining other situations they have come across are also regarded as the indicators of the development of elaboration skills (Allen, 2013). During the observations undertaken in the framework of this study, it was found that teachers used dramatizations as post-reading activities as a follow up to picture story book reading activities.

Switakski (2012) stated that teachers and parents had the biggest responsibility in the development of elaboration in children and stressed that children learn a lot from the dialogues with the teacher and in the family. Teachers can generate dialogues during book reading activities. Pentimonti, Zucker and Justice (2011) reported that interactive reading activities support children's elaboration skills and motivate them to learn. Present study also found that teacher support and reinforcement for children's elaboration skills are significant. Studies in literature also show that teacher support for these skills enhance children's language development. It can be argued that integrating picture story book reading activities with support for children's creativity with activities such as drama and activities to develop motivation to learn will support and develop children's elaboration skills at a higher level.

In Turkey, to equip students with deeper knowledge on print and phonology is not among the objective of preschool education. On the contrary, phonology in preschool includes simple activities designed to ensure readiness for literacy and create awareness. It was identified that the 10 teachers who participated in this study did not utilize the activities that aim to equip students with awareness for print and phonological skills. It was found that teachers only made use of riddles and finger games as preparation for picture story book reading activities. Only two teachers were observed to show students the cover of the book and ask questions that led students to guess the name of the book. It was frequently observed in the study that teachers avoided examining the print in the story text and did not implement any activities that focused on direction of print, starting sounds and rhyming words. During the interviews, teachers stated that they only did activities with children that focused on filling in structured textbook publications designed to equip them with phonological awareness for reading readiness.

It was identified that teacher skills in preparing the environment for reading sessions, managing sessions and motivating students for activities positively contributed to children's language development. According to SABR, it is necessary for teachers to patiently wait for students to settle down before reading activities and ensure a suitable sitting arrangement by using classroom management strategies.

Moreover, it is necessary to arrange the environment for the reading activity beforehand in terms of temperature, light and size. It is imperative to begin the reading activity after it is ensured that students are settled down in a manner that is safe and comfortable and they will not hurt each other. During the activity, teachers should track situations and events that will distract students and prevent them from listening. In SABR, teachers are expected to follow these distractive behaviors and use different methods to ensure student participation and interest by employing verbal warnings, establishing eye contact, changing students' seats and encouraging to listen by means of reinforcement.

Guo, Piasta, Justice and Kaderavek (2010) mentioned that it is important to meet all the needs of children before starting the reading activity so that the activity is not interrupted and they are not distracted. This way, children will be more interested in and attentive to picture story book reading activities and less problems will be encountered during the activity. Cunningham (2010) reported that quality and effective use of preschool education environments increase student participation in activities and therefore ensure motivation for learning. In a study conducted with preschool children, Cunningham (2010) measured the periods of concentration based on the quality of environments and found that classroom management increased the period of concentration. Barbarin, Early, Clifford, Bryant, Frome, Burchinal, Howes and Pianta (2008) presented the effect of quality preschool environments on children's language development. They maintained the most important factor that determined this quality is the teacher. They underlined that fact that teachers had the key role in establishing and developing quality environments and reported that a good preschool teacher should prepare sustainable, practical and creative reading activities that can hold children's interest active for long periods.

It is important to remove negative behavior problems in the classroom to ensure continued student interest in picture story book reding activities. It is necessary to make the class atrractive and ready to learn in all aspects. Torti (2006) examined the effects of classroom environment on children's language and vocabulary development and found that positive and peaceful environments that will be prepared for students support children's language development. Similarly, Barnes (2013), Servizzi (2013) and Rudasill Mortiz, Rimm-Kaufman, Justice and Pence (2010) presented the significance of teachers in creating classroom atmosphere and found that positive relationships between language development and reading environment increase language development.

In their studies, Callahan (2009), Gest, Freeman, Domitrovich and Welsh (2004), Dickinson and Sprague (2001) investigated the characteristics of interactive picture story book reading activities. Preplanning and arranging the environment before the reading activity, making preparations related to the story and using classroom management accurately were found to be important in generating interest for reading activities.

Observation records in this study showed that teachers were attentive to make seating arrangements prior to reading activities. It was found that they tried to make eye contact with children and engaged in activities that would attract student attention. However, it was also observed that teachers sometimes did not hear children's questions, they frequently allowed the same children to speak and contact them, and they did not listen to students' responses at times and cut their answers short. According to SABR, these behaviors caused the teachers not to score on the items related to acting patiently and respectfully to children.

Similar to other studies, present study also found that children's language development was supported when preschool teachers arranged the reading atmosphere/environment and continued the activity by implementing appropriate classroom management strategies. In this context, it can be argued that a positive relationship exists between children's language development and the reading atmosphere. It is believed that the biggest role to ensure this positive relationship lies with the teacher.

Sometimes different materials and tools are required to support children's language development such as picture story books, puppets, dramatization materials and tools, materials for art activities. At times, it can be rather expensive to acquire these materials. A creative teacher or a parent can obtain many materials by using recycled materials found at home. However, acquiring books with different types and shapes, especially the books from quality printing houses is very difficult. Many studies that examined the factors that affected language development in preschool children (Hoff-Ginsburg, 1998; Hoff, 2003; Erdoğan, Şimşek Bekir and Erdoğan Aras, 2005; Erdil, 2010; Manzo, 2011; Güven and Topbaş, 2014) displayed the importance of socio economic status in this respect. Economic conditions of parents also affect children's language development (Dereli and Koçak, 2005; Vernon Feagans, Garett-Peters, Willougby and Mills-Koonce, 2012). When children encounter high level of stimulus from the environment, they show a rapid language development during early childhood. Schools and families with good socio economic status may present children with different and various types of materials support. However, students with lower socio economic status are undeniably deprived in terms of the variety of environmental stimuli. It was identified that children who stayed behind in language development due to socio economic reasons sometimes cannot catch up with others in the future (Schoon, Parsons, Rush and Law, 2010). This situation may negatively affect all other developmental areas. Programs that aim to support early childhood development in many countries target individuals with socio economic deprivation. These programs aim to present opportunities to these children support their development to catch up with their peers.

This study also presented that socio-economic status affected children's language development. Children normally go to schools in the areas in close proximity to their homes and this creates stratification among schools in terms of children's socio-economic status. Although the Turkish Ministry of Education strives to provide all institutions with material support, it is known that this support is not always sufficient. In preschool institutions, education is not limited to school and continues at home with the support of parents. It was found that in this support, socio economic status is as important as productive and quality time spent by parents with their children (Reilly, Wake, Ukoumunne, Bavin, Prior, Cini, Conwmonth, Eadie and Bretherton, 2010). Social relationships, stimulating materials in the environment, interaction of the child with these stimulating materials and tools and quality education not only affect language development but also affect early academic skills (Uyanık and Kandır, 2010).

Based on the findings of this study, it can be claimed that teachers with 2-5 years of experience support children's language development less compared to the teachers with 6-10 or 21 years or more experience. It was identified that children in classrooms taught by teachers with 11-15 years of experience had lower language development years compared to children in classrooms taught by teachers with 6-10 or 21 years or more experience.

During their professional careers, preschool teachers encounter 3-6-year-old or younger children. It is a hard task to spend hours, days, moths and even years with young children. Some of the tasks each preschool teacher should continue doing for years may be listed as being patient, keeping pace with the actions of children, renewing oneself in line with children's interests, being dynamic and being a good role model. Preschool teachers have no breaks or recess. Hence it has been identified that professional burn out level in preschool teachers is higher compared to other teachers (Akman, Taşkın, Özden and Çörtü, 2010). This study found that preschool teachers with 2-5 years of experience support children's language development less compared to others. This result is believed to be related to the factors outlined in Saban, Korkmaz and Akbaşlı's (2004) study for new teachers: (1) reality shock, (2) loneliness in the struggle to achieve better results in the profession and (3) difficulty caused by losing one's ideals. Karaca and Aral (2013) identified that teachers learn how to teach many concepts, develop themselves, realize their shortcomings, acquire classroom management strategies and strive to develop themselves when they have 6-10 years of professional experience. It was found that teachers support and develop students' language development at higher levels compared to their first years in the profession.

It was identified that levels of frustration and burn out are highly increased when teachers have 11-15 years of professional experience. Kandır, Özbey and İnal (2009) stated that continuous routine repetitions in the school system, spending time doing the same thing every day and struggling to make ends meet prevent teachers from focusing on education and training activities. It is believed that these factors cause teachers to support children's development less compared to previous years of their teaching. It is observed that teachers during this period adopt routine behaviors and implement a monotone program without getting out of these established behavior patterns.

Although no significant differences were observed in this respect, this study identified that male children in the sample presented higher level of language development compared to female children. Yenisor (1989) stated that differences in competence based on gender do not carry precise values. While there are differences in language study scores in favor of girls until 4-5 years old, boys make up that difference in advanced ages and gender ceases to be an effective factor. In their study, Yıldırım Doğru, Alabay and Kayılı (2010) found a difference between preschool children's language development scores based on gender in favor of boys. Contrary to Yıldırım Doğru et. al., Acarlar and Dönmez (1992) found in their study that gender difference in language development was in favor of girls. Ataç's (1991) study with disabled children showed that mentally disabled girls learned speaking more easily compared to mentally disabled boys and the biggest difference was observed in 13-14 years. In their study, İpek and Bilgin (2007) identified that there were no significant differences between male and female students in language development level scores they obtained from Peabody Picture Vocabulary Test. In their study, Taner and Başal (2005) compared PPVT mean scores for students with and without preschool education based on gender. They identified that language development level scores for male children were higher than those of female students.

Although many studies in literature present the findings that girls have earlier language development processes compared to boys, other studies show that boys sometimes may progress better than girls. It is believed that these results are based on environmental factors. It can be claimed in the present study that environmental factors may have played an important role related to the finding that language development of boys were higher compared to those of girls.

CONCLUSION

- This study included only preschool teachers employed in 48-60 month classrooms. Therefore, SABR scale can be implemented on teachers teaching different grades and students in different age groups.
- This study focused on children's language development levels and the impact of picture study books was only examined in relation to language

development. In future, studies can be conducted to compare the impact of SABR with inclusion of scales in different developmental areas.

- It was identified in this study that picture story book reading activities are important in language development. Hence, workshops can be organized for teachers to ensure that they can create more creative and attractive activities.
- In-service training activities can be organized for teachers to remind them of important points to consider during picture story book reading activities, to brush up on their prior skills and to have them follow the innovations in the field.
- It is an important need to develop language development tests in Turkish which are reliable, suitable to our culture and with completed norm studies. Therefore, it is suggested that studies are undertaken to fulfill this need in the field of preschool teaching.
- It is observed that educational programs are needed to support children and to develop children's language development, school readiness and literacy awareness. It can be ensured that these types of programs are implemented especially in socially disadvantaged areas.
- Picture story book reading activities that include parents can be planned to have parents support their preschool children's language development and to create awareness by focusing on the importance of language development. In order to strengthen the ties between mother and child and father and child and to support acquisition of reading habits; parents can be provided with information on how to read picture story books, suitable methods and techniques and materials that can be prepared by them.
- Workshops and trainings can be organized to inform teachers and parents about interactive reading activities and how they should be implemented by providing examples.

REFERENCES

Acarlar, F., & Dönmez, N. (1992). 30–47 aylar arasındaki Türk çocuklarının dil yapılarının incelenmesi. *G.Ü. Gazi Eğitim Fakültesi Dergisi*, *8*(3), 163–203.

Adıgüzel, Ö. (2013). *Eğitimde yaratıcı drama*. Ankara: Pegem Akademi Yayıncılık.

Akman, B., Taşkın, N., Özden, Z., & Çörtü, F. (2010). Okul öncesi öğretmenlerinde tükenmişlik üzerine bir çalışma. *İlköğretim Online*, *9*(2), 802-815.

Allen, J. W. (2013). *Storytelling with cultural tools: Children's engagement with features of oral traditions in first nations cultural education programs* (Unpublished Doctoral Dissertation). University of Victoria.

Ataç, F. (1991). *İnsan yaşamında psikolojik gelişim*. İstanbul: Beta Basım Yayım Dağıtım.

Aydın, A. (2012). Turkish adaptation of test of pretended play. *Educational Sciences: Theory and Practice*, *12*(2), 916–925.

Aydoğan, Y. & Koçak, N. (2003). Okul öncesi çocukların dil gelişimine etki eden faktörlerin incelenmesi. *Milli Eğitim Dergisi*, 159.

Ball, E. W., & Blachman, B. A. (1991). Does phoneme awareness training in kindergarten make a difference in early word recognition and developmental spelling? *Reading Research Quarterly*, *24*(1), 49–66. doi:10.1598/RRQ.26.1.3

Barbarin, O. A., Early, D., Clifford, R., Bryant, D., Frome, P., Burchinal, M., & Pianta, R. et al. (2008). Parental conceptions of school readiness: Relation to ethnicity, socioeconomic status, and children's skills. *Early Education and Development*, *19*(5), 671–701. doi:10.1080/10409280802375257

Barnes, M. E. (2013). *Head Start preschool teachers' commenting practices during shared book reading sessions: Describing learning opportunities for children with varying vocabulary abilities* (Unpublished Doctoral Dissertation). University of Vanderbilt.

Beck, I. L., & McKeown, M. G. (2007). Increasing young low-income children's oral vocabulary repertoires through rich and focused instruction. *The Elementary School Journal*, *107*(3), 251–271. doi:10.1086/511706

Benson, K. A. (2013). *An Investigation of the Impact of Small Group Direct Vocabulary Instruction on the Vocabulary Development of Kindergarten Children Living in Poverty* (Unpublished Doctoral Dissertation). Ball State University.

Blank, M., & Solomon, F. (2007). A tutorial language program to develop abstract thinking in socially disadvantaged preschool children. *Child Development*, *39*(2), 379–389. doi:10.2307/1126952 PMID:4172078

Bowerman, M., & Levinson, S. C. (2001). *Language acquisition and conceptional development*. Cambridge University Press. doi:10.1017/CBO9780511620669

Çakmak, T., & Yılmaz, B. (2009). Okul öncesi dönem çocuklarının okuma alışkanlığına hazırlık durumları üzerine bir araştırma: Hacettepe üniversitesi Beytepe anaokulu örneği. *Türk Kütüphaneciliği Dergisi*, *23*(3), 489–509.

Callahan, M. D. (2009). Starting small: Building preschool teacher knowledge that supports early literacy development. *Reading and Writing*, *22*(4), 487–510. doi:10.1007/s11145-009-9164-z

Chomsky, N. (1957). *Syntactic structures*. The Hague: Mouton.

Çocuk, H. E., Yanpar Yelken, T., Emsal Aslantürk, İ., & Güçlü, M. (2013). Okul öncesi eğitim programı dil alanı ile ilgili etkinliklerin uygulanmasına ilişkin okul öncesi öğretmen görüşlerinin belirlenmesi. *The International Journal of Social Sciences (Islamabad)*, *6*(7), 305–320.

Correll, K. (2008). *A program evaluation of a conversational instruction program for the vocabulary development of four-year old student in preschool classes* (Unpublished Doctoral Dissertation). University of Houston.

Crain-Thoreson, C., & Dale, P. S. (1992). Do early talkers become early readers? Linguistic precocity, preschool language, and emergent literacy. *Developmental Psychology*, *28*(3), 421–429. doi:10.1037/0012-1649.28.3.421

Crawford, P. A. (1995). Early literacy: Emerging perspectives. *Journal of Research in Childhood Education*, *10*(1), 71–86. doi:10.1080/02568549509594689

Cunningham, D. D. (2010). Relating preschool quality to children's literacy development. *Early Childhood Education Journal*, *37*(6), 501–507. doi:10.1007/s10643-009-0370-8

Demircan, C. (2006). Tübitak çocuk kitaplığı dizisindeki kitapların dış yapısal ve içyapısal olarak incelenmesi. *Mersin Üniversitesi Eğitim Fakültesi Dergisi*, *2*(1), 12–27.

Dereli, E. & Koçak, N. (2005). Okul öncesi eğitime devam eden 4-6 yaş arasındaki çocukların ifade edici dil düzeylerinin bakım tarzı ve anne- baba eğitim düzeyi açısından incelenmesi. *Selçuk Üniversitesi, Sosyal Bilimler Enstitüsü Dergisi,* (14).

Deretarla Gül, E. (2013). Okul öncesi çocuklara okuma alışkanlığı kazandırma. In M. Gönen (Ed.), Çocuk Edebiyatı (pp. 305-314). Ankara: Eğiten Kitap Yayınevi.

Dickinson, D. K. (2011). Teacher's language practices and academic outcomes of pre school children. *Investing Early. Education, 333.*

Dickinson, D. K., McCabe, A., & Anastasopoulos, L. (2002). *A framework for examining book reading in early childhood classroms*. CIERA Report 1-014.

Dickinson, D. K., & Smith, M. W. (1994). Long term effects of preschool teachers's book readings on low-income children's vocabulary and story comprehension. *Reading Research Quarterly*, *29*(2), 104–122. doi:10.2307/747807

Dickinson, D. K., & Sprague, K. E. (2001). The nature and impact of early childhood care environments on the language and literacy development of children from low-income families. In S.B. Neuman & D.K. Dickinson (Eds.), Handbook of Early Literacy Research (pp. 263-280). Guilford.

Erdil, Z. (2010). Sosyoekonomik olarak risk altında bulunan çocuklara yönelik erken müdahale programları ve akademik başarı ilişkisi. *Sağlık Bilimleri Fakültesi Hemşirelik Dergisi,* 72-78.

Erdoğan, S., Şimşek Bekir, H. & Erdoğan Aras, S. (2005). Alt sosyoekonomik bölgelerde ana sınıfına devam eden 5-6 yaş grubundaki çocukların dil gelişim düzeylerine bazı faktörlerin etkisinin incelenmesi. *Çukurova Üniversitesi Sosyal Bilimler Enstitüsü Dergisi*, *14*(1), 231-246.

Ezell, H. K., & Justice, L. M. (1998). A pilot investigation of parents' questions about print and pictures to preschoolers with language delay. *Child Language Teaching and Therapy*, *14*(3), 273–278.

Gest, S. D., Freeman, N. R., Domitrovich, C. E., & Welsh, J. A. (2004). Shared book reading and children's language comprehension skills: The moderating role of parental discipline practices. *Early Childhood Research Quarterly*, *19*(2), 319–336. doi:10.1016/j.ecresq.2004.04.007

Girolametto, L., Weitzman, E., Lefebvre, P., & Greenberg, J. (2007). The effects of in-service education to promote emergent literacy in child care centers: A feasibility study. *Language, Speech, and Hearing Services in Schools*, *38*(1), 72–83. doi:10.1044/0161-1461(2007/007) PMID:17218537

Gönen, M., Ünüvar, P., Bıçakçı, M., Koçyiğit, S., Yazıcı, Z., Orçan, M., & Özyürek, A. et al. (2010). Okul öncesi öğretmenlerinin dil etkinliklerini uygulama biçimlerinin incelenmesi. *Mehmet Akif Ersoy Eğitim Fakültesi Dergisi*, *10*(19), 23–40.

Guo, Y., Piasta, S. B., Justice, L. M., & Kaderavek, J. N. (2010). Relations among preschool teachers' language and literacy gains. *Teaching and Teacher Education*, *26*, 1094–1103. doi:10.1016/j.tate.2009.11.005

Güven, S., & Topbaş, S. (2014). Erken dil gelişimi testi-üçüncü edisyon'un (test of early language development-third edition) uyarlama, geçerlik ve güvenirlik ön çalışması. *International Journal of Early Childhood Special Education*, *6*(2), 151–172.

Hanbay, O. (2013). *Çocuklarla yabancı dil öğretimi*. Ankara: Anı Yayıncılık.

Hindman, A. H., Wasik, B. A., & Erhart, A. L. (2012). Shared book reading and Head Start preschoolers' vocabulary learning: The role of book-related discussion and curricular connections. *Early Education and Development*, *23*(4), 451–474. do i:10.1080/10409289.2010.537250

Hoff, E. (2003). The specificity of environmental influence: Socioeconomic status affects early vocabulary development via maternal speech. *Child Development*, *74*(5), 1368–1378. doi:10.1111/1467-8624.00612 PMID:14552403

Hoff-Ginsburg, E. (1998). The relation of birth order and socioeconomic status to children's language experience and language development. *Applied Psycholinguistics*, *19*(04), 603–629. doi:10.1017/S0142716400010389

İpek, N. & Bilgin, A. (2007). İlköğretim çağı çocuklarında kelime dağarcığı gelişimi. *İlköğretim Online*, *6*(3), 344-365.

Justice, L. M., Bowles, R., Pence, K., & Gosse, C. (2010). A scalable tool for assessing children's language abilities within a narrative context: The NAP (Narrative Assessment Protocol). *Early Childhood Research Quarterly*, *25*(2), 218–234. doi:10.1016/j.ecresq.2009.11.002

Justice, L. M., & Ezell, H. K. (1999). Vygotskian theory and its application to language assessment: An overview for speech-language pathologists. *Contemporary Issues in Communication Science and Disorders*, *26*, 111–118.

Justice, L. M., & Ezell, H. K. (2002). Use of storybook reading to increase print awareness in at-risk children. *American Journal of Speech-Language Pathology*, *11*(1), 17–29. doi:10.1044/1058-0360(2002/003)

Justice, L. M., Mashburn, A., Hamre, B., & Pianta, R. (2008). Quality of language and literacy instruction in pre-kindergarten programs serving at-risk pupils. *Early Childhood Research Quarterly*, *23*, 51–68. doi:10.1016/j.ecresq.2007.09.004 PMID:22773887

Justice, L. M., Zucker, T. A., & Sofka, A. E. (2010). *Systematic assessment of book reading: SABR manual.* Columbus, OH: The Ohio State University College of Education and Human Ecology.

Kandır, A., Özbey, S., & İnal, G. (2009). A study on the difficulties faced by preschool teachers in the planning and implementation. *The Journal of International Social Research.*, *6*, 373–387.

Karaca, N. H., & Aral, N. (2011). Okul öncesi öğretmen adaylarının öğretmenlik uygulamalarında karşılaştıkları sorunlar. *2nd International Conference on New Trends in Education and Their Implications*, 595-602.

Koçak, N., Ergin, B. & Yalçın, H. (2014). 60-72 Aylık çocukların dil gelişim düzeyleri ve etki eden faktörlerin incelenmesi. *KMÜ Sosyal ve Ekonomik Araştırmalar Dergisi, 16*, 100-106.

La Paro, K. M., Pianta, R. C., & Shulman, M. (2004). The classroom assessment scoring system: Findings from the prekindergarten year. *The Elementary School Journal, 104*(5), 409–426. doi:10.1086/499760

Lee, J. C., Skarakis-Doyle, E., & Dempsey, L. (2011). The Contributions of activity and occupation to young children's comprehension of picture books. *Journal of Occupational Science, 10*(3), 146–149. doi:10.1080/14427591.2003.9686522

Lundberg, I., Larsman, P., & Strid, A. (2012). Development of phonological awareness during the preschool year: The influence of gender and socio-economic status. *Reading and Writing, 25*(2), 305–320. doi:10.1007/s11145-010-9269-4

Manzo, J. C. (2011). *Shared book reading styles and expressive and receptive vocabulary outcomes among low-income latino caregivers and young children* (Unpublished Doctoral Dissertation). Lehigh University.

Mashburn, A. J., Downer, J. T., Hamre, B. K., Justice, L. M., & Pianta, R. C. (2010). Consultation for teachers and children's language and literacy development during Pre-Kindergarten. *Applied Developmental Science, 14*(4), 179–196. doi:10.1080/10888691.2010.516187

Maviş, İ. (2005). Çocukta dil edinim kuralları. In S. Topbaş (Ed.), Dil ve Kavram Gelişimi (pp. 31-61). Ankara: Kök Yayıncılık.

Maybin, J., & Watson, N. J. (2009). Children's literature: approaches and territories. The Open University.

MEB. (2013). *Okul öncesi eğitim programı*. Milli Eğitim Bakanlığı Talim Terbiye Kurumu.

Menyuk, P., & Brisk, E. M. (2005a). Language development in early childhood – the preschool years: 3-5. In Language development and education (pp. 38-58). Palgrave Macmillan.

Neaum, S. (2010). Child development for early childhood studies. In Understanding children's development (pp. 33-41). Glasgow, UK: Learning Matters Ltd.

Nelson, K. (1973). Structure and strategy in learning to talk. *Monographs of the Society for Research in Child Development, 38*(1/2), 149. doi:10.2307/1165788

Oers, B., & Poland, M. (2007). Schematising activities as a means for encouraging young children to think abstractly. *Mathematics Education Research Journal, 19*(2), 10–22. doi:10.1007/BF03217453

Öztan Ulusoy, Y. (2012). Bilgiyi işleme kuramı ve yansımaları. In B. Oral (Ed.), Öğrenme öğretme kuram ve yaklaşımları. Ankara: Pegem Akademi Yayıncılık.

Öztürk, Y. (2013). Sembolik Düşünce; Okul Öncesi Yıllarda Oyun, Dil ve Okuryazarlık. In Erken Çocukluk Döneminde Gelişim (pp. 254-293). Ankara: Nobel Akademik Yayıncılık.

Pentimonti, J. M., & Justice, L. M. (2010). Teachers' use of scaffolding strategies during read alouds in the preschool classroom. *Early Childhood Education Journal*, 1–8.

Pentimonti, J. M., Zucker, T. A., & Justice, L. M. (2011). What are preschool teachers reading in their classrooms? *Reading Psychology, 32*(3), 197–236. doi:10.1080/02702711003604484

Pentimonti, J. M., Zucker, T. A., Justice, L. M., Petscher, Y., Piasta, S. B., & Kaderavek, J. N. (2012). A Standardized tool for assessing the quality of clssroom-based shared reading: Systematic Assessment of Book Reading (SABR). *Early Childhood Research Quarterly, 27*(3), 512–528. doi:10.1016/j.ecresq.2011.12.007

Reese, E., & Cox, A. (1999). Quality of book reading affects children's emergent literacy. *Developmental Psychology, 35*(1), 20–28. doi:10.1037/0012-1649.35.1.20 PMID:9923461

Reilly, S., Wake, M., Ukoumunne, O. C., Bavin, E., Prior, M., Cini, E., & Bretherton, L. et al. (2010). Predicting language outcomes at 4 years of age: Findings from early language in Victoria study. *Pediatrics, 126*(6), e1530–e1537. doi:10.1542/peds.2010-0254 PMID:21059719

Robert, E., & Owens, J. R. (2012). Language development an introduction. In The Territory (pp. 3-35). Upper Saddle River, NJ: Pearson Education Inc.

Roth, F., Troia, A., Wortington, C., & Handy, D. (2006). Promoting awareness of sounds in speech (Pass): The effects of intervention and stimulus characteristics on the blending performance of preschool children with communication impairments. *Learning Disability Quarterly, 29*(2), 64–78. doi:10.2307/30035536

Rudasill Moritz, K., Rimm-Kaufman, S. E., Justice, L. M., & Pence, K. (2010). Temperament and language skills as predictors of teacher-child relationship quality in preschool. *Early Education and Development*, *17*(2), 271–291. doi:10.1207/s15566935eed1702_4

Saban, A., Korkmaz, İ., & Akbaşlı, S. (2004). Öğretmen adaylarının mesleki kaygıları. *Eğitim Araştırmaları*, *5*(17), 198–209.

Schickedanz, J. A. (1999). *Much more than the ABC's: The early stages of reading and writing*. Washington, DC: National Association for the Education of Young Children.

Schoon, İ., Parsons, S., Rush, R., & Law, J. (2010). Childhood language skills and adult literacy: A 29 year follow-up study. *Pediatrics*, *125*(3).

Senemoğlu, N. (2012). Gelişim Öğrenme ve Öğretim. Ankara: Pegem Akademi.

Servizzi, K. M. (2013). *Teachers' cognitive demands and preschool students's use of thinking strategies during interactive book reading* (Unpublished Doctoral Dissertation). Ball State University.

Smith, P. K., Wigboldus, D. H. J., & Dijksterhuis, A. (2008). Abstract thinking increases one's sesnse of power. *Journal of Experimental Social Psychology*, *44*(2), 378–385. doi:10.1016/j.jesp.2006.12.005

Switalski, S. O. (2012). *An investigation of the additive benefits of parent dialogic reading techniques in older preschool children* (Unpublished Doctoral Dissertation). University of Duquesne.

Taner, M., & Başal, H. A. (2005). Farklı sosyoekonomik düzeylerde okul öncesi eğitim alan ve almayan ilköğretim birinci sınıf öğrencilerinin dil gelişimlerinin cinsiyete gore karşılaştırılması. *Eğitim Fakültesi Dergisi*, *18*(2), 395–420.

Torti, C. D. (2006). *The relationship between the quality of the early childhood classroom environment and vocabulary development in young children learning English as a second language* (Unpublished Doctoral Dissertation). Texas A&M University.

Tsao, T. L. (2002). *Perceptual learning style preference and learning strategy use among Taiwanese senior high school EFL learners* (Master's thesis). National Taiwan Normal University.

Uyanık, Ö., & Kandır, A. (2010). Okul öncesi dönemde erken akademik beceriler. *Kuramsal Eğitimbilim*, *3*(2), 118–134.

Vernon-Feagns, L., Garrett-Peters, P., Willoughby, M., & Mills-Koonce, R. (2012). Chaos, poverty, and parenting: Predictors of early language development. *Early Childhood Research Quarterly*, *27*(3), 339–351. doi:10.1016/j.ecresq.2011.11.001 PMID:23049162

Yenisor, E. (1989). *Yuvanın dil gelişimine etkisi*. İstanbul: İstanbul Üniversitesi Çocuk Sağlığı Enstitüsü, Yüksek Lisans Tezi.

Yıldırım Doğru, S. S., Alabay, E., & Kayılı, G. (2010). Determination of word knowledge and comprehension levels in normal developing and learning disorder children. *Elementary Education Online*, *3*(9), 828–840.

Zucker, T. A., Cabell, S. Q., Justice, L. M., Pentimonti, J. M., & Kadaravek, J. N. (2013). The role of frequent, interactive prekindergarten shared reading in the longitudinal development of language and literacy skills. *Developmental Psychology*, *49*(8), 1425–1439. doi:10.1037/a0030347 PMID:23066674

Zucker, T. A., Justice, L. M., Pianta, S. B., & Kaderavek, J. N. (2010). Preschool teachers' literal and inferential questions and children's responses during whole-class shared reading. *Early Childhood Research Quarterly*, *25*(1), 65–83. doi:10.1016/j.ecresq.2009.07.001

Zucker, T. A., & Landry, S. H. (2010). Improving the quality of preschool read alouds: Professional development and coaching that targets book-reading practices. In M. C. McKenna, S. Walpole, & K. Conradi (Eds.), Promoting early reading: Research, resources, and best practices (pp. 78–104). New York, NY: Guilford.

Chapter 11
Bilingual Mental Lexicon and Collocational Processing

Hakan Cangır
Ankara University, Turkey

ABSTRACT

The chapter starts with a definition and models of mental dictionary. It then builds on the bilingual lexical activation models and goes on to discuss formulaic language (collocations in particular). After explaining the basics of formulaic language processing, the author attempts to address the issue of lexical and collocational priming theory by Hoey, which has its roots in cognitive linguistics and usage-based language models. Last but not least, some suggestions for future research are provided in an attempt to address the needs of the lexical research literature in the Turkish setting.

INTRODUCTION

The notion of monolingual and bilingual mental lexicon has intrigued linguists who are interested in cognitive aspects of language processing and psycholinguistics, in particular, for a long time. There have been controversial issues in the literature regarding how the lexicon is organized, if bilinguals have two separate lexicons, and whether both languages of the bilinguals compete for lexical selection during lexical processing etc. Those who have conducted research exploring lexical processing to model the monolingual and bilingual mental lexicons appear to have concentrated on single lexical units only. Although the processing of formulaic expressions has been investigated in many studies, few or almost none of them, to the writer's knowledge, seem to scrutinize cross-linguistic influence and its reflection on the

DOI: 10.4018/978-1-5225-4009-0.ch011

structuring of mental lexicon. Furthermore, while studies exploring collocational processing in English seem to be abound, research investigating the case in a morphologically different language (i.e. Turkish) appears to be lacking. With these controversies and unanswered questions in mind, the chapter attempts to shed light on the monolingual and bilingual mental lexicon models proposed so far, draw the attention of the readers to the processing of formulaic expressions (collocations in particular) and question their possible influence on the organization of the internal lexicon. To this end, this chapter addresses monolingual lexicon models, bilingual mental lexicon models, formulaic language, collocations, and collocational priming, respectively in an attempt to raise awareness about the need to explore cross-linguistic collocational priming, searching for a collocational spreading activation framework at a cross-linguistic level, if any.

Mental Lexicon

Many linguists agree that mental lexicon is defined as systematic representation of words in permanent memory (Carroll, 2004). An analogy is drawn between a physical dictionary and a mental dictionary, but this superficial resemblance is regarded very simplistic considering the psycholinguistic aspect of lexis and the interconnected nature of words in the internal lexicon as opposed to a relatively mechanic representation of words in an actual dictionary where words are provided as lists of items with different senses. The way the language is used by exploiting networks of words is too complex to be reflected in a dictionary alone. As Aitchison (2003) states the lexical items in an actual dictionary are static, whereas the internal dictionary is dynamic. Languages evolve in time and language users' linguistic knowledge also tends to transform, as a result of which the mental representations of words seem to change. A more crucial difference between a traditional dictionary and a mental dictionary can be observed in the accessibility of the linguistic information stored. In a paper dictionary, one can access any lexical entry equally regardless of their frequency, salience, context etc. On the other hand, the lexical items that are stored in our mental dictionary have varying levels of accessibility depending on the item's association with other words, its commonly preferred context, its imageability etc. One last difference can be seen in the form of the stored information. A paper dictionary includes verbal information, whereas the mental dictionary consists not only verbal but also conceptual representation. The internal lexicon is similar to a network of interconnected nodes which are comparable to groups of neurons in the human brain (Aitchison, 2003).

Singleton (1999) thinks that the mental dictionary is an integral part of human long term memory containing the language user's all linguistic knowledge. In a recent and a more comprehensive description, Roux (2013, p.82) states that mental dictionary is "the collective representation of words in the mind drawing together contextual, personal and interpersonal dimensions of meaning" and it helps the language users during acquisition, recalling and while expressing themselves. Although the analogy between a printed dictionary and a mental lexicon help the understanding of the abstract concept of lexical storage and representation in the brain, the supporters of the cognitive approach do not adopt the comparison saying that internal lexicon is a complex cognitive system composed of concepts, their phonological and orthographic linguistic realizations (Gabrys`-Barker, 2005, p.39).

Pickering and Garrod (2013) suggest a new approach to the organization of mental dictionary, which has its roots in the Dynamic Systems Theory (Briggs and Peat, 1989). The evidence based on the conversations indicating that those people taking part in the conversation were exploiting some fixed expression or formulaic phrases, in other words. They claimed that language users employ these phrases as they are since they are stored in the mental lexicon as chunks or bundles. Therefore, this account of the mental lexicon may require taking formulaic language into account while modelling the internal dictionary.

Some linguists like Carrol (2004) attribute the concept mental dictionary to exclusively semantic sub-lexicon, whereas others regard semantic and phonological levels as separate layers of representation. There is, however, a consensus that semantic and formal aspects of a lexical unit are stored separately (Aitchison, 2012). In other words, the semantic and formal features are thought to exist in two different layers, but they are interconnected through an extensive network (Szubko-Sitarek, 2015).

Words can be linked through their meaning; semantically, morphologically or phonologically. That could be seen as one aspect of lexical organization. Words can also be related based on their associative links. Words that are not semantically, morphologically or phonologically related but tend to co-occur frequently in language production is commonly defined as collocations.

There are research studies investigating these associative links in an attempt to provide evidence for an alternative depiction of the mental lexicon. Those studies employ various experimental methodologies, such as priming or association tests (e.g. Durrant and Doherty, 2010; Dijkstra et al. 2010). What they are primarily exploring is the validity of a theory developed by Hoey (2005), collocational priming, which is claimed to be the source of our creative language production. The details of this theory are discussed further in the following sections.

One last important classification to note before moving onto the mental lexicon models is the full listing and decomposition hypotheses. The former asserts that words and their inflected forms are stored separately and as a whole in the form of a list of items. The latter suggests that the words are stored with no morphological markers. The morphological extensions are stored as a separate layer and users tend to decompose lexical units into their affixes and roots during lexical processing and this approach favours a morphologically-governed organization of the lexicon by means of the priming research findings (Harley, 2005).

Having scrutinized the definition of mental lexicon and underlined some broad approaches to the lexical organization in the mind, the chapter will summarize and discuss various models and approaches that have been put forward trying to explain how the mental lexicon is structured; to be more precise, how lexical entries are organized and connected to one another at the semantic level in the mental lexicon in the following section.

MODELS OF MENTAL LEXICON

Lexical representations in the internal lexicon are believed to be linked to one another in different strength and the lexical units belonging to those broader lexical concepts are thought to be in either a syntagmatic or paradigmatic relation with each other. There are models suggested to illustrate these relationships and the ones concentrating mainly on semantic associations will be discussed here.

One of the earlier proposals is the *Hierarchical Model* by Collin's and Quillian (1969). The model suggests that all lexical entries are interrelated, and they are stored and organized hierarchically. As the name suggests, the broadest concepts (i.e. prototypes) are represented as the highest node of the network and like the branches of a tree, other units are lined according to their association to the highest node. To exemplify, the word "dog" stands at the top of the hierarchy and different breeds of dogs or canine types can be represented under the highest node.

Smith et al. (1974) addressed some of the limitations of the *Hierarchical Model* and proposed a new approach highlighting the semantic features of lexical items. *The Semantic Feature Model* assumes that lexical units have characteristic and defining features. Those features are differentiated based on their salience. According to the well-known example, the word "robin" is represented closer to the node "bird" than the word "ostrich" due to the fact that it shares more defining features with the head node "bird". To be more precise, the more defining and salient features a lexical unit shares with another lexical unit, the closer they are represented in the mental dictionary. Therefore, it can be stated that those two models discussed so far seem to differ in that the latter considers semantic features of lexical units as well as the hierarchy and the strength of the relationship between them, whereas the former ignores the semantic consideration. A widely criticized aspect of the model is that although it is good at explaining the organization of concrete concepts, it fails to account for abstract ones due to its focus on semantic features, which lack for abstract lexical entries.

Considering the limitations of the previous models, Collins and Loftus (1975) propounded a new model addressing the inflexible characteristics of the hierarchical perspective. *The Spreading Activation Model* takes the association strength rather than hierarchy into account and it claims that lexical items are interconnected and how closely they are represented depends on the strength of the relationship between them. Thus, according to the model, the word "car" could be linked to the adjective "fast", the verb "drive" and the noun "house" regardless of the hierarchy among them or the semantic features of these items. The idea of spreading assumes that when one sees or hears a word, it seems to prompt the activation of some other nodes which are semantically, phonologically related. The activation appears to cease when it reaches a node where no other relation with other lexical units exist. The proof for spreading activation comes from priming experiments, in which participants are presented with stimuli and their performance in lexical decision is assessed to explore a priming effect. The priming paradigm will be discussed in further details later in the chapter. One of the limitations of the model could be seen as its idiosyncrasy. Every individual appears to have a different organization of his mental dictionary based on his experiences and this internal lexicon depiction is hard to generalize according to many linguists.

Criticizing the lack of explanation for separate levels of lexical organization, Bock and Levelt (1994) proposed a revised version of the spreading activation model including phonological and morphological layers in its representation as well as the semantic component. A more sophisticated proposal to the organization of the mental lexicon was by Seidenberg and McClelland (1989). Their model, which shows resemblance to the *Spreading Activation Model*, assumes that knowledge about words is no different than any other type of knowledge. They compare the links between the lexical units to the neurons in the brain that wire together just like words whose activation spread to other related nodes in the internal lexicon.

In addition to the models illustrating the organization of the monolingual mental dictionary, a great effort has been made to uncover the lexical organization of the bilinguals. There is a growing body of empirical evidence interpreted differently by the researchers and some proposals that have been put forward based on those findings over the years are discussed in the section below.

Bilingual Mental Lexicon

People travel to different countries for various purposes, do business with international partners and get education somewhere other than their native country. Namely, they come into contact with people who are not from their speech community and thus, it can be assumed that learning more than one language is inevitable for those people. The number of bilinguals and multilinguals is increasing every other day due to the requirements of the globalized world. The definition of the term, bilingualism, is not very straightforward, though owing to the relatively subjective nature of language proficiency measures and the fact that it is difficult to draw the line between different levels of proficiency and native-like fluency considering the four different skills of language production.

The definition of bilingualism in the literature has diverged over the years. According to one of the earlier definitions by Bloomfield (1933), bilinguals are those that produce two languages as their native tongue with an equal degree of proficiency. This strict and narrow view of bilingualism was no adopted by others like Weinreich (1953), who basically defined bilinguals as people having a different level of proficiency in two languages. Haugen (1953) had a similar stance on the issue saying bilinguals are those who are fluent in one language and can produce complete meaningful sentences in the other language, despite not having a native-like fluency.

Apart from the disagreement in the definition of bilingualism and the different approaches to the concept, researchers have also been debating regarding the lexical selection process in the bilingual mental lexicon, which will be the main focus of the following paragraph. Two distinct models have been proposed; the language specific (e.g. Costa *et al.*, 1999) vs. language non-specific lexical selection (e.g. Poulisse & Bongaerts, 1994; Hermans *et al.*, 1998). The former view asserts that when a bilingual uses one of the languages, the lexical nodes of the response language are activated and compete for lexical selection, whereas the latter view claims that during language production, lexical nodes of both languages are triggered in the bilingual mental dictionary, which are assumed to share a common conceptual representation and take part in the lexical selection process regardless of the response language. The researchers having a language-specific lexical selection stance accept that both the languages are activated during the process; however, only the lexical items in the response language compete for selection. According to them, as proficiency improves, bilinguals tend to count more on language-specific mechanism. What they fail to explain according the supporters of language non-specific side is the code-switching phenomenon. Language non-specific lexical selection perspective posits that the two languages compete in real time communication and the proof for that could be regarded as code-switching. This view has been supported by a growing body of empirical evidence over the last years. For instance, Dong et al. (2005) provided experimental evidence showing that bilinguals seem to possess a shared conceptual system for the two languages, with links in L1-L2 or L2-L1 direction. The former direction is claimed to be stronger which is named as asymmetry in cross-linguistic priming.

In the light of these discussions (language selective vs. language non-selective and single vs. separate mental lexicons) regarding the bilingual mental processes, there have been attempts to illustrate the lexical representation in the bilingual mental dictionary. The following section aims to provide a brief overview of the illustrations.

Models of Bilingual Mental Lexicon

What has intrigued linguists as much as or even more than the organization of the monolingual mental lexicon is the structuring of the bilingual internal lexicon. Many models have been proposed over the years with differing representations. They all sought to explain the interaction of the two languages during lexical processing on the whole. One of the earlier ones was by Weinreich (1953). He categorized the word knowledge as (a) coordinative, (b) compound, and (c) subordinative. At the coordinative level, a word in L1 and L2 do not share either conceptual or form representation. At the compound level, on the other hand, L1 and L2 word counterparts have the same conceptual representation but a different formal representation. It is at the final, subordinative level that both form and conceptual representations of word knowledge intersect in the bilingual mental lexicon. An illustration of his proposed model can be found in Weinreich (1953). Weinreich's depiction of the bilingual internal lexicon triggered a new perspective and laid the foundations for the *Word Association Model* and *Concept Mediation Model* by Potter et al (1984). The former puts forward a direct association between L1 and L2 at the lexical layer, whereas the latter points at a direct relationship between the conceptual and lexical representations in L1 and L2. The overall depiction of the models can be seen in Potter et al. (1984).

The models discussed above paved the way for a well-recognized and an updated model of bilingual mental dictionary. Kroll and Steward (1994) proposed the *Revised Hierarchical Model*, which highlight the proficiency of the bilinguals and the direction of translation. The rationale behind the model was that as the learners gain proficiency in L2, the strength of the lexical links between L1 and L2 seem to alter. According to the model, the higher the proficiency is, the stronger the links between the concepts and the L2 lexical nodes are. As the model suggests, there are two separate lexical systems in the bilingual mental dictionary, but a shared conceptual system. L1 and L2 words are not only linked at the lexical level, but also at the shared conceptual level. Furthermore, research employing this model in their interpretations claims that the strength of the relationship between the lexical and conceptual layers depend on the proficiency of the bilingual and that L2-L1 direction links appear to be more robust than L1-L2 links (Pavlenko, 2009). A figure reflecting a brief overview of the model discussed above can be observed in Pavlenko (2009).

Another model by De Groot (1992, 1993) emphasizes cross-linguistic variation, which could be considered as one of its strengths. It is claimed that concrete words and cognates are processed faster than abstract ones by the bilinguals, which indicates a shared conceptual store for concrete lexical items and cognates in L1 and L2. The model is thought to account for the organization of mental lexicon of the bilinguals who acquire L2 in its natural setting and are regarded as advanced L2 users better than those who learned L2 in a classroom setting and studied the L2 words by considering their L1 translations. Certain flaws of the models have also been suggested by Pavlenko (2009). Firstly, it fails to explain the developmental aspect of lexical organization. Secondly, it relies on a feature-oriented perspective, which has been rejected by cognitive psychologists due to its failure in explaining prototype and context dependence (e.g. De Groot, 1992). The assumption about the representation of cognates and concrete words in the bilingual mental lexicon can be regarded as another weak aspect of the model since it ignores the possible false friends or cognates with partial equivalence and disregards some empirical evidence suggesting that concrete lexical items can also establish links with partially or entirely different linguistic categories. A brief depiction of the *Distributed Feature Model* can be found in De Groot (1992; 1993).

A relatively recent proposal was from Dong et al. (2005), which adopts the basic features of the *Distributed Features Model* and extends the previous assumption. They state that the links between the L2 form and conceptual representations appear to be not as strong as the connections between the corresponding items in L1. In weaker proficiency levels, L2 form representations are linked to both the shared conceptual system with L1 and L1-specific conceptual system in the bilingual brain. As one gains proficiency, on the whole, the links become stronger in L2 and in particular the relationship between L1-specific conceptual system and L2 form representations weakens. The model is deemed successful due to considering cross-linguistic variation and vocabulary learning procedure in its representation. However, it fails to account for the overall organization of conceptual and lexical representation (Pavlenko, 2009). The illustration of the *Shared Asymmetrical Model* for a better understanding is provided in Dong et al. (2005).

Kroll and Steward again proposed a re-revised version of the model. *The Modified Hierarchical Model* (MHM) can be seen as an extension of the accumulation of the previous models. It possesses all the strengths of the previous depictions as well as integrating new modules explaining further details. For instance, it still retains the developmental perspective of the *Revised Hierarchical Model* and also holds the idea of shared and partially shared representations of lexis, which was present in some other bilingual dictionary models. An important update can be seen in the organization of the conceptual store. Instead of a single conceptual module, which was the case for the previous models, MHM groups conceptual layer into shared,

L1 specific and L2 specific categories, which could shed light on the congruence effect in the priming experiments (Pavlenko, 2009). A detailed illustration of the model for those favouring images is given in Pavlenko (2009).

Another well-acclaimed model was put forward by van Heuven, Dijkstra and Grainger (1998). The model, *Bilingual Interactive Activation* (BIA), has a language non-selective stance in lexical access and supports the view that bilinguals have integrated lexicons. Similar to the perspective of the other interactive lexical activation models, it incorporates the terms resting level, threshold level, parallel bottom-up activation, top-down feedback and inhibition in lexical access. What makes the model different from the others is its claim saying that a language node exists in the mental lexicon which is linked to all the words within a language. In an integrated bilingual mental dictionary, there are two language nodes, both for L1 and L2. Once a word is activated, its activation spreads onto the equivalent language node, which activates all the words in the target language and inhibits the lexical items in the other language. An updated version of the model, the *BIA+* was proposed by Dijkstra and van Heuven (2002). Basic features of the previous model was kept, but two extra layers were added into the representation; the semantic and phonological systems. Furthermore, the expanded version distinguishes between a word identification system and a decision system. It is claimed that lexical access occurs in the word identification module, appears to be automatic and thus, cannot be controlled by the language user consciously.

As the summary above indicates, there have been many attempts to help visualize the bilingual mental lexicon underlining different layers of lexical processing. What all the models have in common seems to be the fact that they concentrate on paradigmatic relations and lack syntagmatic links in their explanation. Wolter and Gyllstad (2011) partly addresses this niche through a framework they proposed emphasizing the collocational links in the mental dictionary. The model titled *Dual Activation of Collocational Connections* stresses the influence of L1 and L2 collocational links on the organization of the internal lexicon. Having a language non-specific stance, they claim that bilinguals activate congruent collocations in L1 and L2 simultaneously in their mental lexicon based on a collocational priming experiment. Faster reaction times for the congruent collocations in particular indicated that L1 collocational knowledge was running in the background to facilitate the processing of L2 collocations. In other words, when a bilingual hears or reads a word in L2, the word triggers not only its L2 collocate but also its L1 counterpart. Their overall assertion was that like the semantically related words, a spreading activation exists between a word and its collocate and the links between congruent L2 and L1 collocations in particular affect this process, which could be regarded as an extension of the model proposed by Collins and Loftus (1975). The two models differ in that the earlier model centres on paradigmatic relations, whereas the Wolter and Gyllstad's proposal (2011) provides interpretations regarding the lexical processing at the syntagmatic level.

This model was the first to claim a syntagmatic relationship in the organization of the mental lexicon and can be regarded as an important attempt. However, the results need to be validated with the help of a cross-linguistic collocational priming experiment which is lacking in the literature. The possible cross-linguistic collocational priming effect and its influence on the way bilingual mental lexicon is organized has been discussed in Cangır and Durrant's (2018 in progress) upcoming research, which hypothesizes that cross-linguistic collocational priming exists in the bilingual (Turkish L1 and English L2) mental lexicon and that congruence, frequency and part of speech are significant indicators of collocational processing at the cross-linguistic level.

The discussion of collocations would be incomplete without explaining formulaic language, which is used as a cover term for multiword units (Wray, 2002). The following section tries to elucidate formulaic language and how collocations are perceived in the domain of formulaic language.

FORMULAIC LANGUAGE

'Formulaic language' defined as 'recurrent multi-word lexical items that have a single meaning or function' is commonly used as an umbrella term for idioms, collocations, and lexical bundles etc. (Schmitt, 2010). Researchers with a usage-based emergentist stance of language assert that formulaic language plays a crucial role in language production because it is ubiquitous in language and it provides a processing advantage to language users. It is further claimed that it makes speech more fluent and help speakers sound more natural (Ellis, 1996).

Formulaic language is also important for second language acquisition and is widely investigated in research studies from different angles. Researchers disagree on the way native and non-native speakers process formulaic language and whether L1 and L2 interact with each other during processing. (Schmitt, 2010). Although it is widely accepted that formulaic sequences are processed holistically and retrieved as chunks during L1 use, which seems to help the language users with fluency (Wray, 2002), the approach regarding their processing in L2 cause controversy. Wray (2002; 2008), for instance, believe that non-native speakers (NNS) process formulaic units different from native speakers (NS). In other words, NNS decompose the lexical chunks into their smallest parts during comprehension and production, whereas NS process them as they are, without paying conscious attention to each unit of the chunk. However, Durrant and Schmitt (2010) concluded based on empirical evidence that the reason behind NS's different collocational processing is their inadequate exposure to the target language, rather than their approach to the acquisition of collocations, which was at odds with Wray's claims.

As Schmitt (2010) states idioms can be seen as a type of formulaic language which have received the most attention although they are merely a small portion of the lexicon and there are more commonly used multiword expressions, such as collocations which have been investigated comprehensively, but not from a cross-linguistic perspective and not from the eyes of a morphologically different language. There have been some attempts in the Turkish context to explore multiword expressions or lexical bundles mainly in writing, though not from a lexical processing perspective. For instance, Öztürk and Köse (2016) examined the use of lexical bundles by Turkish and English post-graduate students and native English faculty members in the foreign language teaching departments. Their small size corpus indicated that Turkish post-graduate students employed much more lexical bundles in their writings than native English students and scholars. Furthermore, they stated that Turkish students seemed to overuse certain lexical bundles and that the expressions that were exploited by the Turkish students did not match with the native language users. In another study by Güngör and Uysal (2016), structural and functional traits of lexical bundles in L1 and L2 research studies were scrutinized. Their results seemed to be in line with Öztürk and Köse's findings (2016) in that they also observed an overuse of specific lexical bundles by Turkish L1 and English L2 writers when compared with the native counterparts. Ortaçtepe (2013) analysed the spoken production of NSs and NNSs (Turkish students) in terms of the use of formulaic expressions in the USA setting, the results of which indicated that American students produced more formulaic expressions than Turkish students and that the expressions that were used by NNSs were more freely generated and thus less native-like. Although the studies do not touch upon the issue of processing of formulaic expressions, the differences observed in NS and NNS language production in spoken and written production may encourage one to question and discuss the possible variations of formulaic language processing by native and non-native speakers on the whole and the role of formulaic expressions in the organization of the bilingual mental lexicon.

More cross-linguistic studies exploring formulaic language with an emphasis on lexical processing needs to be conducted for conclusive results regarding the interaction of the two languages in the bilingual lexicon beyond single word level. The following section will attempt to approach the notion of collocations, which is regarded as the subcategory of formulaic language with the help of two important definitions and provide some research examples focusing on collocations.

Collocations

According to Cruse's illustration (2000), the vocabulary of a language is organized based on two key relations: paradigmatic and syntagmatic. Collocations are classified at the syntagmatic end of the organization, whereas synonyms and antonyms are placed at the paradigmatic end.

The first relation depicted is related with semantic choices in a sentence, while the second heading underlines syntactic links between lexical items. However, it is still debated whether a word and its collocate are only syntactically related or if they have a semantic relation as well. That's why some research studies exploring collocational links integrate semantic association as a separate variable in their analysis or they try to control the semantic link variable (e.g. Cangır and Durrant, 2018 in progress). Durrant and Doherty's (2010) findings also indicated that collocational priming could be restricted to frequently co-occurring word combinations that are also psychological associates and that we may need to adapt our models accordingly.

There are different approaches to the definition of 'collocation'. One of the earlier ones was by Firth (1957). He states:

Meaning by collocation is an abstraction at the syntagmatic level and is not directly concerned with the conceptual or idea approach to the meaning of words. One of the meanings of night is its collocability with dark, and, of dark, of course, collocation with night. (Firth, 1957: 196)

Firth's idea triggered some other linguists, who came up with extended or alternative definitions of collocations. According to Sinclair (1991), collocations are occurrences of two or more words within a short span in a text. His definition can be regarded as a textual interpretation. According to Leech (1974), on the other hand, "collocative meaning consists of the associations a word acquires on account of the meanings of words, which tend to occur in its environment" (p. 20). This definition approach is seen as psychological or associative, which goes hand in hand with Firth (1957) and Aitchison's (2003) stance. Hoey (1991) states "collocation has long been the name given to the relationship a lexical item has with items that appear with greater than random probability in its contextual context" (p. 6-7). His definition has a statistical perspective, which is in line with cognitive linguistics.

In addition to individual definition trials, broader and widely accepted approaches to the definition of collocations have been proposed. The first approach is named as the phraseological approach (Cowie, 1994; Howarth, 1998). In order for a word combination to be termed a true collocation, one of the members of the combination needs to be non-compositional (as in 'strong coffee'). If both the members of the combination are fully compositional, it is called a free combination (as in 'bright light'). On the other hand, if both the lexical items in the combination is non-transparent, the combination is seen as an idiom (as in 'bury the hatchet'). The approach takes semantic transparency as its primary determinant. The second widely acknowledged approach is called statistical approach, which is rooted in corpus linguistics and places emphasis on frequency values provided by statistical measures (Sinclair, 1991). According to the frequency-based or statistically-oriented perspective, the more frequent lexical items co-occur, the more likely they are entrenched in the mental lexicon and can be seen and processed as collocations. Native speakers produce these word combinations automatically, which help them with their fluency and help sound more natural. There are plus and minuses of each approach. The former is criticized due to the fact that it is generally hard to determine the borderline between the transparency levels. However, the fact that semantics is integrated in the classification gives the approach an advantage since it takes competence into account. The latter approach, on the other hand, is criticized owing to its sole concentration on statistics and disregarding the actual experiences of the language users (Howarth, 1998). However, as Henriksen (2013) says the corpus approach (i.e. statistical approach) is one of the best ways to determine which word combinations are collocations because objective criteria; frequency, range and collocational span are adopted. Since each approach has its weakness and they have a complementary nature, much research (e.g. Kjellmer, 1984; Kjellmer, 1987) has adopted both of them in their methodology and come up with lexical items that are regarded as collocations based on the frequency values provided by corpora and their semantic opaqueness. This mixed approach can be seen as a rational attempt considering the strengths and weaknesses of each approach, especially for those who are investigating second language acquisition.

Looking at the issue of lexical processing from another perspective, Hoey's (2005) lexical priming theory attempts to address the psychological reality of collocations and his paradigm is likely to shed light on the different aspects of the organization of mental lexicon. The following section explains his theory in details before discussing the need to explore the existence of lexical priming cross-linguistically.

Lexical and Collocational Priming

Firth's (1957) famous saying "you shall know a word by the company it keeps" (1957: 11) gives a broad overview of collocations. Having its root in Firthian tradition, Hoey's (2005) lexical priming theory opens an alternative window to approach the issue of language production. He asserts that every word is mentally primed for collocational use. In his definition, a collocation is:

a psychological association between words" which is "evidenced by their occurrence together in a corpus more frequently than is rational in terms of random distribution (2005, pp. 3-5)

He believes the psychological relationship can be assessed with the help of 'priming' and he further claims that priming is the source of our creative language system. To give an example, he claims that when a person sees or hears the word "heavy", the word "rain" is prompted and processing of that word in the mental lexicon is easier and faster. As opposed to the Chomskyan view, which (1956) claims humans have an innate and unique grammar device for language acquisition, he believes that grammar does not exist as a separate unit. Rather, grammatical categories emerge from lexical units by dint of priming and this view is closely related with the usage-based models, which have their roots in Cognitive Linguistics (Barlow & Kemmer, 2000). For instance, he posits the articles "a" and "the" seem to be the collocates of the nouns, which stand on their left and these lexical units are processed faster when one faces a noun in language use due to the possible priming effect. Hoey's (2005) view of language learning and production contradicts with Generative Grammar (Chomsky, 1956), which underlines genetic factors, universals and principles in language acquisition, and approaches the issue from a psycholinguistic and cognitive linguistic angle stressing the influence of human inductive reasoning on language production.

Besides his assertions regarding how lexical units prime each other, Hoey (2005) also states that lexical items seem to prime certain grammatical patterns; in other words, lexis and syntax are interrelated. Furthermore, he thinks that discourse is playing a key role in how words and phrases prime each other. To be more precise, lexical units or combinations are primed to appear or not exist in specific kinds of cohesive associations; an inclination which he calls 'textual collocation'. Moreover, he posits that lexical items are primed to exist in specific pragmatic relations like cause-effect and compare-contrast etc.

On the whole, according to Hoey (2005), priming is a natural process that is shaped by the environment we are living in and can be said to have partial individual features since every language user has different experiences. Although priming appears to alter from person to person depending on their experiences, those alterations are adjusted in time so that the language community can use the language in harmony and they can communicate in a standard pattern. His model is considered important since it provides a rational framework attempting to explain the organization of the mental lexicon.

In one of the studies questioning the viability of lexical or collocational priming, Durrant and Doherty (2010) found a partial collocational priming effect with the help of a lexical decision task, which can be seen as a tentative confirmation of Hoey's claims. Their first experiment revealed that there was collocational priming and the findings seemed to correlate with Hoey's assertions. The study was important in that it integrated the frequency variable as a contributing factor to collocational priming and ruled out psychological association. Their second experiment, on the other hand, indicated that priming existed for the associated word pairs but not for high frequency collocations, which was not in line with their first findings. Thus, their results need further investigation and must be treated cautiously.

There is also some research looking into the issue of lexical priming from a cross-linguistic perspective, which appears to shed light on the mental lexicon of the bilinguals. In studies exploring lexical priming cross-linguistically in an attempt to illustrate the organization of the bilingual internal lexicon, semantically related and translation equivalent word pairs are shown to subjects and they are tested with the help of a lexical decision task. The difference between the response times of the target lexical units and the pseudo word pairs reveal the possible priming effect, which help the researchers claim that lexical priming exists in semantically related words or translation equivalents. These findings may give some insights into how words in two languages are interrelated in the bilingual mental lexicon and whether lexical access is language specific or language non-specific, which has been a popular controversial issue in the literature (Pavlenko, 2009).

There are patterns observed in cross-linguistic priming studies. For example, Basnight-Brown & Altarriba (2007) stated that based on the observations in previous studies, translation equivalent words appear to reveal priming effects more often than semantically related words. Additionally, Jiang and Foster (2001) reported that as far as the direction of the priming effect is concerned, L1-L2 direction seemed to show stronger priming effects than L2-L1 direction, which is termed "priming asymmetry"

An important methodological consideration in those studies was SOA (stimulus onset asynchrony), which is the time interval between the prime word and the onset of the target word. Altarriba (1992) found a priming effect in translation equivalent lexical items in a lexical decision task with 200 milliseconds SOA in L1-L2 direction. Likewise, Jiang (1999) detected a priming effect in L1-L2 direction, but not the other way around. The same trend was also observed when masked priming was employed (i.e. SOA 50 milliseconds or less). Another important variable exploited was the difference between the processing of concrete-abstract words and cognates-non-cognates. To exemplify, Jin (1990) incorporated concrete and abstract lexical items into his study and only the concrete items revealed a significant priming effect. Some other studies (e.g. de Groot, 1992b) also stated that participants responded to the translation equivalent items faster if the items were concrete and cognate.

The direction of the priming effect was another noteworthy result in much research. It can be assumed based on a native speaker intuition that when the prime word is in L2 and the target word is in L1, subjects will respond to the target faster mainly because the lexical item is in the native language of the participants. However, as pointed out earlier, priming is stronger in L1-L2 direction, which is called as "asymmetry in priming". It can be attributed to the stronger influence of L1 on L2 or stronger relations in L1-L2 direction rather than the other way around, which reflects itself in lexical priming experiments and gives valuable information about how the mental lexicon of the bilinguals are structured. (see Jiang, 2015 for a comprehensive discussion).

There are some other research studies contradicting the findings discussed so far regarding cross-linguistic lexical priming. For instance, Kim and Davis (2003) concluded based on their findings that there was translation priming for non-cognates in L1-L2 direction, which was at odds with previous studies considering the non-cognate effect. Finkbeiner et al. (2004) found priming in L2-L1 direction in a semantic categorization task, which again disagrees with earlier studies.

It must also be noted that the differences between these research studies focusing on cross-linguistic lexical priming appears to stem from the fact that they have methodological variations and cannot control all the variables, such as different SOA, relatedness proportion, non-word ratio, proficiency level of the participants, native languages of the participants and so on (see Basnight-Brown and Altarriba, 2007 for a comprehensive review).

Different SOA may indicate if the processing of the primes were automatic or conscious. In other words, if a masked priming paradigm is employed (50 milliseconds or less), it is claimed that all the processing is subconscious and the participants are not using any strategies during the experiment. Some researchers (e.g. Jiang, 2012), on the other hand, assert that second language users might need more than 50 milliseconds to subconsciously detect and process a prime in L2, which makes the masked priming application unachievable in particular for those studies exploiting lower proficiency level L2 users. Therefore, researchers aiming to conduct cross-linguistic lexical priming studies in the future need to come up with a rationale for their methodological preferences for their own research purposes. They may even carry out multiple experiments adopting various approaches and test the claims and generalizations made so far.

As has been summarized up to this section, there have been several attempts to model the monolingual and bilingual mental lexicon and there is an ongoing debate whether lexical access is language specific or language non-specific, although the empirical evidence regarding the latter seem to outweigh the former for the time being. Much research some of which have been discussed so far is conducted to investigate the cross-linguistic lexical priming in bilinguals, but none to the writer's knowledge has focused on the collocational priming from a cross-linguistic perspective. The results of a possible research study scrutinizing cross-linguistic collocational priming can give an important insight into how the organization of the mental dictionary can be interpreted.

SUGGESTIONS FOR FURTHER RESEARCH

One of the primary aims of this chapter is to raise interest in research investigating lexical processing and cross-linguistic collocational priming in an agglutinative and an understudied language, Turkish. Future studies in the domain of lexical processing in Turkish have the potential to approach the theories of language use, mainly built on the English language, from the eyes of a morphologically different language. Some of the related topics that have been lacking or underrepresented in the literature based on the observations and readings of this chapter's writer are;

1. The existence of collocational priming in Turkish
2. Frequency effect on collocational priming in Turkish
3. Lexical transparency effect on collocational priming in Turkish
4. Collocational priming with lemmatized lexical items in Turkish
5. Cross-linguistic collocational priming in Turkish L1 and English L2 bilinguals
6. A mental lexicon framework explaining the collocational networks in the bilingual brain

Cangır, Büyükkantarcıoğlu, and Durrant (2017) attempted to test the collocational priming theory in Turkish. The findings indicate a priming effect for both verb+noun and adjective+noun collocations, in line with Hoey's (2005) claims. In addition, there was a significant correlation between frequency (t-score, MI, and delta p) and the priming effect indicating the possible influence of collocational frequency on the processing times. However, as the team states further evidence is required to make even stronger claims. Based on the results, the research team came up with a humble framework, titled "Cross-linguistic collocational spreading activation", which tries to illustrate the collocational links in the mental lexicon.

Research in this domain could be extended by taking lemmatization into account during item development procedures. Lemmatization can be considered important in the investigation of collocational priming in Turkish because lemmatized items are likely to reveal different frequency values than raw lexical items and also lemmatized words are likely to prime different words from non-lemmatized lexical units. Furthermore, the effect of compositionality of the lexical items could provide an alternative insight into collocational processing and the structure of internal lexicon.

Last but not least, collocational priming could be tested from a cross-linguistic perspective, the possible results of which can guide the linguists attempting to model the bilingual (Turkish L1 – English L2, in particular) mental lexicon.

CONCLUSION

The chapter has elaborated the key terminology; mental lexicon, formulaic language, collocations, and collocational priming as well as summarizing earlier and recent models of monolingual and bilingual mental lexicon. In addition, some studies in the related field have been surveyed in an attempt to guide the researchers to possible literature gaps in the domain of collocational processing and the need to explore the issue from a cross-linguistic perspective and from the lenses of an agglutinative language has been underlined.

ACKNOWLEDGMENT

Supported by TUBITAK 2214-A PhD Research Grant (Project ID-1059B141600068).

REFERENCES

Aitchison, J. (2003). *Words in the Mind.* Oxford, UK: Blackwell Publishing.

Aitchison, J. (2012). *Words in the mind: An introduction to the mental lexicon* (4th ed.). John Wiley & Sons.

Altarriba, J. (1992). The representation of translation equiv- alents in bilingual memory. In R. J. Harris (Ed.), *Cognitive processing in bilinguals* (pp. 157–174). Amsterdam: North-Holland. doi:10.1016/S0166-4115(08)61493-4

Barlow, M., & Kemmer, S. (Eds.). (2000). *Usage- Based Models of Language.* CSLI Publications.

Basnight-Brown, D., & Altarriba, J. (2007). Differences in semantic and translation priming across languages: The role of language direction and language dominance. *Memory & Cognition, 35*(5), 953–965. doi:10.3758/BF03193468 PMID:17910179

Bloomfield, L. (1933). *Language.* London: Allen and Unwin.

Bock, K., & Levelt, W. (1994). Language production: Grammatical encoding. In M. A. Gernsbacher (Ed.), *Handbook of psycholinguistics* (pp. 945–984). San Diego, CA: Academic Press.

Briggs, J., & Peat, F. (1989). *Turbulent Mirror: An Illustrated Guide to Chaos Theory and the Science of Wholeness*. New York: Harper & Row.

Cangır, H., Büyükkantarcıoğlu, S. N., & Durrant, P. (2017). Investigating collocational priming in Turkish. *Journal of Language and Linguistic Studies, 13*(2), 465–486.

Cangır, H., & Durrant, P. (2018). *Investigating cross-linguistic collocational priming in Turkish L1-English L2 bilinguals*. Unpublished manuscript.

Carroll, D. W. (2004). *Psychology of Language*. Belmont, WA: Thomson Wadsworth.

Chomsky, N. (1956). Three models for the description of language. *I.R.E. Transactions on Information Theory*, *2*(3), 113–124. doi:10.1109/TIT.1956.1056813

Collins, A. M., & Loftus, E. F. (1975). A spreading-activation theory of semantic processing. *Psychological Review*, *82*(6), 407–428. doi:10.1037/0033-295X.82.6.407

Collins, A. M., & Quillian, M. R. (1969). Retrieval time from semantic memory. *Journal of Verbal Learning and Verbal Behavior*, *8*(2), 240–247. doi:10.1016/S0022-5371(69)80069-1

Costa, A., Miozzo, M., & Caramazza, A. (1999). Lexical selection in bilinguals: Do words in the bilingual's two lexicons compete for selection? *Journal of Memory and Language*, *41*(3), 365–397. doi:10.1006/jmla.1999.2651

Cowie, A. P. (1994). Phraseology. In R. E. Asher (Ed.), *The Encyclopedia of Language and Linguistics*. Oxford, UK: Pergamon.

Cruse, D. A. (2000). *Meaning in Language. An Introduction to Semantics and Pragmatics*. Oxford, UK: Oxford University Press.

De Groot, A. M. B. (1992). Bilingual lexical representation: A closer look at conceptual representations. In R. Frost & I. Katz (Eds.), *Orthography, phonology, morphology, and meaning* (pp. 389–412). Amsterdam: Elsevier. doi:10.1016/S0166-4115(08)62805-8

De Groot, A. M. B. (1993). Word-type effects in bilingual pro- cessing tasks: Support for a mixed-representational system. In R. Schreuder & B. Weltens (Eds.), *The bilingual lexicon* (pp. 27–51). Amsterdam: John Benjamins. doi:10.1075/sibil.6.04gro

Dijkstra, T., Miwa, K., Brummelhuis, B., Sappelli, M., & Baayen, R. H. (2010). How cross-language similarity and task demands affect cognate recognition. *Journal of Memory and Language*, *62*(3), 284–301. doi:10.1016/j.jml.2009.12.003

Dijkstra, T., & Van Heuven, W. (2002). The architecture of the bilingual word recognition system: From identification to decision. *Bilingualism: Language and Cognition*, *5*(03), 175–197. doi:10.1017/S1366728902003012

Dong, Y., Gui, S., & MacWhinney, B. (2005). Shared and separate meanings in the bilingual mental lexicon. *Bilingualism: Language and Cognition*, *8*(3), 221–238. doi:10.1017/S1366728905002270

Durrant, P., & Doherty, A. (2010). Are high-frequency collocations psychologically real? Investigating the thesis of collocational priming. *Corpus Linguistics and Linguistic Theory*, *6*(2), 125–155.

Durrant, P., & Schmitt, N. (2010). Adult learners' retention of collocations from exposure. *Second Language Research*, *26*(2), 163–188. doi:10.1177/0267658309349431

Ellis, N. C. (1996). Sequencing in SLA: Phonological memory, chunking, and points of order. *Studies in Second Language Acquisition*, *18*(01), 91–126. doi:10.1017/S0272263100014698

Finkbeiner, M., Forster, K., Nicol, J., & Nakamura, K. (2004). The role of polysemy in masked semantic and translation priming. *Journal of Memory and Language*, *51*(1), 1–22. doi:10.1016/j.jml.2004.01.004

Firth, J. R. (1957). A synopsis of linguistic theory, 1930–1955. In F. R. Palmer (Ed.), *Selected papers of J.R. Firth*. London: Longmans.

Gabrys´-Barker, D. (2005). *Aspects of multilingual storage, processing and retrieval*. Katowice: University of Silesia Press.

Gungor, F., & Uysal, H. H. (2016). A Comparative Analysis of Lexical Bundles Used by Native and Non-native Scholars. *English Language Teaching*, *9*(6), 176. doi:10.5539/elt.v9n6p176

Harley, T. (2005). *The Psychology of Language from Data to Theory*. New York: Psychology Press.

Haugen, E. (1953). *The Norwegian Language in America*. Philadelphia: University of Pennsylvania Press.

Henriksen, B. (2013). Research on L2 learners ' collocational competence and development – a progress report. *EUROSLA Monographs Series*, *2*, 29–56.

Hermans, D., Bongaerts, T., De Bot, K., & Schreuder, R. (1998). Producing word in a foreign language: Can speakers prevent interference from their first language? *Bilingualism: Language and Cognition*, *1*(3), 213–230. doi:10.1017/S1366728998000364

Hoey, M. (1991). *Patterns of Lexis in Text*. Oxford, UK: Oxford University Press.

Hoey, M. (2005). *Lexical Priming: A New Theory of Words and Language*. Routledge. doi:10.4324/9780203327630

Howarth, P. (1998). Phraseology and second language proficiency. *Applied Linguistics*, *19*(1), 24–44. doi:10.1093/applin/19.1.24

Jiang, N. (1999). Testing processing explanations for the asymmetry in masked cross-language priming. *Bilingualism: Language and Cognition*, *2*(1), 59–75. doi:10.1017/S1366728999000152

Jiang, N. (2012). *Conducting reaction time research in second language studies*. New York: Routledge.

Jiang, N. (2015). Six decades of research on lexical representation and processing in bilinguals. In J. Schwieter (Ed.), The Cambridge Handbook of Bilingual Processing (pp. 27-28). Cambridge, UK: Cambridge University Press. doi:10.1017/CBO9781107447257.002

Jiang, N., & Forster, K. (2001). Cross-language priming asymmetries in lexical decision and episodic recognition. *Journal of Memory and Language*, *44*(1), 32–51. doi:10.1006/jmla.2000.2737

Jin, Y.-S. (1990). Effects of concreteness on cross-language priming in lexical decisions. *Perceptual and Motor Skills*, *70*(3_suppl), 1139–1154. doi:10.2466/pms.1990.70.3c.1139

Kim, J., & Davis, C. (2003). Task effects in masked cross-script translation and phonological priming. *Journal of Memory and Language*, *49*(4), 484–499. doi:10.1016/S0749-596X(03)00093-7

Kjellmer, G. (1984). Some thoughts on collocational distinctiveness. In Corpus Linguistics (pp. 163-171). Amsterdam: Rodopi.

Kjellmer, G. (1987). Aspects of English Collocations. In Corpus Linguistics and Beyond (pp. 133-140). Amsterdam: Rodopi.

Kroll, J. F., & Stewart, E. (1994). Category interference in translation and picture naming: Evidence for asymmetric connections between bilingual memory representations. *Journal of Memory and Language*, *33*(2), 149–174. doi:10.1006/jmla.1994.1008

Leech, G. (1974). *Semantics*. Harmondsworth, UK: Penguin.

Ortaçtepe, D. (2013). Formulaic language and conceptual socialization: The Route to becoming nativelike in L2. *System*, *41*(3), 852–865. doi:10.1016/j.system.2013.08.006

Öztürk, Y., & Köse, D. G. (2016). Turkish and Native English Academic Writers' Use of Lexical Bundles. *Journal of Language and Linguistic Studies*, *12*(1305), 149–165.

Pavlenko, A. (Ed.). (2009). *The bilingual mental lexicon: Interdisciplinary approaches*. Tonawanda, NY: Multilingual Matters.

Pickering, M. J., & Garrod, S. (2013). An integrated theory of language production and comprehension. *Behavioral and Brain Sciences*, *36*(04), 329–347. doi:10.1017/S0140525X12001495 PMID:23789620

Potter, M. C., So, K. F., von Eckardt, B., & Feldman, I. B. (1984). Lexica and conceptual representation in beginning and proficient bilinguals. *Journal of Verbal Learning and Verbal Behavior*, *23*(1), 23–38. doi:10.1016/S0022-5371(84)90489-4

Poulisse, N., & Bongaerts, T. (1994). First language use in second language production. *Applied Linguistics*, *15*(1), 36–57. doi:10.1093/applin/15.1.36

Roux, P. W. (2013). *Words in the mind: Exploring the relationship between word association and lexical development*. Retrieved June 26, 2014, from http://www.rcube.ritsumei.ac.jp/.../8-

Schmitt, N. (2010). *Researching Vocabulary: A Vocabulary Research Manual*. Palgrave Press. doi:10.1057/9780230293977

Seidenberg, M. S., & McClelland, J. L. (1989). A distributed, developmental model of word recognition and naming. *Psychological Review*, *96*(4), 523–568. doi:10.1037/0033-295X.96.4.523 PMID:2798649

Sinclair, J. (1991). *Corpus, Concordance, Collocation*. Oxford University Press.

Singleton, D. (1999). *Exploring the Second Language Mental Lexicon*. Cambridge, UK: CUP. doi:10.1017/CBO9781139524636

Smith, E. E., Shoben, E. J., & Rips, L. J. (1974). Structure and process in semantic memory: A featural model for semantic decisions. *Psychological Review, 81*(3), 214–241. doi:10.1037/h0036351

Szubko-Sitarek, W. (2015). *Multilingual lexical recognition in the mental lexicon of third language users*. Berlin: Springer-Verlag. doi:10.1007/978-3-642-32194-8

Van Heuven, W. J. B., Dijkstra, A., & Grainger, J. (1998). Orthographic neighborhood effects in bilingual word recognition. *Journal of Memory and Language, 39*(3), 458–483. doi:10.1006/jmla.1998.2584

Weinreich, U. (1953). *Languages in contact: Findings and problems*. New York: Linguistic Circle of New York.

Wolter, B., & Gyllstad, H. (2011). Collocational Links in the L2 Mental Lexicon and the Influence of L1 Intralexical Knowledge. *Applied Linguistics, 32*(4), 430–449. doi:10.1093/applin/amr011

Wray, A. (2002). *Formulaic Language and the Lexicon*. Cambridge University Press. doi:10.1017/CBO9780511519772

Wray, A. (2008). *Formulaic language: Pushing the boundaries*. Oxford, UK: Oxford University Press.

Chapter 12
Phonetic Fossilization:
Is It a Matter of Perfection or Intelligibility?

Aicha Rahal
University of Gafsa, Tunisia

ABSTRACT

Fossilization is a common linguistic phenomenon among learners. It presents an obstacle that hinders the process of learning and prevents learners from acquiring the target language. The present chapter explores this phenomenon. It gives an overview of the theory of interlanguage and the concept of fossilization. The chapter presents the history of pronunciation teaching. It also reviews a previous study on pronunciation problems and fossilized errors that face learners of English as a second or a foreign language. The present chapter also raises an important question. It attempts to show the matter behind this linguistic phenomenon. There seems to be different views. Some researchers claim that phonetic fossilization is a matter of intelligibility. Other researchers state that achieving perfection in pronunciation is preferable. Another trend of researchers assumes that fossilization cannot be applied to the multilingual context.

INTRODUCTION

In second language acquisition, it has been claimed that L2 learners develop a unique linguistic system, different from both the first language and the Target Language (TL). This linguistic system is called approximative system (Nemser, 1971), idiosyncratic dialects or transitional dialects (Corder, 1971) and Interlanguage (IL) (Selinker, 1972). The present study mainly focuses on the theory of IL. This linguistic system should be developed to reach the TL. However, previous observations (Kahraman,

DOI: 10.4018/978-1-5225-4009-0.ch012

2012; Smaoui & Rahal 2015; Rahal, 2016) have demonstrated that L2 learners' IL systems often become fossilized and L2 learning process makes no further progress toward the TL. Fossilization can be temporary or permanent. The former refers to persistent errors that are destabilized after corrective feedback and exposure to L2 environment. The latter refers to stable and fixed errors in learners' IL over a period of time.

Fossilization is a linguistic phenomenon that hinders the process of learning and prevents learners from acquiring full level of competence. Many researchers studied fossilization (Han, 2004, 2005), the process of fossilization (Heath, 1998), causes of fossilization (Han, 2005; Wei, 2008), mainly biological factors (Liu, 2012), cognitive factors (Liu, 2012) and psychological factors of fossilization (Chen, 2009), as well as ways to overcome fossilization (Zheng, 2010; Demirezen, 2010; Li, 2009; Qian & Xiao, 2010; Smaoui & Rahal, 2015).

The aim of the present chapter is to address the problem of phonological fossilization by reviewing previous studies on pronunciation errors and persistent phonological errors. It is an attempt to understand this linguistic obstacle.

Interlanguage

The word interlanguage (IL) was advanced by Larry Selinker in 1972 in his eponymous paper *Interlanguage*. It is a central notion in the field of second language acquisition. Stern (1983) states:

The concept of Interlanguage was suggested by Selinker in order to draw attention to the possibility that the learner's language can be regarded as a distinct language variety or system with its own particular characteristics and rules. (as cited in Tanaka, 2000, p.1)

IL is seen as a unique linguistic system, independent in its own right. It differs from both the native language and the target language, but "linked to both native language and the TL by interlangual identifications in the perception of the learner", as Tarone states (2006, p. 749). This means that IL has some characteristics both from the native language and the target language. Selinker (1972) argues, "the sets of utterances from learners of a second language are not identical to the hypothesized corresponding sets of utterances which would have been produced by a native speaker of a target language had he attempted to express the same meaning as the learner" (p.214). Thus, IL is a type of language produced by non-native speakers in the process of learning a second language or a foreign language. IL also refers to "psychological structure latent in the brain" which is activated when one attempts to learn a second language (Selinker, 1972, p.34).

Fossilization

The concept of fossilization was introduced by Larry Selinker in 1972. It is defined as the "linguistic items, rules, and subsystems which speakers of a particular NL will tend to keep in their IL relative to a particular TL, no matter what the age of the learner or amount of explanation and instruction he receives in the TL" (p.215). In his explanation of this linguistic phenomenon, Selinker (1992) states:

Fossilization includes those items, rules, and sub-systems that second language learners tend to retain in their interlanguage while in the process of acquiring a particular target language, and that will only be eliminated with considerable effort for the majority of second language learners, regardless of explanation or instruction.

From the definitions cited above, we can say that fossilization is a stage in which learners cannot make any further progress in their IL towards the TL. And this is clearly cited in Selinker's (1996) definition, where he points that it is "a process whereby the learner creates a cessation of interlanguage learning, thus stopping the TL from developing, it is hypothesized in a permanent way..." (as cited in Han, 2004, p.15).

Han (2004) describes fossilization as the "phenomenon of non-progression of learning despite continuous exposure to input, adequate motivation to learner, and sufficient opportunity for practice" (p.13). Thus, learners fail to achieve native-like competence. Fossilization is the phenomenon of non-progression of learning L2.

According to Ellis (1985), fossilization can be an error or a correct target language form. He believes, "If, when fossilization occurs, the learner has reached a stage of development in which feature x in his interlanguage has assumed the same form as in the target language, the fossilization of the correct forms will occur. If, however, the learner has reached a stage in which feature y still does not have the same form as the target language, the fossilization will manifest itself as error" (as cited in Zheng, 2010, p.148). Fossilization is regarded as a stage in which there is no correspondence between "feature X" and the target language form. It refers to the non-change in learners' transition from L1 and L2. Ellis (2004) states that fossilization is part of IL process which occurs at a certain point in the IL development (as cited in Fauziati, 2011, p.25).

Selinker (1993) argues that fossilization is characterized by some aspects. First, it refers to permanent cessation in the process of learning "far from the target language" (p.16). Second, persistent linguistic features hinder learners from making any progress towards the target norms, "no matter what learners do in terms of further exposure to the TL" (p.17).

It is clear, therefore, that this concept has been studied and interpreted by many researchers and scholars. They used many terms to refer to fossilization, such as cessation of learning, persistent non-target-like performance, learning plateau, backsliding, etc. However, most of them agree that it refers to the inability to fully acquire target language features. It is important to note that there is another term used by Pennington (1999) to refer to fossilization. It is "diminishing returns", which means that at an advanced level, there is less progress in learners' linguistic system. He states that "most adult learners will hardly be able to improve their productive and receptive competence of a new sound system without explicit instruction" (p.428).

However, based on the direct accessibility hypothesis, adult learners learn both first and second language by setting parameters to Universal Grammar (UG). It is seen that UG can be used in the first language, it also can be applied to the L2 learning. This shows the impossibility of the occurrence of the phenomenon of fossilization. To support this argument, Ritchie (1978) tested the operation of the Right Roof Constraint (RRC). He used a grammaticality judgement test. Based on the results, it was found that the RRC is operating. This result shows that UG is accessible to L2 learners.

In a similar vein, there is another study that supports this view. Otsu and Naoi (1986) claim that L2 learners have direct access to UG. They conducted a study on Japanese learners of English as a second language. The aim of the study is to test the operation of the Subject-Dependency Principle in the L2. The participants were 11 female teenagers who had studied English for two years. The subjects were asked to transform 12 declarative sentences that have relative clauses into questions. The findings demonstrated that most of the participants formed the questions correctly. It is clear, therefore, that they were guided by UG (as cited in White, 1989).

Fossilization and Neurological Considerations

It seems that the brain could not function during fossilization. According the Shafaei (2010), fossilization has cognitive, neurological and socio-affective causes. A the neurological level, "fossilizations create certain chemical changes in the chemistry of human brain by generating electrical transactions which work contrary to the neuro-cognitive processes of phonemes and sounds underlying L2 perception and production" (p.378). Han (2004) also suggested many causes of fossilization. These include environmental, cognitive and neuro-biological factors. Neuro-biological causes involve changes in the neural structure of the brain, age, decrease of cerebral plasticity for implicit acquisition, lack of talent and neutral entrenchment (p.29).

Lannerberg (1967) argues that after puberty learners cannot acquire full level of proficiency because "the unilateral function of brains makes the natural language acquisition disappear" (cited in Huang, 2009, p.76). Learners' nerve system which is situated in the left hemisphere of the brain will be restricted. The restriction of the brain will cause interlanguage fossilization. It seems that when fossilization occurs, the left hemisphere of the brain which is devoted to language development stops to function and learners cannot make any progress to reach the TL. According to the critical period hypothesis, language fossilization is inevitable in those individuals who are learning a language beyond this critical period.

Similarly, Scovel (1969) states that there is a clear relationship between lateralization and second language acquisition. He argues that after youthhood, second language learners cannot master native-like pronunciation because "the brain looses its plasticity and lateralization is accomplished" (as cited in Ipek, 2009, p. 159). Based on the lateralization hypothesis, when this plasticity disappeared, native-like L2 learning would become impossible. Johnson and Newport (1989) also points to the onset of puberty as an important moment in terms of the loss of an ability to acquire native-like L2 competence.

It seems that the brain stops to function when fossilization occurs and fossilization happens when the brain ceases to function. Han (2006) uses the terms 'explanans' and 'explanandum' (pp.4-5) to show that fossilization is not only a 'process' but also a 'product'. It is a stage in the process of learning. It occurs when the brain does not function. It is also the result of the brain's loss of plasticity.

Phonological Fossilization

Phonological Fossilization refers to the persistence of phonological rules in learners' IL. This type of fossilization can be result from the incorrect acquisition of L2 pronunciation. For instance, the consonant /θ/ represents a problem for Chinese students because it does not exist in their first language. Therefore, Wei (2008) argues that it is difficult for Chinese learners to pronounce / θ/. They replace it with /s/. They say /snk/ instead of /θnk/.

Definition of Perfection

Perfection means nativeness. Achieving perfection in pronunciation means acquiring native-like speaker. According to *Routledge Dictionary of Languages and Linguistics*, "Native speaker refers to a representative ideal speaker/ listener of a linguistic community" (p.785). The use of the word "ideal" means perfection. It refers to people who have expertise the target pronunciation. The *Dictionary of Linguistics and Phonetics* also defines this notion, stating that "many people do, however, develop 'native-like' command of a foreign language, and in bilingualism one has the case of someone who has a native command of two languages" (p. 322). This indicates that people can master full level of proficiency in pronunciation and they can reach the level of native speakers.

However, Selinker (1972) assumes that second language learners cannot achieve native-like competence. They can only achieve 'attempted learning.' That is they can "express meaning, which he may already have, in a language which he is in the process of learning" (p.210). According to Selinker (1972), there is a small percentage of 5% can succeed in reaching full level of proficiency.

Definition of Intelligibility

Intelligibility has been recognized as the most important aspect of communication and the crucial aspect of L2 speech (Abercrombie, 1949; Crawford, 1987; Nelson, 1982). According to Kenworthy (1987), intelligibility means understandability, that is "being understood by a listener at a given time in a given situation" (p.13). Similarly, Derwing (2010) states that intelligibility refers to the products of "actual understanding" (p.29). Nelson (1982) also notes that "being intelligible means being understood by an interlocutor at a given time in a given situation" (p.59). According to Morley (1991), "Intelligible pronunciation is an essential component of communication competence" (p. 488).

Based on the definitions cited above, it seems that most of the researchers agree that intelligibility refers to the extent to which speaker's speech is understood by a listener (Munro & Derwing, 1995). However, this definition veils the complexity of this term. In this context, Bamgbose (1998) claims that intelligibility is an umbrella term. It includes the three-level system, namely intelligibility, comprehensibility, and interpretability. He further describes it as "a complex of factors comprising recognizing an expression, knowing its meaning, and knowing what that meaning signifies in the sociocultural context" (p. 11). Some researchers (e.g. Munro & Derwing, 1995) suggested a hierarchy of importance: intelligibility, comprehensibility, with accentedness the least important consideration. It seems, therefore, that intelligibility is the focal goal behind teaching pronunciation.

HISTORY OF PRONUNCIATION TEACHING

In the early period of English language teaching, the beginning of 1800's, pronunciation was neglected. The dominant theory was Grammar Translation Method because the main aim of language learning and teaching was to read and write (Celcia-Murcia et al., 1996; Lightbown & Spada, 2006). With the foundation of the International Phonetic Association, pronunciation began to be taught through different techniques, such as imitation and intuition. In the late 1800's, pronunciation gained a special place in language instruction and it was centered on the Direct Method (Celcia-Murcia et al., 1996).

In this period, students tried to imitate their teachers to acquire the target rules and forms. The arrival of Audio-lingualism gave a crucial place to pronunciation because the main interest of language instruction moved to listening and speaking skills (Lightbown & Spada, 2006). Students started learning sounds through listening and practicing minimal pairs (Larsen-Freeman, 1986).

In the 1960s, the situation changed and teaching pronunciation began to decline. The main importance was given to teaching grammar and vocabulary. Some researchers discussed the issues behind the decline of pronunciation teaching. Morley (1991), for instance, argued that the reason is due to teachers who are not satisfied with the principles and methods used to teach this skill.

The emergence of the two humanistic approaches, the Silent Way and the Community Language Teaching, gave an important place to pronunciation. This period is known by its call for a change in the ways and methods of teaching pronunciation. This change was voiced by many researchers, such as Bowen, (1972); Smith and Rafiqzad, (1979); Stevick etal., (1975). After that, pronunciation took its place again in 1980s and especially with the arrival of the communicative approach. It became the center of classroom instruction (Levis, 2007; Setter and Jenkins, 2005). Morley (1991) noted that the 1980's witnessed a "renewed interest in pronunciation teaching principles and practices" (p.487).

The arrival of the communicative approach paved the way for the emergence of 'intelligibility' which had a high priority in language teaching and learning. Pronunciation gained its importance and became an integral part in language teaching (García-Lecumberri and Gallardo, 2003; Pennington, 1996; Fraser, 2006).

Pronunciation Problems That Face Learners of English

There are a number of studies that investigated pronunciation problems that face learners of English as a second or a foreign language. Naama (2011), for instance, has analyzed errors made by Yemeni University students in English consonant-clusters system. Five categories of consonant clusters have been investigated, namely initial-consonant clusters that are made up of two consonants, initial-consonant clusters which are made up of three consonants, final consonant clusters which are made up of two consonants, and final consonant clusters that are made up of three and four consonants.

The first category shows that 26 of 45 students were unable to pronounce the initial-consonant clusters which are made up of two consonants. They inserted the short vowel /i/ in pronouncing them. For instance, they say /pilei/ for play. The second category also shows that they tend to insert the vowel /i/ in words such as /

spilendid/ for "splendid" and /ispired/ for "spired." The third category demonstrates that most of the students do not pronounce the final consonant cluster /-kt/ correctly. They pronounce it as /pikid/.They have not yet acquired the rule that the /-d/ sound has to be pronounced /t/ if it is preceded by the voiceless sound /k/.The fourth and fifth categories show that no one could pronounce the final consonant clusters that are made up of three or four consonants. For example, no one could pronounce the word "sixths" correctly. The subjects tend to insert a short vowel among the four consonant clusters like /siksi/. According to Naama (2011), the mother tongue is the major cause of interlingual phonological errors of Yemeni University students. Another reason beyond making errors in English consonant-clusters is the absence of using teaching aids. Students have to listen to cassettes, videos, etc. Naama (2011) also states that incompetent instructors affect students' pronunciation.

Hassan (2012) also studied the pronunciation problems of Sudanese learners of English. The aim of the study was to identify the errors of pronunciation among English learners and their major reasons. The participants were all the students of English at the Sudan University of Science and Technology. The results of the study showed that many Sudanese learners did not pronounce the following consonants /p, v, ð, θ/. Some Sudanese learners mispronounced /a, e, i, o, u/ sounds. They pronounced / dʒ / instead of /ʒ/ and / ʃ / in place of /tʃ/. The results suggest that the main reasons of the errors were the difference between the sound system of both languages, Arabic and English, mother tongue interference, insufficient practices and inconsistency of English vowels.

Along the same line as Hassan, Pal (2013) conducted a study on mother tongue interference on spoken English. The study identified the sounds of Hindi that affected the acquisition of English pronunciation. The participants were Indian learners, and Hindi is their mother tongue. The findings showed Hindi learners of English faced different pronunciation problems, namely fricative sounds, plural markers, consonants clusters, vowel sounds which have different spellings and words which display sound and spelling disparity. The results of the investigation also indicated that errors resulted from L1 interference.

Similarly, Maniruzzaman (2005) has conducted a study on phonological errors made by Bengali learners of English. He tried to identify the major problems and show the factors behind them. The results revealed that Bengali learners committed errors in pronouncing monophthongs, diphthongs and consonants. Monophthongal errors include mispronunciation of long vowels, mispronunciation of contrastive vowels and the schwa sound. Diphthongal errors include omission of the first part of monophthongs. Consonant errors involve the use of Bengali bilabial stops in place of English labio-dental fricatives, the use of Bengali alveolar retroflex stops in place of English alveolar plosives and the use of Bengali dental stops in place of English inter-dental fricatives.

Moreover, O'Connor (2003) reported that there are many pronunciation problems faced Arab learners of English. These problems involve consonants and vowels. Consonant difficulties include the confusion between /f/ and /v/, /b/ and /p/ and / t ʃ / and / dʒ /. They also replaced / ŋ / by / ŋk/ and / ŋg/.Vowel difficulties include the confusion between /i/ and /e/ sounds, /ʌ/ and /ɔ/ sounds, /ɔ: / and /ʌ/ or /ɔ/ sounds. Arab learners also did not make the distinction between /æ/ and /a: / sounds. Further, they replaced /3:/ by /ʌ/ and /e/ and / iə, eə, ʊə/ by / i:, ei, u: /. Tahereen (2015) also conducted a study on the problems in teaching pronunciation in Bangladesh. The results showed that the students tend to use local accents in pronouncing English. For instance, students from Chittagong, Sylhet and Nookhali are confused between /e/ and /ae/. They also use /f/ or /c/ sounds in place of /p/ because they are influenced by the dialect of Dhaka.

Furthermore, Lin (2014) investigated pronunciation variations that face learners of English as a second language. The study focused on the major problems in English articulation of five groups, namely Vietnamese, Japanese, Arab, Chinese and Spanish speakers of English. The results demonstrated that the first group has a problem with the pronunciation of final consonants. The second group added vowels to English words that end with consonants. The third group tended to insert a vowel sound when the stems have onset consonant clusters. The fourth group pronounced short vowels in place of long vowels. The fifth group has a problem in pronouncing these sounds: /f/, /v/ and /r/.

STUDIES ON FOSSILIZED PHONETIC ERRORS, CAUSES, AND SOLUTIONS

Fossilization is one of the obstacles that prevent learners from reaching the target language and achieving a full level of proficiency. Researchers tried to study this linguistic obstacle. Some of them focused on investigating phonetic fossilization. Another trend of researchers attempted to identify the major causes and the possible solutions.

Phonetic Fossilization

Considerable amount of second language researchers has focused on studying phonological fossilization. Demirezen (2008) has studied many fossilized vowel sounds. He examined the fossilized pronunciation of the /æ/ phoneme. He claimed that this phoneme represents a problem for Turkish English language students. The findings showed that Turkish learners pronounced /ʌ/ sound in place of /æ/ sound because the latter does not exist in Modern Standard Turkish. Demirezen (2005a) further conducted a study on the fossilized pronunciation of /v/ and /w/ sounds. The result showed that Turkish teachers and trainees mispronounced the /w/ sound as /v/ sound. This should be due to mother tongue interference.

Moreover, Demirezen (2005 b) studied the /ɔ/ and /ow/ sounds of Turkish students of the English language. He claimed that these sounds have always been a fossilized mistake. According to the researcher, Turkish students "do not give the required lip rounding in its articulation" (p.73). The causes of this problem are the absence of pronunciation teaching method and the absence of courses in phonetics, phonology and intonation.

Furthermore, Demirezen (2010) conducted a study on the difficulties in articulating the schwa sound. The study was conducted at Hacettep University, Ankara. The subjects of the study were 81 students. The findings indicated that the schwa sound is a fossilized sound in the speech of Turkish students. It was replaced by the /e/ and /ʊ/ sounds. The result also showed that the fossilization of the schwa sound can be attributed to NL interference and the lack of awareness.

The studies cited above demonstrated the existence of phonetic fossilization in the speech of the subjects. However, they do not clarify the methodology. In other words, they do not show how they reached the findings. It is difficult to prove the existence of fossilization without studying learners' IL overtime. Researchers need to show non-change in learners' linguistic systems. These studies also provide a number of fossilized sounds. The question is whether these sounds can affect communication and lead to confusion between the interlocutors. According to Jenkins (2000), some of the above sounds do not represent a problem of comprehensibility and understandability. She summarizes the main features of pronunciation which are necessary for intelligibility, as follows:

1. Consonant sounds except voiced/voiceless th and dark l
2. Vowel length contrasts (e.g. the difference between the vowels in 'pitch' and 'peach')
3. Restrictions on consonant deletion (in particular, not omitting sounds at the beginning an in the middle of words)
4. Nuclear (or tonic) stress production/placement

Similarly, Baker and Farr (1997) studied the fossilized pronunciation of French speakers of English. The subjects were 14 students. They were divided into two groups: Control group and experimental group. The aim of the study was to show the role of instruction in destabilizing fossilization. The findings of the first group showed that 28.6% of the subjects maintained the same level of pronunciation, 28.6% of them did not show improvement over the ten week period and 42.8% of them showed improvement in their pronunciation. The findings of the second group showed that the pronunciation of 71.4% of the participants improved and 28.6% of them maintained the same level of pronunciation over the ten week period. Therefore, the experimental group showed more improvement in their pronunciation. However, control group showed the existence of fossilization. Based on the findings, it seems that L2 environment is one way to fight fossilization.

Baker and Farr's (1997) study conducted a cross-sectional approach to show the existence of fossilization and a corrective feedback approach to show the role of instruction in rehabilitating fossilization. However, the cross sectional approach is used to examine errors from a single point in time. It is an insufficient tool for studying the development of the process of learning. The need for further longitudinal studies and pretest-posttest experimental studies is therefore evident.

Hişmanoğlu (2007) also conducted a study on the fossilized pronunciation of the /ɔ:/ and /ɔ/ sounds. The participants were Turkish learners of English. The study showed that Turkish learners tended to pronounce /oʊ/ in place of the /ɔ: / and /ɔ/ sounds. Based on the results, the fossilized sound is due to mother tongue interference. The researcher proposed the audio-articulation method to avoid persistent errors. He gave an example of a lesson plan to help Turkish learners get rid of their fossilization.

Similarly, Kahraman (2012) carried out a study on the fossilized pronunciation of the vowel phoneme /æ/ and the ways to overcome this. Based on the findings, most Turkish learners of English articulated /æ/ sound as /e/. They were also confused between the mid-back unrounded vowel phoneme /ʌ/ and the front low spread vowel /æ/. Kahraman (2012) also proposed the audio-articulation method to remedy fossilization.

In studies of Tunisian English students, Rahal (2014) conducted a research on the fossilized pronunciation of the schwa sound. The participants of the study were 5 English students from the department of English of Gafsa, Tunisia. The findings of the study showed that the subjects fossilized the /e/, /ɔ: / and /a: / sounds in place of the schwa sound. The results also revealed that fossilization is due to L1 interference, inconsistency of English vowels and lack of knowing the production of English phonetics.

Though the findings of this study showed that Tunisian students have a problem with articulating the schwa sound, a few additional issues need to be taken into consideration. First, the period of the longitudinal study was rather short. Therefore, the study did not provide any evidence for long-term changes. The persistent errors can be destabilized. So we can speak about temporary fossilization or stabilization. Second, the study indicated that Tunisian students fossilized some sounds in place of the schwa sound. However, it did not elaborate more on where the problem is because the schwa sound has a family: Is the problem with the Schwi, the schwu, or the schwr. Finally, the results did not provide a clear explanation of the factors behind fossilization.

Similarly, Smaoui and Rahal (2015) studied the fossilized pronunciation of the /3:/ sound in the speech of intermediate Tunisian English students. The participants of the study were 10 students from the department of English of Kairouan, Tunisia. The results showed that most of the subjects fossilized the /ɔ: / sound in place of the /3:/ sound. Based on the findings, fossilization can be attributed to the effect of French sounds, limited exposure to L2 environment and lack of practice. The researchers proposed the audio-articulation method to remedy fossilization.

Recently, Rahal (2016) has conducted a study on the fossilized pronunciation of Advanced Tunisian English students. The participants of the study were 20 students from the English department of Kairouan. The researcher used an eighteen-month longitudinal study to try to show the existence of fossilization. Based on the results, the subjects made a number of errors in times 1, 2 and 3. The longitudinal study showed that there are errors that disappeared and there are a number of errors that repeated in times 2 and 3.

The findings also showed that phonetic fossilization is the result of a number of factors, including mother tongue interference, effect of French sounds, inconsistency of English vowels, limited exposure to L2 environment, insufficient corrective feedback and insufficient knowledge of the production of English sounds. According to the results, fossilization can be remedied by the use of dictionaries to check the phonetic transcription, the adoption of new teaching methods, the integration of technology in teaching pronunciation and sufficient corrective feedback.

Although Smaoui and Rahal (2015) and Rahal (2016) investigated Tunisian students' ILs longitudinally, the studies still have their limitations. They investigated segmental features of pronunciation and they neglected supra-segmental features. Both features play an important role in creating the global sounds of a language. The studies also focused on the effect of interference from first language on learners' pronunciation. That is they studied fossilization from the psychological perspective. But, in the literature, there are also the sociolinguistic uses of the word interference which refers to language contact and the effect of one language on the acquisition of the other.

It is worth noting that the studies cited above have demonstrated that L2 learners fail to achieve native-like competence and their persistent errors remain in their IL systems overtime. However, some researchers (e.g. Fauziati, 2011; Ricard, 1986) argue that learners' linguistic system can stop developing at a certain stage but after treatment learners can master target forms or rules. Ricard (1986) states that "students who have been speaking English for years can go beyond fossilized pronunciation habits" (p.249). This means that learners' IL can be characterized by a momentary halt and fossilization can be destabilized.

Demirezen and Topal (2015) also studied fossilized pronunciation errors from the perspective of Turkish teachers. The participants were 30 teachers from different universities in Turkey. According to the results, most of the subjects considered that persistent pronunciation errors are rehabilitable. They also agreed that trainings are important to help learners overcome fossilization.

Causes of Fossilization and Ways to Remedy Fossilization

Another literature of fossilization has tried to identify the major causes of fossilization and the possible solutions to overcome it. Graham (1990) conducted a study on de-fossilizing persistent pronunciation errors. The participants of the study were six Asian engineers and scientists. The researcher proposed a course of 15 class sessions. This model of treatment is based on learners themselves and the corrective feedback given to them. Based on the findings, it seems clear that the participants showed improvement in their pronunciation.

Like Graham (1990), Murphy (1991) believes that overcoming pronunciation errors relies on learners themselves. He states that "improvement in pronunciation depends up significant commitment of both time and energy from learners themselves" (p.95). This means that learners' awareness and engagement can help them avoid fossilized pronunciation. According to Valette (1991), giving appropriate and accurate input can save learners from fossilization. The input is of three types: Teacher input, recorded input and student input. For teacher input, proficient teachers should teach beginning classes to help them acquire accurate linguistic input. Recorded input involves the use of videos as an effective way to avoid fossilization. Learners should listen to videos by native speakers to master target sounds. Listening is a way to be in contact with natural language. Student input is manifested in communicative interaction between students to master TL rules.

Based on the above studies, we can argue that learners' awareness is important to avoid fossilization. In this respect, Tahereen (2015) states that "Learners' awareness is very important in developing good pronunciation" (p.13). However, teachers should also be aware of their students' pronunciation problems. If teachers are aware of these problems, they will adopt the appropriate teaching method to deal with fossilized errors.

Valette (1991) argued that recorded input like videos is important in helping learners' overcome fossilization. A question that should be raised is whether the integration of internet resources can help students to destabilize their fossilized pronunciation. Some researchers (for example Lui, 2012) believe that the dominance of technology can affect student-teacher interaction. It minimizes communicative interaction in the classroom and without teachers' correction; learners acquire incorrect sounds and rules.

Wei (2008) also conducted research on the factors of fossilization and the possible suggestions to avoid this phenomenon. The researcher mentioned Selinker's five processes as the main sources of fossilization. The study suggested three solutions to reduce this obstacle. These include the selection of the appropriate strategy for learners' performance, sufficient input and natural exposure to TL environment.

Furthermore, Xinguang and Xiuquin (2015) conducted a study on the causes of the fossilized errors made by Chinese college students and the possible solutions to overcome them. The subjects were 180 students from the University of Jinan in China. The findings showed that fossilization is attributable to various factors. It can be the result of lack of interest, insufficient teaching methods, mother tongue interference and the transfer of training. Based on the results, fossilization can be remedied by both teachers' and learners' effort. Learners should cultivate themselves with the TL culture and teachers should choose good teaching methods that are appropriate for their learners.

Zheng (2010) also proposed a model of instruction for destabilizing fossilization. The researcher noted that the model consisted of five curriculums. First, teachers should understand the needs of students to select the appropriate teaching materials and strategies. Second, testing learners' proficiency is important to know their levels. Third, motivating learners is also necessary. Fourth, teachers should adopt learning strategies that combine attitude, approaches and techniques to improve learners' language learning. Fifth, teachers should develop learners' language competence and pragmatic strategies.

Zheng's (2010) study suggested a pedagogical model for overcoming fossilization. This model has its strengthens. It takes into account the needs of learners. It also gives an important key to help learners overcome fossilization which is motivation. However, the literature of fossilization still needs empirical studies to show the effectiveness of such methods or techniques in rehabilitating fossilized errors. In other words, researchers should move from theory to focus on experimental investigation.

It is worth mentioning that the identification of the causes behind fossilization can help teachers to draw the suitable teaching methods and to use the appropriate materials. Based on the studies reviewed so far, there has been a general agreement on the role of pedagogy in stabilizing fossilized errors. However, there are also other activities that can help learners to overcome their fossilized errors. Eliasi (2013) perceived repetition as one way to reduce fossilization. Other researchers (e.g. Malmeer and Araghi, 2013) showed the significant role of extensive reading in avoiding fossilization.

Although the literature reviewed so far has demonstrated that researchers tried to study the phenomenon of fossilization, its causes and the solutions to avoid this linguistic obstacle, an important question needs to be studied. Trying to know the problem behind phonetic fossilization can help both teachers and learners understand it and try to find solutions to overcome it.

WHAT IS THE MATTER BEHIND PHONETIC FOSSILIZATION?

As mentioned above, fossilization refers to the cessation of learners' linguistic system overtime. It occurs when learners acquire non-target norms. The raised question revolves around the problem behind fossilized phonetic errors. Some researchers see that this linguistic phenomenon is a matter of intelligibility. Maniruzzaman (2005), for instance, states that the replacement of phonemes leads to huge confusion and misunderstanding between the listener and the speaker. Researchers (Celcia-Murcia et al., 1996; Jenkins, 2000; Seidlhofer, 2001) have emphasized the centrality of intelligibility as a key component in communication. They claimed that intelligibility is the most important goal of pronunciation teaching. Ur (1996) supports this view and he states that "the aim of the pronunciation is not to achieve a perfect imitation of native accent, but simply to get the learner to pronounce accurately enough to be easily and comfortably comprehensible to other (component) speakers" (p.52).

Achieving perfection in pronunciation and phonetics seems to be preferable. Some linguists, such as Thornbury, Harmer, Cook, Marianne, Donna and Janet argue that most of the teachers and learners want to be perfectionist or try to be like the natives. But it is not desirable. In this case, intelligibility can be more important. Hawlader (2011) agrees that "high goal of achieving perfection in pronunciation" (p.275) is not important. Teachers and learners should concentrate more on making their speech clear and intelligible to the interlocutor. According to Morley (1991), the "notions of perfection and native-like pronunciation" are type of "imposing and perpetuating false standards" (p.499). Smith and Rafiqzad (1979) say that "the native speaker was always found to be among the least intelligible speakers" (p. 395). Morley (1991) further states that the aim of pronunciation should be changed from 'perfection' pronunciation to more realistic aims, such as developing functional intelligibility, communicability, increased self-confidence, the development of speech monitoring abilities and speech modification strategies for use beyond the classroom (p. 500).

It seems that most of the researchers agree that perfection is not necessary for intercultural communication. Most of them argue that intelligibility is the real goal behind identifying learners' pronunciation problems and studying learners' fossilized errors. There is a need for understandability. Rahal (2016), for instance, studied fossilized phonetic errors in the speech of Tunisian English students. She gave examples of fossilized sounds that present a problem in communication. One of these examples is the use of short /i/ in place of long /i: /. She states that if the speaker pronounces the "i" in "live" as long /i: /, the listener will understand "leave" not "live". This creates a huge confusion.

Seidlhofer (2005) argues that teaching Standard English is not very realistic, given that it is not a language variety easy to define. She argues that "in terms of numbers of speakers and domains of use, an insistence on Standard English as the only option for all purposes is… difficult to justify" (p.159). The raised question paves the path for another deep and crucial question: Is there Standard English nowadays? This question opens a debate between monocentrists (e.g. Selinker) and pluralists (e.g. Kachru). According to pluralist, there is no fossilization. All learners' errors are varieties of English. They are 'innovation' to use Jenkins' term. However, monocentrists believe in the existence of error and fossilization.

FUTURE RESEARCH DIRECTIONS

Future research should move to practice to show how such fossilized sounds cause problems of communication. There is also a pressing need for empirical studies to measure intelligibility and to identify the exact persistent sounds that impede communication.

Further, there is a need for classroom activities to raise learners' awareness on the importance of pronunciation. Teachers and learners should understand that "pronunciation is not an optional extra for the language learner, any more than grammar, vocabulary or any other aspect of language is. If a learner's general aim is to talk intelligibly to others in another language, a reasonable pronunciation is important" (as cited in Maniruzzaman, 2005, p.1).

CONCLUSION

The present chapter tries to review and clarify some key concepts in psycholinguistics and in second or foreign language acquisition. It presents the theory of Interlanguage and the phenomenon of fossilization. It also tries to show fossilization in the branch of phonetics.

Based on the study results, the history of teaching pronunciation shows that this skill was not given its real place. In some periods, there was a total decline and neglect of pronunciation in classroom instruction. This seems to be one of the main reasons behind the occurrence of pronunciation problems and phonetic fossilization. Pronunciation should be an integral component of the teaching curriculum like the other skills.

It is worth mentioning that a considerable amount of studies have been conducted to show the existence of persistent phonetic errors. Former studies showed that intelligibility is a central goal of pronunciation teaching. It seems that there is no need for native-like speaker. Learners need to produce intelligible pronunciation to facilitate communication.

The study still has its limitations. It needs more empirical investigations to study this linguistic issue and to provide more examples of how fossilized sounds can lead to misunderstanding and confusion between the interlocutors.

REFERENCES

Abercrombie, D. (1949). Teaching pronunciation. *English Language Teaching*, *3*(5), 113–122. doi:10.1093/elt/III.5.113

Bamgbose, A. (1998). Torn between the norms: Innovations in world Englishes. *World Englishes*, *17*(1), 1–17. doi:10.1111/1467-971X.00078

Bowen, J. D. (1972). Contextualizing Pronunciation Practice in the ESOL Classroom. *TESOL Quarterly*, *6*(1), 83–94. doi:10.2307/3585862

Bussman, H. (Ed.). (1996). *Routledge Dictionary of Language and Linguistics*. London: Routledge.

Celce-Murcia, M., Brinton, D. M., & Goodwin, J. M. (1996). *Teaching pronunciation: A reference for teachers of English to speakers of other languages*. New York: Cambridge University Press.

Chen, C. L. A. (2009). First Language Influence and Fossilization in Second Language Vocabulary Acquisition. *Columbia University Working Papers in TESOL & Applied Linguistics*, *9*(2), 65–67.

Corder, S. P. (1967). The significance of learner's errors. *International Review of Applied Linguistics in Language Teaching*, *5*(4), 161–170.

Crawford, W. W. (1987). The pronunciation monitor: L2 acquisition considerations and pedagogical priorities. In J. Morley (Ed.), *Current perspectives on pronunciation: Practices anchored in theory* (pp. 101–121). Washington, DC: TESOL.

Crystal, D. (Ed.). (2008). *Dictionary of Linguistics and Phonetics*. Hong Kong: Blackwell Publishing Ltd. doi:10.1002/9781444302776

Demirezen, M. (2005a). Rehabilitating a fossilized pronunciation error: The /v/ and /w/ contrast by using the audio articulation method in teacher training in Turkey. *Journal of Language and Linguistic Studies*, *1*(2), 183–192.

Demirezen, M. (2005b). The /ɔ/ and /ow/ contrast: Curing a fossilized pronunciation error of Turkish teacher trainees of English language. *Journal of Arts and Sciences*, *1*(3), 71–84.

Demirezen, M. (2008). The /æ/ and /ʌ/ phonemes as fossilized pronunciation errors for Turkish English language teachers and students: Undoing the fossilized pronunciation error. *Journal of Language and Linguistic Studies*, *4*(2), 73–82.

Demirezen, M. (2010). The principles and application of the audio-lingual pronunciation rehabilitation model in foreign language teacher education. *Journal of Language and Linguistic Studies*, *6*(2), 127–147.

Demirezen, M. (2010). The Order of Consonant Fossilization of the English Language Consonants for Turkish English Teachers and Students. *E-Proceedings of the International Online Language Conference*.

Demirezen, M., & Topal, I. H. (2015). Fossilized Pronunciation Errors from the Perspectives of Turkish Teachers of English and their Implications. *Procedia: Social and Behavioral Sciences*, *199*, 793–800. doi:10.1016/j.sbspro.2015.07.613

Eliasi, A., & Vahidi Borji, H. (2013). Task repetition and noticing as a route to semester-long destabilization: A cross-sectional study of Iranian EFL learners' oral output. *International Journal of Applied Linguistics and English Literature*, *2*(3), 21–28. doi:10.7575/aiac.ijalel.v.2n.3p.21

Fauziati, E. (2003). Interlanguage errors in English textbooks for junior high school students in Surakarta. *TEFLIN Journal*, *14*(2), 1–10.

Fauziati, E. (2011). Interlanguage and error fossilization: A study of Indonesian students learning English as a foreign language. *Indonesian Journal of Applied Linguistics*, *1*(1), 23–38. doi:10.17509/ijal.v1i1.97

Fraser, H. (2006). Helping teachers help students with pronunciation: A cognitive approach. *Prospect: A Journal of Australian TESOL*, *21*, 80-94.

García-Lecumberri, L., & Gallardo del Puerto, F. (2003). English FL sounds in school learners of different ages. In G. Mayo & L. García Lecumberri (Eds.), *Age and the acquisition of English as a foreign language* (pp. 115–135). Clevedon, UK: Multilingual Matters.

Graham, J. (1990). *Changing fossilized speech: What does it take?* Paper presented at the 1990 San Francisco TESOL Convention, San Francisco, CA.

Han, J., Yu, B., & Zhang, W. (2012). The effect of Chinese dialects on English pronunciation of high school students in China. *Journal of Teacher Education*, *1*(3), 225–230.

Han, Z. (2004a). *What is fossilization? In Fossilization in Adult Second Language Acquisition* (pp. 12–23). Toronto: Multilingual Matters.

Han, Z. (2004b). *Behavioral reflexes and causal variables. In Fossilization in Adult Second Language Acquisition* (pp. 25–42). Toronto: Multilingual Matters.

Han, Z.-H., & Odlin, T. (2006). *Studies of Fossilization in Second Language Acquisition*. Clevedon, UK: Multilingual Matters.

Hassan, S. I. (2012). *Pronunciation Problems of Sudanese Learners of English* (Published M.A. Thesis). Open University of Sudan.

Hişmanoğlu, M. (2007). The /ɔ:/ and /oʊ/ Contrast as a fossilized pronunciation error of Turkish learners of English and solutions to the problem. *Journal of Language and Linguistic Studies*, *3*(1), 98–115.

Howlader, M. R. (2010). Teaching English pronunciation in countries where English is a second language: Bangladesh perspective. *ASA University Review*, *4*(2), 233–244.

Huang, Q. (2009). Probe into the internal mechanism of interlanguage fossilization. *English Language Teaching*, *2*(2), 75–77. doi:10.5539/elt.v2n2p75

Ipek, H. (2009). Comparing and contrasting first and second language acquisition. *English Language Teaching*, *2*(2), 155–163. doi:10.5539/elt.v2n2p155

Jenkins, J. (2000). *The Phonology of English as an International Language*. Oxford, UK: Oxford University Press.

Johnson, J., & Newport, E. (1989). Critical period effects in second language learning: The influence of maturational state on the acquisition of English as a second language. *Cognitive Psychology*, *21*(1), 60–99. doi:10.1016/0010-0285(89)90003-0 PMID:2920538

Kahraman, A. (2012). Defosilization of /æ/ phoneme pronunciation of non-native EFL teachers. *Journal of Language Teaching and Research*, *3*(3), 379–385. doi:10.4304/jltr.3.3.379-385

Larsen-Freeman, D. (1986). *Techniques and Principles in Language Teaching*. Oxford, UK: Oxford University Press.

Levis, J. (2007). Computer technology in teaching and researching pronunciation. *Annual Review of Applied Linguistics*, *27*, 184–202. doi:10.1017/S0267190508070098

Li, D. (2009). Activating strategies to fossilization for English learners in China. *English Language Teaching*, *2*(4), 75–77. doi:10.5539/elt.v2n4p75

Lightbown, P. M., & Spada, N. (2006). *How languages are learned*. London: Oxford University Press.

Lin, L. (2014). Understanding pronunciation variations facing ESL students. *International Journal of Humanities and Social Science*, *4*(1), 16–20.

Lui, Y. (2012). *On fossilization of non-English majors' speaking ability in multimedia assisted English class*. Paper presented at the International Conference on Education Technology and Computer, China. Retrieved from http://www.ipcsit.com/vol43/037-ICETC2012-T1045.pdf

Maniruzzaman, M. (2005). *Phonetic and phonological problems encountered by the Bengali speaking EFL learner: How can they be overcome?* Dhaka: Department of English at East West University.

Morley, J. (1991). The pronunciation component in teaching English to speakers of other languages. *TESOL Quarterly*, *25*(3), 481–520. doi:10.2307/3586981

Munro, J., & Derwing, M. (1995). Foreign accent, comprehensibility and intelligibility in the speech of second language learners. *Language Learning*, *45*(1), 73–97. doi:10.1111/j.1467-1770.1995.tb00963.x

Naama, A. (2011). An analysis of errors made by Yemeni University students in the English consonants-clusters system. *Damaxus University Journal*, *27*(3), 145–161.

Nelson, C. (1982). Intelligibility and non-native varieties of English. In B. B. Kachru (Ed.), *The other tongue: English across cultures* (pp. 58–73). Urbana, IL: University of Illinois Press.

Pennington, M. C. (1996). *Phonology in English language teaching: An international approach*. London: Longman.

Pennington, M. C. (1999). Computer aided pronunciation pedagogy: Promise, limitations, directions. *Computer Assisted Language Learning*, *12*(5), 427–440. doi:10.1076/call.12.5.427.5693

Rahal, A. (2014). The fossilized pronunciation of the schwa sound in the speech of Advanced Tunisian English learners: Problem and causes. *International Journal of Humanities and Cultural Studies*, *1*(1), 1–6.

Rahal, A. (2016). *Phonetic Fossilization in the Speech of Advanced Tunisian English Students: The English Department of Kairouan as a case study* (Unpublished MA thesis). Faculty of Letters and Humanities of Kairouan.

Ritchie, W. (1978). The Right Roof Constraint in an adult-acquired language. In W. Ritchie (Ed.), *Second language acquisition research: Issues and implications*. London: Academic Press.

Selinker, L. (1972). Interlanguage. *International Journal of Applied Linguistics*, *10*, 203–230.

Selinker, L. (1992). *Rediscovering Interlanguage*. London: Longman Group UK Limited.

Selinker, L. (1996). *Fossilization: What We Think We Know*. London: Longman Group UK Limited.

Setter, J., & Jenkins, J. (2005). State-of-the-art review article. *Language Teaching*, *38*(1), 1–17. doi:10.1017/S026144480500251X

Smaoui, Ch., & Rahal, A. (2015). The *Fossilized Pronunciation* of the /3:/ Sound in the Speech of Intermediate *Tunisian* English Students: Problem, Reasons and Suggested Solution. *International Journal of English Language and Translation Studies*, *3*(1), 70–79.

Smith, L. E., & Rafiqzad, K. (1979). English for cross-cultural communication: The question of intelligibility. *TESOL Quarterly*, *5*(3), 371–380. doi:10.2307/3585884

Stevick, E., Morley, J., & Wallace Robinett, B. (1975). Round robin on the teaching of pronunciation. *TESOL Quarterly*, *9*(1), 81–88. doi:10.2307/3586016

Tahereen, T. (2015). Challenges in teaching pronunciation at tertiary level in Bangladesh. *International Journal of English language & Translation Studies, 3*(1), 9-20. Retrieved from http://www.eltsjournal.org

Ur, P. (1996). *A course in language teaching: practice and theory*. Cambridge, UK: Cambridge University Press.

Valette, R. M. (1991). Proficiency and the prevention of fossilization. *Modern Language Journal*, *75*(3), 325–328. doi:10.1111/j.1540-4781.1991.tb05363.x

Wei, X. (2008). Implication of IL fossilization in second language acquisition. *English Language Teaching*, *1*(1), 127–131. doi:10.5539/elt.v1n1p127

White, L. (1986). Implications of parametric variation for adult second language acquisition: An investigation of the 'pro-drop' parameter. In V. Cook (Ed.), *Experimental approaches to second language acquisition*. Oxford, UK: Pergamon.

Xiao, Z., & Qian, M. (2010). Strategies for preventing and resolving temporary fossilization in second language acquisition. *English Language Teaching*, *3*(1), 180–183.

Xinguang, S., & Xiuquin, X. (2015). A study of fossilization in Chinese college students' English learning. *Advances in Social Sciences Research Journal*, *2*(1), 54–60. doi:10.14738/assrj.21.678

Zhang, F., & Yin, P. (2009). A Study of Pronunciation Problems of English Learners in China. *Asian Social Science*, *5*(6), 141–146. doi:10.5539/ass.v5n6p141

Zheng, Y. (2010). On some models of instruction for overcoming fossilization in English learning. *Journal of Language Teaching and Research*, *1*(2), 148–150. Retrieved from http://ojs.academypublisher.com/index.php/jltr/article/viewFile/0102148150/1659

KEY TERMS AND DEFINITIONS

Fossilization: A key concept in interlanguage theory. It refers to permanent stop in learning.

Intelligibility: The ability to understand and to be understood by a listener in a situation. It can refer to understandability.

Phonetic Fossilization: Refers to pronunciation errors that become permanent, stable, and fixed in learners' IL overtime.

Phonetics: The science of the production of sounds. It deals with how consonants and vowels are produced and pronounced. It involves studying the place and the manner of articulation of consonants and the description of vowels in terms of the height of the tongue, part of the tongue, and lips rounding.

Related References

To continue our tradition of advancing academic research, we have compiled a list of recommended IGI Global readings. These references will provide additional information and guidance to further enrich your knowledge and assist you with your own research and future publications.

Abdelaziz, H. A. (2013). From content engagement to cognitive engagement: Toward an immersive web-based learning model to develop self-questioning and self-study skills. *International Journal of Technology Diffusion*, *4*(1), 16–32. doi:10.4018/jtd.2013010102

Acha, V., Hargiss, K. M., & Howard, C. (2013). The relationship between emotional intelligence of a leader and employee motivation to job performance. *International Journal of Strategic Information Technology and Applications*, *4*(4), 80–103. doi:10.4018/ijsita.2013100105

Agrawal, P. R. (2014). Digital information management: preserving tomorrow's memory. In S. Dhamdhere (Ed.), *Cloud computing and virtualization technologies in libraries* (pp. 22–35). Hershey, PA: IGI Global. doi:10.4018/978-1-4666-4631-5.ch002

Akram, H. A., & Mahmood, A. (2014). Predicting personality traits, gender and psychopath behavior of Twitter users. *International Journal of Technology Diffusion*, *5*(2), 1–14. doi:10.4018/ijtd.2014040101

Akyol, Z. (2013). Metacognitive development within the community of inquiry. In Z. Akyol & D. Garrison (Eds.), *Educational communities of inquiry: Theoretical framework, research and practice* (pp. 30–44). Hershey, PA: IGI Global. doi:10.4018/978-1-4666-2110-7.ch003

Albers, M. J. (2012). How people read. In *Human-information interaction and technical communication: Concepts and frameworks* (pp. 367–397). Hershey, PA: IGI Global. doi:10.4018/978-1-4666-0152-9.ch011

Albers, M. J. (2012). What people bring with them. In *Human-information interaction and technical communication: Concepts and frameworks* (pp. 61–113). Hershey, PA: IGI Global. doi:10.4018/978-1-4666-0152-9.ch003

Ally, M. (2012). Designing mobile learning for the user. In B. Khan (Ed.), *User interface design for virtual environments: Challenges and advances* (pp. 226–235). Hershey, PA: IGI Global. doi:10.4018/978-1-61350-516-8.ch014

Almeida, L., Menezes, P., & Dias, J. (2013). Augmented reality framework for the socialization between elderly people. In M. Cruz-Cunha, I. Miranda, & P. Gonçalves (Eds.), *Handbook of research on ICTs for human-centered healthcare and social care services* (pp. 430–448). Hershey, PA: IGI Global. doi:10.4018/978-1-4666-3986-7.ch023

Alonso, E., & Mondragón, E. (2011). Computational models of learning and beyond: Symmetries of associative learning. In E. Alonso & E. Mondragón (Eds.), *Computational neuroscience for advancing artificial intelligence: Models, methods and applications* (pp. 316–332). Hershey, PA: IGI Global. doi:10.4018/978-1-60960-021-1.ch013

Ancarani, A., & Di Mauro, C. (2013). The human side of supply chains: A behavioural perspective of supply chain risk management. In *Supply chain management: Concepts, methodologies, tools, and applications* (pp. 1453–1476). Hershey, PA: IGI Global. doi:10.4018/978-1-4666-2625-6.ch086

Andres, H. P. (2013). Collaborative technology and dimensions of team cognition: Test of a second-order factor model. *International Journal of Information Technology Project Management, 4*(3), 22–37. doi:10.4018/jitpm.2013070102

Arora, A. S., Raisinghani, M. S., Leseane, R., & Thompson, L. (2013). Personality scales and learning styles: Pedagogy for creating an adaptive web-based learning system. In M. Raisinghani (Ed.), *Curriculum, learning, and teaching advancements in online education* (pp. 161–182). Hershey, PA: IGI Global. doi:10.4018/978-1-4666-2949-3.ch012

Ashcraft, D., & Treadwell, T. (2010). The social psychology of online collaborative learning: The good, the bad, and the awkward. In web-based education: concepts, methodologies, tools and applications (pp. 1146-1161). Hershey, PA: IGI Global. doi:10.4018/978-1-61520-963-7.ch078

Aston, J. (2013). Database narrative, spatial montage, and the cultural transmission of memory: An anthropological perspective. In D. Harrison (Ed.), *Digital media and technologies for virtual artistic spaces* (pp. 150–158). Hershey, PA: IGI Global. doi:10.4018/978-1-4666-2961-5.ch011

Asunka, S. (2013). Collaborative online learning in non-formal education settings in the developing world: A best practice framework. In V. Wang (Ed.), *Technological applications in adult and vocational education advancement* (pp. 186–201). Hershey, PA: IGI Global. doi:10.4018/978-1-4666-2062-9.ch015

Attia, M. (2014). The role of early learning experience in shaping teacher cognition and technology use. In P. Breen (Ed.), *Cases on teacher identity, diversity, and cognition in higher education* (pp. 1–21). Hershey, PA: IGI Global. doi:10.4018/978-1-4666-5990-2.ch001

Ávila, I., Menezes, E., & Braga, A. M. (2014). Strategy to support the memorization of iconic passwords. In K. Blashki & P. Isaias (Eds.), *Emerging research and trends in interactivity and the human-computer interface* (pp. 239–259). Hershey, PA: IGI Global. doi:10.4018/978-1-4666-4623-0.ch012

Bachvarova, Y., & Bocconi, S. (2014). Games and social networks. In T. Connolly, T. Hainey, E. Boyle, G. Baxter, & P. Moreno-Ger (Eds.), *Psychology, pedagogy, and assessment in serious games* (pp. 204–219). Hershey, PA: IGI Global. doi:10.4018/978-1-4666-4773-2.ch010

Bagley, C. A., & Creswell, W. H. (2013). The role of social media as a tool for learning. In E. McKay (Ed.), *ePedagogy in online learning: New developments in web mediated human computer interaction* (pp. 18–38). Hershey, PA: IGI Global. doi:10.4018/978-1-4666-3649-1.ch002

Balogh, Š. (2014). Forensic analysis, cryptosystem implementation, and cryptology: Methods and techniques for extracting encryption keys from volatile memory. In S. Sadkhan Al Maliky & N. Abbas (Eds.), *Multidisciplinary perspectives in cryptology and information security* (pp. 381–396). Hershey, PA: IGI Global. doi:10.4018/978-1-4666-5808-0.ch016

Banas, J. R., & Brown, C. A. (2012). Web 2.0 visualization tools to stimulate generative learning. In D. Polly, C. Mims, & K. Persichitte (Eds.), *Developing technology-rich teacher education programs: Key issues* (pp. 77–90). Hershey, PA: IGI Global. doi:10.4018/978-1-4666-0014-0.ch006

Bancroft, J., & Wang, Y. (2013). A computational simulation of the cognitive process of children knowledge acquisition and memory development. In Y. Wang (Ed.), *Cognitive informatics for revealing human cognition: Knowledge manipulations in natural intelligence* (pp. 111–127). Hershey, PA: IGI Global. doi:10.4018/978-1-4666-2476-4.ch008

Bartsch, R. A. (2011). Social psychology and instructional technology. In *Instructional design: Concepts, methodologies, tools and applications* (pp. 1237–1244). Hershey, PA: IGI Global. doi:10.4018/978-1-60960-503-2.ch508

Bertolotti, T. (2013). Facebook has it: The irresistible violence of social cognition in the age of social networking. In R. Luppicini (Ed.), *Moral, ethical, and social dilemmas in the age of technology: Theories and practice* (pp. 234–247). Hershey, PA: IGI Global. doi:10.4018/978-1-4666-2931-8.ch016

Berwick, R. C. (2013). Songs to syntax: Cognition, combinatorial computation, and the origin of language. In Y. Wang (Ed.), *Cognitive informatics for revealing human cognition: Knowledge manipulations in natural intelligence* (pp. 70–80). Hershey, PA: IGI Global. doi:10.4018/978-1-4666-2476-4.ch005

Best, C., O'Neill, B., & Gillespie, A. (2014). Assistive technology for cognition: An updated review. In G. Naik & Y. Guo (Eds.), *Emerging theory and practice in neuroprosthetics* (pp. 215–236). Hershey, PA: IGI Global. doi:10.4018/978-1-4666-6094-6.ch011

Bhattacharya, A. (2014). Organisational justice perception: A work attitude modifier. In N. Ray & K. Chakraborty (Eds.), *Handbook of research on strategic business infrastructure development and contemporary issues in finance* (pp. 296–322). Hershey, PA: IGI Global. doi:10.4018/978-1-4666-5154-8.ch021

Biggiero, L. (2012). Practice vs. possession: Epistemological implications on the nature of organizational knowledge and cognition. In M. Mora, O. Gelman, A. Steenkamp, & M. Raisinghani (Eds.), *Research methodologies, innovations and philosophies in software systems engineering and information systems* (pp. 82–105). Hershey, PA: IGI Global. doi:10.4018/978-1-4666-0179-6.ch005

Bishop, J. (2014). The psychology of trolling and lurking: The role of defriending and gamification for increasing participation in online communities using seductive narratives. In J. Bishop (Ed.), *Gamification for human factors integration: Social, education, and psychological issues* (pp. 162–179). Hershey, PA: IGI Global. doi:10.4018/978-1-4666-5071-8.ch010

Blasko, D. G., Lum, H. C., White, M. M., & Drabik, H. B. (2014). Individual differences in the enjoyment and effectiveness of serious games. In T. Connolly, T. Hainey, E. Boyle, G. Baxter, & P. Moreno-Ger (Eds.), *Psychology, pedagogy, and assessment in serious games* (pp. 153–174). Hershey, PA: IGI Global. doi:10.4018/978-1-4666-4773-2.ch008

Borah, P. (2014). Interaction of incivility and news frames in the political blogosphere: Consequences and psychological mechanisms. In A. Solo (Ed.), *Handbook of research on political activism in the information age* (pp. 407–424). Hershey, PA: IGI Global. doi:10.4018/978-1-4666-6066-3.ch024

Borri, D., & Camarda, D. (2011). Spatial ontologies in multi-agent environmental planning. In J. Yearwood & A. Stranieri (Eds.), *Technologies for supporting reasoning communities and collaborative decision making: Cooperative approaches* (pp. 272–295). Hershey, PA: IGI Global. doi:10.4018/978-1-60960-091-4.ch015

Boukhobza, J. (2013). Flashing in the cloud: Shedding some light on NAND flash memory storage systems. In D. Kyriazis, A. Voulodimos, S. Gogouvitis, & T. Varvarigou (Eds.), *Data intensive storage services for cloud environments* (pp. 241–266). Hershey, PA: IGI Global. doi:10.4018/978-1-4666-3934-8.ch015

Boyle, E. (2014). Psychological aspects of serious games. In T. Connolly, T. Hainey, E. Boyle, G. Baxter, & P. Moreno-Ger (Eds.), *Psychology, pedagogy, and assessment in serious games* (pp. 1–18). Hershey, PA: IGI Global. doi:10.4018/978-1-4666-4773-2.ch001

Boyle, E., Terras, M. M., Ramsay, J., & Boyle, J. M. (2014). Executive functions in digital games. In T. Connolly, T. Hainey, E. Boyle, G. Baxter, & P. Moreno-Ger (Eds.), *Psychology, pedagogy, and assessment in serious games* (pp. 19–46). Hershey, PA: IGI Global. doi:10.4018/978-1-4666-4773-2.ch002

Breen, P. (2014). Philosophies, traditional pedagogy, and new technologies: A report on a case study of EAP teachers' integration of technology into traditional practice. In P. Breen (Ed.), *Cases on teacher identity, diversity, and cognition in higher education* (pp. 317–341). Hershey, PA: IGI Global. doi:10.4018/978-1-4666-5990-2.ch013

Buchanan, A. (2014). Protective factors in family relationships. In M. Merviö (Ed.), *Contemporary social issues in east Asian societies: Examining the spectrum of public and private spheres* (pp. 76–85). Hershey, PA: IGI Global. doi:10.4018/978-1-4666-5031-2.ch004

Burke, M. E., & Speed, C. (2014). Knowledge recovery: Applications of technology and memory. In M. Michael & K. Michael (Eds.), *Uberveillance and the social implications of microchip implants: Emerging technologies* (pp. 133–142). Hershey, PA: IGI Global. doi:10.4018/978-1-4666-4582-0.ch005

Burusic, J., & Karabegovic, M. (2014). The role of students' personality traits in the effective use of social networking sites in the educational context. In G. Mallia (Ed.), *The social classroom: Integrating social network use in education* (pp. 224–243). Hershey, PA: IGI Global. doi:10.4018/978-1-4666-4904-0.ch012

Caixinha, A., Magalhães, V., & Alexandre, I. M. (2013). Do you remember, or have you forgotten? In R. Martinho, R. Rijo, M. Cruz-Cunha, & J. Varajão (Eds.), *Information systems and technologies for enhancing health and social care* (pp. 136–146). Hershey, PA: IGI Global. doi:10.4018/978-1-4666-3667-5.ch009

Carbonaro, N., Cipresso, P., Tognetti, A., Anania, G., De Rossi, D., Pallavicini, F., & Riva, G. et al. (2014). Psychometric assessment of cardio-respiratory activity using a mobile platform. *International Journal of Handheld Computing Research*, *5*(1), 13–29. doi:10.4018/ijhcr.2014010102

Castellani, M. (2011). Cognitive tools for group decision making: The repertory grid approach revisited. In J. Yearwood & A. Stranieri (Eds.), *Technologies for supporting reasoning communities and collaborative decision making: Cooperative approaches* (pp. 172–192). Hershey, PA: IGI Global. doi:10.4018/978-1-60960-091-4.ch010

Cawthon, S. W., Harris, A., & Jones, R. (2010). Cognitive apprenticeship in an online research lab for graduate students in psychology. *International Journal of Web-Based Learning and Teaching Technologies*, *5*(1), 1–15. doi:10.4018/jwltt.2010010101

Cederborg, T., & Oudeyer, P. (2014). Learning words by imitating. In *Computational linguistics: Concepts, methodologies, tools, and applications* (pp. 1674–1704). Hershey, PA: IGI Global. doi:10.4018/978-1-4666-6042-7.ch084

Cervantes, J., Rodríguez, L., López, S., Ramos, F., & Robles, F. (2013). Cognitive process of moral decision-making for autonomous agents. *International Journal of Software Science and Computational Intelligence*, *5*(4), 61–76. doi:10.4018/ijssci.2013100105

Chadwick, D. D., Fullwood, C., & Wesson, C. J. (2014). Intellectual disability, identity, and the internet. In *Assistive technologies: Concepts, methodologies, tools, and applications* (pp. 198–223). Hershey, PA: IGI Global. doi:10.4018/978-1-4666-4422-9.ch011

Chan, E. C., Baciu, G., & Mak, S. C. (2010). Cognitive location-aware information retrieval by agent-based semantic matching. *International Journal of Software Science and Computational Intelligence*, *2*(3), 21–31. doi:10.4018/jssci.2010070102

Chen, C. (2014). Differences between visual style and verbal style learners in learning English. *International Journal of Distance Education Technologies*, *12*(1), 91–104. doi:10.4018/ijdet.2014010106

Chen, K., & Barthès, J. A. (2012). Giving personal assistant agents a case-based memory. In Y. Wang (Ed.), *Developments in natural intelligence research and knowledge engineering: Advancing applications* (pp. 287–304). Hershey, PA: IGI Global. doi:10.4018/978-1-4666-1743-8.ch021

Chen, S., Tai, C., Wang, T., & Wang, S. G. (2011). Social simulation with both human agents and software agents: An investigation into the impact of cognitive capacity on their learning behavior. In S. Chen, Y. Kambayashi, & H. Sato (Eds.), *Multi-agent applications with evolutionary computation and biologically inspired technologies: Intelligent techniques for ubiquity and optimization* (pp. 95–117). Hershey, PA: IGI Global. doi:10.4018/978-1-60566-898-7.ch006

Chiriacescu, V., Soh, L., & Shell, D. F. (2013). Understanding human learning using a multi-agent simulation of the unified learning model. *International Journal of Cognitive Informatics and Natural Intelligence*, *7*(4), 1–25. doi:10.4018/ijcini.2013100101

Christen, M., Alfano, M., Bangerter, E., & Lapsley, D. (2013). Ethical issues of 'morality mining': Moral identity as a focus of data mining. In H. Rahman & I. Ramos (Eds.), *Ethical data mining applications for socio-economic development* (pp. 1–21). Hershey, PA: IGI Global. doi:10.4018/978-1-4666-4078-8.ch001

Cipresso, P., Serino, S., Gaggioli, A., & Riva, G. (2014). Modeling the diffusion of psychological stress. In J. Rodrigues (Ed.), *Advancing medical practice through technology: Applications for healthcare delivery, management, and quality* (pp. 178–204). Hershey, PA: IGI Global. doi:10.4018/978-1-4666-4619-3.ch010

Code, J. (2013). Agency and identity in social media. In S. Warburton & S. Hatzipanagos (Eds.), *Digital identity and social media* (pp. 37–57). Hershey, PA: IGI Global. doi:10.4018/978-1-4666-1915-9.ch004

Combs, R. M., & Mazur, J. (2014). 3D modeling in a high school computer visualization class: Enacting a productive, distributed social learning environment. In *K-12 education: Concepts, methodologies, tools, and applications* (pp. 1020–1040). Hershey, PA: IGI Global. doi:10.4018/978-1-4666-4502-8.ch061

Cook, R. G., & Sutton, R. (2014). Administrators' assessments of online courses and student retention in higher education: Lessons learned. In S. Mukerji & P. Tripathi (Eds.), *Handbook of research on transnational higher education* (pp. 138–150). Hershey, PA: IGI Global. doi:10.4018/978-1-4666-4458-8.ch008

Correa, T., Bachmann, I., Hinsley, A. W., & Gil de Zúñiga, H. (2013). Personality and social media use. In E. Li, S. Loh, C. Evans, & F. Lorenzi (Eds.), *Organizations and social networking: Utilizing social media to engage consumers* (pp. 41–61). Hershey, PA: IGI Global. doi:10.4018/978-1-4666-4026-9.ch003

Cowell, R. A., Bussey, T. J., & Saksida, L. M. (2011). Using computational modelling to understand cognition in the ventral visual-perirhinal pathway. In E. Alonso & E. Mondragón (Eds.), *Computational neuroscience for advancing artificial intelligence: Models, methods and applications* (pp. 15–45). Hershey, PA: IGI Global. doi:10.4018/978-1-60960-021-1.ch002

Crespo, R. G., Martíne, O. S., Lovelle, J. M., García-Bustelo, B. C., Díaz, V. G., & Ordoñez de Pablos, P. (2014). Improving cognitive load on students with disabilities through software aids. In *Assistive technologies: Concepts, methodologies, tools, and applications* (pp. 1255–1268). Hershey, PA: IGI Global. doi:10.4018/978-1-4666-4422-9.ch066

Cró, M. D., Andreucci, L., Pinho, A. M., & Pereira, A. (2013). Resilience and psychomotricity in preschool education: A study with children that are socially, culturally, and economically disadvantaged. In M. Cruz-Cunha, I. Miranda, & P. Gonçalves (Eds.), *Handbook of research on ICTs for human-centered healthcare and social care services* (pp. 366–378). Hershey, PA: IGI Global. doi:10.4018/978-1-4666-3986-7.ch019

Cummings, J. J., & Ross, T. L. (2013). Optimizing the psychological benefits of choice: information transparency and heuristic use in game environments. In R. Ferdig (Ed.), *Design, utilization, and analysis of simulations and game-based educational worlds* (pp. 142–157). Hershey, PA: IGI Global. doi:10.4018/978-1-4666-4018-4.ch009

Curumsing, M. K., Pedell, S., & Vasa, R. (2014). Designing an evaluation tool to measure emotional goals. *International Journal of People-Oriented Programming, 3*(1), 22–43. doi:10.4018/ijpop.2014010102

Cuzzocrea, F., Murdaca, A. M., & Oliva, P. (2013). Using precision teaching method to improve foreign language and cognitive skills in university students. In A. Cartelli (Ed.), *Fostering 21st century digital literacy and technical competency* (pp. 201–211). Hershey, PA: IGI Global. doi:10.4018/978-1-4666-2943-1.ch014

DaCosta, B., & Seok, S. (2010). Human cognition in the design of assistive technology for those with learning disabilities. In S. Seok, E. Meyen, & B. DaCosta (Eds.), *Handbook of research on human cognition and assistive technology: Design, accessibility and transdisciplinary perspectives* (pp. 1–20). Hershey, PA: IGI Global. doi:10.4018/978-1-61520-817-3.ch001

DaCosta, B., & Seok, S. (2010). Multimedia design of assistive technology for those with learning disabilities. In S. Seok, E. Meyen, & B. DaCosta (Eds.), *Handbook of research on human cognition and assistive technology: Design, accessibility and transdisciplinary perspectives* (pp. 43–60). Hershey, PA: IGI Global. doi:10.4018/978-1-61520-817-3.ch003

Danielsson, U., & Öberg, K. D. (2011). Psychosocial life environment and life roles in interaction with daily use of information communication technology boundaries between work and leisure. In D. Haftor & A. Mirijamdotter (Eds.), *Information and communication technologies, society and human beings: Theory and framework (Festschrift in honor of Gunilla Bradley)* (pp. 266–282). Hershey, PA: IGI Global. doi:10.4018/978-1-60960-057-0.ch020

Daradoumis, T., & Lafuente, M. M. (2014). Studying the suitability of discourse analysis methods for emotion detection and interpretation in computer-mediated educational discourse. In H. Lim & F. Sudweeks (Eds.), *Innovative methods and technologies for electronic discourse analysis* (pp. 119–143). Hershey, PA: IGI Global. doi:10.4018/978-1-4666-4426-7.ch006

De Simone, C., Marquis, T., & Groen, J. (2013). Optimizing conditions for learning and teaching in K-20 education. In V. Wang (Ed.), *Handbook of research on teaching and learning in K-20 education* (pp. 535–552). Hershey, PA: IGI Global. doi:10.4018/978-1-4666-4249-2.ch031

Deka, G. C. (2014). Significance of in-memory computing for real-time big data analytics. In P. Raj & G. Deka (Eds.), *Handbook of research on cloud infrastructures for big data analytics* (pp. 352–369). Hershey, PA: IGI Global. doi:10.4018/978-1-4666-5864-6.ch014

Demirbilek, M. (2010). Cognitive load and disorientation issues in hypermedia as assistive technology. In S. Seok, E. Meyen, & B. DaCosta (Eds.), *Handbook of research on human cognition and assistive technology: Design, accessibility and transdisciplinary perspectives* (pp. 109–120). Hershey, PA: IGI Global. doi:10.4018/978-1-61520-817-3.ch007

Derrick, M. G. (2013). The inventory of learner persistence. In M. Bocarnea, R. Reynolds, & J. Baker (Eds.), *Online instruments, data collection, and electronic measurements: Organizational advancements* (pp. 271–290). Hershey, PA: IGI Global. doi:10.4018/978-1-4666-2172-5.ch016

Doolittle, P. E., McNeill, A. L., Terry, K. P., & Scheer, S. B. (2011). Multimedia, cognitive load, and pedagogy. In *Instructional design: Concepts, methodologies, tools and applications* (pp. 1564–1585). Hershey, PA: IGI Global. doi:10.4018/978-1-60960-503-2.ch706

Dourlens, S., & Ramdane-Cherif, A. (2013). Cognitive memory for semantic agents architecture in robotic interaction. In Y. Wang (Ed.), *Cognitive informatics for revealing human cognition: Knowledge manipulations in natural intelligence* (pp. 82–97). Hershey, PA: IGI Global. doi:10.4018/978-1-4666-2476-4.ch006

Dubbels, B. (2011). Cognitive ethnography: A methodology for measure and analysis of learning for game studies. *International Journal of Gaming and Computer-Mediated Simulations*, *3*(1), 68–78. doi:10.4018/jgcms.2011010105

Dunbar, N. E., Wilson, S. N., Adame, B. J., Elizondo, J., Jensen, M. L., Miller, C. H., & Burgoon, J. K. et al. (2013). MACBETH: Development of a training game for the mitigation of cognitive bias. *International Journal of Game-Based Learning*, *3*(4), 7–26. doi:10.4018/ijgbl.2013100102

Dunham, A. H., & Burt, C. D. (2012). Mentoring and the transfer of organizational memory within the context of an aging workforce: Cultural implications for competitive advantage. In *Organizational learning and knowledge: Concepts, methodologies, tools and applications* (pp. 3076–3099). Hershey, PA: IGI Global. doi:10.4018/978-1-60960-783-8.ch817

Durrington, V. A., & Du, J. (2013). Learning tasks, peer interaction, and cognition process an online collaborative design model. *International Journal of Information and Communication Technology Education*, *9*(1), 38–50. doi:10.4018/jicte.2013010104

Duţu, A. (2014). Understanding consumers' behaviour change in uncertainty conditions: A psychological perspective. In F. Musso & E. Druica (Eds.), *Handbook of research on retailer-consumer relationship development* (pp. 45–69). Hershey, PA: IGI Global. doi:10.4018/978-1-4666-6074-8.ch004

Dwyer, P. (2013). Measuring collective cognition in online collaboration venues. In N. Kock (Ed.), *Interdisciplinary applications of electronic collaboration approaches and technologies* (pp. 46–61). Hershey, PA: IGI Global. doi:10.4018/978-1-4666-2020-9.ch004

Egan, R. G., & Zhou, M. (2011). Re-conceptualizing calibration using trace methodology. In G. Dettori & D. Persico (Eds.), *Fostering self-regulated learning through ICT* (pp. 71–88). Hershey, PA: IGI Global. doi:10.4018/978-1-61692-901-5.ch005

El-Farargy, N. (2013). Refresher training in clinical psychology supervision: A blended learning approach. In A. Benson, J. Moore, & S. Williams van Rooij (Eds.), *Cases on educational technology planning, design, and implementation: A project management perspective* (pp. 295–317). Hershey, PA: IGI Global. doi:10.4018/978-1-4666-4237-9.ch016

El Louadi, M., & Tounsi, I. (2010). Do organizational memory and information technology interact to affect organizational information needs and provision? In M. Jennex (Ed.), *Ubiquitous developments in knowledge management: Integrations and trends* (pp. 1–20). Hershey, PA: IGI Global. doi:10.4018/978-1-60566-954-0.ch001

Estrada-Hernández, N., & Stachowiak, J. R. (2010). Evaluating systemic assistive technology needs. In S. Seok, E. Meyen, & B. DaCosta (Eds.), *Handbook of research on human cognition and assistive technology: Design, accessibility and transdisciplinary perspectives* (pp. 239–250). Hershey, PA: IGI Global. doi:10.4018/978-1-61520-817-3.ch016

Fitzpatrick, M., & Theoharis, R. (2010). Assistive technology for deaf and hard of hearing students. In S. Seok, E. Meyen, & B. DaCosta (Eds.), *Handbook of research on human cognition and assistive technology: Design, accessibility and transdisciplinary perspectives* (pp. 179–191). Hershey, PA: IGI Global. doi:10.4018/978-1-61520-817-3.ch012

Francis, A. G. Jr, Mehta, M., & Ram, A. (2012). Emotional memory and adaptive personalities. In *Machine learning: Concepts, methodologies, tools and applications* (pp. 1292–1313). Hershey, PA: IGI Global. doi:10.4018/978-1-60960-818-7.ch507

Gagliardi, F. (2014). A cognitive machine-learning system to discover syndromes in erythemato-squamous diseases. In J. Rodrigues (Ed.), *Advancing medical practice through technology: Applications for healthcare delivery, management, and quality* (pp. 66–101). Hershey, PA: IGI Global. doi:10.4018/978-1-4666-4619-3.ch005

Gaines, B. R., & Shaw, M. L. (2013). Sociocognitive inquiry. In *Data mining: Concepts, methodologies, tools, and applications* (pp. 1688–1708). Hershey, PA: IGI Global. doi:10.4018/978-1-4666-2455-9.ch088

Gardner, M. K., & Hill, R. D. (2013). Training older adults to improve their episodic memory: Three different approaches to enhancing numeric memory. In R. Zheng, R. Hill, & M. Gardner (Eds.), *Engaging older adults with modern technology: Internet use and information access needs* (pp. 191–211). Hershey, PA: IGI Global. doi:10.4018/978-1-4666-1966-1.ch010

Ghili, S., Nazarian, S., Tavana, M., Keyvanshokouhi, S., & Isaai, M. T. (2013). A complex systems paradox of organizational learning and knowledge management. *International Journal of Knowledge-Based Organizations*, *3*(3), 53–72. doi:10.4018/ijkbo.2013070104

Gibson, D. (2012). Designing a computational model of learning. In *Machine learning: Concepts, methodologies, tools and applications* (pp. 147–174). Hershey, PA: IGI Global. doi:10.4018/978-1-60960-818-7.ch203

Gibson, M., Renaud, K., Conrad, M., & Maple, C. (2013). Music is the key: Using our enduring memory for songs to help users log on. In *IT policy and ethics: Concepts, methodologies, tools, and applications* (pp. 1018–1037). Hershey, PA: IGI Global. doi:10.4018/978-1-4666-2919-6.ch046

Godine, N., & Barnett, J. E. (2013). The use of telepsychology in clinical practice: Benefits, effectiveness, and issues to consider. *International Journal of Cyber Behavior, Psychology and Learning*, *3*(4), 70–83. doi:10.4018/ijcbpl.2013100105

Gökçay, D. (2011). Emotional axes: Psychology, psychophysiology and neuroanatomical correlates. In D. Gökçay & G. Yildirim (Eds.), *Affective computing and interaction: Psychological, cognitive and neuroscientific perspectives* (pp. 56–73). Hershey, PA: IGI Global. doi:10.4018/978-1-61692-892-6.ch003

Goswami, R., Jena, R. K., & Mahapatro, B. B. (2013). Psycho-social impact of shift work: A study of ferro-alloy industries in Orissa. In P. Ordóñez de Pablos (Ed.), *Business, technology, and knowledge management in Asia: Trends and innovations* (pp. 166–174). Hershey, PA: IGI Global. doi:10.4018/978-1-4666-2652-2.ch013

Graff, M. (2011). Can cognitive style predict how individuals use web-based learning environments? In *Instructional design: Concepts, methodologies, tools and applications* (pp. 1553–1563). Hershey, PA: IGI Global. doi:10.4018/978-1-60960-503-2.ch705

Griffiths, M., Kuss, D. J., & Ortiz de Gortari, A. B. (2013). Videogames as therapy: A review of the medical and psychological literature. In M. Cruz-Cunha, I. Miranda, & P. Gonçalves (Eds.), *Handbook of research on ICTs and management systems for improving efficiency in healthcare and social care* (pp. 43–68). Hershey, PA: IGI Global. doi:10.4018/978-1-4666-3990-4.ch003

Guger, C., Sorger, B., Noirhomme, Q., Naci, L., Monti, M. M., & Real, R. ... Cincotti, F. (2014). Brain-computer interfaces for assessment and communication in disorders of consciousness. In G. Naik & Y. Guo (Eds.), Emerging theory and practice in neuroprosthetics (pp. 181-214). Hershey, PA: IGI Global. doi:10.4018/978-1-4666-6094-6.ch010

Güngör, H. (2014). Adolescent suicides as a chaotic phenomenon. In Ş. Erçetin & S. Banerjee (Eds.), *Chaos and complexity theory in world politics* (pp. 306–324). Hershey, PA: IGI Global. doi:10.4018/978-1-4666-6070-0.ch022

Hai-Jew, S. (2013). Interpreting "you" and "me": Personal voices, PII, biometrics, and imperfect/perfect electronic memory in a democracy. In C. Akrivopoulou & N. Garipidis (Eds.), *Digital democracy and the impact of technology on governance and politics: New globalized practices* (pp. 20–37). Hershey, PA: IGI Global. doi:10.4018/978-1-4666-3637-8.ch003

Hainey, T., Connolly, T. M., Chaudy, Y., Boyle, E., Beeby, R., & Soflano, M. (2014). Assessment integration in serious games. In T. Connolly, T. Hainey, E. Boyle, G. Baxter, & P. Moreno-Ger (Eds.), *Psychology, pedagogy, and assessment in serious games* (pp. 317–341). Hershey, PA: IGI Global. doi:10.4018/978-1-4666-4773-2.ch015

Hainey, T., Soflano, M., & Connolly, T. M. (2014). A randomised controlled trial to evaluate learning effectiveness using an adaptive serious game to teach SQL at higher education level. In T. Connolly, T. Hainey, E. Boyle, G. Baxter, & P. Moreno-Ger (Eds.), *Psychology, pedagogy, and assessment in serious games* (pp. 270–291). Hershey, PA: IGI Global. doi:10.4018/978-1-4666-4773-2.ch013

Haque, J., Erturk, M., Arslan, H., & Moreno, W. (2011). Cognitive aeronautical communication system. *International Journal of Interdisciplinary Telecommunications and Networking, 3*(1), 20–35. doi:10.4018/jitn.2011010102

Hauge, J. B., Boyle, E., Mayer, I., Nadolski, R., Riedel, J. C., Moreno-Ger, P., & Ritchie, J. et al. (2014). Study design and data gathering guide for serious games' evaluation. In T. Connolly, T. Hainey, E. Boyle, G. Baxter, & P. Moreno-Ger (Eds.), *Psychology, pedagogy, and assessment in serious games* (pp. 394–419). Hershey, PA: IGI Global. doi:10.4018/978-1-4666-4773-2.ch018

Haykin, S. (2013). Cognitive dynamic systems. In Y. Wang (Ed.), *Cognitive informatics for revealing human cognition: Knowledge manipulations in natural intelligence* (pp. 250–260). Hershey, PA: IGI Global. doi:10.4018/978-1-4666-2476-4.ch016

Henderson, A. M., & Sabbagh, M. A. (2014). Learning words from experience: An integrated framework. In *Computational linguistics: Concepts, methodologies, tools, and applications* (pp. 1705–1727). Hershey, PA: IGI Global. doi:10.4018/978-1-4666-6042-7.ch085

Hendrick, H. W. (2011). Cognitive and organizational complexity and behavior: Implications for organizational design and leadership. In D. Haftor & A. Mirijamdotter (Eds.), *Information and communication technologies, society and human beings: Theory and framework (Festschrift in honor of Gunilla Bradley)* (pp. 147–159). Hershey, PA: IGI Global. doi:10.4018/978-1-60960-057-0.ch013

Henrie, K. M., & Miller, D. W. (2013). An examination of mediation: Insights into the role of psychological mediators in the use of persuasion knowledge. In R. Eid (Ed.), *Managing customer trust, satisfaction, and loyalty through information communication technologies* (pp. 106–117). Hershey, PA: IGI Global. doi:10.4018/978-1-4666-3631-6.ch007

Ho, W. C., Dautenhahn, K., Lim, M., Enz, S., Zoll, C., & Watson, S. (2012). Towards learning 'self' and emotional knowledge in social and cultural human-agent interactions. In *Virtual learning environments: Concepts, methodologies, tools and applications* (pp. 1426–1445). Hershey, PA: IGI Global. doi:10.4018/978-1-4666-0011-9.ch705

Holt, L., & Ziegler, M. F. (2013). Promoting team learning in the classroom. In V. Wang (Ed.), *Technological applications in adult and vocational education advancement* (pp. 94–105). Hershey, PA: IGI Global. doi:10.4018/978-1-4666-2062-9.ch008

Honey, R. C., & Grand, C. S. (2011). Application of connectionist models to animal learning: Interactions between perceptual organization and associative processes. In E. Alonso & E. Mondragón (Eds.), *Computational neuroscience for advancing artificial intelligence: Models, methods and applications* (pp. 1–14). Hershey, PA: IGI Global. doi:10.4018/978-1-60960-021-1.ch001

Hoppenbrouwers, S., Schotten, B., & Lucas, P. (2012). Towards games for knowledge acquisition and modeling. In R. Ferdig & S. de Freitas (Eds.), *Interdisciplinary advancements in gaming, simulations and virtual environments: Emerging trends* (pp. 281–299). Hershey, PA: IGI Global. doi:10.4018/978-1-4666-0029-4.ch018

Huang, C., Liang, C., & Lin, E. (2014). A study on emotion releasing effect with music and color. In F. Cipolla-Ficarra (Ed.), *Advanced research and trends in new technologies, software, human-computer interaction, and communicability* (pp. 23–31). Hershey, PA: IGI Global. doi:10.4018/978-1-4666-4490-8.ch003

Huang, W. D., & Tettegah, S. Y. (2014). Cognitive load and empathy in serious games: A conceptual framework. In J. Bishop (Ed.), *Gamification for human factors integration: Social, education, and psychological issues* (pp. 17–30). Hershey, PA: IGI Global. doi:10.4018/978-1-4666-5071-8.ch002

Huijnen, C. (2011). The use of assistive technology to support the wellbeing and independence of people with memory impairments. In J. Soar, R. Swindell, & P. Tsang (Eds.), *Intelligent technologies for bridging the grey digital divide* (pp. 65–79). Hershey, PA: IGI Global. doi:10.4018/978-1-61520-825-8.ch005

Huseyinov, I. N. (2014). Fuzzy linguistic modelling in multi modal human computer interaction: Adaptation to cognitive styles using multi level fuzzy granulation method. In *Assistive technologies: Concepts, methodologies, tools, and applications* (pp. 1481–1496). Hershey, PA: IGI Global. doi:10.4018/978-1-4666-4422-9.ch077

Hussey, H. D., Fleck, B. K., & Richmond, A. S. (2014). Promoting active learning through a flipped course design. In J. Keengwe, G. Onchwari, & J. Oigara (Eds.), *Promoting active learning through the flipped classroom model* (pp. 23–46). Hershey, PA: IGI Global. doi:10.4018/978-1-4666-4987-3.ch002

Ilin, R., & Perlovsky, L. (2010). Cognitively inspired neural network for recognition of situations. *International Journal of Natural Computing Research, 1*(1), 36–55. doi:10.4018/jncr.2010010102

Ilin, R., & Perlovsky, L. (2011). Cognitive based distributed sensing, processing, and communication. In B. Igelnik (Ed.), *Computational modeling and simulation of intellect: Current state and future perspectives* (pp. 131–161). Hershey, PA: IGI Global. doi:10.4018/978-1-60960-551-3.ch006

Jenkins, J. L., Durcikova, A., & Burns, M. B. (2013). Simplicity is bliss: Controlling extraneous cognitive load in online security training to promote secure behavior. *Journal of Organizational and End User Computing, 25*(3), 52–66. doi:10.4018/joeuc.2013070104

Jennings, D. J., Alonso, E., Mondragón, E., & Bonardi, C. (2011). Temporal uncertainty during overshadowing: A temporal difference account. In E. Alonso & E. Mondragón (Eds.), *Computational neuroscience for advancing artificial intelligence: Models, methods and applications* (pp. 46–55). Hershey, PA: IGI Global. doi:10.4018/978-1-60960-021-1.ch003

Jin, S., DaCosta, B., & Seok, S. (2014). Social skills development for children with autism spectrum disorders through the use of interactive storytelling games. In B. DaCosta & S. Seok (Eds.), *Assistive technology research, practice, and theory* (pp. 144–159). Hershey, PA: IGI Global. doi:10.4018/978-1-4666-5015-2.ch010

Johnson, R. D., De Ridder, D., & Gillett, G. (2014). Neurosurgery to enhance brain function: Ethical dilemmas for the neuroscientist and society. In S. Thompson (Ed.), *Global issues and ethical considerations in human enhancement technologies* (pp. 96–118). Hershey, PA: IGI Global. doi:10.4018/978-1-4666-6010-6.ch006

Johnson, V., & Price, C. (2010). A longitudinal case study on the use of assistive technology to support cognitive processes across formal and informal educational settings. In S. Seok, E. Meyen, & B. DaCosta (Eds.), *Handbook of research on human cognition and assistive technology: Design, accessibility and transdisciplinary perspectives* (pp. 192–198). Hershey, PA: IGI Global. doi:10.4018/978-1-61520-817-3.ch013

Kalyuga, S. (2012). Cognitive load aspects of text processing. In C. Boonthum-Denecke, P. McCarthy, & T. Lamkin (Eds.), *Cross-disciplinary advances in applied natural language processing: Issues and approaches* (pp. 114–132). Hershey, PA: IGI Global. doi:10.4018/978-1-61350-447-5.ch009

Kammler, D., Witte, E. M., Chattopadhyay, A., Bauwens, B., Ascheid, G., Leupers, R., & Meyr, H. (2012). Automatic generation of memory interfaces for ASIPs. In S. Virtanen (Ed.), *Innovations in embedded and real-time systems engineering for communication* (pp. 79–100). Hershey, PA: IGI Global. doi:10.4018/978-1-4666-0912-9.ch005

Khan, T. M. (2011). Theory of mind in autistic children: multimedia based support. In P. Ordóñez de Pablos, J. Zhao, & R. Tennyson (Eds.), *Technology enhanced learning for people with disabilities: Approaches and applications* (pp. 167–179). Hershey, PA: IGI Global. doi:10.4018/978-1-61520-923-1.ch012

Khetrapal, N. (2010). Cognition meets assistive technology: Insights from load theory of selective attention. In S. Seok, E. Meyen, & B. DaCosta (Eds.), *Handbook of research on human cognition and assistive technology: Design, accessibility and transdisciplinary perspectives* (pp. 96–108). Hershey, PA: IGI Global. doi:10.4018/978-1-61520-817-3.ch006

Khetrapal, N. (2010). Cognitive science helps formulate games for moral education. In K. Schrier & D. Gibson (Eds.), *Ethics and game design: Teaching values through play* (pp. 181–196). Hershey, PA: IGI Global. doi:10.4018/978-1-61520-845-6.ch012

Kickmeier-Rust, M. D., Mattheiss, E., Steiner, C., & Albert, D. (2011). A psycho-pedagogical framework for multi-adaptive educational games. *International Journal of Game-Based Learning, 1*(1), 45–58. doi:10.4018/ijgbl.2011010104

Kiel, L. D., & McCaskill, J. (2013). Cognition and complexity: An agent-based model of cognitive capital under stress. In S. Banerjee (Ed.), *Chaos and complexity theory for management: Nonlinear dynamics* (pp. 254–268). Hershey, PA: IGI Global. doi:10.4018/978-1-4666-2509-9.ch012

Kiili, K., & Perttula, A. (2013). A design framework for educational exergames. In S. de Freitas, M. Ott, M. Popescu, & I. Stanescu (Eds.), *New pedagogical approaches in game enhanced learning: Curriculum integration* (pp. 136–158). Hershey, PA: IGI Global. doi:10.4018/978-1-4666-3950-8.ch008

Kiliç, F. (2011). Structuring of knowledge and cognitive load. In G. Kurubacak & T. Yuzer (Eds.), *Handbook of research on transformative online education and liberation: Models for social equality* (pp. 370–382). Hershey, PA: IGI Global. doi:10.4018/978-1-60960-046-4.ch020

Kim, E. B. (2011). Student personality and learning outcomes in e-learning: An introduction to empirical research. In S. Eom & J. Arbaugh (Eds.), *Student satisfaction and learning outcomes in e-learning: An introduction to empirical research* (pp. 294–315). Hershey, PA: IGI Global. doi:10.4018/978-1-60960-615-2.ch013

Kinsell, C. (2010). Investigating assistive technologies using computers to simulate basic curriculum for individuals with cognitive impairments. In S. Seok, E. Meyen, & B. DaCosta (Eds.), *Handbook of research on human cognition and assistive technology: Design, accessibility and transdisciplinary perspectives* (pp. 61–75). Hershey, PA: IGI Global. doi:10.4018/978-1-61520-817-3.ch004

Kirwan, G., & Power, A. (2012). Can forensic psychology contribute to solving the problem of cybercrime? In G. Kirwan & A. Power (Eds.), *The psychology of cyber crime: Concepts and principles* (pp. 18–36). Hershey, PA: IGI Global. doi:10.4018/978-1-61350-350-8.ch002

Klippel, A., Richter, K., & Hansen, S. (2013). Cognitively ergonomic route directions. In *Geographic information systems: Concepts, methodologies, tools, and applications* (pp. 250–257). Hershey, PA: IGI Global. doi:10.4018/978-1-4666-2038-4.ch017

Knafla, B., & Champandard, A. J. (2012). Behavior trees: Introduction and memory-compact implementation. In A. Kumar, J. Etheredge, & A. Boudreaux (Eds.), *Algorithmic and architectural gaming design: Implementation and development* (pp. 40–66). Hershey, PA: IGI Global. doi:10.4018/978-1-4666-1634-9.ch003

Kokkinos, C. M., Antoniadou, N., Dalara, E., Koufogazou, A., & Papatziki, A. (2013). Cyber-bullying, personality and coping among pre-adolescents. *International Journal of Cyber Behavior, Psychology and Learning*, *3*(4), 55–69. doi:10.4018/ijcbpl.2013100104

Konrath, S. (2013). The empathy paradox: Increasing disconnection in the age of increasing connection. In R. Luppicini (Ed.), *Handbook of research on technoself: Identity in a technological society* (pp. 204–228). Hershey, PA: IGI Global. doi:10.4018/978-1-4666-2211-1.ch012

Kopp, B., & Mandl, H. (2012). Supporting virtual collaborative learning using collaboration scripts and content schemes. In *Virtual learning environments: Concepts, methodologies, tools and applications* (pp. 470–487). Hershey, PA: IGI Global. doi:10.4018/978-1-4666-0011-9.ch303

Kumar, S., Singhal, D., & Murthy, G. R. (2013). Doubly cognitive architecture based cognitive wireless sensor networks. In N. Chilamkurti (Ed.), *Security, design, and architecture for broadband and wireless network technologies* (pp. 121–126). Hershey, PA: IGI Global. doi:10.4018/978-1-4666-3902-7.ch009

Kutaula, S., & Talwar, V. (2014). Integrating psychological contract and service-related outcomes in emerging economies: A proposed conceptual framework. In A. Goyal (Ed.), *Innovations in services marketing and management: Strategies for emerging economies* (pp. 291–306). Hershey, PA: IGI Global. doi:10.4018/978-1-4666-4671-1.ch016

Kyriakaki, G., & Matsatsinis, N. (2014). Pedagogical evaluation of e-learning websites with cognitive objectives. In D. Yannacopoulos, P. Manolitzas, N. Matsatsinis, & E. Grigoroudis (Eds.), *Evaluating websites and web services: Interdisciplinary perspectives on user satisfaction* (pp. 224–240). Hershey, PA: IGI Global. doi:10.4018/978-1-4666-5129-6.ch013

Kyritsis, M., Gulliver, S. R., & Morar, S. (2014). Cognitive and environmental factors influencing the process of spatial knowledge acquisition within virtual reality environments. *International Journal of Artificial Life Research*, *4*(1), 43–58. doi:10.4018/ijalr.2014010104

Laffey, J., Stichter, J., & Schmidt, M. (2010). Social orthotics for youth with ASD to learn in a collaborative 3D VLE. In S. Seok, E. Meyen, & B. DaCosta (Eds.), *Handbook of research on human cognition and assistive technology: Design, accessibility and transdisciplinary perspectives* (pp. 76–95). Hershey, PA: IGI Global. doi:10.4018/978-1-61520-817-3.ch005

Lai, S., & Han, H. (2014). Behavioral planning theory. In J. Wang (Ed.), *Encyclopedia of business analytics and optimization* (pp. 265–272). Hershey, PA: IGI Global. doi:10.4018/978-1-4666-5202-6.ch025

Lawson, D. (2013). Analysis and use of the life styles inventory 1 and 2 by human synergistics international. In M. Bocarnea, R. Reynolds, & J. Baker (Eds.), *Online instruments, data collection, and electronic measurements: Organizational advancements* (pp. 76–96). Hershey, PA: IGI Global. doi:10.4018/978-1-4666-2172-5.ch005

Lee, L., & Hung, J. C. (2011). Effect of teaching using whole brain instruction on accounting learning. In Q. Jin (Ed.), *Distance education environments and emerging software systems: New technologies* (pp. 261–282). Hershey, PA: IGI Global. doi:10.4018/978-1-60960-539-1.ch016

Levin, I., & Kojukhov, A. (2013). Personalization of learning environments in a post-industrial class. In M. Pătruţ & B. Pătruţ (Eds.), *Social media in higher education: Teaching in web 2.0* (pp. 105–123). Hershey, PA: IGI Global. doi:10.4018/978-1-4666-2970-7.ch006

Li, A., Li, H., Guo, R., & Zhu, T. (2013). MobileSens: A ubiquitous psychological laboratory based on mobile device. *International Journal of Cyber Behavior, Psychology and Learning*, *3*(2), 47–55. doi:10.4018/ijcbpl.2013040104

Li, R. (2013). Traditional to hybrid: Social media's role in reshaping instruction in higher education. In A. Sigal (Ed.), *Advancing library education: Technological innovation and instructional design* (pp. 65–90). Hershey, PA: IGI Global. doi:10.4018/978-1-4666-3688-0.ch005

Li, X., Lin, Z., & Wu, J. (2014). Language processing in the human brain of literate and illiterate subjects. In *Computational linguistics: Concepts, methodologies, tools, and applications* (pp. 1391–1400). Hershey, PA: IGI Global. doi:10.4018/978-1-4666-6042-7.ch068

Li, X., Ouyang, Z., & Luo, Y. (2013). The cognitive load affects the interaction pattern of emotion and working memory. *International Journal of Cognitive Informatics and Natural Intelligence*, *6*(2), 68–81. doi:10.4018/jcini.2012040104

Lin, T., Li, X., Wu, Z., & Tang, N. (2013). Automatic cognitive load classification using high-frequency interaction events: An exploratory study. *International Journal of Technology and Human Interaction*, *9*(3), 73–88. doi:10.4018/jthi.2013070106

Linek, S. B. (2011). As you like it: What media psychology can tell us about educational game design. In P. Felicia (Ed.), *Handbook of research on improving learning and motivation through educational games: Multidisciplinary approaches* (pp. 606–632). Hershey, PA: IGI Global. doi:10.4018/978-1-60960-495-0.ch029

Linek, S. B., Marte, B., & Albert, D. (2014). Background music in educational games: Motivational appeal and cognitive impact. In J. Bishop (Ed.), *Gamification for human factors integration: Social, education, and psychological issues* (pp. 259–271). Hershey, PA: IGI Global. doi:10.4018/978-1-4666-5071-8.ch016

Logeswaran, R. (2011). Neural networks in medicine. In *Clinical technologies: Concepts, methodologies, tools and applications* (pp. 744–765). Hershey, PA: IGI Global. doi:10.4018/978-1-60960-561-2.ch308

Low, R. (2011). Cognitive architecture and instructional design in a multimedia context. In *Instructional design: Concepts, methodologies, tools and applications* (pp. 496–510). Hershey, PA: IGI Global. doi:10.4018/978-1-60960-503-2.ch301

Low, R., Jin, P., & Sweller, J. (2014). Instructional design in digital environments and availability of mental resources for the aged subpopulation. In *Assistive technologies: Concepts, methodologies, tools, and applications* (pp. 1131–1154). Hershey, PA: IGI Global. doi:10.4018/978-1-4666-4422-9.ch059

Lu, J., & Peng, Y. (2014). Brain-computer interface for cyberpsychology: Components, methods, and applications. *International Journal of Cyber Behavior, Psychology and Learning*, *4*(1), 1–14. doi:10.4018/ijcbpl.2014010101

Ludvig, E. A., Bellemare, M. G., & Pearson, K. G. (2011). A primer on reinforcement learning in the brain: Psychological, computational, and neural perspectives. In E. Alonso & E. Mondragón (Eds.), *Computational neuroscience for advancing artificial intelligence: Models, methods and applications* (pp. 111–144). Hershey, PA: IGI Global. doi:10.4018/978-1-60960-021-1.ch006

Lützenberger, M. (2014). A driver's mind: Psychology runs simulation. In D. Janssens, A. Yasar, & L. Knapen (Eds.), *Data science and simulation in transportation research* (pp. 182–205). Hershey, PA: IGI Global. doi:10.4018/978-1-4666-4920-0.ch010

Mancha, R., Yoder, C. Y., & Clark, J. G. (2013). Dynamics of affect and cognition in simulated agents: Bridging the gap between experimental and simulation research. *International Journal of Agent Technologies and Systems*, *5*(2), 78–96. doi:10.4018/jats.2013040104

Manchiraju, S. (2014). Predicting behavioral intentions toward sustainable fashion consumption: A comparison of attitude-behavior and value-behavior consistency models. In H. Kaufmann & M. Panni (Eds.), *Handbook of research on consumerism in business and marketing: Concepts and practices* (pp. 225–243). Hershey, PA: IGI Global. doi:10.4018/978-1-4666-5880-6.ch011

Mancilla, R. L. (2013). Getting smart about split attention. In B. Zou, M. Xing, Y. Wang, M. Sun, & C. Xiang (Eds.), *Computer-assisted foreign language teaching and learning: Technological advances* (pp. 210–229). Hershey, PA: IGI Global. doi:10.4018/978-1-4666-2821-2.ch012

Manrique-de-Lara, P. Z. (2013). Does discretionary internet-based behavior of instructors contribute to student satisfaction? An empirical study on 'cybercivism'. *International Journal of Cyber Behavior, Psychology and Learning*, *3*(1), 50–66. doi:10.4018/ijcbpl.2013010105

Markov, K., Vanhoof, K., Mitov, I., Depaire, B., Ivanova, K., Velychko, V., & Gladun, V. (2013). Intelligent data processing based on multi-dimensional numbered memory structures. In X. Naidenova & D. Ignatov (Eds.), *Diagnostic test approaches to machine learning and commonsense reasoning systems* (pp. 156–184). Hershey, PA: IGI Global. doi:10.4018/978-1-4666-1900-5.ch007

Martin, J. N. (2014). How can we incorporate relevant findings from psychology into systems methods? *International Journal of Systems and Society*, *1*(1), 1–11. doi:10.4018/ijss.2014010101

Mayer, I., Bekebrede, G., Warmelink, H., & Zhou, Q. (2014). A brief methodology for researching and evaluating serious games and game-based learning. In T. Connolly, T. Hainey, E. Boyle, G. Baxter, & P. Moreno-Ger (Eds.), *Psychology, pedagogy, and assessment in serious games* (pp. 357–393). Hershey, PA: IGI Global. doi:10.4018/978-1-4666-4773-2.ch017

Mazumdar, B. D., & Mishra, R. B. (2011). Cognitive parameter based agent selection and negotiation process for B2C e-commerce. In V. Sugumaran (Ed.), *Intelligent, adaptive and reasoning technologies: New developments and applications* (pp. 181–203). Hershey, PA: IGI Global. doi:10.4018/978-1-60960-595-7.ch010

McLaren, I. (2011). APECS: An adaptively parameterised model of associative learning and memory. In E. Alonso & E. Mondragón (Eds.), *Computational neuroscience for advancing artificial intelligence: Models, methods and applications* (pp. 145–164). Hershey, PA: IGI Global. doi:10.4018/978-1-60960-021-1.ch007

McMurray, B., Zhao, L., Kucker, S. C., & Samuelson, L. K. (2013). Pushing the envelope of associative learning: Internal representations and dynamic competition transform association into development. In L. Gogate & G. Hollich (Eds.), *Theoretical and computational models of word learning: Trends in psychology and artificial intelligence* (pp. 49–80). Hershey, PA: IGI Global. doi:10.4018/978-1-4666-2973-8.ch003

Mena, R. J. (2014). The quest for a massively multiplayer online game that teaches physics. In T. Connolly, T. Hainey, E. Boyle, G. Baxter, & P. Moreno-Ger (Eds.), *Psychology, pedagogy, and assessment in serious games* (pp. 292–316). Hershey, PA: IGI Global. doi:10.4018/978-1-4666-4773-2.ch014

Misra, S. (2011). Cognitive complexity measures: An analysis. In A. Dogru & V. Biçer (Eds.), *Modern software engineering concepts and practices: Advanced approaches* (pp. 263–279). Hershey, PA: IGI Global. doi:10.4018/978-1-60960-215-4.ch011

Mok, J. (2010). Social and distributed cognition in collaborative learning contexts. In S. Dasgupta (Ed.), *Social computing: Concepts, methodologies, tools, and applications* (pp. 1838–1854). Hershey, PA: IGI Global. doi:10.4018/978-1-60566-984-7.ch121

Moore, J. E., & Love, M. S. (2013). An examination of prestigious stigma: The case of the technology geek. In B. Medlin (Ed.), *Integrations of technology utilization and social dynamics in organizations* (pp. 48–73). Hershey, PA: IGI Global. doi:10.4018/978-1-4666-1948-7.ch004

Moore, M. J., Nakano, T., Suda, T., & Enomoto, A. (2013). Social interactions and automated detection tools in cyberbullying. In L. Caviglione, M. Coccoli, & A. Merlo (Eds.), *Social network engineering for secure web data and services* (pp. 67–87). Hershey, PA: IGI Global. doi:10.4018/978-1-4666-3926-3.ch004

Moseley, A. (2014). A case for integration: Assessment and games. In T. Connolly, T. Hainey, E. Boyle, G. Baxter, & P. Moreno-Ger (Eds.), *Psychology, pedagogy, and assessment in serious games* (pp. 342–356). Hershey, PA: IGI Global. doi:10.4018/978-1-4666-4773-2.ch016

Mpofu, S. (2014). Memory, national identity, and freedom of expression in the information age: Discussing the taboo in the Zimbabwean public sphere. In A. Solo (Ed.), *Handbook of research on political activism in the information age* (pp. 114–128). Hershey, PA: IGI Global. doi:10.4018/978-1-4666-6066-3.ch007

Mulvey, F., & Heubner, M. (2014). Eye movements and attention. In *Assistive technologies: Concepts, methodologies, tools, and applications* (pp. 1030–1054). Hershey, PA: IGI Global. doi:10.4018/978-1-4666-4422-9.ch053

Munipov, V. (2011). Psychological and social problems of automation and computerization. In D. Haftor & A. Mirijamdotter (Eds.), *Information and communication technologies, society and human beings: Theory and framework (Festschrift in honor of Gunilla Bradley)* (pp. 136–146). Hershey, PA: IGI Global. doi:10.4018/978-1-60960-057-0.ch012

Najjar, M., & Mayers, A. (2012). A cognitive computational knowledge representation theory. In *Machine learning: Concepts, methodologies, tools and applications* (pp. 1819–1838). Hershey, PA: IGI Global. doi:10.4018/978-1-60960-818-7.ch708

Nakamura, H. (2011). Cognitive decline in patients with Alzheimer's disease: A six-year longitudinal study of mini-mental state examination scores. In J. Wu (Ed.), *Early detection and rehabilitation technologies for dementia: Neuroscience and biomedical applications* (pp. 107–111). Hershey, PA: IGI Global. doi:10.4018/978-1-60960-559-9.ch013

Nankee, C. (2010). Switch technologies. In S. Seok, E. Meyen, & B. DaCosta (Eds.), *Handbook of research on human cognition and assistive technology: Design, accessibility and transdisciplinary perspectives* (pp. 157–168). Hershey, PA: IGI Global. doi:10.4018/978-1-61520-817-3.ch010

Nap, H. H., & Diaz-Orueta, U. (2014). Rehabilitation gaming. In J. Bishop (Ed.), *Gamification for human factors integration: Social, education, and psychological issues* (pp. 122–147). Hershey, PA: IGI Global. doi:10.4018/978-1-4666-5071-8.ch008

Naranjo-Saucedo, A. B., Suárez-Mejías, C., Parra-Calderón, C. L., González-Aguado, E., Böckel-Martínez, F., & Yuste-Marco, A. … Marco, A. (2014). Interactive games with robotic and augmented reality technology in cognitive and motor rehabilitation. In Robotics: Concepts, methodologies, tools, and applications (pp. 1233-1254). Hershey, PA: IGI Global. doi:10.4018/978-1-4666-4607-0.ch059

Ndinguri, E., Machtmes, K., Hatala, J. P., & Coco, M. L. (2014). Learning through immersive virtual environments: An organizational context. In J. Keengwe, G. Schnellert, & K. Kungu (Eds.), *Cross-cultural online learning in higher education and corporate training* (pp. 185–199). Hershey, PA: IGI Global. doi:10.4018/978-1-4666-5023-7.ch010

Ninaus, M., Witte, M., Kober, S. E., Friedrich, E. V., Kurzmann, J., & Hartsuiker, E. … Wood, G. (2014). Neurofeedback and serious games. In T. Connolly, T. Hainey, E. Boyle, G. Baxter, & P. Moreno-Ger (Eds.), Psychology, pedagogy, and assessment in serious games (pp. 82-110). Hershey, PA: IGI Global. doi:10.4018/978-1-4666-4773-2.ch005

Nobre, F. S. (2012). The roles of cognitive machines in customer-centric organizations: Towards innovations in computational organizational management networks. In F. Nobre, D. Walker, & R. Harris (Eds.), *Technological, managerial and organizational core competencies: Dynamic innovation and sustainable development* (pp. 653–674). Hershey, PA: IGI Global. doi:10.4018/978-1-61350-165-8.ch035

Norris, S. E. (2014). Transformative curriculum design and program development: Creating effective adult learning by leveraging psychological capital and self-directedness through the exercise of human agency. In V. Wang & V. Bryan (Eds.), *Andragogical and pedagogical methods for curriculum and program development* (pp. 118–141). Hershey, PA: IGI Global. doi:10.4018/978-1-4666-5872-1.ch007

Norris, S. E., & Porter, T. H. (2013). Self-monitoring scale. In M. Bocarnea, R. Reynolds, & J. Baker (Eds.), *Online instruments, data collection, and electronic measurements: Organizational advancements* (pp. 118–133). Hershey, PA: IGI Global. doi:10.4018/978-1-4666-2172-5.ch007

O'Connell, R. M. (2014). Mind mapping for critical thinking. In L. Shedletsky & J. Beaudry (Eds.), *Cases on teaching critical thinking through visual representation strategies* (pp. 354–386). Hershey, PA: IGI Global. doi:10.4018/978-1-4666-5816-5.ch014

Okrigwe, B. N. (2010). Cognition and learning. In S. Seok, E. Meyen, & B. DaCosta (Eds.), *Handbook of research on human cognition and assistive technology: Design, accessibility and transdisciplinary perspectives* (pp. 388–400). Hershey, PA: IGI Global. doi:10.4018/978-1-61520-817-3.ch027

Ong, E. H., & Khan, J. Y. (2013). Cognitive cooperation in wireless networks. In M. Ku & J. Lin (Eds.), *Cognitive radio and interference management: Technology and strategy* (pp. 179–204). Hershey, PA: IGI Global. doi:10.4018/978-1-4666-2005-6.ch010

Orlova, M. (2014). Social psychology of health as a social-psychological situation. In Ş. Erçetin & S. Banerjee (Eds.), *Chaos and complexity theory in world politics* (pp. 331–335). Hershey, PA: IGI Global. doi:10.4018/978-1-4666-6070-0.ch024

Orr, K., & McGuinness, C. (2014). What is the "learning" in games-based learning? In T. Connolly, T. Hainey, E. Boyle, G. Baxter, & P. Moreno-Ger (Eds.), Psychology, pedagogy, and assessment in serious games (pp. 221-242). Hershey, PA: IGI Global. doi:10.4018/978-1-4666-4773-2.ch011

Ortiz Zezzatti, C. A., Martínez, J., Castillo, N., González, S., & Hernández, P. (2012). Improve card collection from memory alpha using sociolinguistics and Japanese puzzles. In C. Ortiz Zezzatti, C. Chira, A. Hernandez, & M. Basurto (Eds.), *Logistics management and optimization through hybrid artificial intelligence systems* (pp. 310–326). Hershey, PA: IGI Global. doi:10.4018/978-1-4666-0297-7.ch012

Ota, N., Maeshima, S., Osawa, A., Kawarada, M., & Tanemura, J. (2011). Prospective memory impairment in remembering to remember in mild cognitive impairment and healthy subjects. In J. Wu (Ed.), *Early detection and rehabilitation technologies for dementia: Neuroscience and biomedical applications* (pp. 98–106). Hershey, PA: IGI Global. doi:10.4018/978-1-60960-559-9.ch012

Ouwehand, K., van Gog, T., & Paas, F. (2013). The use of gesturing to facilitate older adults' learning from computer-based dynamic visualizations. In R. Zheng, R. Hill, & M. Gardner (Eds.), *Engaging older adults with modern technology: Internet use and information access needs* (pp. 33–58). Hershey, PA: IGI Global. doi:10.4018/978-1-4666-1966-1.ch003

Özel, S. (2012). Utilizing cognitive resources in user interface designs. In B. Khan (Ed.), *User interface design for virtual environments: Challenges and advances* (pp. 115–123). Hershey, PA: IGI Global. doi:10.4018/978-1-61350-516-8.ch007

Parsons, T. D., & Courtney, C. G. (2011). Neurocognitive and psychophysiological interfaces for adaptive virtual environments. In M. Ziefle & C. Röcker (Eds.), *Human-centered design of e-health technologies: Concepts, methods and applications* (pp. 208–233). Hershey, PA: IGI Global. doi:10.4018/978-1-60960-177-5.ch009

Peden, B. F., & Tiry, A. M. (2013). Using web surveys for psychology experiments: A case study in new media technology for research. In N. Sappleton (Ed.), *Advancing research methods with new technologies* (pp. 70–99). Hershey, PA: IGI Global. doi:10.4018/978-1-4666-3918-8.ch005

Perakslis, C. (2014). Willingness to adopt RFID implants: Do personality factors play a role in the acceptance of uberveillance? In M. Michael & K. Michael (Eds.), *Uberveillance and the social implications of microchip implants: Emerging technologies* (pp. 144–168). Hershey, PA: IGI Global. doi:10.4018/978-1-4666-4582-0.ch006

Pereira, G., Brisson, A., Dias, J., Carvalho, A., Dimas, J., & Mascarenhas, S. ... Paiva, A. (2014). Non-player characters and artificial intelligence. In T. Connolly, T. Hainey, E. Boyle, G. Baxter, & P. Moreno-Ger (Eds.), Psychology, pedagogy, and assessment in serious games (pp. 127-152). Hershey, PA: IGI Global. doi:10.4018/978-1-4666-4773-2.ch007

Pereira, R., Hornung, H., & Baranauskas, M. C. (2014). Cognitive authority revisited in web social interaction. In M. Pańkowska (Ed.), *Frameworks of IT prosumption for business development* (pp. 142–157). Hershey, PA: IGI Global. doi:10.4018/978-1-4666-4313-0.ch010

Phebus, A. M., Gitlin, B., Shuffler, M. L., & Wildman, J. L. (2014). Leading global virtual teams: The supporting role of trust and team cognition. In E. Nikoi & K. Boateng (Eds.), *Collaborative communication processes and decision making in organizations* (pp. 177–200). Hershey, PA: IGI Global. doi:10.4018/978-1-4666-4478-6.ch010

Plunkett, D., Banerjee, R., & Horn, E. (2010). Supporting early childhood outcomes through assistive technology. In S. Seok, E. Meyen, & B. DaCosta (Eds.), *Handbook of research on human cognition and assistive technology: Design, accessibility and transdisciplinary perspectives* (pp. 339–359). Hershey, PA: IGI Global. doi:10.4018/978-1-61520-817-3.ch024

Prakash, S., Vaish, A., Coul, N., Saravana, G. K., Srinidhi, T. N., & Botsa, J. (2014). Child security in cyberspace through moral cognition. In *Cyber behavior: Concepts, methodologies, tools, and applications* (pp. 1946–1958). Hershey, PA: IGI Global. doi:10.4018/978-1-4666-5942-1.ch102

Prescott, J., & Bogg, J. (2013). Self, career, and gender issues: A complex interplay of internal/external factors. In *Gendered occupational differences in science, engineering, and technology careers* (pp. 79–111). Hershey, PA: IGI Global. doi:10.4018/978-1-4666-2107-7.ch004

Prescott, J., & Bogg, J. (2013). Stereotype, attitudes, and identity: Gendered expectations and behaviors. In *Gendered occupational differences in science, engineering, and technology careers* (pp. 112–135). Hershey, PA: IGI Global. doi:10.4018/978-1-4666-2107-7.ch005

Pressey, A., Salciuviene, L., & Barnes, S. (2013). Uncovering relationships between emotional states and higher-order needs: Enhancing consumer emotional experiences in computer-mediated environment. *International Journal of Online Marketing*, *3*(1), 31–46. doi:10.4018/ijom.2013010103

Qin, X., Li, C., Chen, H., Qin, B., Du, X., & Wang, S. (2014). In memory data processing systems. In J. Wang (Ed.), *Encyclopedia of business analytics and optimization* (pp. 1182–1191). Hershey, PA: IGI Global. doi:10.4018/978-1-4666-5202-6.ch109

Ramos, I., & Oliveira e Sá, J. (2014). Organizational memory: The role of business intelligence to leverage the application of collective knowledge. In H. Rahman & R. de Sousa (Eds.), *Information systems and technology for organizational agility, intelligence, and resilience* (pp. 206–223). Hershey, PA: IGI Global. doi:10.4018/978-1-4666-5970-4.ch010

Ratten, V. (2013). The development of social e-enterprises, mobile communication and social networks: A social cognitive perspective of technological innovation. *Journal of Electronic Commerce in Organizations, 11*(3), 68–77. doi:10.4018/jeco.2013070104

Reddy, Y. B. (2013). Nanocomputing in cognitive radio networks to improve the performance. In N. Meghanathan & Y. Reddy (Eds.), *Cognitive radio technology applications for wireless and mobile ad hoc networks* (pp. 173–193). Hershey, PA: IGI Global. doi:10.4018/978-1-4666-4221-8.ch010

Redien-Collot, R., & Lefebvre, M. R. (2014). SMEs' leaders: Building collective cognition and competences to trigger positive strategic outcomes. In K. Todorov & D. Smallbone (Eds.), *Handbook of research on strategic management in small and medium enterprises* (pp. 143–158). Hershey, PA: IGI Global. doi:10.4018/978-1-4666-5962-9.ch008

Remmele, B., & Whitton, N. (2014). Disrupting the magic circle: The impact of negative social gaming behaviours. In T. Connolly, T. Hainey, E. Boyle, G. Baxter, & P. Moreno-Ger (Eds.), *Psychology, pedagogy, and assessment in serious games* (pp. 111–126). Hershey, PA: IGI Global. doi:10.4018/978-1-4666-4773-2.ch006

Renaud, P., Chartier, S., Fedoroff, P., Bradford, J., & Rouleau, J. L. (2011). The use of virtual reality in clinical psychology research. In *Clinical technologies: Concepts, methodologies, tools and applications* (pp. 2073–2093). Hershey, PA: IGI Global. doi:10.4018/978-1-60960-561-2.ch805

Revett, K. (2012). Cognitive biometrics: A novel approach to continuous person authentication. In I. Traore & A. Ahmed (Eds.), *Continuous authentication using biometrics: Data, models, and metrics* (pp. 105–136). Hershey, PA: IGI Global. doi:10.4018/978-1-61350-129-0.ch006

Rødseth, I. (2011). A motive analysis as a first step in designing technology for the use of intuition in criminal investigation. In A. Mesquita (Ed.), *Sociological and philosophical aspects of human interaction with technology: Advancing concepts* (pp. 276–298). Hershey, PA: IGI Global. doi:10.4018/978-1-60960-575-9.ch015

Rothblatt, M. (2014). Mindclone technoselves: Multi-substrate legal identities, cyber-psychology, and biocyberethics. In *Cyber behavior: Concepts, methodologies, tools, and applications* (pp. 1199–1216). Hershey, PA: IGI Global. doi:10.4018/978-1-4666-5942-1.ch062

Rückemann, C. (2013). Integrated information and computing systems for advanced cognition with natural sciences. In C. Rückemann (Ed.), *Integrated information and computing systems for natural, spatial, and social sciences* (pp. 1–26). Hershey, PA: IGI Global. doi:10.4018/978-1-4666-2190-9.ch001

Rudnianski, M., & Kravcik, M. (2014). The road to critical thinking and intelligence analysis. In T. Connolly, T. Hainey, E. Boyle, G. Baxter, & P. Moreno-Ger (Eds.), *Psychology, pedagogy, and assessment in serious games* (pp. 47–61). Hershey, PA: IGI Global. doi:10.4018/978-1-4666-4773-2.ch003

Rufer, R., & Adams, R. H. (2012). Adapting three-dimensional-virtual world to reach diverse learners in an MBA program. In H. Yang & S. Yuen (Eds.), *Handbook of research on practices and outcomes in virtual worlds and environments* (pp. 606–619). Hershey, PA: IGI Global. doi:10.4018/978-1-60960-762-3.ch033

Saadé, R. G. (2010). Cognitive mapping decision support for the design of web-based learning environments. *International Journal of Web-Based Learning and Teaching Technologies*, *5*(3), 36–53. doi:10.4018/jwltt.2010070103

Saeed, N., & Sinnappan, S. (2014). Comparing learning styles and technology acceptance of two culturally different groups of students. In T. Issa, P. Isaias, & P. Kommers (Eds.), *Multicultural awareness and technology in higher education: Global perspectives* (pp. 244–264). Hershey, PA: IGI Global. doi:10.4018/978-1-4666-5876-9.ch012

Samuelson, L. K., Spencer, J. P., & Jenkins, G. W. (2013). A dynamic neural field model of word learning. In L. Gogate & G. Hollich (Eds.), *Theoretical and computational models of word learning: Trends in psychology and artificial intelligence* (pp. 1–27). Hershey, PA: IGI Global. doi:10.4018/978-1-4666-2973-8.ch001

Sanjram, P. K., & Gupta, M. (2013). Task difficulty and time constraint in programmer multitasking: An analysis of prospective memory performance and cognitive workload. *International Journal of Green Computing*, *4*(1), 35–57. doi:10.4018/jgc.2013010103

Sato, Y., Ji, Z., & van Dijk, S. (2013). I think I have heard that one before: Recurrence-based word learning with a robot. In L. Gogate & G. Hollich (Eds.), *Theoretical and computational models of word learning: Trends in psychology and artificial intelligence* (pp. 327–349). Hershey, PA: IGI Global. doi:10.4018/978-1-4666-2973-8.ch014

Scalzone, F., & Zontini, G. (2013). Thinking animals and thinking machines in psychoanalysis and beyond. In F. Orsucci & N. Sala (Eds.), *Complexity science, living systems, and reflexing interfaces: New models and perspectives* (pp. 44–68). Hershey, PA: IGI Global. doi:10.4018/978-1-4666-2077-3.ch003

Schafer, S. B. (2013). Fostering psychological coherence: With ICTs. In M. Cruz-Cunha, I. Miranda, & P. Gonçalves (Eds.), *Handbook of research on ICTs for human-centered healthcare and social care services* (pp. 29–47). Hershey, PA: IGI Global. doi:10.4018/978-1-4666-3986-7.ch002

Scheiter, K., Wiebe, E., & Holsanova, J. (2011). Theoretical and instructional aspects of learning with visualizations. In *Instructional design: Concepts, methodologies, tools and applications* (pp. 1667–1688). Hershey, PA: IGI Global. doi:10.4018/978-1-60960-503-2.ch710

Seo, K. K., Byk, A., & Collins, C. (2011). Cognitive apprenticeship inspired simulations. In *Gaming and simulations: Concepts, methodologies, tools and applications* (pp. 346–358). Hershey, PA: IGI Global. doi:10.4018/978-1-60960-195-9.ch202

Serenko, N. (2014). Informational, physical, and psychological privacy as determinants of patient behaviour in health care. In V. Michell, D. Rosenorn-Lanng, S. Gulliver, & W. Currie (Eds.), *Handbook of research on patient safety and quality care through health informatics* (pp. 1–20). Hershey, PA: IGI Global. doi:10.4018/978-1-4666-4546-2.ch001

Shibata, T. (2013). A human-like cognitive computer based on a psychologically inspired VLSI brain model. In J. Wu (Ed.), *Technological advancements in biomedicine for healthcare applications* (pp. 247–266). Hershey, PA: IGI Global. doi:10.4018/978-1-4666-2196-1.ch027

Shirkhodaee, M., & Rezaee, S. (2013). Evaluating the persuasive and memory effects of viral advertising. *International Journal of Online Marketing*, *3*(3), 51–61. doi:10.4018/ijom.2013070104

Simzar, R., & Domina, T. (2014). Attending to student motivation through critical practice: A recommendation for improving accelerated mathematical learning. In S. Lawrence (Ed.), *Critical practice in P-12 education: Transformative teaching and learning* (pp. 66–116). Hershey, PA: IGI Global. doi:10.4018/978-1-4666-5059-6.ch004

Smart, P. R., Engelbrecht, P. C., Braines, D., Strub, M., & Giammanco, C. (2010). The network-extended mind. In D. Verma (Ed.), *Network science for military coalition operations: Information exchange and interaction* (pp. 191–236). Hershey, PA: IGI Global. doi:10.4018/978-1-61520-855-5.ch010

Smith, M. A. (2011). Functions of unconscious and conscious emotion in the regulation of implicit and explicit motivated behavior. In D. Gökçay & G. Yildirim (Eds.), *Affective computing and interaction: Psychological, cognitive and neuroscientific perspectives* (pp. 25–55). Hershey, PA: IGI Global. doi:10.4018/978-1-61692-892-6.ch002

Soliman, F. (2014). Could knowledge, learning, and innovation gaps be spiralling? In F. Soliman (Ed.), *Learning models for innovation in organizations: Examining roles of knowledge transfer and human resources management* (pp. 1–29). Hershey, PA: IGI Global. doi:10.4018/978-1-4666-4884-5.ch001

Somyürek, S. (2012). Interactive learning in workplace training. In J. Jia (Ed.), *Educational stages and interactive learning: From kindergarten to workplace training* (pp. 498–514). Hershey, PA: IGI Global. doi:10.4018/978-1-4666-0137-6.ch027

Spadaro, L., Timpano, F., Marino, S., & Bramanti, P. (2013). Telemedicine and Alzheimer disease: ICT-based services for people with Alzheimer disease and their caregivers. In V. Gulla, A. Mori, F. Gabbrielli, & P. Lanzafame (Eds.), *Telehealth networks for hospital services: New methodologies* (pp. 191–206). Hershey, PA: IGI Global. doi:10.4018/978-1-4666-2979-0.ch013

Spiegel, T. (2014). An overview of cognition roles in decision-making. In J. Wang (Ed.), *Encyclopedia of business analytics and optimization* (pp. 74–84). Hershey, PA: IGI Global. doi:10.4018/978-1-4666-5202-6.ch008

Stachon, Z., & Šašinka, C. (2012). Human cognition: People in the world and world in their minds. In T. Podobnikar & M. Čeh (Eds.), *Universal ontology of geographic space: Semantic enrichment for spatial data* (pp. 97–122). Hershey, PA: IGI Global. doi:10.4018/978-1-4666-0327-1.ch005

Stefurak, J. R., Surry, D. W., & Hayes, R. L. (2011). Technology in the supervision of mental health professionals: Ethical, interpersonal, and epistemological implications. In D. Surry, R. Gray Jr, & J. Stefurak (Eds.), *Technology integration in higher education: Social and organizational aspects* (pp. 114–131). Hershey, PA: IGI Global. doi:10.4018/978-1-60960-147-8.ch009

Stieglitz, S. (2014). The American memory project. In J. Krueger (Ed.), *Cases on electronic records and resource management implementation in diverse environments* (pp. 106–116). Hershey, PA: IGI Global. doi:10.4018/978-1-4666-4466-3.ch006

Suárez, M. G., & Gumiel, C. G. (2014). The use of sensorial marketing in stores: Attracting clients through their senses. In F. Musso & E. Druica (Eds.), *Handbook of research on retailer-consumer relationship development* (pp. 258–274). Hershey, PA: IGI Global. doi:10.4018/978-1-4666-6074-8.ch014

Sugiura, M. (2013). A cognitive neuroscience approach to self and mental health. In J. Wu (Ed.), *Biomedical engineering and cognitive neuroscience for healthcare: Interdisciplinary applications* (pp. 1–10). Hershey, PA: IGI Global. doi:10.4018/978-1-4666-2113-8.ch001

Sujo-Montes, L. E., Armfield, S. W., Yen, C., & Tu, C. (2014). The use of ubiquitous learning for children with Down Syndrome. In F. Neto (Ed.), *Technology platform innovations and forthcoming trends in ubiquitous learning* (pp. 160–176). Hershey, PA: IGI Global. doi:10.4018/978-1-4666-4542-4.ch009

Tamba, H. (2013). Workers' mental health problems and future perspectives in Japan: Psychological job stress research. In J. Wu (Ed.), *Biomedical engineering and cognitive neuroscience for healthcare: Interdisciplinary applications* (pp. 370–379). Hershey, PA: IGI Global. doi:10.4018/978-1-4666-2113-8.ch038

Tatachari, S., Manikandan, K. S., & Gunta, S. (2014). A synthesis of organizational learning and knowledge management literatures. In M. Chilton & J. Bloodgood (Eds.), *Knowledge management and competitive advantage: Issues and potential solutions* (pp. 122–147). Hershey, PA: IGI Global. doi:10.4018/978-1-4666-4679-7.ch008

Taxén, L. (2010). Cognitive grounding. In L. Taxen (Ed.), *Using activity domain theory for managing complex systems* (pp. 108–124). Hershey, PA: IGI Global. doi:10.4018/978-1-60566-192-6.ch006

Te'eni, D. (2012). Knowledge for communicating knowledge. In *Organizational learning and knowledge: Concepts, methodologies, tools and applications* (pp. 1656–1665). Hershey, PA: IGI Global. doi:10.4018/978-1-60960-783-8.ch501

Terras, M. M., & Ramsay, J. (2014). E-learning, mobility, and time: A psychological framework. In E. Barbera & P. Reimann (Eds.), *Assessment and evaluation of time factors in online teaching and learning* (pp. 63–90). Hershey, PA: IGI Global. doi:10.4018/978-1-4666-4651-3.ch003

Thapa, A. (2013). A study on worker's perceptions of psychological capital on their earnings. *International Journal of Applied Behavioral Economics*, *2*(3), 27–42. doi:10.4018/ijabe.2013070103

Thatcher, A., & Ndabeni, M. (2013). A psychological model to understand e-adoption in the context of the digital divide. In *Digital literacy: Concepts, methodologies, tools, and applications* (pp. 1402–1424). Hershey, PA: IGI Global. doi:10.4018/978-1-4666-1852-7.ch074

Thompson, K., & Markauskaite, L. (2014). Identifying group processes and affect in learners: A holistic approach to assessment in virtual worlds in higher education. In S. Kennedy-Clark, K. Everett, & P. Wheeler (Eds.), *Cases on the assessment of scenario and game-based virtual worlds in higher education* (pp. 175–210). Hershey, PA: IGI Global. doi:10.4018/978-1-4666-4470-0.ch006

Titus, C. S. (2013). The use of developmental psychology in ethics: Beyond Kohlberg and Seligman? In F. Doridot, P. Duquenoy, P. Goujon, A. Kurt, S. Lavelle, N. Patrignani, & A. Santuccio et al. (Eds.), *Ethical governance of emerging technologies development* (pp. 266–286). Hershey, PA: IGI Global. doi:10.4018/978-1-4666-3670-5.ch018

Tiwary, U. S., & Siddiqui, T. J. (2014). Working together with computers: Towards a general framework for collaborative human computer interaction. In *Assistive technologies: Concepts, methodologies, tools, and applications* (pp. 141–162). Hershey, PA: IGI Global. doi:10.4018/978-1-4666-4422-9.ch008

Tomono, A. (2013). Display technology of images with scents and its psychological evaluation. In T. Nakamoto (Ed.), *Human olfactory displays and interfaces: Odor sensing and presentation* (pp. 429–445). Hershey, PA: IGI Global. doi:10.4018/978-1-4666-2521-1.ch022

Torres, G., Jaime, K., & Ramos, F. (2013). Brain architecture for visual object identification. *International Journal of Cognitive Informatics and Natural Intelligence*, *7*(1), 75–97. doi:10.4018/jcini.2013010104

Trajkovski, G., Stojanov, G., Collins, S., Eidelman, V., Harman, C., & Vincenti, G. (2011). Cognitive robotics and multiagency in a fuzzy modeling framework. In G. Trajkovski (Ed.), *Developments in intelligent agent technologies and multi-agent systems: Concepts and applications* (pp. 132–152). Hershey, PA: IGI Global. doi:10.4018/978-1-60960-171-3.ch009

Tran, B. (2014). Rhetoric of play: Utilizing the gamer factor in selecting and training employees. In T. Connolly, T. Hainey, E. Boyle, G. Baxter, & P. Moreno-Ger (Eds.), *Psychology, pedagogy, and assessment in serious games* (pp. 175–203). Hershey, PA: IGI Global. doi:10.4018/978-1-4666-4773-2.ch009

Tran, B. (2014). The psychology of consumerism in business and marketing: The macro and micro behaviors of Hofstede's cultural consumers. In H. Kaufmann & M. Panni (Eds.), *Handbook of research on consumerism in business and marketing: Concepts and practices* (pp. 286–308). Hershey, PA: IGI Global. doi:10.4018/978-1-4666-5880-6.ch014

Travica, B. (2014). Homo informaticus. In *Examining the informing view of organization: Applying theoretical and managerial approaches* (pp. 34–66). Hershey, PA: IGI Global. doi:10.4018/978-1-4666-5986-5.ch002

Twomey, K. E., Horst, J. S., & Morse, A. F. (2013). An embodied model of young children's categorization and word learning. In L. Gogate & G. Hollich (Eds.), *Theoretical and computational models of word learning: Trends in psychology and artificial intelligence* (pp. 172–196). Hershey, PA: IGI Global. doi:10.4018/978-1-4666-2973-8.ch008

Ursyn, A. (2014). Cognitive processes involved in visual thought. In *Perceptions of knowledge visualization: Explaining concepts through meaningful images* (pp. 131–173). Hershey, PA: IGI Global. doi:10.4018/978-1-4666-4703-9.ch005

Ursyn, A. (2014). Communication through many senses. In *Perceptions of knowledge visualization: Explaining concepts through meaningful images* (pp. 25–60). Hershey, PA: IGI Global. doi:10.4018/978-1-4666-4703-9.ch002

Ursyn, A. (2014). Four trapped in an elevator. In *Computational solutions for knowledge, art, and entertainment: Information exchange beyond text* (pp. 322–329). Hershey, PA: IGI Global. doi:10.4018/978-1-4666-4627-8.ch016

Usart, M., & Romero, M. (2014). Time factor assessment in game-based learning: Time perspective and time-on-task as individual differences between players. In T. Connolly, T. Hainey, E. Boyle, G. Baxter, & P. Moreno-Ger (Eds.), *Psychology, pedagogy, and assessment in serious games* (pp. 62–81). Hershey, PA: IGI Global. doi:10.4018/978-1-4666-4773-2.ch004

Usoro, A., Majewski, G., & Bloom, L. (2012). Individual and collaborative approaches in e-learning design. In *Virtual learning environments: Concepts, methodologies, tools and applications* (pp. 1110–1130). Hershey, PA: IGI Global. doi:10.4018/978-1-4666-0011-9.ch514

van den Brink, J. C. (2014). How positive psychology can support sustainable project management. In *Sustainable practices: Concepts, methodologies, tools and applications* (pp. 958–973). Hershey, PA: IGI Global. doi:10.4018/978-1-4666-4852-4.ch053

van der Helden, J., & Bekkering, H. (2014). The role of implicit and explicit feedback in learning and the implications for distance education techniques. In T. Yuzer & G. Eby (Eds.), *Handbook of research on emerging priorities and trends in distance education: Communication, pedagogy, and technology* (pp. 367–384). Hershey, PA: IGI Global. doi:10.4018/978-1-4666-5162-3.ch025 van Mierlo, C. M., Jarodzka, H., Kirschner, F., & Kirschner, P. A. (2012). Cognitive load theory in e-learning. In Z. Yan (Ed.), *Encyclopedia of cyber behavior* (pp. 1178–1211). Hershey, PA: IGI Global. doi:10.4018/978-1-4666-0315-8.ch097

van Rosmalen, P., Wilson, A., & Hummel, H. G. (2014). Games for and by teachers and learners. In T. Connolly, T. Hainey, E. Boyle, G. Baxter, & P. Moreno-Ger (Eds.), *Psychology, pedagogy, and assessment in serious games* (pp. 243–269). Hershey, PA: IGI Global. doi:10.4018/978-1-4666-4773-2.ch012

Vega, J., Perdices, E., & Cañas, J. M. (2014). Attentive visual memory for robot localization. In Robotics: Concepts, methodologies, tools, and applications (pp. 785-811). Hershey, PA: IGI Global. doi:10.4018/978-1-4666-4607-0.ch038

Vinther, J. (2012). Cognitive skills through CALL-enhanced teacher training. In F. Zhang (Ed.), *Computer-enhanced and mobile-assisted language learning: Emerging issues and trends* (pp. 158–187). Hershey, PA: IGI Global. doi:10.4018/978-1-61350-065-1.ch008

Vogel, E. H., & Ponce, F. P. (2011). Empirical issues and theoretical mechanisms of Pavlovian conditioning. In E. Alonso & E. Mondragón (Eds.), *Computational neuroscience for advancing artificial intelligence: Models, methods and applications* (pp. 81–110). Hershey, PA: IGI Global. doi:10.4018/978-1-60960-021-1.ch005

Vragov, R. (2013). Detecting behavioral biases in mixed human-proxy online auction markets. *International Journal of Strategic Information Technology and Applications, 4*(4), 60–79. doi:10.4018/ijsita.2013100104

Wagner, C. L., & Delisi, J. (2010). Multi-sensory environments and augmentative communication tools. In S. Seok, E. Meyen, & B. DaCosta (Eds.), *Handbook of research on human cognition and assistive technology: Design, accessibility and transdisciplinary perspectives* (pp. 121–131). Hershey, PA: IGI Global. doi:10.4018/978-1-61520-817-3.ch008

Walk, A. M., & Conway, C. M. (2014). Two distinct sequence learning mechanisms for syntax acquisition and word learning. In *Computational linguistics: Concepts, methodologies, tools, and applications* (pp. 540–560). Hershey, PA: IGI Global. doi:10.4018/978-1-4666-6042-7.ch025

Wang, H. (2014). A guide to assistive technology for teachers in special education. In *Assistive technologies: Concepts, methodologies, tools, and applications* (pp. 12–25). Hershey, PA: IGI Global. doi:10.4018/978-1-4666-4422-9.ch002

Wang, J. (2012). Organizational learning and technology. In V. Wang (Ed.), *Encyclopedia of e-leadership, counseling and training* (pp. 154–170). Hershey, PA: IGI Global. doi:10.4018/978-1-61350-068-2.ch012

Wang, K. Y. (2014). Mixing metaphors: Sociological and psychological perspectives on virtual communities. In *Cross-cultural interaction: Concepts, methodologies, tools and applications* (pp. 116–132). Hershey, PA: IGI Global. doi:10.4018/978-1-4666-4979-8.ch008

Wang, Y. (2013). Neuroinformatics models of human memory: Mapping the cognitive functions of memory onto neurophysiological structures of the brain. *International Journal of Cognitive Informatics and Natural Intelligence*, *7*(1), 98–122. doi:10.4018/jcini.2013010105

Wang, Y. (2013). The cognitive mechanisms and formal models of consciousness. *International Journal of Cognitive Informatics and Natural Intelligence*, *6*(2), 23–40. doi:10.4018/jcini.2012040102

Wang, Y. (2013). Towards the synergy of cognitive informatics, neural informatics, brain informatics, and cognitive computing. In Y. Wang (Ed.), *Cognitive informatics for revealing human cognition: Knowledge manipulations in natural intelligence* (pp. 1–19). Hershey, PA: IGI Global. doi:10.4018/978-1-4666-2476-4.ch001

Wang, Y., Berwick, R. C., Haykin, S., Pedrycz, W., Kinsner, W., & Baciu, G. … Gavrilova, M. L. (2013). Cognitive informatics and cognitive computing in year 10 and beyond. In Y. Wang (Ed.), Cognitive informatics for revealing human cognition: Knowledge manipulations in natural intelligence (pp. 140-157). Hershey, PA: IGI Global. doi:10.4018/978-1-4666-2476-4.ch010

Wang, Y., Fariello, G., Gavrilova, M. L., Kinsner, W., Mizoguchi, F., Patel, S., & Tsumoto, S. et al. (2013). Perspectives on cognitive computers and knowledge processors. *International Journal of Cognitive Informatics and Natural Intelligence*, *7*(3), 1–24. doi:10.4018/ijcini.2013070101

Wang, Y., Patel, S., & Patel, D. (2013). The cognitive process and formal models of human attentions. *International Journal of Software Science and Computational Intelligence*, *5*(1), 32–50. doi:10.4018/ijssci.2013010103

Wang, Y., Pedrycz, W., Baciu, G., Chen, P., Wang, G., & Yao, Y. (2012). Perspectives on cognitive computing and applications. In Y. Wang (Ed.), *Breakthroughs in software science and computational intelligence* (pp. 1–12). Hershey, PA: IGI Global. doi:10.4018/978-1-4666-0264-9.ch001

Wang, Y., Widrow, B. C., Zhang, B., Kinsner, W., Sugawara, K., Sun, F., & Zhang, D. et al. (2013). Perspectives on the field of cognitive informatics and its future development. In Y. Wang (Ed.), *Cognitive informatics for revealing human cognition: Knowledge manipulations in natural intelligence* (pp. 20–34). Hershey, PA: IGI Global. doi:10.4018/978-1-4666-2476-4.ch002

Was, C. A., & Woltz, D. J. (2013). Implicit memory and aging: Adapting technology to utilize preserved memory functions. In R. Zheng, R. Hill, & M. Gardner (Eds.), *Engaging older adults with modern technology: Internet use and information access needs* (pp. 1–19). Hershey, PA: IGI Global. doi:10.4018/978-1-4666-1966-1.ch001

Wei, H. (2013). A neural dynamic model based on activation diffusion and a micro-explanation for cognitive operations. *International Journal of Cognitive Informatics and Natural Intelligence*, *6*(2), 1–22. doi:10.4018/jcini.2012040101

Wexler, R. H., & Roff-Wexler, S. (2013). The evolution and development of self in virtual worlds. *International Journal of Cyber Behavior, Psychology and Learning*, *3*(1), 1–6. doi:10.4018/ijcbpl.2013010101

Wickramasinghe, N. (2012). Knowledge economy for innovating organizations. In *Organizational learning and knowledge: Concepts, methodologies, tools and applications* (pp. 2298–2309). Hershey, PA: IGI Global. doi:10.4018/978-1-60960-783-8.ch616

Widrow, B. C., & Aragon, J. (2012). Cognitive memory: Human like memory. In Y. Wang (Ed.), *Breakthroughs in software science and computational intelligence* (pp. 84–99). Hershey, PA: IGI Global. doi:10.4018/978-1-4666-0264-9.ch006

Widyanto, L., & Griffiths, M. (2013). An empirical study of problematic internet use and self-esteem. In R. Zheng (Ed.), *Evolving psychological and educational perspectives on cyber behavior* (pp. 82–95). Hershey, PA: IGI Global. doi:10.4018/978-1-4666-1858-9.ch006

Wilson, M. S., & Pascoe, J. (2010). Using software to deliver language intervention in inclusionary settings. In S. Seok, E. Meyen, & B. DaCosta (Eds.), *Handbook of research on human cognition and assistive technology: Design, accessibility and transdisciplinary perspectives* (pp. 132–156). Hershey, PA: IGI Global. doi:10.4018/978-1-61520-817-3.ch009

Wilson, S., & Haslam, N. (2013). Reasoning about human enhancement: Towards a folk psychological model of human nature and human identity. In R. Luppicini (Ed.), *Handbook of research on technoself: Identity in a technological society* (pp. 175–188). Hershey, PA: IGI Global. doi:10.4018/978-1-4666-2211-1.ch010

Wilson, S. G. (2014). Enhancement and identity: A social psychological perspective. In S. Thompson (Ed.), *Global issues and ethical considerations in human enhancement technologies* (pp. 241–256). Hershey, PA: IGI Global. doi:10.4018/978-1-4666-6010-6.ch014

Winsor, D. L. (2012). The epistemology of young children. In S. Blake, D. Winsor, & L. Allen (Eds.), *Child development and the use of technology: Perspectives, applications and experiences* (pp. 21–44). Hershey, PA: IGI Global. doi:10.4018/978-1-61350-317-1.ch002

Winsor, D. L., & Blake, S. (2012). Socrates and Descartes meet the E*Trade baby: The impact of early technology on children's developing beliefs about knowledge and knowing. In S. Blake, D. Winsor, & L. Allen (Eds.), *Child development and the use of technology: Perspectives, applications and experiences* (pp. 1–20). Hershey, PA: IGI Global. doi:10.4018/978-1-61350-317-1.ch001

Yakavenka, H. (2012). Developing professional competencies through international peer learning communities. In V. Dennen & J. Myers (Eds.), *Virtual professional development and informal learning via social networks* (pp. 134–154). Hershey, PA: IGI Global. doi:10.4018/978-1-4666-1815-2.ch008

Yamaguchi, M., & Shetty, V. (2013). Evaluating the psychobiologic effects of fragrances through salivary biomarkers. In T. Nakamoto (Ed.), *Human olfactory displays and interfaces: Odor sensing and presentation* (pp. 359–369). Hershey, PA: IGI Global. doi:10.4018/978-1-4666-2521-1.ch017

Yan, Z., & Zheng, R. Z. (2013). Growing from childhood into adolescence: The science of cyber behavior. In R. Zheng (Ed.), *Evolving psychological and educational perspectives on cyber behavior* (pp. 1–14). Hershey, PA: IGI Global. doi:10.4018/978-1-4666-1858-9.ch001

Yildirim, G., & Gökçay, D. (2011). Problems associated with computer-mediated communication cognitive psychology and neuroscience perspectives. In D. Gökçay & G. Yildirim (Eds.), *Affective computing and interaction: Psychological, cognitive and neuroscientific perspectives* (pp. 244–261). Hershey, PA: IGI Global. doi:10.4018/978-1-61692-892-6.ch011

Younan, Y., Joosen, W., Piessens, F., & Van den Eynden, H. (2012). Improving memory management security for C and C. In K. Khan (Ed.), *Security-aware systems applications and software development methods* (pp. 190–216). Hershey, PA: IGI Global. doi:10.4018/978-1-4666-1580-9.ch011

Yu, C., & Smith, L. B. (2013). A sensory-motor solution to early word-referent learning. In L. Gogate & G. Hollich (Eds.), *Theoretical and computational models of word learning: Trends in psychology and artificial intelligence* (pp. 133–152). Hershey, PA: IGI Global. doi:10.4018/978-1-4666-2973-8.ch006

Yu, J., Chen, Z., Lu, J., Liu, T., Zhou, L., Liu, X., . . . Chui, D. (2013). The important role of lipids in cognitive impairment. In Bioinformatics: Concepts, methodologies, tools, and applications (pp. 268-272). Hershey, PA: IGI Global. doi:10.4018/978-1-4666-3604-0.ch014

Yu, Y., Yang, J., & Wu, J. (2013). Cognitive functions and neuronal mechanisms of tactile working memory. In J. Wu (Ed.), *Biomedical engineering and cognitive neuroscience for healthcare: Interdisciplinary applications* (pp. 89–98). Hershey, PA: IGI Global. doi:10.4018/978-1-4666-2113-8.ch010

Zelinski, E. M. (2013). How interventions might improve cognition in healthy older adults. *International Journal of Gaming and Computer-Mediated Simulations*, *5*(3), 72–82. doi:10.4018/jgcms.2013070105

Zhang, J., Luo, X., Lu, L., & Liu, W. (2013). An acquisition model of deep textual semantics based on human reading cognitive process. *International Journal of Cognitive Informatics and Natural Intelligence*, *6*(2), 82–103. doi:10.4018/jcini.2012040105

Zheng, R. Z. (2013). Effective online learning for older people: A heuristic design approach. In R. Zheng, R. Hill, & M. Gardner (Eds.), *Engaging older adults with modern technology: Internet use and information access needs* (pp. 142–159). Hershey, PA: IGI Global. doi:10.4018/978-1-4666-1966-1.ch008

Zhou, M., & Xu, Y. (2013). Challenges to use recommender systems to enhance meta-cognitive functioning in online learners. In *Data mining: Concepts, methodologies, tools, and applications* (pp. 1916–1935). Hershey, PA: IGI Global. doi:10.4018/978-1-4666-2455-9.ch099

Ziaeehezarjeribi, Y., & Graves, I. (2013). Behind the MASK: Motivation through avatar skills and knowledge. In R. Ferdig (Ed.), *Design, utilization, and analysis of simulations and game-based educational worlds* (pp. 225–239). Hershey, PA: IGI Global. doi:10.4018/978-1-4666-4018-4.ch014

Zoss, A. M. (2014). Cognitive processes and traits related to graphic comprehension. In M. Huang & W. Huang (Eds.), *Innovative approaches of data visualization and visual analytics* (pp. 94–110). Hershey, PA: IGI Global. doi:10.4018/978-1-4666-4309-3.ch005

Compilation of References

Abercrombie, D. (1949). Teaching pronunciation. *English Language Teaching*, *3*(5), 113–122. doi:10.1093/elt/III.5.113

Abu-Rabia, S. (2001). Testing the interdependence hypothesis among native adult bilingual Russian-English students. *Journal of Psycholinguistic Research*, *30*(4), 437–455. doi:10.1023/A:1010425825251 PMID:11529524

Abutalebi, J., & Green, D. (2007). Bilingual Language Production: The Neurocognition of Language Representation and Control. *Journal of Neurolinguistics*, *20*(3), 242–275. doi:10.1016/j.jneuroling.2006.10.003

Acarlar, F., & Dönmez, N. (1992). 30–47 aylar arasındaki Türk çocuklarının dil yapılarının incelenmesi. *G.Ü. Gazi Eğitim Fakültesi Dergisi*, *8*(3), 163–203.

Adıgüzel, Ö. (2013). *Eğitimde yaratıcı drama*. Ankara: Pegem Akademi Yayıncılık.

Aitchison, J. (2003). *Words in the Mind*. Oxford, UK: Blackwell Publishing.

Aitchison, J. (2012). *Words in the mind: An introduction to the mental lexicon* (4th ed.). John Wiley & Sons.

Akmajian, A., Demers, R., Farmer, A., & Harnish, R. (2001). *An Introduction to Language and Communication*. Library of Congress Cataloging-in-Publication Data.

Akman, B., Taşkın, N., Özden, Z., & Çörtü, F. (2010). Okul öncesi öğretmenlerinde tükenmişlik üzerine bir çalışma. *İlköğretim Online*, *9*(2), 802-815.

Alario, F.-X., & Ferrand, L. (1999). A set of 400 pictures standardized for French: Norms for name agreement, image agreement, familiarity, visual complexity, image variability, and age of acquisition. *Behavior Research Methods, Instruments, & Computers*, *31*(3), 531–552. doi:10.3758/BF03200732 PMID:10502875

Allen, J. W. (2013). *Storytelling with cultural tools: Children's engagement with features of oral traditions in first nations cultural education programs* (Unpublished Doctoral Dissertation). University of Victoria.

Altarriba, J. (1992). The representation of translation equiv- alents in bilingual memory. In R. J. Harris (Ed.), *Cognitive processing in bilinguals* (pp. 157–174). Amsterdam: North-Holland. doi:10.1016/S0166-4115(08)61493-4

Altarriba, J., & Basnight-Brown, D. M. (2007). Methodological considerations in performing semantic-and translation-priming experiments across languages. *Behavior Research Methods*, *39*(1), 1–18. doi:10.3758/BF03192839 PMID:17552467

Althusser, L. (1999). *Ideologia e Aparelhos Ideológicos do Estado. In Um mapa da ideologia* (pp. 105–142). Rio de Janeiro: Contraponto.

Altınkamış, F., Altan, A., & Sofu, H. 2013. Properties of relative clauses in child directed speech [İlgi Tümceciklerinin Çocuğa Yöneltilmiş Konuşmadaki Özellikleri]. *Proceedings of the 27th National Linguistics Conference*, 51-60.

Arabski, J. (2006). Language transfer in language learning and language contact. In J. Arabski (Ed.), *Cross-linguistic influences in the second language lexicon* (pp. 12–21). Clevedon, UK: Multilingual Matters.

Aragao, R. (2011). Beliefs and emotions in foreign language learning. *System*, *39*(3), 302–313. doi:10.1016/j.system.2011.07.003

Arnold, J. (1999). *Affect in language learning*. Cambridge, UK: Cambridge University Press.

Aron, A. R. (2007). The Neural Basis of Inhibition in Cognitive Control. *The Neuroscientist*, *13*(3), 214–228. doi:10.1177/1073858407299288 PMID:17519365

Ataç, F. (1991). *İnsan yaşamında psikolojik gelişim*. İstanbul: Beta Basım Yayım Dağıtım.

August, D., Carlo, M., Dressler, C., & Snow, C. (2008). The critical role of vocabulary development for English language learners. *Learning Disabilities Research & Practice*, *20*(1), 50–57. doi:10.1111/j.1540-5826.2005.00120.x

Ayçiçeği-Dinn, A., & Caldwell-Harris, C. (2009). *Emotion-memory effects in bilingual speakers: A levels-of-processing approach*. Bilingualism.

Aydın, A. (2012). Turkish adaptation of test of pretended play. *Educational Sciences: Theory and Practice*, *12*(2), 916–925.

Aydoğan, Y. & Koçak, N. (2003). Okul öncesi çocukların dil gelişimine etki eden faktörlerin incelenmesi. *Milli Eğitim Dergisi*, 159.

Baayen, H., Piepenbrock, R., & van Rijn, H. (1993). *The CELEX database on CD-ROM*. Philadelphia: Linguistic Data Consortium.

Bajo, M. T., Puerta-Melguizo, M. C., & Macizo, P. (2003). The locus of semantic interference in picture naming. *Psicológica (Valencia)*, *24*, 31–55. doi:10.1037/a0033745

Bajo, M.-T. (1988). Semantic facilitation with picture and words. *Journal of Experimental Psychology. Learning, Memory, and Cognition*, *14*(4), 579–589. doi:10.1037/0278-7393.14.4.579 PMID:2972797

Ball, E. W., & Blachman, B. A. (1991). Does phoneme awareness training in kindergarten make a difference in early word recognition and developmental spelling? *Reading Research Quarterly*, *24*(1), 49–66. doi:10.1598/RRQ.26.1.3

Baloyannis, S. J. (2009). Neuroscience and Philosophy. *Encephalos, 46*(1), 5-20. Retrieved on January 25, 2017, from: file:///C:/Users/Dion%C3%A9ia/Downloads/Philosophy%20and%20 Neurosciencesl%20(1).pdf

Baluch, B., & Besner, D. (1991). Visual word recognition: Evidence for strategic control of lexical and nonlexical routines in oral reading. *Journal of Experimental Psychology. Learning, Memory, and Cognition*, *17*(4), 644–652. doi:10.1037/0278-7393.17.4.644

Baluch, B., & Besner, D. (2001). Basic processes in reading: Semantics affects speeded naming of high-frequency words in an alphabetic script. *Canadian Journal of Experimental Psychology*, *55*(1), 63–69. doi:10.1037/h0087353 PMID:11301729

Bamgbose, A. (1998). Torn between the norms: Innovations in world Englishes. *World Englishes*, *17*(1), 1–17. doi:10.1111/1467-971X.00078

Barbarin, O. A., Early, D., Clifford, R., Bryant, D., Frome, P., Burchinal, M., & Pianta, R. et al. (2008). Parental conceptions of school readiness: Relation to ethnicity, socioeconomic status, and children's skills. *Early Education and Development*, *19*(5), 671–701. doi:10.1080/10409280802375257

Barca, L., Burani, C., & Arduino, L. S. (2002). Word naming times and psycholinguistic norms for Italian nouns. *Behavior Research Methods, Instruments, & Computers*, *34*(3), 424–434. doi:10.3758/BF03195471 PMID:12395559

Barhudarov, S. E., & Dosycheva, E. I. (1940). *Грамматика русского языка. Часть первая. Фонетика и морфология* [Russian grammar. Part one. Phonetics and morphology]. Moscow, Russia: State Educational and Pedagogical Publishing.

Barlow, M., & Kemmer, S. (Eds.). (2000). *Usage- Based Models of Language*. CSLI Publications.

Barnes, M. E. (2013). *Head Start preschool teachers' commenting practices during shared book reading sessions: Describing learning opportunities for children with varying vocabulary abilities* (Unpublished Doctoral Dissertation). University of Vanderbilt.

Barry, C., Hirsch, K. W., Johnston, R. A., & Williams, C. L. (2001). Age of acquisition, word frequency, and the locus of repetition priming of picture naming. *Journal of Memory and Language*, *44*(3), 350–375. doi:10.1006/jmla.2000.2743

Barry, C., Morrison, C. M., & Ellis, A. W. (1997). Naming the Snodgrass and Vanderwart pictures: Effects of age of acquisition, frequency, and name agreement. *The Quarterly Journal of Experimental Psychology: Section A*, *50*(3), 560–585. doi:10.1080/783663595

Basnight-Brown, D. M., & Altarriba, J. (2007). *Methodological considerations in performing semantic-and translation-priming experiments across languages*. Academic Press.

Basnight-Brown, D., & Altarriba, J. (2007). Differences in semantic and translation priming across languages: The role of language direction and language dominance. *Memory & Cognition*, *35*(5), 953–965. doi:10.3758/BF03193468 PMID:17910179

Bates, E., Burani, C., D'Amico, S., & Barca, L. (2001). Word reading and picture naming in Italian. *Memory & Cognition*, *29*(7), 986–999. doi:10.3758/BF03195761 PMID:11820758

Beck, I. L., & McKeown, M. G. (2007). Increasing young low-income children's oral vocabulary repertoires through rich and focused instruction. *The Elementary School Journal*, *107*(3), 251–271. doi:10.1086/511706

Beel, R., & Felder, J. (2013). Phonological adaptations of English loanwords in Turkish. *Other Undergraduate Scholarship*. Retrieved from http://digitalcommons.liberty.edu/eml_undergrad_schol/2

Benson, K. A. (2013). *An Investigation of the Impact of Small Group Direct Vocabulary Instruction on the Vocabulary Development of Kindergarten Children Living in Poverty* (Unpublished Doctoral Dissertation). Ball State University.

Bernard, M. E. (2006). It's Time We Teach Social-Emotional Competence as well as We Teach Academic Competence. *Reading & Writing Quarterly*, *22*(2), 103–119. doi:10.1080/10573560500242184

Besner, D. (1999). Basic processes in reading: Multiple routines in localist and connectionist models. In P. A. McMullen & R. M. Klein (Eds.), *Converging methods for understanding reading and dyslexia*. Cambridge, MA: MIT Press.

Besner, D., & Smith, M. C. (1992). Basic Processes in reading: Is the orthographic depth hypothesis sinking? In R. Frost & L. Katz (Eds.), *Advances in psychology: orthography, phonology, morphology and meaning*. North-Holland. doi:10.1016/S0166-4115(08)62788-0

Bhatia, T. K. (2006). Author. In T. K. Bhatia & W. C. Ritchie (Eds.), The Handbook of Bilingualism (pp. 5-6). Blackwell.

Bialystok, E. (2001). Metalinguistic aspects of bilingual processing. *Annual Review of Applied Linguistics*, *21*, 169–181. doi:10.1017/S0267190501000101

Bialystok, E., & Hakuta, K. (1994). *In other words: The science and psychology of second-language acquisition*. New York: Basic Books.

Biarnès, J. (1998). O ser e as letras: da voz à letra, um caminho que construímos todos. Revista da Faculdade de Educação-USP, 24(2).

Biggs, T. C., & Marmurek, H. H. (1990). Picture and word naming: Is facilitation due to processing overlap? *The American Journal of Psychology, 103*(1), 81–110. doi:10.2307/1423260

Birkner, V. (2016). Revisiting Input an Output Hypotheses in Second Language Learning. *Asian Education Studies, 1*(1).

Blackford, T., Holcomb, P. J., Grainger, J., & Kuperberg, G. R. (2012). A funny thing happened on the way to articulation: N400 attenuation despite behavioral interference in picture naming. *Cognition, 123*(1), 84–99. doi:10.1016/j.cognition.2011.12.007 PMID:22245030

Blakemore, D. (1992). *Understanding Utterances*. Oxford, UK: Blackwell.

Blank, M., & Solomon, F. (2007). A tutorial language program to develop abstract thinking in socially disadvantaged preschool children. *Child Development, 39*(2), 379–389. doi:10.2307/1126952 PMID:4172078

Bloomfield, L. (1933). *Language*. London: Allen and Unwin.

Bock, K., & Levelt, W. (1994). Language production: Grammatical encoding. In M. A. Gernsbacher (Ed.), *Handbook of psycholinguistics* (pp. 945–984). San Diego, CA: Academic Press.

Bogka, N., Masterson, J., Druks, J., Fragkioudaki, M., Chatziprokopiou, E. S., & Economou, K. (2003). Object and action picture naming in English and Greek. *The European Journal of Cognitive Psychology, 15*(3), 371–403. doi:10.1080/09541440303607

Bonin, P., Chalard, M., Meot, A., & Fayol, M. (2002). The determinants of spoken and written picture naming latencies. *British Journal of Psychology, 93*(1), 89–114. doi:10.1348/000712602162463 PMID:11839103

Bonin, P., Fayol, M., & Chalard, M. (2001). Age of acquisition and word frequency in written picture naming. *Quarterly Journal of Experimental Psychology, 54*(2), 469–489. doi:10.1080/713755968 PMID:11394057

Bowen, J. D. (1972). Contextualizing Pronunciation Practice in the ESOL Classroom. *TESOL Quarterly, 6*(1), 83–94. doi:10.2307/3585862

Bowerman, M., & Levinson, S. C. (2001). *Language acquisition and conceptional development*. Cambridge University Press. doi:10.1017/CBO9780511620669

Brase, J., & Raman, I. (2009). The Role of Age of Acquisition in Picture and Word Naming in German. Presented at the Annual Cognitive Section Meeting, BPS, Hertfordshire, UK.

Brewster, J. (1991). What is Good Primary Practice? In C. Brumfit, J. Moon, & R. Tongue (Eds.), Teaching English to Children-From Practice to Principle. London: Longman.

Brewster, J., Ellis, G., & Girard, D. (2002). *The Primary English Teacher's Guide*. London: Pearson Education Limited.

Briggs, J., & Peat, F. (1989). *Turbulent Mirror: An Illustrated Guide to Chaos Theory and the Science of Wholeness*. New York: Harper & Row.

Bril, A., & Green, R. (2013). Bilingual Stroop in English Speakers with Russian as a Second Language: Exploring the Model of the Bilingual Mind. *FIVE: The Claremont Colleges Journal of Undergraduate Academic Writing*, *2*(1), 3. doi:10.5642/five.20130201.03

Broselow, E. (2009). Stress adaptation in loanword phonology: Perception and learnability. In Phonology in perception (pp. 191–234). New York: Mouton de Gruyter.

Brown, D. (2007). *Principles of language learning and teaching*. White Plains, NY: Pearson Education.

Brown, G. D. A., & Watson, F. L. (1987). First in, first out: Word learning age and spoken word frequency as predictors of word familiarity and word naming latency. *Memory & Cognition*, *15*(3), 208–216. doi:10.3758/BF03197718 PMID:3600260

Brown, H. D. (2000). *Principles of Language Learning and Teaching*. NewYork: Longman.

Brysbaert, M., Ameel, E., & Storms, G. (2014). Bilingual Semantic Memory: A New Hypothesis. In *Foundations of Bilingual Memory* (pp. 133–146). New York: Springer. doi:10.1007/978-1-4614-9218-4_7

Brysbaert, M., Lange, M., & Van Wijnendaele, I. (2000). The effects of age-of-acquisition and frequency-of-occurrence in visual word recognition: Further evidence from the Dutch language. *The European Journal of Cognitive Psychology*, *12*(1), 65–85. doi:10.1080/095414400382208

Brysbaert, M., Van Wijnendaele, I., & De Deyne, S. (2000). Age-of-acquisition is a significant variable in semantic tasks. *Acta Psychologica*, *104*, 215–226. doi:10.1016/S0001-6918(00)00021-4 PMID:10900706

Buğa, D. (2016). Central Language Hypothesis in the Decision-Making Process. In B. Christiansen & E. Lechman (Eds.), *Neuroeconomics and Decision-Making Process* (pp. 66–83). Hershey, PA: IGI Global. doi:10.4018/978-1-4666-9989-2.ch004

Bussman, H. (Ed.). (1996). *Routledge Dictionary of Language and Linguistics*. London: Routledge.

Butler, Y. G. (2012). What Level of English Proficiency Do Elementary School Teachers Need to Attain to Teach EFL? Case Studies from Korea, Taiwan, and Japan. *TESOL Quarterly*, *38*(2), 245–278. doi:10.2307/3588380

Bybee, J. L., & Hopper, P. J. (2001). *Frequency and the emergence of linguistic structure*. John Benjamins Publishing. doi:10.1075/tsl.45

Çakmak, T., & Yılmaz, B. (2009). Okul öncesi dönem çocuklarının okuma alışkanlığına hazırlık durumları üzerine bir araştırma: Hacettepe üniversitesi Beytepe anaokulu örneği. *Türk Kütüphaneciliği Dergisi*, *23*(3), 489–509.

Callahan, M. D. (2009). Starting small: Building preschool teacher knowledge that supports early literacy development. *Reading and Writing*, *22*(4), 487–510. doi:10.1007/s11145-009-9164-z

Cameron, L. (2001). *Teaching Languages to Young Learners*. Cambridge, UK: Cambridge University Press. doi:10.1017/CBO9780511733109

Campos, R., & Furtado, J. (2011). *Desafios da avaliação de programas e serviços em saúde*. EBC, Empresa Brasil de Comunicação. Retrieved on June 28, 2018, from: http://www.ebc.com.br/noticias/internacional/2013/06/relatorio-do-unicef-aponta-exclusao-da-crianca-com-deficiencia

Cangır, H., & Durrant, P. (2018). *Investigating cross-linguistic collocational priming in Turkish L1-English L2 bilinguals*. Unpublished manuscript.

Cangır, H., Büyükkantarcıoğlu, S. N., & Durrant, P. (2017). Investigating collocational priming in Turkish. *Journal of Language and Linguistic Studies*, *13*(2), 465–486.

Carroll, D. W. (2004). *Psychology of Language*. Belmont, WA: Thomson Wadsworth.

Carr, T. H., McCauley, C., Sperber, R. D., & Parmelee, C. M. (1982). Words, pictures, and priming: On semantic activation, conscious identification, and the automaticity of nformation processing. *Journal of Experimental Psychology. Human Perception and Performance*, *8*(6), 757–777. doi:10.1037/0096-1523.8.6.757 PMID:6218234

Castello, D. (2015). *First Language Acquisition and Classroom Language Learning: Similarities and Differences* (Master's thesis). University of Birmingham.

Celaya, M. L., & Torras, M. R. (2001). L1 influence and EFL vocabulary: do children rely more on L1 than adult learners? In *Proceedings of the 25thAEDEAN Meeting*. University of Granada.

Celce-Murcia, M. (1991). *Teaching English as a Second or Foreign Language*. Boston: Heinle & Heinle Publishers.

Celce-Murcia, M., Brinton, D. M., & Goodwin, J. M. (1996). *Teaching pronunciation: A reference for teachers of English to speakers of other languages*. New York: Cambridge University Press.

Çelik, M. (2007). *Linguistics for Students of English Book I*. EDM Publishing.

Chateau, D., & Lupker, S. J. (2003). Strategic effects in word naming: Examining the route-emphasis versus time-criterion accounts. *Journal of Experimental Psychology. Human Perception and Performance*, *29*(1), 139–151. doi:10.1037/0096-1523.29.1.139 PMID:12669753

Chauncey, K., Grainger, J., & Holcomb, P. J. (2008). Code-Switching Effects In Bilingual Word Recognition: A Masked Priming Study with Event-Related Potentials. *Brain and Language*, *105*(3), 161–174. doi:10.1016/j.bandl.2007.11.006 PMID:18191445

Chauncey, K., Holcomb, P. J., & Grainger, J. (2009). Primed picture naming within and across languages: An ERP investigation. *Cognitive, Affective & Behavioral Neuroscience*, *3*(3), 286–303. doi:10.3758/CABN.9.3.286 PMID:19679764

Chen, B., You, W., & Zhou, H. (2007a). Age of acquisition effects in reading Chinese: Evidence in favor of the semantic hypothesis. *Acta Psychologica Sinica*, *39*(1), 9–17.

Chen, B., Zhou, H., Dunlap, S., & Perfetti, C. A. (2007b). Age of acquisition effects in reading Chinese: Evidence in favour of the arbitrary mapping hypothesis. *British Journal of Psychology*, *98*(3), 499–516. doi:10.1348/000712606X165484 PMID:17705943

Chen, C. L. A. (2009). First Language Influence and Fossilization in Second Language Vocabulary Acquisition. *Columbia University Working Papers in TESOL & Applied Linguistics*, *9*(2), 65–67.

Chen, H. C., & Ho, C. (1986). Development of stroop interference in Chinese-English bilinguals. *Journal of Experimental Psychology. Learning, Memory, and Cognition*, *12*(3), 397–401. doi:10.1037/0278-7393.12.3.397

Cherry, B. J. (2003). Memory, Explicit / Implicit. In H. Withaker (Ed.), *Concise Encyclopedia of Brain and Language* (pp. 332–334). Oxford, UK: Elsevier.

Chiyuki, I., & Kenstowicz, M. (2009). Mandarin loanwords in Yanbian Korean II: Tones. *Language Research*, *45*(1), 85–109.

Chomsky, N. (1956). Three models for the description of language. *I.R.E. Transactions on Information Theory*, *2*(3), 113–124. doi:10.1109/TIT.1956.1056813

Chomsky, N. (1957). *Syntactic structures*. The Hague: Mouton.

Chomsky, N. (1965). *Aspects Of The Theory Of Syntax*. The M.I.T. Press.

Chomsky, N. (1975). *Reflections on Language*. New York: Pantheon Books.

Chomsky, N. (2006). *Language and Mind*. New York: Cambridge University Press. doi:10.1017/CBO9780511791222

Christoffels, I. K., Firk, C., & Schiller, N. O. (2007). Bilingual Language Control: An event-related brain potential study. *Brain Research*, 193. PMID:17391649

Cicogna, P., & Bosinelli, M. (2001). Consciousness During Dreams. *Consciousness and Cognition*, *10*(1), 26–41. doi:10.1006/ccog.2000.0471 PMID:11273624

Çocuk, H. E., Yanpar Yelken, T., Emsal Aslantürk, İ., & Güçlü, M. (2013). Okul öncesi eğitim programı dil alanı ile ilgili etkinliklerin uygulanmasına ilişkin okul öncesi öğretmen görüşlerinin belirlenmesi. *The International Journal of Social Sciences (Islamabad)*, *6*(7), 305–320.

Coello, Y., & Bartolo, A. (2013). *Language and Action in Cognitive Neuroscience*. New York: Psychology Press.

Collins, A. M., & Loftus, E. F. (1975). A spreading-activation theory of semantic processing. *Psychological Review*, *82*(6), 407–428. doi:10.1037/0033-295X.82.6.407

Collins, A. M., & Quillian, M. R. (1969). Retrieval time from semantic memory. *Journal of Verbal Learning and Verbal Behavior*, *8*(2), 240–247. doi:10.1016/S0022-5371(69)80069-1

Colomé, A. (2001). Lexical activation in bilinguals' speech production: Language-specific or language-independent? *Journal of Memory and Language, 45*(4), 721–736. doi:10.1006/jmla.2001.2793

Coltheart, M. (1978). Lexical access in simple reading tasks. Strategies of Information Processing, 151-216.

Coltheart, M. (1978). Lexical access in simple reading tasks. In G. Underwood (Ed.), *Strategies of information processing*. San Diego, CA: Academic Press.

Coltheart, M., Curtis, B., Atkins, P., & Haller, M. (1993). Models of reading aloud: Dual route and parallel distributed processing approaches. *Psychological Review, 100*(4), 589–608. doi:10.1037/0033-295X.100.4.589

Coltheart, M., & Rastle, K. (1994). Serial processing in Reading aloud: Evidence for Dual-route Models of Reading. *Journal of Experimental Psychology. Human Perception and Performance, 20*(6), 1197–1211. doi:10.1037/0096-1523.20.6.1197

Common European Framework for Languages. (2001). Strasbourg, France: Academic Press.

Cook, V. (2013). *Second Language Learning and Language Teaching*. New York: Routledge.

Corder, S. P. (1967). The significance of learner's errors. *International Review of Applied Linguistics in Language Teaching, 5*(4), 161–170.

Correll, K. (2008). *A program evaluation of a conversational instruction program for the vocabulary development of four-year old student in preschool classes* (Unpublished Doctoral Dissertation). University of Houston.

Costa, A., Caramazza, A., & Sebastián-Gallés, N. (2000). The cognate facilitation effect: Implications for models of lexical access. *Journal of Experimental Psychology: Learning, Memory, and Cognition, 26*, 1283–1296. doi: 1037TO278-7393.26.5.1283

Costa, A., & Caramazza, A. (1999). Is lexical selection in bilingual speech production language-specific? Further evidence from Spanish–English and English–Spanish bilinguals. *Bilingualism: Language and Cognition, 2*(3), 231–244. doi:10.1017/S1366728999000334

Costa, A., Colomé, A., Gómez, O., & Sebastián–Gallés, N. (2003). Another look at cross-language competition in bilingual speech production: Lexical and phonological factors. *Bilingualism: Language and Cognition, 6*(3), 167–179. doi:10.1017/S1366728903001111

Costa, A., Miozzo, M., & Caramazza, A. (1999). Lexical selection in bilinguals: Do words in the bilingual's two lexicons compete for selection? *Journal of Memory and Language, 41*(3), 365–397. doi:10.1006/jmla.1999.2651

Costa, A., & Pickering, M. J. (2016). Do Bilinguals Automatically Activate Their Native Language When They Are Not Using It? *Cognitive Science*. PMID:27766658

Cowie, A. P. (1994). Phraseology. In R. E. Asher (Ed.), *The Encyclopedia of Language and Linguistics*. Oxford, UK: Pergamon.

Crain-Thoreson, C., & Dale, P. S. (1992). Do early talkers become early readers? Linguistic precocity, preschool language, and emergent literacy. *Developmental Psychology*, *28*(3), 421–429. doi:10.1037/0012-1649.28.3.421

Crawford, P. A. (1995). Early literacy: Emerging perspectives. *Journal of Research in Childhood Education*, *10*(1), 71–86. doi:10.1080/02568549509594689

Crawford, W. W. (1987). The pronunciation monitor: L2 acquisition considerations and pedagogical priorities. In J. Morley (Ed.), *Current perspectives on pronunciation: Practices anchored in theory* (pp. 101–121). Washington, DC: TESOL.

Cruse, D. A. (2000). *Meaning in Language. An Introduction to Semantics and Pragmatics*. Oxford, UK: Oxford University Press.

Crystal, D. (1997). *The Cambridge Encyclopedia of Language*. Cambridge, UK: Cambridge University Press.

Crystal, D. (2008). Two thousand million? *English Today*, *24*(01), 3–6. doi:10.1017/S0266078408000023

Crystal, D. (Ed.). (2008). *Dictionary of Linguistics and Phonetics*. Hong Kong: Blackwell Publishing Ltd. doi:10.1002/9781444302776

Cubberley, P. (2002). *Russian: A linguistic introduction*. Cambridge, MA: Cambridge University Press.

Cuetos, F., Ellis, A. W., & Alvarez, B. (1999). Naming times for the Snodgrass and Vanderwart pictures in Spanish. *Behavior Research Methods, Instruments, & Computers*, *31*(4), 650–558. doi:10.3758/BF03200741 PMID:10633980

Cunningham, D. D. (2010). Relating preschool quality to children's literacy development. *Early Childhood Education Journal*, *37*(6), 501–507. doi:10.1007/s10643-009-0370-8

Dawaele, J.-M., & Pavlenko, A. (2001-2003). *Web questionnaire bilingualism and emotions*. University of London.

De Groot, A. M. B. (1992). Bilingual lexical representation: A closer look at conceptual representations. In R. Frost & I. Katz (Eds.), *Orthography, phonology, morphology, and meaning* (pp. 389–412). Amsterdam: Elsevier. doi:10.1016/S0166-4115(08)62805-8

De Groot, A. M. B. (1993). Word-type effects in bilingual pro- cessing tasks: Support for a mixed-representational system. In R. Schreuder & B. Weltens (Eds.), *The bilingual lexicon* (pp. 27–51). Amsterdam: John Benjamins. doi:10.1075/sibil.6.04gro de Groot, A. M., Delmaar, P., & Lupker, S. J. (2000). The processing of interlexical homographs in translation recognition and lexical decision: Support for non-selective access to bilingual memory. *The Quarterly Journal of Experimental Psychology: Section A*, *53*(2), 397–428. doi:10.1080/713755891 PMID:10881612

Dehmell, A. (2006). Making a European area of lifelong learning a reality? Some critical reflections on the European Union's lifelong learning policies. *Comparative Education*, *42*(1), 49–62. doi:10.1080/03050060500515744

Demircan, C. (2006). Tübitak çocuk kitaplığı dizisindeki kitapların dış yapısal ve içyapısal olarak incelenmesi. *Mersin Üniversitesi Eğitim Fakültesi Dergisi*, *2*(1), 12–27.

Demirezen, M. (2005a). Rehabilitating a fossilized pronunciation error: The /v/ and /w/ contrast by using the audio articulation method in teacher training in Turkey. *Journal of Language and Linguistic Studies*, *1*(2), 183–192.

Demirezen, M. (2005b). The / ɔ/ and /ow/ contrast: Curing a fossilized pronunciation error of Turkish teacher trainees of English language. *Journal of Arts and Sciences*, *1*(3), 71–84.

Demirezen, M. (2008). The /æ/ and /ʌ/ phonemes as fossilized pronunciation errors for Turkish English language teachers and students: Undoing the fossilized pronunciation error. *Journal of Language and Linguistic Studies*, *4*(2), 73–82.

Demirezen, M. (2010). The Order of Consonant Fossilization of the English Language Consonants for Turkish English Teachers and Students. *E-Proceedings of the International Online Language Conference.*

Demirezen, M. (2010). The principles and application of the audio-lingual pronunciation rehabilitation model in foreign language teacher education. *Journal of Language and Linguistic Studies*, *6*(2), 127–147.

Demirezen, M., & Topal, I. H. (2015). Fossilized Pronunciation Errors from the Perspectives of Turkish Teachers of English and their Implications. *Procedia: Social and Behavioral Sciences*, *199*, 793–800. doi:10.1016/j.sbspro.2015.07.613

Denham, S. A., Bassett, H. H., & Zinssen, K. (2012). Early childhood teachers as socializers of young children's emotional competence. *Early Childhood Education*, *40*(3), 137–143. doi:10.1007/s10643-012-0504-2

Dereli, E. & Koçak, N. (2005). Okul öncesi eğitime devam eden 4-6 yaş arasındaki çocukların ifade edici dil düzeylerinin bakım tarzı ve anne- baba eğitim düzeyi açısından incelenmesi. *Selçuk Üniversitesi, Sosyal Bilimler Enstitüsü Dergisi,* (14).

Deretarla Gül, E. (2013). Okul öncesi çocuklara okuma alışkanlığı kazandırma. In M. Gönen (Ed.), Çocuk Edebiyatı (pp. 305-314). Ankara: Eğiten Kitap Yayınevi.

Dewaele, J.-M. (2006). Expressing Anger in Multiple Languages. In A. Pavlenko (Ed.), *Bilingual Minds: Emotional Experience, Expression and Representation.* Multilingual Matters Ltd.

Dewaele, J.-M. (2008). The emotional weight of "I love you" in multilinguals' languages. *Journal of Pragmatics, 40*(10), 1753–1780. doi:10.1016/j.pragma.2008.03.002

Dewaele, J.-M. (2013). Multilingualism and Emotions. In C. A. Chapelle (Ed.), *The Encyclopedia of Applied Linguistics.* Blackwell Publishing.

Dickinson, D. K., & Sprague, K. E. (2001). The nature and impact of early childhood care environments on the language and literacy development of children from low-income families. In S.B. Neuman & D.K. Dickinson (Eds.), Handbook of Early Literacy Research (pp. 263-280). Guilford.

Dickinson, D. K., McCabe, A., & Anastasopoulos, L. (2002). *A framework for examining book reading in early childhood classroms.* CIERA Report 1-014.

Dickinson, D. K. (2011). Teacher's language practices and academic outcomes of pre school children. *Investing Early. Education, 333.*

Dickinson, D. K., & Smith, M. W. (1994). Long term effects of preschool teachers's book readings on low-income children's vocabulary and story comprehension. *Reading Research Quarterly, 29*(2), 104–122. doi:10.2307/747807

Dijkstra, T., Miwa, K., Brummelhuis, B., Sappelli, M., & Baayen, R. H. (2010). How cross-language similarity and task demands affect cognate recognition. *Journal of Memory and Language, 62*(3), 284–301. doi:10.1016/j.jml.2009.12.003

Dijkstra, T., & Van Heuven, W. (2002). The architecture of the bilingual word recognition system: From identification to decision. *Bilingualism: Language and Cognition, 5*(03), 175–197. doi:10.1017/S1366728902003012

Dijkstra, T., Van Jaarsveld, H., & Brinke, S. T. (1998). Interlingual homograph recognition: Effects of task demands and language intermixing. *Bilingualism: Language and Cognition, 1*(01), 51–66. doi:10.1017/S1366728998000121

Dimitropoulou, M., Duñabeitia, J. A., Blitsas, P., & Carreiras, M. (2009). A standardized set of 260 pictures for Modern Greek: Norms for name agreement, age of acquisition, and visual complexity. *Behavior Research Methods, 41*(2), 584–589. doi:10.3758/BRM.41.2.584 PMID:19363201

Dong, Y., Gui, S., & MacWhinney, B. (2005). Shared and separate meanings in the bilingual mental lexicon. *Bilingualism: Language and Cognition, 8*(3), 221–238. doi:10.1017/S1366728905002270

Dörnyei, Z. (2005). The psychology of the language learner: Individual differences in second language acquisition. Mahwah, NJ: Erlbaum.

Dörnyei, Z. (2003). Attitudes, orientations, and motivations in language learning: Advances in theory, research, and applications. *Language Learning, 53*(S1), 3–32. doi:10.1111/1467-9922.53222

Doughty, C. J., & Long, M. H. (2005). *The Handbook of Second Language Acquisition.2003*. Blackwell Publishing. doi:10.1111/b.9781405132817.2005.x

Durlak, J. A., Weissberg, R. P., Dymnicki, A. B., Taylor, R. D., & Schellinger, K. B. (2011). The impact of enhancing students' social and emotional learning: A meta-analysis of school-based universal interventions. *Child Development*, *82*(1), 405–432. doi:10.1111/j.1467-8624.2010.01564.x PMID:21291449

Durrant, P., & Doherty, A. (2010). Are high-frequency collocations psychologically real? Investigating the thesis of collocational priming. *Corpus Linguistics and Linguistic Theory*, *6*(2), 125–155.

Durrant, P., & Schmitt, N. (2010). Adult learners' retention of collocations from exposure. *Second Language Research*, *26*(2), 163–188. doi:10.1177/0267658309349431

Durso, F. T., & Johnson, M. K. (1979). Facilitation in naming and categorizing repeated pictures and words. *Journal of Experimental Psychology. Human Learning and Memory*, *5*(5), 449–459. doi:10.1037/0278-7393.5.5.449

Dyer, F. (1971). Color-naming interference in monolinguals and bilinguals. *Journal of Verbal Learning and Verbal Behavior*, *10*(3), 297–302. doi:10.1016/S0022-5371(71)80057-9

Edwards, J. (2006). Foundations of Bilingualism. In T. Bhatia & W. Ritchie (Eds.), *The Handbook of Bilingualism* (pp. 5–29). Oxford, UK: Blackwell. doi:10.1002/9780470756997.ch1

Egorov, T. G. (2006). *Психология овладения навыком чтения* [The psychology of reading acquisition]. St. Petersburg, Russia: KARO.

Ehri, L. C., & Ryan, E. B. (1980). Performance of bilinguals in a picture-word interference task. *Journal of Psycholinguistic Research*, *9*(3), 285–302. doi:10.1007/BF01067243 PMID:7391998

Eliasi, A., & Vahidi Borji, H. (2013). Task repetition and noticing as a route to semester-long destabilization: A cross-sectional study of Iranian EFL learners' oral output. *International Journal of Applied Linguistics and English Literature*, *2*(3), 21–28. doi:10.7575/aiac.ijalel.v.2n.3p.21

Ellis, A. W., & Lambon Ralph, M. A. (2000). Age of acquisition effects in adult lexical processing reflect loss of placticity in maturing systems: Insights from connectionist networks. *Journal of Experimental Psychology. Learning, Memory, and Cognition*, *26*(5), 1103–1123. doi:10.1037/0278-7393.26.5.1103 PMID:11009247

Ellis, N. C. (1996). Sequencing in SLA: Phonological memory, chunking, and points of order. *Studies in Second Language Acquisition*, *18*(01), 91–126. doi:10.1017/S0272263100014698

Ellis, N. C. (2002). Frequency Effects in language processing. *Studies in Second Language Acquisition*, 143–188.

Ellis, R. (1994). *The Study of Second Language Acquisition*. Shangai: Shangai Foreign Language Education Press.

Ellis, R. (2008). *The study of second language acquisition*. Oxford, UK: Oxford University Press.

Erdil, Z. (2010). Sosyoekonomik olarak risk altında bulunan çocuklara yönelik erken müdahale programları ve akademik başarı ilişkisi. *Sağlık Bilimleri Fakültesi Hemşirelik Dergisi,* 72-78.

Erdoğan, S., Şimşek Bekir, H. & Erdoğan Aras, S. (2005). Alt sosyoekonomik bölgelerde ana sınıfına devam eden 5-6 yaş grubundaki çocukların dil gelişim düzeylerine bazı faktörlerin etkisinin incelenmesi. *Çukurova Üniversitesi Sosyal Bilimler Enstitüsü Dergisi, 14*(1), 231-246.

Ezell, H. K., & Justice, L. M. (1998). A pilot investigation of parents' questions about print and pictures to preschoolers with language delay. *Child Language Teaching and Therapy, 14*(3), 273–278.

Fauziati, E. (2003). Interlanguage errors in English textbooks for junior high school students in Surakarta. *TEFLIN Journal, 14*(2), 1–10.

Fauziati, E. (2011). Interlanguage and error fossilization: A study of Indonesian students learning English as a foreign language. *Indonesian Journal of Applied Linguistics, 1*(1), 23–38. doi:10.17509/ijal.v1i1.97

Finkbeiner, M., Forster, K., Nicol, J., & Nakamura, K. (2004). The role of polysemy in masked semantic and translation priming. *Journal of Memory and Language, 51*(1), 1–22. doi:10.1016/j.jml.2004.01.004

Firth, J. R. (1957). A synopsis of linguistic theory, 1930–1955. In F. R. Palmer (Ed.), *Selected papers of J.R. Firth*. London: Longmans.

Flege, J. (1995). Second-language speech learning: theory, findings and problems. In W. Strange (Ed.), *Speech perception and linguistic experience: issues in cross-language research* (pp. 233–273). Timonium, MD: York Press.

Foley, J., & Thompson, L. (2003). *Language Learning: A lifelong process*. London: Arnold Hodder Healine Group.

Foster, R. P. (1996). The bilingual self—thoughts from a scientific positivist or pragmatic psychoanalyst? *Psychoanalytic Dialogues*, 142–143.

Foucault, M. (1967). *As palavras e as coisas, tradução de António Ramos Rosa*. Lisboa: Portugália Editora.

Foucault, M. (1969). *Qu'est-cequ'unauteur? conferência pronunciada na Sociedade Francesa de Filosofia em 22 de fevereiro de 1969, Littoral, n. 9, Márcia Gatto e Clarice Gato (trad.)*. Paris: Eres. (Original work published 1963)

Foucault, M. (1995). *Arqueologia do saber, Luiz Felipe Baeta Neves (trad.)*. Rio de Janeiro: Ed. Forense Universitária.

Foucault, M. (1996). *A ordem do discurso, Laura Fraga de Almeida Sampaio (trad.)*. São Paulo: Loyola.

Foucault, M. (2004). *A hermenêutica do sujeito, Márcio Alves Fonseca e Salma TannusMuchail (trad.)*. São Paulo: Martins Fontes.

Francis, W. S. (1999). Cognitive integration of language and memory in bilinguals: Semantic representation. *Psychological Bulletin, 125*(2), 193–222. doi:10.1037/0033-2909.125.2.193 PMID:10087936

Fraser, H. (2006). Helping teachers help students with pronunciation: A cognitive approach. *Prospect: A Journal of Australian TESOL, 21*, 80-94.

Frederiksen, J. R., & Kroll, J. F. (1976). Spelling and sound: Approaches to the internal lexicon. *Journal of Experimental Psychology. Human Perception and Performance, 2*(3), 361–379. doi:10.1037/0096-1523.2.3.361

Frenck, C., & Pynte, J. (1987). Semantic representations and surface forms: A look at across-language priming in bilinguals. *Journal of Psycholinguistic Research, 16*(4), 383–396. doi:10.1007/BF01069290

Fromkin, V., Rodman, R., & Hyamas, N. (2003). *An Introduction to Language*. Heinle.

Gabrys´-Barker, D. (2005). *Aspects of multilingual storage, processing and retrieval*. Katowice: University of Silesia Press.

Gabrys-Barker, D. (2006). The interaction of languages in the lexical search of multilingual language users. In J. Arabski (Ed.), *Cross-linguistic influences in the second language lexicon* (pp. 144–166). Clevedon, UK: Multilingual Matters.

García-Lecumberri, L., & Gallardo del Puerto, F. (2003). English FL sounds in school learners of different ages. In G. Mayo & L. García Lecumberri (Eds.), *Age and the acquisition of English as a foreign language* (pp. 115–135). Clevedon, UK: Multilingual Matters.

Gardner, R. C., & MacIntyre, P. D. (1991). An instrumental motivation in language study: Who says it isn't effective? *Studies in Second Language Acquisition, 13*(01), 57–72. doi:10.1017/S0272263100009724

Gardner, R. C., & MacIntyre, P. D. (1993). On the measurement of affective variables in second language learning. *Language Learning, 43*(2), 157–194. doi:10.1111/j.1467-1770.1992.tb00714.x

Garret, N. (1986). The problem with grammar: what kind can the language learner use? *Modern Language Journal, 70*, 133–149.

Garret, P., & Young, R. F. (2009). Theorizing affect in foreign language learning: An analysis of one learner's response to a communicative Portuguese course. *Modern Language Journal, 93*(2), 209–226. doi:10.1111/j.1540-4781.2009.00857.x

Gass, S. M. (2013). *Second language acquisition*. New York: Routledge.

Gass, S. M., & Selinker, L. (2008). *Second Language Acquisition*. New York: Routledge.

Gaufey, G. (1998). *El lazo especular. Unestudiotraversero de launidad imaginaria, trad.* Graciela Leguizamón, Argentina: Edelp SA.

Gennari, S. P., & MacDonalds, M. C. (2008). Semantic indeterminacy in object relative clauses. *Journal of Memory and Language*, *58*(2), 161–187. doi:10.1016/j.jml.2007.07.004 PMID:19724662

Gerhand, S., & Barry, C. (1999). Age-of-Acquisition and frequency effects in speeded word naming. *Cognition*, *73*(2), B27–B36. doi:10.1016/S0010-0277(99)00052-9 PMID:10580164

Gernsbacher, A. M. (1984). Resolving 20 Years of Inconsistent Interactions Between Lexical Familiarity and Orthography, Concreteness and Polysemy. *Journal of Experimental Psychology. General*, *113*(2), 256–281. doi:10.1037/0096-3445.113.2.256 PMID:6242753

Gest, S. D., Freeman, N. R., Domitrovich, C. E., & Welsh, J. A. (2004). Shared book reading and children's language comprehension skills: The moderating role of parental discipline practices. *Early Childhood Research Quarterly*, *19*(2), 319–336. doi:10.1016/j.ecresq.2004.04.007

Ghyselinck, M., Custers, R., & Brysbaert, M. (2004). The Effect of Age of Acquisition in Visual Word Processing: Further Evidence for the Semantic Hypothesis. *Journal of Experimental Psychology. Learning, Memory, and Cognition*, *30*(2), 550–554. doi:10.1037/0278-7393.30.2.550 PMID:14979824

Gilhooly, K. J., & Logie, R. H. (1980). Age of acquisition, imagery, concreteness, familiarity and ambiguity measures for 1944 words. *Behavior Research Methods and Instrumentation*, *12*(4), 395–427. doi:10.3758/BF03201693

Girolametto, L., Weitzman, E., Lefebvre, P., & Greenberg, J. (2007). The effects of in-service education to promote emergent literacy in child care centers: A feasibility study. *Language, Speech, and Hearing Services in Schools*, *38*(1), 72–83. doi:10.1044/0161-1461(2007/007) PMID:17218537

Glaser, W. R., & Dungelhoff, F. J. (1984). The time course of picture-word interference. *Journal of Experimental Psychology. Human Perception and Performance*, *10*(5), 640–654. doi:10.1037/0096-1523.10.5.640 PMID:6238124

Gollan, T. H., & Acenas, L. A. (2004). What is TOT? Cognate and translation effects on tip-of-the-tongue states in Spanish–English and Tagalog–English bilinguals. *Journal of Experimental Psychology. Learning, Memory, and Cognition*, *30*(1), 246–269. doi:10.1037/0278-7393.30.1.246 PMID:14736310

Gönen, M., Ünüvar, P., Bıçakçı, M., Koçyiğit, S., Yazıcı, Z., Orçan, M., & Özyürek, A. et al. (2010). Okul öncesi öğretmenlerinin dil etkinliklerini uygulama biçimlerinin incelenmesi. *Mehmet Akif Ersoy Eğitim Fakültesi Dergisi*, *10*(19), 23–40.

Gordon, B. (1985). Subjective frequency and the lexical decision latency function: Implications for mechanisms of lexical access. *Journal of Memory and Language*, *24*(6), 631–645. doi:10.1016/0749-596X(85)90050-6

Graham, J. (1990). *Changing fossilized speech: What does it take?* Paper presented at the 1990 San Francisco TESOL Convention, San Francisco, CA.

Green, K. (2016). The Human Brain Does Not Need High Levels of Motivation to Learn a Foreign Language: Motivation Has Had its Day. *Advances in Language and Literary Studies¸ 7*(5).

Grigorenko, E. L. (2010). *Report on the Russian Language for the world dyslexia forum.* Yale University, Columbia University, and Moscow State University, Russia.

Grosjean, F. (1997). The Bilingual Individual. *Interpreting, 2*(1-2), 163–187. doi:10.1075/intp.2.1-2.07gro

Grosjean, F. (2013). Bilingualism: A Short Introduction. In F. Grosjean & P. Li (Eds.), *The Psycholinguistics of Bilingualism* (pp. 5–25). Wiley-Blackwell.

Guimarães, E. (2002). *Semântica do acontecimento: um estudo enunciativo da designação.* Campinas, SP: Pontes.

Gungor, F., & Uysal, H. H. (2016). A Comparative Analysis of Lexical Bundles Used by Native and Non-native Scholars. *English Language Teaching, 9*(6), 176. doi:10.5539/elt.v9n6p176

Guo, Y., Piasta, S. B., Justice, L. M., & Kaderavek, J. N. (2010). Relations among preschool teachers' language and literacy gains. *Teaching and Teacher Education, 26*, 1094–1103. doi:10.1016/j.tate.2009.11.005

Gut, U. (2009). *Non-native Speech: a corpus-based analysis of phonological and phonetic properties of L2 English and German.* Frankfurt, Germany: Peter Lang. doi:10.3726/978-3-653-01155-5

Güven, S., & Topbaş, S. (2014). Erken dil gelişimi testi-üçüncü edisyon'un (test of early language development-third edition) uyarlama, geçerlik ve güvenirlik ön çalışması. *International Journal of Early Childhood Special Education, 6*(2), 151–172.

Hallam, S. (2009). An Evaluation of the Social and Emotional Aspects of Learning (SEAL) Programme: Promoting Positive Behaviour, Effective Learning and Well-being in Primary School Children. *Oxford Review of Education, 35*(3), 313–330. doi:10.1080/03054980902934597

Halliwell, S. (1992). *Teaching English in the Primary Classroom.* London: Longman.

Hanbay, O. (2013). *Çocuklarla yabancı dil öğretimi.* Ankara: Anı Yayıncılık.

Han, J., Yu, B., & Zhang, W. (2012). The effect of Chinese dialects on English pronunciation of high school students in China. *Journal of Teacher Education, 1*(3), 225–230.

Han, Z. (2004a). *What is fossilization? In Fossilization in Adult Second Language Acquisition* (pp. 12–23). Toronto: Multilingual Matters.

Han, Z. (2004b). *Behavioral reflexes and causal variables. In Fossilization in Adult Second Language Acquisition* (pp. 25–42). Toronto: Multilingual Matters.

Han, Z.-H., & Odlin, T. (2006). *Studies of Fossilization in Second Language Acquisition*. Clevedon, UK: Multilingual Matters.

Haraway, D., & Kunzru, H. (2014). *A cyborg manifesto: science, technology, and socialist-feminism in the late twentieth century. Antropologia do ciborgue: as vertigens do pós-humano, Tadeu, T., (organização e tradução). Acesso em 23 de janeiro de 2014*. Retrieved from http://mairakubik.files.wordpress.com/2012/06/86532011-haraway-donna-kunzru-hari-antropologia-do-ciborgue-as-vertigens-do-pos-humano-org-tomaz-tadeu.pdf

Harley, T. (2005). *The Psychology of Language from Data to Theory*. New York: Psychology Press.

Harley, T. A. (2008). *The Psychology of Language*. New York: Psychology Press.

Harley, T. A. (2013). *The psychology of language: From data to theory*. New York: Psychology Press.

Harmer, J. (2007). *The Practice of English Language Teaching*. Pearson Longman.

Haroche, C. (1992). *Fazer dizer, querer dizer*. São Paulo: Hucitec.

Harris, C. L., Gleason, J. B., & Ayçiçeği, A. (2006). When is a First Language More emotional? Psychophysiological Evidence from Bilingual Speakers. In A. Pavlenko (Eds.), Bilingual Minds: Emotional Experience, Expression and Representation (pp. 257-279). Multilingual Matters.

Hassan, S. I. (2012). *Pronunciation Problems of Sudanese Learners of English* (Published M.A. Thesis). Open University of Sudan.

Haugen, E. (1953). *The Norwegian Language in America*. Philadelphia: University of Pennsylvania Press.

Havelka, J., & Tomita, I. (2006). Age of acquisition in naming Japanese words. *Visual Cognition*, *13*(7/8), 981–991. doi:10.1080/13506280544000156

Headinjury. (2015). Retrieved on February 3, 2015, from: http://www.headinjury.com/rehabcognitive.html

Henriksen, B. (2013). Research on L2 learners ' collocational competence and development – a progress report. *EUROSLA Monographs Series*, *2*, 29–56.

Hermans, D., Bongaerts, T., De Bot, K., & Schreuder, R. (1998). Producing words in a foreign language: Can speakers prevent interference from their first language? *Bilingualism: Language and Cognition*, *1*(3), 213–229. doi:10.1017/S1366728998000364

Hernandez, A. (2016). *Bilingual Brain*. Houston, TX: University of Houston.

Hindman, A. H., Wasik, B. A., & Erhart, A. L. (2012). Shared book reading and Head Start preschoolers' vocabulary learning: The role of book-related discussion and curricular connections. *Early Education and Development*, *23*(4), 451–474. doi:10.1080/10409289.2010.537250

Hino, Y., & Lupker, S. J. (1996). Effects of Polysemy in Lexical Decision and Naming: An Alternative to Lexical Accounts. *Journal of Experimental Psychology. Human Perception and Performance, 22*(6), 1331–1356. doi:10.1037/0096-1523.22.6.1331

Hişmanoğlu, M. (2007). The /ɔ:/ and /oʊ/ Contrast as a fossilized pronunciation error of Turkish learners of English and solutions to the problem. *Journal of Language and Linguistic Studies, 3*(1), 98–115.

Hoey, M. (1991). *Patterns of Lexis in Text.* Oxford, UK: Oxford University Press.

Hoey, M. (2005). *Lexical Priming: A New Theory of Words and Language*. Routledge. doi:10.4324/9780203327630

Hoff, E., & Core, C. (2013). Input and Language development in bilingually developing children. *Seminars in Speech and Language, 34*, 215-226. DOI: 10.1055/S-OO33-1353448

Hoff, E., Coard, W., & Senor, M. (2013). *Bilingual Parent's Child-directed Speech in two languages: Do native and non-native input differ?* Poster presented at Society for Research in Child Development Biennial Meeting, Seattle, WA.

Hoff, E. (2003). The specificity of environmental influence: Socioeconomic status affects early vocabulary development via maternal speech. *Child Development, 74*(5), 1368–1378. doi:10.1111/1467-8624.00612 PMID:14552403

Hoff, E. (2006). How social contexts support and shape language development. *Developmental Review, 26*(1), 55–88. doi:10.1016/j.dr.2005.11.002

Hoff, E., Core, C., Place, S., Rumiche, R., Señor, M., & Parra, M. (2012). Dual language exposure and early bilingual development. *Journal of Child Language, 39*(01), 1–27. doi:10.1017/S0305000910000759 PMID:21418730

Hoff, E., Welsh, S., Place, S., & Ribot, K. M. (2014). Bilingual environments, bilingual input, and bilingual development. In T. Grüter & J. Paradis (Eds.), *Input and Experience in Bilingual Development.* Amsterdam, The Netherlands: John Benjamins Publishing Company.

Hoff-Ginsburg, E. (1998). The relation of birth order and socioeconomic status to children's language experience and language development. *Applied Psycholinguistics, 19*(04), 603–629. doi:10.1017/S0142716400010389

Hoshino, N. (2006). *A psycholinguistic study of native language constraints on speaking words in a second language* (Doctoral dissertation). Pennsylvania State University. Retrieved from https://etda.libraries.psu.edu/paper/7316/

Houmanfar, R., Hayes, L. J., & Herbst, S. A. (2005). An Analog study of first language dominance and interference over second language. *Analysis of Verbal Behavior, 21*(1), 75–98. doi:10.1007/BF03393011 PMID:22477315

Houwer, A. D. (2016). Bilingual language input environments, intake, maturity and practice. *Bilingualism: Language and Cognition.*

Howarth, P. (1998). Phraseology and second language proficiency. *Applied Linguistics, 19*(1), 24–44. doi:10.1093/applin/19.1.24

Howlader, M. R. (2010). Teaching English pronunciation in countries where English is a second language: Bangladesh perspective. *ASA University Review, 4*(2), 233–244.

Hromek, R., & Roffey, S. (2009). Promoting Social and Emotional Learning With Games: It's Fun and We Learn Things. *Simulation & Gaming, 20*(10), 1–18.

Huang, Q. (2009). Probe into the internal mechanism of interlanguage fossilization. *English Language Teaching, 2*(2), 75–77. doi:10.5539/elt.v2n2p75

Huebler, F., & Lu, W. (2013). *Adult and Youth Literacy: National, Regional and Global Trends, 1985-2015.* Academic Press.

Hutchison, K. A. (2003). Is semantic priming due to association strength or feature overlap? A microanalytic review. *Psychonomic Bulletin & Review, 10*(4), 785–813. doi:10.3758/BF03196544 PMID:15000531

Huttenlocher, J., Waterfall, H. R., Vasilyeva, M., Vevea, J., & Hedges, L. (2010). Sources of variability in children's language growth. *Cognitive Psychology, 61*(4), 343–365. doi:10.1016/j.cogpsych.2010.08.002 PMID:20832781

Iliev, I. G. (2013). Short History of the Cyrillic Alphabet. *International Journal of Russian Studies, 2*(2), 1–65.

Imai, Y. (2010). Emotions in SLA: New insights from collaborative learning for an EFL classroom. *Modern Language Journal, 94*(2), 278–292. doi:10.1111/j.1540-4781.2010.01021.x

İnanç, B. Y., Bilgin, M., & Atıcı, M. K. (2007). *Gelişim Psikolojisi: Çocuk ve Ergen Gelişimi.* Ankara: PegemA Yayıncılık.

İpek, N. & Bilgin, A. (2007). İlköğretim çağı çocuklarında kelime dağarcığı gelişimi. *İlköğretim Online, 6*(3), 344-365.

Ipek, H. (2009). Comparing and contrasting first and second language acquisition. *English Language Teaching, 2*(2), 155–163. doi:10.5539/elt.v2n2p155

Irwin, D. I., & Lupker, S. J. (1983). Semantic priming of pictures and words: A levels of processing approach. *Journal of Verbal Learning and Verbal Behavior, 22*(1), 45–60. doi:10.1016/S0022-5371(83)80005-X

Ivanova, I., Murillo, M., Montoya, R. I., & Gollan, T. H. (2016). Does Bilingual Language Control Decline in Older Age? *Linguistic Approaches to Bilingualism, 6*(1-2), 86–118. doi:10.1075/lab.15003.iva PMID:28090222

Jared, D., & Kroll, J.F. (2001). Do bilinguals activate phonological representations in one or both of their languages when naming words? *Journal of Memory and Language, 44*, 2-31.

Jarvis, S., & Pavlenko, A. (2008). *Crosslinguistic influence in language and cognition*. London: Routledge.

Jenkins, J. (2000). *The Phonology of English as an International Language*. Oxford, UK: Oxford University Press.

Jiang, N. (2015). Six decades of research on lexical representation and processing in bilinguals. In J. Schwieter (Ed.), The Cambridge Handbook of Bilingual Processing (pp. 27-28). Cambridge, UK: Cambridge University Press. doi:10.1017/CBO9781107447257.002

Jiang, N. (1999). Testing processing explanations for the asymmetry in masked cross-language priming. *Bilingualism: Language and Cognition*, *2*(1), 59–75. doi:10.1017/S1366728999000152

Jiang, N. (2012). *Conducting reaction time research in second language studies*. New York: Routledge.

Jiang, N., & Forster, K. (2001). Cross-language priming asymmetries in lexical decision and episodic recognition. *Journal of Memory and Language*, *44*(1), 32–51. doi:10.1006/jmla.2000.2737

Jin, Y.-S. (1990). Effects of concreteness on cross-language priming in lexical decisions. *Perceptual and Motor Skills*, *70*(3_suppl), 1139–1154. doi:10.2466/pms.1990.70.3c.1139

Johnson, J., & Newport, E. (1989). Critical period effects in second language learning: The influence of maturational state on the acquisition of English as a second language. *Cognitive Psychology*, *21*(1), 60–99. doi:10.1016/0010-0285(89)90003-0 PMID:2920538

Johnstone, R. (2002). *Addressing the age factor: Some implications for languages policy*. Strasburg: Council of Europe.

Johnston, R. A., & Barry, C. (2006). Age of acquisition and lexical processing. *Visual Cognition*, *13*(7-8), 789–845. doi:10.1080/13506280544000066

Joseph, E. G., & Strain, P. S. (2003). Comprehensive Evidence-Based Social- Emotional Curricula for Young Children: An Analysis of Efficacious Adoption Potential. *TECSE*, *23*(2), 65–76.

Juhasz, B. J. (2005). Age-of-Acquisition Effects in Word and Picture Identification. *Psychological Bulletin*, *131*(5), 684–712. doi:10.1037/0033-2909.131.5.684 PMID:16187854

Justice, L. M., Bowles, R., Pence, K., & Gosse, C. (2010). A scalable tool for assessing children's language abilities within a narrative context: The NAP (Narrative Assessment Protocol). *Early Childhood Research Quarterly*, *25*(2), 218–234. doi:10.1016/j.ecresq.2009.11.002

Justice, L. M., & Ezell, H. K. (1999). Vygotskian theory and its application to language assessment: An overview for speech-language pathologists. *Contemporary Issues in Communication Science and Disorders*, *26*, 111–118.

Justice, L. M., & Ezell, H. K. (2002). Use of storybook reading to increase print awareness in at-risk children. *American Journal of Speech-Language Pathology*, *11*(1), 17–29. doi:10.1044/1058-0360(2002/003)

Justice, L. M., Mashburn, A., Hamre, B., & Pianta, R. (2008). Quality of language and literacy instruction in pre-kindergarten programs serving at-risk pupils. *Early Childhood Research Quarterly*, *23*, 51–68. doi:10.1016/j.ecresq.2007.09.004 PMID:22773887

Justice, L. M., Zucker, T. A., & Sofka, A. E. (2010). *Systematic assessment of book reading: SABR manual*. Columbus, OH: The Ohio State University College of Education and Human Ecology.

Kahraman, A. (2012). Defosilization of /æ/ phoneme pronunciation of non-native EFL teachers. *Journal of Language Teaching and Research*, *3*(3), 379–385. doi:10.4304/jltr.3.3.379-385

Kandır, A., Özbey, S., & İnal, G. (2009). A study on the difficulties faced by preschool teachers in the planning and implementation. *The Journal of International Social Research.*, *6*, 373–387.

Karaca, N. H., & Aral, N. (2011). Okul öncesi öğretmen adaylarının öğretmenlik uygulamalarında karşılaştıkları sorunlar. *2nd International Conference on New Trends in Education and Their Implications*, 595-602.

Kaur, S. (2016). *Lexical representation and processing in Bodo–Assamese bilinguals* (Unpublished doctoral thesis). Indian Institute of Technology Guwahati, India.

Kay, G. (1995). English loanwords in Japanese. *World Englishes*, *14*(1), 67–76. doi:10.1111/j.1467-971X.1995.tb00340.x

Kecskes, I., & Albertazzi, L. (2007). *Cognitive Aspects of Bilingualism*. Dordrecht: Springer. doi:10.1007/978-1-4020-5935-3

Kellerman, E., & Sharwood, S. (1986). *Crosslinguistic influence in second language: an introduction*. Oxford, UK: Pergamon.

Kerek E., & Niemi P. (2009b). Learning to read in Russian: effects of orthographic complexity. *Journal of Research in Reading, Volume, 32*(2), 157–179. DOI: 10.1111/j.1467-9817.2008.01390.x

Kerek, E., & Niemi, P. (2009a). Russian orthography and learning to read. *Reading in a Foreign Language*, *21*(1), 1–21.

Kim, J., & Davis, C. (2003). Task effects in masked cross-script translation and phonological priming. *Journal of Memory and Language*, *49*(4), 484–499. doi:10.1016/S0749-596X(03)00093-7

Kim, K. H., Relkin, N. R., Lee, K.-M., & Hirch, J. (1997). Distinct cortical areas associated with native and second languages. *Nature*, *388*(6638), 171–174. doi:10.1038/40623 PMID:9217156

Kim, T. (2011). Korean elementary school students' English learning demotivation: A comparative survey study. *Asia Pacific Education Review*, *12*(1), 1–11. doi:10.1007/s12564-010-9113-1

Kinoshita, S., & Lupker, S. J. (2002). Effects of filler type in naming: Change in time-criterion or attentional control pathways? *Memory & Cognition*, *30*(8), 1277–1287. doi:10.3758/BF03213409 PMID:12661858

Kinoshita, S., & Lupker, S. J. (2007). Switch costs when reading aloud words and nonwords. *Psychonomic Bulletin & Review*, *14*(3), 449–454. doi:10.3758/BF03194087 PMID:17874586

Kjellmer, G. (1984). Some thoughts on collocational distinctiveness. In Corpus Linguistics (pp. 163-171). Amsterdam: Rodopi.

Kjellmer, G. (1987). Aspects of English Collocations. In Corpus Linguistics and Beyond (pp. 133-140). Amsterdam: Rodopi.

Koçak, N., Ergin, B. & Yalçın, H. (2014). 60-72 Aylık çocukların dil gelişim düzeyleri ve etki eden faktörlerin incelenmesi. *KMÜ Sosyal ve Ekonomik Araştırmalar Dergisi*, *16*, 100-106.

Kornev, A. N. (1995). *Дислексия и дисграфия у детей* [Dyslexia and dysgraphia in children]. St. Petersburg, Russia: MiM.

Kornev, A. N. (2003). *Нарушения чтения и письма у детей* [Difficulties in reading and writing in children]. St. Petersburg, Russia: Rech.

Kornev, A. N., Rakhlin, N., & Grigorenko, E. L. (2010). Dyslexia From a Cross-Linguistic and Cross-Cultural Perspective: The Case of Russian and Russia. *Learning Disabilities (Weston, Mass.)*, *8*(1), 41–69.

Kroll, J. F., Dijkstra, A., Janssen, N., & Schreifers, H. (2000). *Selecting the language in which to speak: Experiments on lexical access in bilingual production*. Paper presented at the 41st Annual meeting on the Psychonomic Society, New Orleans, LA.

Kroll, J. F., & Stewart, E. (1994). Category interference in translation and picture naming: Evidence for asymmetric connections between bilingual memory representations. *Journal of Memory and Language*, *33*(2), 149–174. doi:10.1006/jmla.1994.1008

La Heij, W., Dirkx, J., & Kramer, J. (1990). Categorical interference and associative priming in picture naming. *British Journal of Psychology*, *81*(4), 511–525. doi:10.1111/j.2044-8295.1990.tb02376.x

La Paro, K. M., Pianta, R. C., & Shulman, M. (2004). The classroom assessment scoring system: Findings from the prekindergarten year. *The Elementary School Journal*, *104*(5), 409–426. doi:10.1086/499760

Lacan, J. (1998). Formulações sobre a causalidade psíquica. In Escritos (pp. 152-194). Rio de Janeiro: Jorge Zahar.

Lacan, J. (1998). *Função e campo da fala e da linguagem em psicanálise, Escritos*. Rio de Janeiro: Jorge Zahar. (Original work published 1953)

Lacan, J. (1998). *O estádio do espelho como formador da função do eu, Escritos, Vera Ribeiro (trad.)*. Rio de Janeiro: Jorge Zahar. (Original work published 1949)

Larsen-Freeman, D. (1986). *Techniques and Principles in Language Teaching*. Oxford, UK: Oxford University Press.

Lee, N., & Schumann, J. H. (2005). The interactional instinct: The evolution and acquisition of language. Congress of the International Association for applied Linguistics, Madison, WI.

Leech, G. (1974). *Semantics*. Harmondsworth, UK: Penguin.

Lee, J. C., Skarakis-Doyle, E., & Dempsey, L. (2011). The Contributions of activity and occupation to young children's comprehension of picture books. *Journal of Occupational Science, 10*(3), 146–149. doi:10.1080/14427591.2003.9686522

Lee, J. H., & Macaro, E. (2013). Investigating Age in the Use of L1 or English-Only Instruction: Vocabulary Acquisition by Korean EFL Learners. *Modern Language Journal, 97*(4), 887–901. doi:10.1111/j.1540-4781.2013.12044.x

Lemhöfer, K., Dijkstra, T., Schriefers, H., Baayen, R. H., Grainger, J., & Zwitserlood, P. (2008). Native language influences on word recognition in a second language: A megastudy. *Journal of Experimental Psychology. Learning, Memory, and Cognition, 34*(1), 12–31. doi:10.1037/0278-7393.34.1.12 PMID:18194052

Lemos, C. (2002). Das vicissitudes da fala da criança e de sua investigação. *Cadernos de Estudos Linguísticos, 42*. Retrieved on October 13, 2012, from: http://www.iel.unicamp.br/revista/index.php/cel/article/view/1599/1178

Levelt, W. J. (2013). *A History of Psycholinguistics*. Oxford University Press.

Levelt, W. J., Roelofs, A., & Meyer, A. S. (1999). A theory of lexical access in speech production. *Behavioral and Brain Sciences, 22*(01), 1–75. doi:10.1017/S0140525X99001776 PMID:11301520

Levis, J. (2007). Computer technology in teaching and researching pronunciation. *Annual Review of Applied Linguistics, 27*, 184–202. doi:10.1017/S0267190508070098

Li, D. (2009). Activating strategies to fossilization for English learners in China. *English Language Teaching, 2*(4), 75–77. doi:10.5539/elt.v2n4p75

Lieberman, P. (2002). Human Language and Our Reptilian Brain: The Subcortical Bases of Speech, Syntax and Thought *Language in Society, 31*(4), 609–612.

Lightbown, P. M., & Spada, N. (2006). *How languages are learned*. London: Oxford University Press.

Lightbown, P., & Spada, N. (1999). *How Languages are Learned*. Oxford, UK: Oxford University Press.

Lindquist, K. A., MacCormack, J., & Shablack, H. (2015). The Role of Language in Emotion: Predictions From Psychological Constructionism. *Frontiers in Psychology*, *6*. doi:10.3389/fpsyg.2015.00444 PMID:25926809

Lin, L. (2014). Understanding pronunciation variations facing ESL students. *International Journal of Humanities and Social Science*, *4*(1), 16–20.

Liu, Y. (2016). The emotional geographies of language teaching. *Teacher Development*, *20*(4), 482–497. doi:10.1080/13664530.2016.1161660

Long, M. H. (1983). Native speaker/non-native speaker conversation in the second language classroom. *Working Papers in English as a Second Language.*

Lopez, M. N., & Cardenas, M. A. F. (2014). Emotions and their effects in a language learning Mexican context. *System*, *42*, 298–307. doi:10.1016/j.system.2013.12.006

Lui, Y. (2012). *On fossilization of non-English majors' speaking ability in multimedia assisted English class*. Paper presented at the International Conference on Education Technology and Computer, China. Retrieved from http://www.ipcsit.com/vol43/037-ICETC2012-T1045.pdf

Lundberg, I., Larsman, P., & Strid, A. (2012). Development of phonological awareness during the preschool year: The influence of gender and socio-economic status. *Reading and Writing*, *25*(2), 305–320. doi:10.1007/s11145-010-9269-4

Lupker, S. J. (1982). The role of phonetic and orthographic similarity in picture-word interference. *Canadian Journal of Psychology*, *36*(3), 349–367. doi:10.1037/h0080652 PMID:7172126

Lupker, S. J., Brown, P., & Colombo, L. (1997). Strategic control in a naming task: Changing routes or changing deadlines? *Journal of Experimental Psychology. Learning, Memory, and Cognition*, *23*(3), 570–590. doi:10.1037/0278-7393.23.3.570

Lyashevskaya, O., & Sharov, S. (2009). *The frequency dictionary of modern Russian language.* Moscow, Russia: Azbukovnik.

Ma, A. (2012). A study of the shaping of the 'emotion and attitude' domain in the new English language curriculum of China through an EFL textbook. *Pedagogy, Culture & Society*, *20*(2), 231–250. doi:10.1080/14681366.2012.688764

Macaro, E. (2001). *Learning Strategies in Foreign and Second Language Classrooms*. London: Continuum.

MacLeod, C. M. (1991). Half a century of research on the Stroop effect: An integrative review. *Psychological Bulletin*, *109*(2), 163–203. doi:10.1037/0033-2909.109.2.163 PMID:2034749

MacWhinney, B. (2000). *The CHILDES project: Tools for analyzing talk* (3rd ed.). Mahwah, NJ: Erlbaum.

Mägiste, E. (1984b). Stroop tasks and dichotic translation: The development of interference patterns in bilinguals. *Journal of Experimental Psychology. Learning, Memory, and Cognition*, *10*, 304–315. doi:10.1037/0278-7393.10.2.304

Mägiste, E. (1985). Development of intra- and interlingual interference in bilinguals. *Journal of Psycholinguistic Research*, *14*, 137–154. doi:10.1007/BF01067626

Major, R. C. (2008). Transfer in second language phonology. *Phonology and Second Language Acquisition*, *36*, 63-94.

Maniruzzaman, M. (2005). *Phonetic and phonological problems encountered by the Bengali speaking EFL learner: How can they be overcome?* Dhaka: Department of English at East West University.

Manzo, J. C. (2011). *Shared book reading styles and expressive and receptive vocabulary outcomes among low-income latino caregivers and young children* (Unpublished Doctoral Dissertation). Lehigh University.

Marchman, V. A., Martinez, L. Z., Hurtado, N., Grüter, T., & Fernald, A. (2016). Caregiver talk to young Spanish-English bilinguals: Comparing direct observation and parent-report measures of dual-language exposure. *Developmental Science*, 1–13. PMID:27197746

Marian, V., Blumenfeld, H. K., Mizrahi, E., Kania, U., & Cordes, A.-K. (2013). Multilingual Stroop performance: Effects of trilingualism and proficiency on inhibitory control. *International Journal of Multilingualism*, *10*(1), 82–104. doi:10.1080/14790718.2012.708037 PMID:24039546

Mashburn, A. J., Downer, J. T., Hamre, B. K., Justice, L. M., & Pianta, R. C. (2010). Consultation for teachers and children's language and literacy development during Pre-Kindergarten. *Applied Developmental Science*, *14*(4), 179–196. doi:10.1080/10888691.2010.516187

Maviş, İ. (2005). Çocukta dil edinim kuralları. In S. Topbaş (Ed.), Dil ve Kavram Gelişimi (pp. 31-61). Ankara: Kök Yayıncılık.

Maybin, J., & Watson, N. J. (2009). Children's literature: approaches and territories. The Open University.

McNamara, T. P., & Holbrook, J. B. (2003). *Semantic memory and priming*. Handbook of psychology. doi:10.1002/0471264385.wei0416

Meadows, B., & Marumatsu, Y. (2007). Native speaker or non-native speaker teacher? a report of student preferences in four different foreign language classrooms. *Arizona Working Papers in SLA & Testing*, (14), 95-109.

MEB. (2013). *Okul öncesi eğitim programı*. Milli Eğitim Bakanlığı Talim Terbiye Kurumu.

Menyuk, P., & Brisk, E. M. (2005a). Language development in early childhood – the preschool years: 3-5. In Language development and education (pp. 38-58). Palgrave Macmillan.

Meyer, D. E., & Schvaneveldt, R. W. (1971). Facilitation in recognizing pairs of words: Evidence of a dependence between retrieval operations. *Journal of Experimental Psychology, 90*(2), 227–234. doi:10.1037/h0031564 PMID:5134329

Miaille, M. (1979). *Uma Introdução Crítica ao Direito* (A. Prata, Trans.). Lisboa: Moraes Editores.

Molnar, M., Ibáñez-Molina, A., & Carreiras, M. (2015). Interlocutor Identitiy Affects Language Activation in Bilinguals. *Journal of Memory and Language, 81*, 91–104. doi:10.1016/j.jml.2015.01.002

Monaghan, J., & Ellis, A. W. (2002a). What exactly interacts with spelling-sound consistency in word naming? *Journal of Experimental Psychology. Learning, Memory, and Cognition, 28*(1), 183–206. doi:10.1037/0278-7393.28.1.183 PMID:11827080

Monaghan, J., & Ellis, A. W. (2002b). Age of acquisition and the completeness of phonological representations. *Reading and Writing, 15*(7/8), 759–788. doi:10.1023/A:1020958722472

Monsell, S., Patterson, K. E., Graham, A., Hughes, C. H., & Milroy, R. (1992). Lexical and sublexical translation of spelling to sound: Strategic anticipation of lexical status. *Journal of Experimental Psychology. Learning, Memory, and Cognition, 18*(3), 452–467. doi:10.1037/0278-7393.18.3.452

Monte-Serrat, D. (2013). *Letramento e discurso jurídico, Tese defendida no Departamento de Psicologia da Faculdade de Filosofia, Ciências e Letras da Universidade de São Paulo, Campus Ribeirão Preto, FFCLRP-USP, em junho de. Orientadora Profa. Dra. Leda VerdianiTfouni.* Disponível na Biblioteca Digital de Teses e Dissertações da Universidade de São Paulo: http://www.teses.usp.br/teses/disponiveis/59/59137/tde-14032013-104350/

Monte-Serrat, D. (2015). *Relatório de pesquisa como Pesquisadora Colaboradora em Linguística, do Instituto de Estudos da Linguagem da Universidade Estadual de Campinas - IEL-UNICAMP, supervisora Profa. Dra. Maria Irma HadlerCoudry.* Não publicado.

Morley, J. (1991). The pronunciation component in teaching English to speakers of other languages. *TESOL Quarterly, 25*(3), 481–520. doi:10.2307/3586981

Morrison, C. M., & Ellis, A. W. (1999). Age of acquisition, lexical processing and ageing: Changes across the lifespan. In *Proceedings of the 21st Annual Meeting of the Cognitive Science Society*. Mahwah, NJ: Lawrence Erlbaum Associates.

Morrison, C. M., & Ellis, A. W. (2000). Real age of acquisition effects in word naming and lexical decision. *British Journal of Psychology, 91*(2), 167–180. doi:10.1348/000712600161763 PMID:10832512

Morrison, C. M., Ellis, A. W., & Quinlan, P. T. (1992). Age of acquisition, not word frequency, affects object naming, not object recognition. *Memory & Cognition, 20*(6), 705–714. doi:10.3758/BF03202720 PMID:1435273

Morton, J. (1969). Interaction of information in word recognition. *Psychological Review*, *76*(2), 165–178. doi:10.1037/h0027366

Munro, J., & Derwing, M. (1995). Foreign accent, comprehensibility and intelligibility in the speech of second language learners. *Language Learning*, *45*(1), 73–97. doi:10.1111/j.1467-1770.1995.tb00963.x

Naama, A. (2011). An analysis of errors made by Yemeni University students in the English consonants-clusters system. *Damaxus University Journal*, *27*(3), 145–161.

Naigles, L. R., & Hoff-Ginsberg, E. (1998). Why are some verbs learned before other verbs-Effects of input frequency and structure on children's early verb use. *Journal of Child Language*, *25*(1), 95–120. doi:10.1017/S0305000997003358 PMID:9604570

Neaum, S. (2010). Child development for early childhood studies. In Understanding children's development (pp. 33-41). Glasgow, UK: Learning Matters Ltd.

Neely, J. H. (1991). Semantic priming effects in visual word recognition: A selective review of current findings and theories. *Basic Processes in Reading: Visual Word Recognition, 11*, 264-336.

Neely, J. H. (1977). Semantic priming and retrieval from lexical memory: Roles of inhibitionless spreading activation and limited-capacity attention. *Journal of Experimental Psychology. General*, *106*(3), 226–254. doi:10.1037/0096-3445.106.3.226

Neely, J. H., & Kahan, T. A. (2001). Is semantic activation automatic? A critical re-evaluation. In H. L. Roediger III, J. S. Nairne, I. Neath, & A. M. Surprenant (Eds.), *Science conference series. The nature of remembering: Essays in honor of Robert G. Crowder* (pp. 69–93). Academic Press. doi:10.1037/10394-005

Nelson, C. (1982). Intelligibility and non-native varieties of English. In B. B. Kachru (Ed.), *The other tongue: English across cultures* (pp. 58–73). Urbana, IL: University of Illinois Press.

Nelson, K. (1973). Structure and strategy in learning to talk. *Monographs of the Society for Research in Child Development*, *38*(1/2), 149. doi:10.2307/1165788

Nemati, M., & Taghizadeh, M. (2013). Exploring Similarities and Differences between L1 and L2. *International Research Journal of Applied and Basic Sciences*, *4*(9), 2477–2483.

Neuner, G. (2002). *Policy Approaches to English. Language Policies*. Council of Europe.

Nickels, L., Biedermann, B., Fieder, N., & Schiller, N. O. (2015). The Lexical-Syntactic Representation of Numbers. *Language, Cognition and Neuroscience*, *30*(3), 287–304. doi:10.1080/23273798.2013.879191

Ni, H. (2012). The effects of affective factors in SLA and pedagogical implications. *Theory and Practice in Language Studies*, *2*(7), 1508–1513. doi:10.4304/tpls.2.7.1508-1513

Niolaki, G. Z., Masterson, J., & Terzopoulos, A. R. (2014). Spelling improvement through letter-sound and whole-word training in two multilingual Greek-and English-speaking children. *Multilingual Education*, *4*(1), 1–23. doi:10.1186/s13616-014-0020-3

Nishimoto, T., Miyawaki, K., Ueda, T., Une, Y., & Takahashi, M. (2005). Japanese normative set of 359 pictures. *Behavior Research Methods*, *37*(3), 398–416. doi:10.3758/BF03192709 PMID:16405135

Nisi, M., Longoni, A. M., & Snodgrass, J. G. (2000). Italian measurement on the relation of name, familiarity, and acquisition age for the 260 figures of Snodgrass and Vanderwart. *Giornale Italiano di Psicologia*, *27*, 205–218.

Norris, A. J. (2003). Looking at clasrrom management through a social and emotional learning lens. *Theory into Practice*, *42*(4), 313–318. doi:10.1207/s15430421tip4204_8

O'Grady, W. (2011). Relative Clauses: Processing and acquisition. In E. Kidd (Ed.), *The Acquisition of Relative Clauses: Processing, Typology and function*. John Benjamins Publishing Company. doi:10.1075/tilar.8.03gra

Odlin, T. (1989). *Language Transfer*. Cambridge, UK: Cambridge University Press. doi:10.1017/CBO9781139524537

Oers, B., & Poland, M. (2007). Schematising activities as a means for encouraging young children to think abstractly. *Mathematics Education Research Journal*, *19*(2), 10–22. doi:10.1007/BF03217453

Ortaçtepe, D. (2013). Formulaic language and conceptual socialization: The Route to becoming nativelike in L2. *System*, *41*(3), 852–865. doi:10.1016/j.system.2013.08.006

Ortega, L. (2009). *Understanding second language acquisition*. London: Hodder Education.

Ostrower, F. (2013). *Acasos e criação artística*. Campinas: Ed. Unicamp.

Öztan Ulusoy, Y. (2012). Bilgiyi işleme kuramı ve yansımaları. In B. Oral (Ed.), Öğrenme öğretme kuram ve yaklaşımları. Ankara: Pegem Akademi Yayıncılık.

Öztürk, Y. (2013). Sembolik Düşünce; Okul Öncesi Yıllarda Oyun, Dil ve Okuryazarlık. In Erken Çocukluk Döneminde Gelişim (pp. 254-293). Ankara: Nobel Akademik Yayıncılık.

Öztürk, Y., & Köse, D. G. (2016). Turkish and Native English Academic Writers' Use of Lexical Bundles. *Journal of Language and Linguistic Studies*, *12*(1305), 149–165.

Paap, K. R., & Noel, R. W. (1991). Dual-rote models of print to sound: Still a good horse race. *Psychological Research*, *53*(1), 13–24. doi:10.1007/BF00867328

Padilha, A. M. (2000). *Bianca. O ser simbólico: para além dos limites da deficiência mental.* Tese de Doutorado, Faculdade de Educaçāo, UNICAMP, 2000. Retrieved on March 3, 2014, from: http://www.vigotski.net/ditebras/padilha.pdf

Paivio, A., Clark, J. M., & Lambert, W. E. (1988). Bilingual dual-coding theory and semantic repetition effects on recall. *Journal of Experimental Psychology. Learning, Memory, and Cognition*, *14*(1), 163–172. doi:10.1037/0278-7393.14.1.163

Paivio, A., Yuille, J. C., & Madigan, S. A. (1968). Concreteness, imagery and meaningfulness values for 925 words. *Journal of Experimental Psychology Monograph*, *76*(3).

Paradis, J. (2011). Individual differences in child English second language acquisition: Comparing child-Internal and child-external factors. *Linguistic Approaches to Bilingualism*, *1*(3), 213–237. doi:10.1075/lab.1.3.01par

Paradis, J., & Jia, R. (2016). Bilingual children's long-term outcomes in English as a second language: Language environment factors shape individual differences in catching up with monolinguals. *Developmental Science*, 1–15. PMID:27320539

Parker, F., & Riley, K. (2005). *Linguistics for Non-Linguists*. Pearson.

Park, S. J., & Abelmann, N. (2004). Class and Cosmopolitan Striving: Mothers' Management of English Education in South Korea. *Anthropological Quarterly*, *77*(4), 645–672. doi:10.1353/anq.2004.0063

Patton, M. (1997). *Utilizaton-focused evaluation: the new century text* (3rd ed.). Thousand Oaks, CA: Sage Publications.

Pavlenko, A. (2005). *Emotions and Multilingualism*. New York: Cambridge University Press.

Pavlenko, A. (Ed.). (2009). *The bilingual mental lexicon: Interdisciplinary approaches*. Tonawanda, NY: Multilingual Matters.

Pêcheux, M. (1998). *Semântica e Discurso: uma crítica à afirmação do óbvio*. Campinas: Ed. Unicamp.

Pêcheux, M. (2002). *O Discurso: estrutura ou acontecimento?* (3rd ed.). Campinas, SP: Pontes.

Pêcheux, M., & Fichant, M. (1971). *Sur l'histoire des sciences*. Paris: Maspero.

Pêcheux, M., & Fuchs, C. (1997). *A propósito da análise automática do discurso: atualização e perspectivas. In Por uma análise automática do discurso - uma introdução à obra de Michel Pêcheux*. Campinas: UNICAMP. (Original work published 1975)

Pennington, M. C. (1996). *Phonology in English language teaching: An international approach*. London: Longman.

Pennington, M. C. (1999). Computer aided pronunciation pedagogy: Promise, limitations, directions. *Computer Assisted Language Learning*, *12*(5), 427–440. doi:10.1076/call.12.5.427.5693

Pentimonti, J. M., & Justice, L. M. (2010). Teachers' use of scaffolding strategies during read alouds in the preschool classroom. *Early Childhood Education Journal*, 1–8.

Pentimonti, J. M., Zucker, T. A., & Justice, L. M. (2011). What are preschool teachers reading in their classrooms? *Reading Psychology*, *32*(3), 197–236. doi:10.1080/02702711003604484

Pentimonti, J. M., Zucker, T. A., Justice, L. M., Petscher, Y., Piasta, S. B., & Kaderavek, J. N. (2012). A Standardized tool for assessing the quality of clssroom-based shared reading: Systematic Assessment of Book Reading (SABR). *Early Childhood Research Quarterly*, *27*(3), 512–528. doi:10.1016/j.ecresq.2011.12.007

Perlovsky, L. (2009). Language and Cognition. *Neural Networks*, *22*(3), 247–257. doi:10.1016/j.neunet.2009.03.007 PMID:19419838

Perlovsky, L. (2009). Language and Emotions: Emotional Sapir-Whorf Hypothesis. *Neural Networks*, *22*(5-6), 518–526. doi:10.1016/j.neunet.2009.06.034 PMID:19616406

Pickering, M. J., & Garrod, S. (2013). An integrated theory of language production and comprehension. *Behavioral and Brain Sciences*, *36*(04), 329–347. doi:10.1017/S0140525X12001495 PMID:23789620

Pind, J., Jónsdóttir, H., Tryggvadóttir, H. B., & Jónsson, F. (2000). Icelandic norms for the Snodgrass and Vanderwart (1980) pictures: Name and image agreement, familiarity, and age of acquisition. *Scandinavian Journal of Psychology*, *41*(1), 41–48. doi:10.1111/1467-9450.00169 PMID:10731842

Pinter, A. (2006). *Teaching Young Language Learners*. Oxford, UK: Oxford University Press.

Place, S. & Hoff, E. (2015). Effects and non-effects of input in bilingual environments on dual language skills in 2 1/2-year-olds. *Bilingualism: Language and Cognition*.

Place, S., & Hoff, E. (2011). Properties of dual language exposure that influence 2-year-olds' bilingual proficiency. *Child Development*, *82*(6), 1834–1849. doi:10.1111/j.1467-8624.2011.01660.x PMID:22004372

Potter, M. C., So, K. F., Von Eckardt, B., & Feldman, L. B. (1984). Lexical and conceptual representation in beginning and proficient bilinguals. *Journal of Verbal Learning and Verbal Behavior*, *23*(1), 23–38. doi:10.1016/S0022-5371(84)90489-4

Poulisse, N., & Bongaerts, T. (1994). First language use in second language production. *Applied Linguistics*, *15*(1), 36–57. doi:10.1093/applin/15.1.36

Preston, M. S., & Lambert, W. E. (1969). Interlingual interference in a bilingual version of the Stroop color-word task. *Journal of Verbal Learning and Verbal Behavior*, *8*(2), 295–301. doi:10.1016/S0022-5371(69)80079-4

Rahal, A. (2016). *Phonetic Fossilization in the Speech of Advanced Tunisian English Students: The English Department of Kairouan as a case study* (Unpublished MA thesis). Faculty of Letters and Humanities of Kairouan.

Rahal, A. (2014). The fossilized pronunciation of the schwa sound in the speech of Advanced Tunisian English learners: Problem and causes. *International Journal of Humanities and Cultural Studies*, *1*(1), 1–6.

Raman, I. (2006). On the Age of Acquisition Effects in Word Naming and Orthographic Transparency: Mapping specific or universal? *Visual Cognition*, *13*(7/8), 1044–1053. doi:10.1080/13506280500153200

Raman, I., & Baluch, B. (2001). Semantic Effects as a Function of Reading Skill in Word Naming of a Transparent Orthography. *Reading and Writing*, *14*(7/8), 599–614. doi:10.1023/A:1012004729180

Raman, I., Baluch, B., & Besner, D. (2004). On the Control of Visual Word Recognition: Changing Routes Versus Changing Deadlines. *Memory & Cognition*, *32*(3), 489–500. doi:10.3758/BF03195841 PMID:15285131

Raman, I., Baluch, B., & Sneddon, P. (1996). What is the cognitive system's preferred route for deriving phonology from print? *European Psychologist*, *1*(3), 221–227. doi:10.1027/1016-9040.1.3.221

Raman, I., Raman, E., Ikier, S., Kilecioglu, E., Uzun, D., & Zeyveli, S. (under review). Differential Effects of Age of Acquisition and Frequency on Memory. *Evidence from Free Recall of Pictures and Words in Turkish.*

Raman, I., Raman, E., & Mertan, B. (2014). A standardised set of 260 pictures for Turkish: Norms of name and image agreement, age of acquisition, visual complexity and conceptual familiarity. *Behavior Research Methods*, *46*(2), 588–595. doi:10.3758/s13428-013-0376-4 PMID:23943583

Rastle, K., & Coltheart, M. (1999). Serial and strategic effects in reading aloud. *Journal of Experimental Psychology. Human Perception and Performance*, *25*(2), 482–503. doi:10.1037/0096-1523.25.2.482

Reese, E., & Cox, A. (1999). Quality of book reading affects children's emergent literacy. *Developmental Psychology*, *35*(1), 20–28. doi:10.1037/0012-1649.35.1.20 PMID:9923461

Reeve, J. M. (2005). *Understanding motivation and emotion*. Hoboken, NJ: John Wiley & Sons.

Reilly, S., Wake, M., Ukoumunne, O. C., Bavin, E., Prior, M., Cini, E., & Bretherton, L. et al. (2010). Predicting language outcomes at 4 years of age: Findings from early language in Victoria study. *Pediatrics*, *126*(6), e1530–e1537. doi:10.1542/peds.2010-0254 PMID:21059719

Reinders, H. (2012). *Towards a definition of intake in second language acquisition*. Applied Research in English.

Reynolds, M., & Besner, D. (2008). Contextual Effects on Reading Aloud: Evidence for Pathway Control. *Journal of Experimental Psychology. Learning, Memory, and Cognition*, *34*(1), 50–64. doi:10.1037/0278-7393.34.1.50 PMID:18194054

Richard, J. C., & Rodgers, T. S. (2001). Approaches and Methods in Language Teaching. United States of America. Cambridge. doi:10.1017/CBO9780511667305

Richards, J. C., & Schmidt, R. (2002). *Longman dictionary of language teaching and applied linguistics* (3rd ed.). London: Longman.

Ringbom, H. (1987). *The role of the first language in foreign language learning*. Clevedon, UK: Multilingual Matters.

Ringbom, H. (2006). The Importance of different types of similarity in transfer studies. In J. Arabski (Ed.), *Cross-linguistic influences in the second language lexicon* (pp. 36–45). Clevedon, UK: Multilingual Matters.

Ringbom, H. (2007). The importance of cross-linguistic similarities. *Language Teaching*, *31*(9), 3–5.

Ritchie, W. (1978). The Right Roof Constraint in an adult-acquired language. In W. Ritchie (Ed.), *Second language acquisition research: Issues and implications*. London: Academic Press.

Rivera, T. (2009). *Ensaio sobre o espaço e o sujeito. Lygia Clark e a psicanálise*. Retrieved on August 3, 2009, from: http://www.scielo.br/scielo.php?pid=S1516-14982008000200004&script=sci_arttext

Robert, E., & Owens, J. R. (2012). Language development an introduction. In The Territory (pp. 3-35). Upper Saddle River, NJ: Pearson Education Inc.

Roberts, S. G. (2013). *Evolutionary approach to bilingualism* (PhD thesis). University of Edinburgh, United Kingdom.

Rodriguez-Fornelss, A., Van der Lugt, A., Rotte, M., Britti, B., Heinze, H. J., & Münte, T. F. (2005). Second language interferes with word production in fluent bilinguals: Brain potential and functional imaging evidence. *Journal of Cognitive Neuroscience*, *17*(3), 422–433. doi:10.1162/0898929053279559 PMID:15814002

Roelofs, A. (1992). A spreading-activation theory of lemma retrieval in speaking: Modeling attentional control in the Stroop task. *Psychological Review*, *110*, 88–125. doi:10.1037/0033-295X.110.1.88 PMID:12529058

Roelofs, A. (2009). Attention and Facilitation: Converging Information Versus Inadvertent Reading in Stroop Task Performance. *Journal of Experimental Psychology. Learning, Memory, and Cognition*, *36*(2), 411–422. doi:10.1037/a0018523 PMID:20192539

Rosinski, R. R. (1977). Picture-word interference is semantically based. *Child Development*, *48*(2), 643–647. doi:10.2307/1128667

Rosinski, R. R., Golinkoff, R. M., & Kukish, K. S. (1975). Automatic semantic processing in a picture-word interference task. *Child Development*, *46*(1), 247–253. doi:10.2307/1128859

Rosselli, M., Ardila, A., Santisi, M. N., Arecco, M. D. R., Salvatierra, J., Conde, A., & Lenis, B. O. N. I. E. (2002). Stroop effect in Spanish–English bilinguals. *Journal of the International Neuropsychological Society*, *8*(06), 819–827. doi:10.1017/S1355617702860106 PMID:12240746

Rossion, B., & Pourtois, G. (2004). Revisiting Snodgrass and Vanderwart's object pictorial set: The role of surface detail in basic-level object recognition. *Perception*, *33*(2), 217–236. doi:10.1068/p5117 PMID:15109163

Roth, F., Troia, A., Wortington, C., & Handy, D. (2006). Promoting awareness of sounds in speech (Pass): The effects of intervention and stimulus characteristics on the blending performance of preschool children with communication impairments. *Learning Disability Quarterly*, *29*(2), 64–78. doi:10.2307/30035536

Roudinesco, E. (1998). *Dicionário de psicanálise, trad.* Vera Ribeiro, Brazil: Jorge Zahar.

Roux, P. W. (2013). *Words in the mind: Exploring the relationship between word association and lexical development.* Retrieved June 26, 2014, from http://www.rcube.ritsumei.ac.jp/.../8-

Rudasill Moritz, K., Rimm-Kaufman, S. E., Justice, L. M., & Pence, K. (2010). Temperament and language skills as predictors of teacher-child relationship quality in preschool. *Early Education and Development*, *17*(2), 271–291. doi:10.1207/s15566935eed1702_4

Saban, A., Korkmaz, İ., & Akbaşlı, S. (2004). Öğretmen adaylarının mesleki kaygıları. *Eğitim Araştırmaları*, *5*(17), 198–209.

Sanfeliù, M. C., & Fernandez, A. (1996). A set of 254 Snodgrass–Vanderwart pictures standardized for Spanish: Norms for name agreement, image agreement, familiarity, and visual complexity. *Behavior Research Methods, Instruments, & Computers*, *28*(4), 537–555. doi:10.3758/BF03200541

Scarborough, D. L., Gerard, L., & Cortese, C. (1984). Independence of lexical access in bilingual word recognition. *Journal of Verbal Learning and Verbal Behavior*, *23*(1), 84–99. doi:10.1016/S0022-5371(84)90519-X

Scarcella, R. C., & Oxford, R. L. (1992). *The Tapestry of Language Learning: The Individual in the Communicative Classroom.* Heinle & Heinle.

Schickedanz, J. A. (1999). *Much more than the ABC's: The early stages of reading and writing.* Washington, DC: National Association for the Education of Young Children.

Schmidt, R. (1995). *Attention and Awareness in Foreign Language Learning.* Second Language Teaching & Curriculum Center University of Hawaii.

Schmitt, N. (2010). *Researching Vocabulary: A Vocabulary Research Manual.* Palgrave Press. doi:10.1057/9780230293977

Schonell, F. J. (1971). *Reading and Spelling Tests.* Edinburgh, UK: Oliver and Boyd.

Schoonbaert, S., Duyck, W., Brysbaert, M., & Hartsuiker, R. J. (2009). Semantic and translation priming from a first language to a second and back: Making sense of the findings. *Memory & Cognition*, *37*(5), 569–586. doi:10.3758/MC.37.5.569 PMID:19487749

Schoon, İ., Parsons, S., Rush, R., & Law, J. (2010). Childhood language skills and adult literacy: A 29 year follow-up study. *Pediatrics*, *125*(3).

Schrauf, W. R., & Rubin, D. C. (1998). Bilingual Autobiographical Memory in Older Adult Immigrants: A Test of Cognitive Explanations of the Reminiscence Bump. *Journal of Memory and Language, 39*(3), 437–457. doi:10.1006/jmla.1998.2585

Schriefers, H., Meyer, A. S., & Levelt, W. J. (1990). Exploring the time course of lexical access in language production: Picture-word interference studies. *Journal of Memory and Language, 29*(1), 86–102. doi:10.1016/0749-596X(90)90011-N

Scott, W. A., & Ytreberg, L. H. (1997). *Teaching English to Children.* London: Longman.

Scovel, T. (1999). The younger the better myth and bilingual education. In R. Gonzales (Ed.), *Language Ideologies. Critical Perspectives on the English only Movement.* Urbana, IL: National Council of Teachers of English.

Seidenberg, M. S., & McClelland, J. L. (1989). A distributed, developmental model of word recognition and naming. *Psychological Review, 96*(4), 523–568. doi:10.1037/0033-295X.96.4.523 PMID:2798649

Selinker, L. (1972). Interlanguage. *International Journal of Applied Linguistics, 10*, 203–230.

Selinker, L. (1992). *Rediscovering Interlanguage.* London: Longman Group UK Limited.

Selinker, L. (1996). *Fossilization: What We Think We Know.* London: Longman Group UK Limited.

Senemoğlu, N. (2012). Gelişim Öğrenme ve Öğretim. Ankara: Pegem Akademi.

Senemoğlu, N. (2011). *Gelişim, Öğrenme ve Öğretim: Kuramdan Uygulamaya.* Ankara: Pegem Akademi.

Servizzi, K. M. (2013). *Teachers' cognitive demands and preschool students's use of thinking strategies during interactive book reading* (Unpublished Doctoral Dissertation). Ball State University.

Setter, J., & Jenkins, J. (2005). State-of-the-art review article. *Language Teaching, 38*(1), 1–17. doi:10.1017/S026144480500251X

Shanks, K., & Hoff, E. (2015). *Qualities of Mothers' Native and Non-native Child-directed Speech in Spanish- English Bilingual Households.* Poster presented at BUCLD.

Shi, X. (2007). Intercultural Language Socialization: Theory and Methodology. *Intercultural Communication Studies, 16*(1), 230.

Sholl, A., Sankaranarayanan, A., & Kroll, J. F. (1995). Transfer between picture naming and translation: A test of asymmetries in bilingual memory. *Psychological Science, 6*(1), 45–49. doi:10.1111/j.1467-9280.1995.tb00303.x

Signorini, I. (2001). Construindo com a escrita "outras cenas de fala". In *Signorini (org.), Investigando a relação oral/escrito e as teorias do letramento* (pp. 97–134). Campinas: Mercado das Letras.

Silva, R., & Brandão, D. (2011). Nas rodas da avaliação educadora. In R. Campos & J. Furtado (Eds.), Desafios da avaliação de programas e serviços em saúde. Unicamp.

Silva, M. (2001). *Alfabetização, escrita e colonização, InHistória das ideias linguísticas*. Ed. Unemat.

Silverberg, S., & Samuel, A. G. (2004). The effect of age of second language acquisition on the representation and processing of second language words. *Journal of Memory and Language*, *51*(3), 381–398. doi:10.1016/j.jml.2004.05.003

Simon-Maeda, A. (1995). Language awareness: Use/misuse of loan-words in the English language in Japan. *The Internet TESL Journal, 1*(2). Retrieved from http://www.aitech.ac.jp/~iteslj/

Sinclair, J. (1991). *Corpus, Concordance, Collocation*. Oxford University Press.

Singleton, D. (1999). *Exploring the Second Language Mental Lexicon*. Cambridge, UK: CUP. doi:10.1017/CBO9781139524636

Smaoui, Ch., & Rahal, A. (2015). The *Fossilized Pronunciation* of the /3:/ Sound in the Speech of Intermediate *Tunisian* English Students: Problem, Reasons and Suggested Solution. *International Journal of English Language and Translation Studies*, *3*(1), 70–79.

Smith, E. E., Shoben, E. J., & Rips, L. J. (1974). Structure and process in semantic memory: A featural model for semantic decisions. *Psychological Review*, *81*(3), 214–241. doi:10.1037/h0036351

Smith, L. E., & Rafiqzad, K. (1979). English for cross-cultural communication: The question of intelligibility. *TESOL Quarterly*, *5*(3), 371–380. doi:10.2307/3585884

Smith, M. C., & Magee, L. E. (1980). Tracing the time course of picture-word processing. *Journal of Experimental Psychology. General*, *4*(4), 373–392. doi:10.1037/0096-3445.109.4.373 PMID:6449530

Smith, P. K., Wigboldus, D. H. J., & Dijksterhuis, A. (2008). Abstract thinking increases one's sesnse of power. *Journal of Experimental Social Psychology*, *44*(2), 378–385. doi:10.1016/j.jesp.2006.12.005

Snodgrass, J. G., & Vanderwart, M. (1980). A standardized set of 260 pictures: Norms for name agreement, image agreement, familiarity, and visual complexity. *Journal of Experimental Psychology. Human Learning and Memory*, *6*(2), 174–215. doi:10.1037/0278-7393.6.2.174 PMID:7373248

Sperber, R. D., McCauley, C., Ragain, R. D., & Weil, C. M. (1979). Semantic priming effects on picture and word processing. *Memory & Cognition*, *7*(5), 339–345. doi:10.3758/BF03196937

Sroufe, A., Cooper, R., & Marshall, M. (1996). *Child Development: It's Nature and Course*. New York: McGraw-Hill, Inc.

Starkey, H. (2002). Guide for the development of language education policies in Europe, from linguistic diversity to plurilingual education In *Reference Study in Democratic Citizenship, Languages, Diversity and Human Rights.* Council of Europe. Retrieved August 9, 2010, from http://www.coe.int/t/dg4/linguistics/Source/StarkeyEN.pdf

Starreveld, P. A., & La Heij, W. (1995). Semantic interference, orthographic facilitation, and their interaction in naming tasks. *Journal of Experimental Psychology. Learning, Memory, and Cognition, 21*(3), 686–698. doi:10.1037/0278-7393.21.3.686

Starreveld, P. A., & La Heij, W. (1996). Time-course analysis of semantic and orthographic context effects in picture naming. *Journal of Experimental Psychology. Learning, Memory, and Cognition, 22*(4), 896–918. doi:10.1037/0278-7393.22.4.896

Stevick, E., Morley, J., & Wallace Robinett, B. (1975). Round robin on the teaching of pronunciation. *TESOL Quarterly, 9*(1), 81–88. doi:10.2307/3586016

Strain, E., Patterson, K., & Seidenberg, M. S. (1995). Semantic effects in single word naming. *Journal of Experimental Psychology. Learning, Memory, and Cognition, 21*(5), 1140–1154. doi:10.1037/0278-7393.21.5.1140 PMID:8744959

Strijkers, K., & Costa, A. (2016). On Words and Brains: Linking psycholinguistics with neural dynamics in speech production. *Language, Cognition and Neuroscience, 31*(4), 524–535. doi:10.1080/23273798.2016.1158845

Stroop, J. R. (1935). Studies in interference in serial verbal reactions. *Journal of Experimental Psychology, 18*(6), 643–661. doi:10.1037/h0054651

Sucaromana, U. (2012). Contribution to language teaching and learning: A review of emotional intelligence. *English Language Teaching, 5*(9), 54–57. doi:10.5539/elt.v5n9p54

Sumiya, H., & Healy, A. F. (2004). Phonology in the bilingual Stroop effect. *Memory & Cognition, 32*(5), 752–758. doi:10.3758/BF03195865 PMID:15552352

Switalski, S. O. (2012). *An investigation of the additive benefits of parent dialogic reading techniques in older preschool children* (Unpublished Doctoral Dissertation). University of Duquesne.

Szubko-Sitarek, W. (2015). *Multilingual lexical recognition in the mental lexicon of third language users.* Berlin: Springer-Verlag. doi:10.1007/978-3-642-32194-8

Tabossi, P., & Laghi, L. (1992). Semantic priming in the pronunciation of words in two writing systems: Italian and English. *Memory & Cognition, 20*(3), 303–313. doi:10.3758/BF03199667 PMID:1508055

Tahereen, T. (2015). Challenges in teaching pronunciation at tertiary level in Bangladesh. *International Journal of English language & Translation Studies, 3*(1), 9-20. Retrieved from http://www.eltsjournal.org

Tanck, S. (2002). Speech act sets of refusal and complaint: A comparison of native and non-native English speakers' production. Studies in Second Language Acquisition.

Taner, M., & Başal, H. A. (2005). Farklı sosyoekonomik düzeylerde okul öncesi eğitim alan ve almayan ilköğretim birinci sınıf öğrencilerinin dil gelişimlerinin cinsiyete gore karşılaştırılması. *Eğitim Fakültesi Dergisi, 18*(2), 395–420.

Tarone, E. (2006). Interlanguage. Elsevier Ltd.

Tfouni, L., & Carreira. (2010, July). O sujeito submetido à linguagem. *Revista Investigações da Universidade Federal de Pernambuco, 20*(2).

Tfouni, L., & Monte-Serrat, D. (2010). Letramento e Discurso Jurídico. In *Virgínia Colares*. Recife: Ed universitária da UFPE.

Tfouni, L., Carvalho, & Monte-Serrat, D. (2017). *A prática da oralidade como lugar de resistência*. Submetido à RevistaEducaçãoemFoco UEMG.

Tfouni, L. (1992). *Letramento e analfabetismo, Tese de Livre-Docência*. Ribeirão Preto: FFCLRP-USP.

Tfouni, L. (2005). *Letramento e alfabetização*. São Paulo: Ed. Cortez.

The Anatomy of the Brain. (2015). Retrieved on April 12, 2015, from: http://psychology.about.com/od/biopsychology/ss/brainstructure_2.htm

The Brain and Its Functions. (2015). Retrieved on April 9, 2015, from: http://mybrainonline.ca/?page=3

Therriault, D. J., Yaxley, R. H., & Zwaan, R. A. (2009). The role of color diagnosticity in object recognition and representation. *Cognitive Processing, 10*(4), 335–342. doi:10.1007/s10339-009-0260-4 PMID:19471986

Torti, C. D. (2006). *The relationship between the quality of the early childhood classroom environment and vocabulary development in young children learning English as a second language* (Unpublished Doctoral Dissertation). Texas A&M University.

Traxler, M. J., & Gernsbacher, M. A. (2006). *Handbook of Psycholinguistics*. Oxford, UK: Elsevier.

Trewhella, J. (2016). *The challenges and opportunities for multidisciplinary research in a world of complex interdependent systems*. Retrieved on September 16, 2016, from: https://globalhighered.wordpress.com/2009/06/26/multidisciplinary-research-an-essential-driver-for-innovation/

Tsao, T. L. (2002). *Perceptual learning style preference and learning strategy use among Taiwanese senior high school EFL learners* (Master's thesis). National Taiwan Normal University.

Tsaparina, D., Bonin, P., & Méot, A. (2011). Russian norms for name agreement, image agreement for the colorized version of the Snodgrass and Vanderwart pictures and age of acquisition, conceptual familiarity, and imageability scores for modal object names. *Behavior Research Methods, 43*(4), 1085–1099. doi:10.3758/s13428-011-0121-9 PMID:21717267

Tsujimura, N. (1996). *An introduction to Japanese linguistics*. Oxford, UK: Blackwell publishing.

Tzelgov, J., Henik, A., & Leiser, D. (1990). Controlling Stroop interference: Evidence from a bilingual task. *Journal of Experimental Psychology, 16*, 760–771.

Ur, P. (1996). *A course in language teaching: practice and theory*. Cambridge, UK: Cambridge University Press.

Uyanık, Ö., & Kandır, A. (2010). Okul öncesi dönemde erken akademik beceriler. *Kuramsal Eğitimbilim, 3*(2), 118–134.

Valette, R. M. (1991). Proficiency and the prevention of fossilization. *Modern Language Journal, 75*(3), 325–328. doi:10.1111/j.1540-4781.1991.tb05363.x

Valian, V., & Lyman, C. (2013). Young children's acquisition of wh-questions: The role of structured input. *Journal of Child Language, 30*(1), 117–143. doi:10.1017/S0305000902005457 PMID:12718295

Van Heuven, W. J. B., Dijkstra, A., & Grainger, J. (1998). Orthographic neighborhood effects in bilingual word recognition. *Journal of Memory and Language, 39*(3), 458–483. doi:10.1006/jmla.1998.2584

Verga, L., & Kotz, S. A. (2013). How relevant is social interaction in second language learning? *Frontiers in Human Neuroscience, 7*, 550–560. doi:10.3389/fnhum.2013.00550 PMID:24027521

Vernon-Feagns, L., Garrett-Peters, P., Willoughby, M., & Mills-Koonce, R. (2012). Chaos, poverty, and parenting: Predictors of early language development. *Early Childhood Research Quarterly, 27*(3), 339–351. doi:10.1016/j.ecresq.2011.11.001 PMID:23049162

Voga, M., & Grainger, J. (2007). Cognate status and cross-script translation priming. *Memory & Cognition, 35*(5), 938–952. doi:10.3758/BF03193467 PMID:17910178

Volkovyskaya, E., Raman, I., & Baluch, B. (under review). Age of Acquisition (AoA) effect in monolingual Russian speakers and bilingual Russian (L1) - English (L2) speakers in a free recall task. *Writing Systems Research Journal*.

Vygotsky, L. S. (1978). *Mind in society: The development of higher psychological processes*. Cambridge, MA: Harvard University Press.

Wang, Y. (2015). *Negative Transfer of Mother Language in English Compositions by Jiujiang University Students*. Academic Press. doi:10.1051/shsconf/20151401008

Weber, G. (1997). Top Language. *Language Monthly*, (3).

Weber-Fox, C. M., & Neville, H. J. (1999). Functional neural subsystems are differentially affected by delays in second-language immersion: ERP and behavioral evidence in bilingual speakers. In D. Birdsong (Ed.), *New perspectives on the critical period for second language acquisition*. Mahwah, NJ: Lawrence Erlbaum.

Weekes, B. S., Shu, H., Hao, M., Liu, Y., & Tan, L. H. (2007). Predictors of timed picture naming in Chinese. *Behavior Research Methods, 39*(2), 335–342. doi:10.3758/BF03193165 PMID:17695362

Wei, L. (2000). *The Bilingual Reader*. London: Routledge. doi:10.4324/9780203461341

Wei, L., & Moyer, M. G. (2008). *The Blackwell Guide to Research Methods in Bilingualism and Multilingualism*. Oxford, UK: Blackwell Publishing. doi:10.1002/9781444301120

Weinreich, U. (1953). *Languages in contact: Findings and problems*. New York: Linguistic Circle of New York.

Wei, X. (2008). Implication of IL fossilization in second language acquisition. *English Language Teaching, 1*(1), 127–131. doi:10.5539/elt.v1n1p127

Wells, J. B., Christiansen, M. H., Race, D. S., Acheson, D. J., & MacDonals, M. C. (2009). Experience and sentence processing: Statistical learning and relative clause comprehension. *Cognitive Psychology, 58*(2), 250–271. doi:10.1016/j.cogpsych.2008.08.002 PMID:18922516

Whitaker, H. (2010). *Concise Encyclopedia of Brain and Language*. Oxford, UK: Elsevier.

White, L. (1986). Implications of parametric variation for adult second language acquisition: An investigation of the 'pro-drop' parameter. In V. Cook (Ed.), *Experimental approaches to second language acquisition*. Oxford, UK: Pergamon.

Wiechmann, D., Steinfeld, J., & Kerz, E. 2013. Modeling bilingual children's acquisition of complex sentences in German. In M. Knauff, M. Pauen, N. Sebanz, & I. Wachsmuth (eds.), *Proceedings of the 35th Annual Conference of the Cognitive Science Society* (pp. 3753-3758). Austin, TX: Cognitive Science Society.

Wolter, B., & Gyllstad, H. (2011). Collocational Links in the L2 Mental Lexicon and the Influence of L1 Intralexical Knowledge. *Applied Linguistics, 32*(4), 430–449. doi:10.1093/applin/amr011

Woods, C. (2006). Bilingualism, Scribal Learning, and the Death of Sumerian. In S. L. Sanders (Ed.), Margins of Writing, Origins of Culture (pp. 91–120). Chicago: Academic Press.

Wray, A. (2002). *Formulaic Language and the Lexicon*. Cambridge University Press. doi:10.1017/CBO9780511519772

Wray, A. (2008). *Formulaic language: Pushing the boundaries*. Oxford, UK: Oxford University Press.

Wuillemin, D., Richardson, B., & Lynch, J. (1994). Right hemisphere involvement in processing later-learned languages in multilinguals. *Brain and Language, 46*(4), 620–636. doi:10.1006/brln.1994.1034 PMID:8044679

Xiao, Z., & Qian, M. (2010). Strategies for preventing and resolving temporary fossilization in second language acquisition. *English Language Teaching, 3*(1), 180–183.

Xinguang, S., & Xiuquin, X. (2015). A study of fossilization in Chinese college students' English learning. *Advances in Social Sciences Research Journal*, *2*(1), 54–60. doi:10.14738/assrj.21.678

Yamazaki, M., Ellis, A. W., Morrison, C. M., & Lambon Ralph, M. (1997). Two age of acquisition effects in the reading of Japanese Kanji. *British Journal of Psychology*, *88*(3), 407–421. doi:10.1111/j.2044-8295.1997.tb02648.x

Yenisor, E. (1989). *Yuvanın dil gelişimine etkisi*. İstanbul: İstanbul Üniversitesi Çocuk Sağlığı Enstitüsü, Yüksek Lisans Tezi.

Yıldırım Doğru, S. S., Alabay, E., & Kayılı, G. (2010). Determination of word knowledge and comprehension levels in normal developing and learning disorder children. *Elementary Education Online*, *3*(9), 828–840.

Yule, G. (2014). The Study of Language. Cambridge University Press.

Zeidner, M., Roberts, R. D., & Matthews, G. (2002). Can Emotional Intelligence be Schooled? A Critical Review. *Educational Psychologist*, *37*(4), 215–231. doi:10.1207/S15326985EP3704_2

Zevin, J. D., & Balota, D. A. (2000). Priming and attentional control of lexical and sublexical pathways during naming. *Journal of Experimental Psychology. Learning, Memory, and Cognition*, *26*(1), 121–135. doi:10.1037/0278-7393.26.1.121 PMID:10682293

Zhang, F., & Yin, P. (2009). A Study of Pronunciation Problems of English Learners in China. *Asian Social Science*, *5*(6), 141–146. doi:10.5539/ass.v5n6p141

Zhao, L. (2015). The influence of learners' motivation and attitdes on second language teaching. *Theory and Practice in Language Studies*, *5*(11), 2333–2339. doi:10.17507/tpls.0511.18

Zheng, Y. (2010). On some models of instruction for overcoming fossilization in English learning. *Journal of Language Teaching and Research*, *1*(2), 148–150. Retrieved from http://ojs.academypublisher.com/index.php/jltr/article/viewFile/0102148150/1659

Zucker, T. A., & Landry, S. H. (2010). Improving the quality of preschool read alouds: Professional development and coaching that targets book-reading practices. In M. C. McKenna, S. Walpole, & K. Conradi (Eds.), Promoting early reading: Research, resources, and best practices (pp. 78–104). New York, NY: Guilford.

Zucker, T. A., Cabell, S. Q., Justice, L. M., Pentimonti, J. M., & Kadaravek, J. N. (2013). The role of frequent, interactive prekindergarten shared reading in the longitudinal development of language and literacy skills. *Developmental Psychology*, *49*(8), 1425–1439. doi:10.1037/a0030347 PMID:23066674

Zucker, T. A., Justice, L. M., Pianta, S. B., & Kaderavek, J. N. (2010). Preschool teachers' literal and inferential questions and children's responses during whole-class shared reading. *Early Childhood Research Quarterly*, *25*(1), 65–83. doi:10.1016/j.ecresq.2009.07.001

About the Contributors

Duygu Buğa is an English Language Teacher and Researcher. She graduated from English Language Teaching division of Istanbul University. She is interested in linguistics, psychology and cognitive science. She is also Research Volunteer in Language and Cognition Lab, Koç University. She wants to propose academic/experimental studies in psycholinguistics, neurolinguistics and cognitive science.

Muhlise Ögeyik is a Professor at the Faculty of Education, Trakya University. She has been working at English Language Teaching Department. She holds PhD. degree in English Language Teaching. Her special research interest areas are: foreign language teacher training, strategy education, methodology, culture teaching, research design and methodology.

* * *

Aslı Altan graduated from Boğaziçi University in 2000. She completed her MA in Linguistics in 2002 and her PhD in 2008. She has various publications, conference presentations on acquisition of Turkish as a native language and teaching Turkish as a foreign language.

Bahman Baluch is Associate Professor in Psychology at Middlesex University. His teaching interests are Cognitive Psychology; Psychological aspects of infertility; children's human figure drawings; Research Methods.

Hakan Cangır, PhD candidate, is a lecturer at Ankara University, School of Foreign Languages in Turkey. He teaches EFL courses at the preparatory school and pursues his PhD research at Hacettepe University, Linguistics Department. His research interests are lexical processing in L1 and L2, the organization of the mental lexicon and the use and building of corpora for educational purposes.

Nur Erdem Cebeci holds an MA degree in language teaching. She is working at Trakya University. Her research interests are teaching English to young learners, linguistics, and research methods.

Mübeccel Gönen is currently working as a professor in Education Faculty / Department of Primary Education, Hacettepe University. Her main interests include early childhood development, language development, storybook reading, early childhood programme and children literature.

Erika Hoff directs the Language Development Lab which comprises several projects aimed at identifying the human abilities and human experiences that contribute to language development. Her main focus is a NICHD-funded longitudinal study of English monolingual and Spanish-English bilingual children from the age of 2 ½ to 10 years. She studies factors in children's early language experiences and early language development that predict successful oral language and literacy outcomes.

Sugandha Kaur obtained her Master's degree in Linguistics from Gauhati University, India in 2007. From 2008-2016, she worked at the Indian Institute of Technology Guwahati, India, first as a project fellow, and then as a PhD scholar. For her doctoral thesis, she investigated how Bodo-Assamese bilinguals negotiate the representation and processing of words in two languages in one mind and one brain.

Dionéia Monte-Serrat had her undergraduate degrees in Languages and Law. She was editor for International Journal of Research and Methodology in Social Science, IJRMSS (USA-Malasia). She is collaborating researcher at IEL-UNICAMP. She had her doctoral degree in Psychology, FFCLRP-USP and the programme was partly completed at Université Paris III, Sorbonne Nouvelle (2010, CAPES-BEX). Her internship was at École des Hautes Études en Sciences Sociales, Paris (2012, FAPESP). Dionéia is faculty member at Universidade de Ribeirão Preto.

Aicha Rahal is a Tunisian researcher in English linguistics. She holds an MA in English linguistics from the Faculty of Letters and Humanities of Kairouan, Tunisia and a BA in English from the Higher Institute of Applied Studies in Humanities of Gafsa, Tunisia. She was a former online teacher assistant and course moderator in the US Department of State and University of Oregon. She currently teaches English at the Higher Institute of Sciences and Energy Technology, Department of Sciences of Education, Gafsa and the Private Higher School of Engineers of Gafsa, Tunisia.

Ilhan Raman is a Chartered Psychologist is Programme Leader in MSc in Applied Psychology (at London, Dubai and Mauritius) and a Senior Lecturer at Middlesex University, UK with research expertise in experimental psychology, psycholinguistics and neuropsychology of language. Raman's academic career spans over two decades and she holds a BSc(Hons) in Psychology and a PhD in Cognitive Psychology from Middlesex University, UK supported by a scholarship. Her research explores the extent to which underpinning cognitive processes in reading are shaped by the nature of writing systems. To date, she has conducted pioneering psycholinguistic research by employing the unique characteristics of the Turkish orthography which has been the subject of peer reviewed publications, invited keynote talks, public seminars and international collaborations. Her research interests cover understanding cognitive processes involved in reading in orthographies other than English; reading and spelling in children and adults; dyslexia; the development of normative and diagnostic tools to assess literacy skills; bilingualism and the neuropsychology of language after brain damage. Raman holds full membership to numerous professional bodies and is an Associate Fellow of the British Psychological Society, a member of the Experimental Psychology Society, and a Fellow of the Higher Education Academy in the UK.

Bidisha Som is a linguist, currently working as an Associate Professor at the Indian Institute of Technology Guwahati. She did her PhD in Linguistics from Jawaharlal Nehru University, New Delhi on the moribund Great Andamanese language. Her current research interests are language processing in monolingual and bilingual context, effect of culture on language and cognition, sociolinguistics and documentation of lesser known languages in the context of North East Indian languages.

Gülüzar Şule Tepetaş Cengiz is graduate from Hacettepe University PhD programme. She is currently working as an Assistant Professor at the Department of Child Development, Abant Izzet Baysal University, Turkey. Her main interests include early childhood development, language development, storyline method, preschool teacher education, dialogic reading and concept development.

Evgenia Volkovyskaya is a PhD candidate at the Department of Psychology, Middlesex University and also Associate Lecturer at the Open University.

Işıl Gamze Yıldız holds a PhD degree on language education. She works at Trakya University, English Language Education Department as Research Assistant. Her research interest areas are linguistics, second language education, research methods in language teaching.

Index

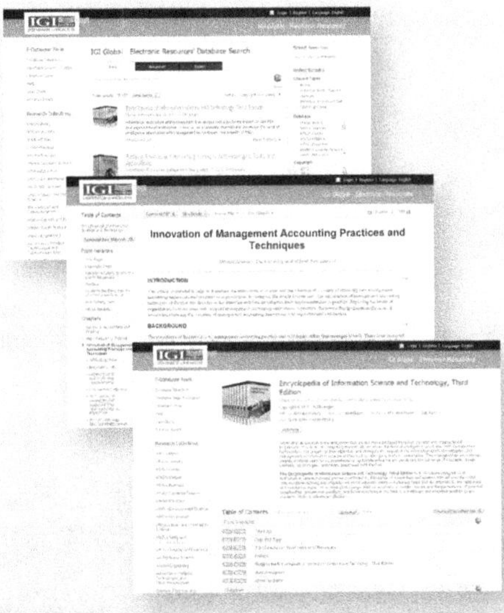
Innovation of Management Accounting Practices and Techniques

www.ingramcontent.com/pod-product-compliance
Lightning Source LLC
LaVergne TN
LVHW081346300926
849161LV00008B/2081